THE COLOUR DICTIONARY OF

# GEMSTONES & MINERALS

CW01645393

THE COLOUR DICTIONARY OF

# GEMSTONES & MINERALS

MICHAEL O'DONOGHUE

ORBIS PUBLISHING · LONDON

# ACKNOWLEDGMENTS

The authors and publishers wish to thank J A D Cotton for the loan of equipment and J Winter for assistance with the text.

The photographs in this book were taken by Carlo Bevilacqua and supplied by courtesy of Istituto Geografico de Agostini, Novara, except those on the following pages:

*12* (centre right) De Beers. *14* (top left) Angelo Hornak/Orbis. *44* (bottom) Archivio Foto B. *53* (top) Angelo Hornak/Orbis. *68* (both) Angelo Hornak/Orbis. *80* (bottom right) Archivio Foto B. *87* (top) NERC copyright, reproduced by permission of the Director, Institute of Geological Sciences. *123* (top) Angelo Hornak/Orbis. *131* (top) Angelo Hornak/Orbis. *144* (bottom) G Mazza. *145* C Annunziata.

First published in Great Britain by Orbis Publishing Limited, London 1976 as part of *The Encyclopedia of Minerals and Gemstones*

© Orbis Publishing Limited, London and Istituto Geografico de Agostini, S.p.A., Novara 1976, 1982

All rights reserved. No part of this publication may be reproduced, stored in a retrieval system, or transmitted, in any form or by any means, electronic, mechanical, photocopying or otherwise, without prior permission of the publishers. Such permission, if granted, is subject to a fee depending on the nature of the use.

Printed in Czechoslovakia

ISBN: 0-85613-414-7

Title-page photograph: characteristic rosettes of wavellite from Barnstaple, England, showing a fibrous radiating structure.
Opposite: gold on quartz from California.

## CONTENTS

# INTRODUCTION

*Left: Magnificent hexagonal crystals of chalybite, an iron carbonate. The triangular 'growth shadows' that are visible represent the form of the crystals at an earlier stage in their development*

The following pages contain the essential information on over one thousand minerals. These are nearly half of all those known to science, and they include all those that the vast majority of mineralogists will ever be able to examine, whether they be enthusiastic collectors or professionals.

The ordering of so many entries presents difficulties; there are many different systems of classification of minerals, and all are arbitrary to some extent. In large part these entries follow the order of the Chemical Index of Minerals (CIM) published by the British Museum (Natural History) in London. The first section of CIM consists of the elements and their alloys; further minerals are entered according to traditional subdivisions into oxides, sulphates, silicates, phosphates and so on. They are further grouped by their metals, according to their atomic weight.

The ordering of the entries here departs from CIM to make clearer some of the important relationships among minerals. Members of the main mineral families are grouped together. Each such family begins with a general introduction describing some of its chemical properties. Within each group the minerals are listed according to CIM; and minerals not belonging to the main families are listed according to CIM too.

To find a particular mineral in this section, consult the Index. Under each mineral name in the Index there are often several page numbers—numbers in bold type refer to this reference section.

If you have a sample of a mineral of whose identity you are unsure, you should consult the Identification Tables in the following section. When you think you know the name of the mineral you can find its entry by consulting the Index.

Details of cutting and polishing minerals are included here whenever the mineral is suitable for fashioning and is likely to be available to the ordinary lapidary. Information has not been provided when the mineral is very rare, too difficult to work or too easily damaged to be worth fashioning.

The information here has been compiled from many detailed works of reference, which are listed in the Bibliography of this Dictionary. Of necessity they are expressed in a condensed form. The technical terms that have been used are explained fully in the appropriate sections of this book. Brief definitions of them will be found in the Glossary. Most are easy to understand and are necessary to anyone with a serious interest in minerals.

The information in the entries is listed in the same order throughout: name of mineral; chemical composition; general properties; mode of occurrence; localities in which it is found; mode of treatment; fashioning details.

*Name*. Usually this is the name given in CIM. Chemical designations have been used rather than more fanciful ones—rutile (synthetic) in preference to titania, for example. The spellings of names follow CIM; thus pyrite, baryte and sylvine replace the older pyrites, barytes and sylvite.

*Composition*. In a few cases, such as psilomelane and limonite, the exact composition of a mineral is uncertain. In these cases, it has been described in words; otherwise it would have been necessary to give several formulae.

*General properties*. Here the mineral's *crystal system*—the basic arrangement of its atoms—is specified. Six systems are used, rather than seven; this means that crystals that some authors describe as belonging to the trigonal system are here classified under the hexagonal system. This usage is the more modern one. The usual shape of the mineral's crystals, its *habit*, is described too, together with its *lustre* and *colour*. *Twinning* is mentioned when it is a conspicuous feature—crystals are described as twinned when they appear in two parts, which are mirror images of each other, or which interpenetrate.

The *cleavage*, or tendency to splitting along certain directions, is mentioned here. It is an important way of identifying minerals, and it is important to a collector to know about cleavage before he attempts to separate a sample from other minerals. It is even more important to the cutter of stones, since a stone with a cleavage can shatter when it is polished in certain directions. The *hardness* of the mineral is specified here, according to Mohs' scale, which runs from 1 (talc) to 10 (diamond). It is an important guide to the identity of a mineral, and is comparatively easy to test. *Specific gravity*, SG, is the density of a mineral, its mass per unit volume; it is given here in grams per cubic centimetre, gm/cm$^3$. A careful series of measurements is needed to make accurate determinations of it, but it is again a good method of getting at a mineral's identity.

*Occurrence*. Each mineral occurs in association with characteristic companion minerals and in characteristic geological circumstances; atacamite, for example, is found in the oxidized zones of copper deposits, often with cuprite and malachite.

*Localities*. Very often a mineral is known from only a few sites, and then the discussion of its mode of occurrence merges with the description of these localities. In general, the localities have been included in which outstanding specimens are to be found, or the particular place that has given its name to the mineral. Sometimes the places mentioned are the only known places of occurrence of the mineral; more often, they are a selection from localities too numerous to list. All place names have been modernized where necessary, and as far as possible their spellings follow the usage of the Universal Postal Union. To find a particular site the collector must consult the mineralogical literature of the area he is interested in.

*Treatment*. In most cases the best treatment for a mineral species is to leave it alone. Do not attempt to clean any of the minerals listed here unless a treatment procedure is described. In certain cases fragility or unfavourable reaction to certain acids used in fashioning has been mentioned. Where some cleaning agent has been found to be particularly useful, such as alcohol for the cleaning of fibrous material, it has been mentioned.

*Fashioning*. Details of fashioning stones that are of interest to lapidaries are given here (provided by Colin Winter). They include the kinds of shapes that the mineral can be cut into, whether faceted or cabochon (rounded); how it splits, and how readily; what angles facets should be cut at so that the light rays follow paths that give the maximum fire and colour to the stone; and the mineral's sensitivity to heat—an important consideration, since stones are heated during fashioning, both deliberately, when mounted with wax, and unavoidably, owing to friction when being ground and polished.

At the end of the section, a few materials of organic origin, such as jet and amber, are listed for their aesthetic appeal.

Wherever possible, minerals that are especially important, interesting or attractive, or simply very common, have been illustrated with photographs. No amount of verbal description of the appearance of a mineral can replace one good picture—to the mineral enthusiast, the next-best thing to holding a sample in his hands.

# THE MINERAL KINGDOM

*Above: Copper from Lake Superior, Michigan. This crystal shows the enlarged faces of the rhombic dodecahedron, in this example out of proportion*

*Above right: This copper specimen shows dendritic (plant-like) habit and is from Houghton, Michigan*

## Elements and Alloys

### Copper Cu

Native copper occurs in small amounts only, the mineral being almost always secondary in origin. It crystallizes in the cubic system but crystals are rare; when found they are cubic or rhombdodecahedral. Dendritic or filiform habit is far more common. The colour is copper-red with a brown tarnish, the lustre metallic, and the streak copper-red. It is ductile and malleable with a hackly fracture. H 2.5–3.0; SG 8.9.

*Occurrence.* Copper may occur in basaltic lavas, sandstones and conglomerates, and is recovered by the reduction of copper minerals or solutions. It is found in veins and beds in association with chalcopyrite, chalcocite, cuprite, malachite and azurite. It often occurs in the vicinity of igneous rocks.

*Localities.* Occurs in dendritic forms in limestone at Turnisk, USSR; as crystals in Cornwall; at Wallaroo, South Australia and Broken Hill, New South Wales. Found in sandstone at Corocoro, Bolivia, and at Cananea, Mexico. In the USA copper is found in abundance in the Keweenaw area of north Michigan; at the Copper Queen mine, Bisbee, Arizona and at Georgetown, New Mexico.

*Treatment.* Copper specimens should be cleaned with water as they are readily attacked by acids, especially nitric. Black deposits of copper oxide may be removed by the use of a solution of one part by weight sodium hydroxide, three parts potassium sodium tartrate and 20 parts distilled water.

### Silver Ag

Silver is a member of the cubic crystal system but crystals are rare, the mineral occurring more commonly as dendritic wires or as scales. The colour is silver-white, tarnishing quickly to black. The streak is silver-white and the lustre metallic. It is malleable and ductile with a hackly fracture. H 2.5–3.0; SG 10.1–11.1

*Occurrence.* Found in hydrothermal veins, where it may have been formed by the action of hot waters on silver sulphides, or of metallic sulphides or arsenides on silver chloride. It occurs disseminated in various metallic sulphides.

*Localities.* Silver is found at Kongsberg, Norway, sometimes as fine, large specimens; at Freiberg, E. Germany; Příbram, Czechoslovakia; Broken Hill, New South Wales; Chanarcillo, Atacama, Chile; and in the states of Guanajuato and Chihuahua, Mexico. In the USA silver occurs at Keweenaw, Michigan, in association with copper ores, and at Butte, Montana, as well as Colorado, Arizona and Idaho. In Canada it occurs at Cobalt, Ontario.

*Treatment.* Dissolves readily in nitric acid, hot sulphuric acid, and aqua regia. Tarnish may be removed electrolytically or with sodium cyanide or potassium cyanide. These compounds should be used with the utmost care, since they are dangerous. The tendency of silver to tarnish is greatly increased when it is stored in the neighbourhood of sulphur-bearing agents.

*Right: This silver specimen from Secci, Sarrabus, Sardinia, is called filiform from its threadlike appearance*

**Gold Au**

Gold crystals are rare; they belong to the cubic system and when found may be octahedra, cubes or rhombdodecahedra. Gold is more commonly found as grains, in dendritic forms or as nuggets, which are irregular lumps with rounded surfaces. Twinning is common. The colour is golden yellow, lighter when there is a high silver content; the streak is a similar colour. The lustre is metallic. Gold is ductile and is the only highly malleable yellow mineral. Gold is usually alloyed with varying amounts of silver and may also contain some copper. Electrum contains up to 20% silver and rhodite contains some rhodium. Porpezite contains palladium. H 2.5–3.0; SG of pure gold 19.3; SG of alloyed gold 15.6–19.3

*Occurrence.* Gold is quite widely distributed in igneous, sedimentary and metamorphic rock, and in sea water. Auriferous quartz is a major source for gold and occurs in hydrothermal veins. In examining this type of occurrence care should be taken not to confuse gold with pyrite, which is superficially similar. Alluvial deposits, which contain gold released from rocks by the action of weathering, are good areas for the prospector. Consolidated deposits such as those in the Witwatersrand, South Africa, are the major economic gold producers. The Republic of South Africa is in fact the world's largest producer of gold, being responsible for over half the total annual production.

*Localities.* Apart from South Africa, gold is found in Rhodesia, Egypt and Ghana. Also found in Wales and sparingly in some other parts of Great Britain; in the Ural Mountains, in Czechoslovakia and Romania; in the Alps of South Island, New Zealand; from Charters Towers, Queensland, from Bendigo and Ballarat, Victoria and from Kalgoorlie in Western Australia. In the USA gold is often obtained by individual prospectors by placer mining. It is found along the mountain ranges of the western states, including California, Colorado, Nevada and Alaska. In Canada deposits occur at the Klondike, Yukon Territory, in Nova Scotia and Ontario.

*Treatment.* Gold is dissolved only by aqua regia and iron stains may be removed by any convenient acid. Quartz may be removed by strong hydrofluoric acid.

*Above: Gold on quartz from California. Such a specimen would command very high prices, owing to the large amount of gold visible*

*Left: Another fine example of gold on quartz, also from California*

*Left: Silver showing dendritic form; strictly speaking it is reticular dendritic since the 'branches' form a mesh. From the Harz Mountains, Germany*

*Right: Native mercury from Lucca, Italy. This form is extremely rare as mercury is normally found in the combined state*

**Mercury Hg**

Mercury is rare in the metallic state, usually being of secondary origin and obtained from cinnabar. It crystallizes at $-40°C$ and shows a hexagonal structure. It is tin-white with a brilliant metallic lustre and is found in small fluid globules. SG 13.6

*Occurrence.* Mercury is usually found as small isolated drops although it may sometimes occur as large fluid masses in rock cavities, usually in regions of volcanic activity. Deposits from hot springs occasionally contain mercury as well as cinnabar.

*Localities.* Mercury is found at Idrija and Mount Avala, Yugoslavia and near Landsberg, W. Germany. It also occurs in the United States, in California and Texas; and in Spain and Italy.

*Treatment.* Occurs naturally in such small drops that cleaning would not be attempted. In large quantities it is highly poisonous and all activity associated with it should be carried out in very well-ventilated conditions.

**Amalgam**

Amalgam is the alpha-phase of the system Ag–Hg. The gamma-phase is moschellandsbergite. Amalgam is a member of the cubic crystal system and is found as dodecahedra and in a massive form. The colour and streak are silver-white; the lustre is brilliant metallic. H 3.0–3.5; SG 13.7–14.1

*Occurrence.* Amalgam is rare and found in mercury or silver deposits as grains or scattered crystals.

*Localities.* Fine crystals from Landsberg, W. Germany; and Coquimbo, Chile.

**Diamond C**

The transparent, crystalline form of carbon, diamond is polymorphous with graphite. It crystallizes in the cubic system and occurs as octahedra, dodecahedra or icositetrahedra; twinning is common but cube forms are rare. There is a perfect octahedral cleavage and the fracture is conchoidal. Many stones are found as worn pebbles. Some stones may display anomalous birefringence and some may luminesce. The colour of diamond may be white, yellow, pink, green, blue, brown, red or black. There is a white streak. The lustre is adamantine and the stones often feel greasy. Investigation of the absorption spectrum and luminescence of diamond have led scientists to place the material into five classes:

*Type 1.* Nitrogen contained in platelet form; the majority of all natural diamonds.

*Type 1b.* Nitrogen contained in dispersed form.

*Type 2a.* Stones with no significant nitrogen.

*Type 2b.* Diamonds with no nitrogen but containing aluminium; all natural blue stones are of this type.

*Type 3.* The meteoric diamond with a hexagonal structure, named lonsdaleite.

Diamonds are graded both when rough and after cutting, different systems being used for each type of appraisal. Many

*Above right: Crystals of diamond, some displaying the characteristic forms (particularly the octahedron) of the cubic system. Note the high lustre*

*Right: A single crystal of diamond in its matrix. The faces are curved*

*Far right: Diamond in its parent rock of kimberlite from Kimberley, South Africa*

shades of white are recognised for the cut stones, though the term blue-white has fallen into disuse; the best quality stones are called 'finest white' or 'river' according to the country where the grading takes place. Cape stones are yellow in appearance – not a bright yellow but a perceptible off-white. H 10; SG 3.52; RI 2.42, dispersion 0.044

*Occurrence.* Diamond occurs in alluvial gravel deposits associated with quartz, corundum, platinum, zircon and other minerals. The other main type of occurrence is in the 'pipes'; these are composed of kimberlite, in which the most prominent mineral is serpentinized olivine. Diamond is randomly distributed in the pipes.

*Localities.* Diamonds are found in India, the celebrated Golconda mines being in the Madras area; in Brazil, from Diamantina, Minas Gerais; from South Africa in a number of areas including Kimberley, Pretoria (the Premier mine is in this area), and Jagersfontein in the Orange Free State. Also found in Tanzania, Sierra Leone, Ghana, Zaire, Botswana, South-West Africa, Angola and Guinea. Other sources are Australia, Borneo, Guyana, Venezuela and Siberia, where the Mir pipe is one of the largest in the world, and parts of the US.

*Treatment.* Diamond is unaffected by acids and crystals may be cleaned by boiling in concentrated hydrofluoric acid.

*Fashioning. Uses*: faceting, impure or badly coloured material used as abrasive; *cleavage*: perfect, octahedral; brittle; *cutting angles*: crown 34° 30', pavilion 40° 45'; *heat sensitivity*: very low.

**Graphite C**

Graphite, sometimes called black lead, crystallizes in the hexagonal system as flat six-sided crystals, but is usually found massive. There is a perfect basal cleavage. Both graphite and diamond are pure carbon; the phenomenon of widely differing forms in substances of identical chemical composition is called *polymorphism*. Graphite has a typically greasy feel and will mark paper; it is black and gives a black streak. The lustre is dull metallic. It is sectile and is easily scratched. H 1–2; SG 2.1–2.3

*Occurrence.* Graphite occurs in flakes in metamorphic rocks that themselves are derived from rocks containing carbon. It also occurs in veins and pegmatites.

*Localities.* Found in the Irkutsk area of Siberia, and in Sri Lanka, where it occurs in veins. Graphite crystals occur in limestone at Pargas, Finland; a compact form has been mined at Borrowdale, Cumbria; graphite suitable for pencils comes from Sonora, Mexico. In the USA a major locality is at Ticonderoga, New York State, where it is found in quartzites and with quartz in small veins running through gneiss.

**Lead Pb**

Native lead occurs only rarely, and sometimes contains some silver or antimony. It is a member of the cubic crystal system and forms thin plates and small globular masses of a grey colour. It is soft enough to be scratched with the fingernail, is very malleable and somewhat ductile. The lustre is metallic. H 1.5; SG 11.4

*Occurrence.* Very rare as native metal. Occurs in compact limestone with hematite, and in gold placers.

*Localities.* Lead is found in Sweden at the Harstig mine, Pajsberg; from the gold placers of the Ural Mountains, USSR; from Mexico near Veracruz; and from Franklin, New Jersey.

*Treatment.* Any acid apart from nitric can be used as a cleaning agent.

**Arsenic As**

Arsenic is found as light grey reniform or botryoidal masses; it may also be stalactitic. Crystals of the hexagonal system with rhombohedral form are occasionally found. There is a perfect cleavage. The lustre is metallic and the streak light grey. It may smell of garlic when struck with a hammer or on heating. It tarnishes quickly to a darker grey. H 3.5; SG 5.7

*Occurrence.* Arsenic occurs in hydrothermal veins and often contains some silver, iron, gold or bismuth as traces; it may also contain antimony. It is sometimes accompanied by ores of nickel and cobalt.

*Localities.* Fine reniform masses occur at St Andreasberg in the Harz Mountains. Also from the silver mines at Ste. Marie-aux-Mines in Alsace, France, and from Fukui Prefecture, Japan, where globular masses of rhombohedral crystals are found. It occurs in Arizona, and in the Montreal area of Canada.

*Treatment.* Arsenic is attacked by acids except hydrofluoric, which may therefore be used to remove adhering material. It is not possible to remove the tarnish.

**Domeykite $Cu_3As$**

Domeykite is a copper arsenide closely related to mohawkite, which contains Ni and Co. It is a member of the cubic crystal system; reniform and botryoidal forms are found. White to grey in colour, it tarnishes easily. The lustre is metallic. H 3.0–3.5; SG 7.9–8.1

*Occurrence.* With copper ores.

*Left: Graphite, one of the forms of carbon, from Siberia. The other form is diamond*

*Left: Native arsenic in massive form*

*Right: Hopper crystals of bismuth. Natural bismuth rarely shows its crystal form as well as does this synthetic specimen*

*Far right: Sulphur crystal from Perticara, Italy*

*Localities.* Domeykite has been found in several localities in Chile, and from the Mohawk mine, Keweenaw County, Michigan; also from Lake Superior, Ontario.
*Treatment.* Brown coating will eventually form; impossible to remove permanently.

**Algodonite**
Some workers do not consider this copper compound as a separate mineral as there is a close resemblance to domeykite. The formula $Cu_6As$ has been proposed. It is silver-white to steel-grey in colour, tarnishing quickly to brown on exposure to light. H 4; SG 8.3
*Localities.* Algodonite has been found in Chile and from the area of Lake Superior.

**Antimony Sb**
Antimony belongs to the hexagonal system, but is commonly found massive and reniform, with granular forms also occurring. Polysynthetic twinning may also be displayed. There is a perfect cleavage. It is light-grey with a metallic lustre and grey streak. H 3.0–3.5; SG 6.7
*Occurrence.* Antimony occurs in hydrothermal metal-bearing veins and is frequently associated with silver and arsenic. It is often accompanied by stibnite and sphalerite.
*Localities.* Near Sala, Sweden; St. Andreasberg in the Harz Mountains, Germany; Příbram, Czechoslovakia; Chile and Borneo. Occurs in the USA in California, and in Canada at South Ham, Quebec and Prince William, New Brunswick.
*Treatment.* Any acid apart from sulphuric may be used as a cleaning agent.

*Above right: Native antimony. It is normally found massive like this. Well-formed crystals are rare*

**Horsfordite**
Horsfordite, an antimonide of copper, has been given the formula $Cu_6Sb$. An alternative is $Cu_5Sb$. SG 8.8
*Localities.* Near Mytilene, Greece.

**Bismuth Bi**
Bismuth, a silver-white mineral, which becomes reddish with tarnish, crystallizes in the hexagonal crystal system. Crystals are rare and the massive forms are those usually encountered. It may be found granular or arborescent. The lustre is metallic and the streak silver-white. Cleavage is perfect. H 2.5; SG 9.8.
*Occurrence.* Bismuth is comparatively rare, the metal being commonly obtained from the smelting of gold and silver. It occurs naturally in veins in granite and gneiss, often accompanying ores of cobalt and silver; it is deposited hydrothermally.
*Localities.* Major deposits of economic importance are at San Baldomero, Bolivia and in other areas in the vicinity of La Paz; also found in E. Germany. There are important deposits in North Queensland and New South Wales. Some bismuth occurs in Devon and Cornwall, California, South Dakota and Colorado.

**Sulphur S**
The commonest form of sulphur, alpha-sulphur, crystallizes in the orthorhombic crystal system; but the mineral is polymorphous and beta-sulphur and gamma-sulphur or rosickyite, both monoclinic, are found. The orthorhombic form commonly occurs as acute pyramidal crystals but may also be tabular; massive forms are found and also granular aggregates. The lustre is resinous and there is a white streak. The crystals are coloured a bright yellow and are slightly sectile and rather brittle. H 1.5–2.5; SG 2.0–2.1; RI 1.958, 2.038, 2.245, with a strong birefringence.
*Occurrence.* Sulphur is associated with volcanic activity and occurs in gases given off at fumaroles. It is also formed by the decomposition of hydrogen sulphide in hot springs, which may result from the action of acid water on metallic sulphates or from the reduction of sulphates such as gypsum. It is most commonly found in sedimentary rocks of Tertiary age, associated most fre-

*Right: Sulphur crystals from Sicily showing a group of bipyramids*

quently with gypsum and limestone.
*Localities.* The finest crystals come from Girgenti, Sicily and adjoining localities; it is also common in volcanic regions of Japan, Iceland, Hawaii, Mexico and the Andes. There are large deposits of economic importance in Louisiana and Texas, where it is associated with evaporate deposits, particularly salt domes.
*Treatment.* Sulphur is extremely sensitive to heat, so that the warmth of the hand may cause it to crack. It should not be exposed to bright sunlight for the same reason. It is not advisable to attempt to clean this mineral.

**Tellurium Te**
Tellurium occurs as prismatic crystals of the hexagonal system and is also found massive. It has a perfect prismatic cleavage, is tin-white in colour and has a similar streak. The lustre is metallic. It gives a red solution in warm concentrated sulphuric acid. H 2.0–2.5; SG 6.2
*Occurrence.* Occurs in hydrothermal vein deposits.
*Localities.* Tellurium has been found in Romania, Western Australia, the United States, particularly Colorado, and Mexico.

**Iron Fe**
Native iron is rare. It is found either as a terrestrial form, in which it occurs as grains and masses in rocks; or as meteoritic iron, forming the entire mass or a matrix in which silicate minerals are embedded, or as grains or scales throughout the meteorite. Kamacite is a form of meteoritic iron and is the cubic alpha-phase of the Fe–Ni system with up to 6% Ni. Metakamacite is an unstable phase of similar composition, while taenite is the gamma-phase, with upwards of 33% Fe. The terrestrial form, awaruite, is Ni, Fe, with 60% or more Ni. Iron is grey to black, with a metallic lustre; it is strongly magnetic and malleable. H 4.5; SG 7.3–7.8
*Localities.* Terrestrial iron is found in basalt at Disco Island, West Greenland and in small grains with pyrrhotite near Kassel, W. Germany. Awaruite is found in Awarua Bay in South Island, New Zealand, where it is associated with gold and platinum.
*Treatment.* Iron dissolves rapidly in acids, especially nitric. This reaction gives off dangerous fumes of nitrogen oxides. Native iron may oxidize in moist conditions and should be stored with a dehydrating agent such as silica gel.

**Iridosmine Os, Ir**
This is the osmiridium-rich member of the system Os–Ir, in which the osmium content exceeds 35%; a synonym is iridium-osmine. It crystallizes in the hexagonal system and occurs as flattened grains of a metallic white colour. It has a metallic lustre, is slightly malleable and somewhat brittle. A variety with osmium content from 35% to 50% is nevyanskite and another, with osmium content from 50% to 80% is sysertskite. H 6–7; SG 19.3–21.1
*Occurrence.* Iridosmine occurs with platinum and contains this and such metals as rhodium and ruthenium.
*Localities.* Chocó area of Colombia and in the Ural mountains, USSR; in Australia at Platina, New South Wales, and in Oregon, California and British Columbia; with gold at Witwatersrand, South Africa.
*Treatment.* Any dilute acid may be used as a cleaning agent.

**Osmiridium Ir, Os**
This is the cubic, iridium-rich phase of the system Os–Ir, with osmium less than 35%. Data as for iridosmine, above.

**Platinum Pt**
Platinum, a precious metal, is rare in its native form, being alloyed with iron, iridium, rhodium, palladium, osmium and other metals. It crystallizes in the cubic system but is most commonly found as grains. It has a metallic lustre and a steel-grey to whitish streak. It is malleable and ductile. It is sometimes magnetic and occasionally shows polarity. H 4–4.5; SG 14–19 (native mineral); 21–22 (pure).
*Occurrence.* Platinum is usually found in granules or nuggets resulting from the erosion of platinum-bearing rocks. Associated minerals are chromite, magnetite, zircon and corundum, and the various platinum metals.
*Localities.* The most important locality, now said to be nearing exhaustion, is in the Ural Mountains; there the primary sources are ultrabasic igneous rocks, including dunites (olivine-rich rocks). Outside the Ural Mountains, platinum has been found in the Chocó area of Colombia, near the river Pinto. It occurs in the Broken Hill area of New South Wales and in New Zealand and the Transvaal. In the USA platinum has been found in North Carolina and California (in placer deposits) and in Canada from the Kamloops area, British Columbia.
*Treatment.* Any acid apart from aqua regia can be used as a cleaning agent.

**Dyscrasite $Ag_3Sb$**
Dyscrasite is an important silver mineral. It belongs to the orthorhombic crystal system although crystals – often found as pseudo-hexagonal twins – are rare, the mineral normally being found massive. It is silver in colour and shows a similar streak; it has a metallic lustre. It may be sectile. A yellow or black tarnish sometimes appears. H 3.5–4.0; SG 9.4–10.0
*Occurrence.* Frequently with silver ores.
*Localities.* An important West German source is at Wolfach in the Black Forest, in West Germany. Crystals associated with calcite are found in the Harz Mountains, Germany. Other localities are Atacama, Chile and Cobalt, Ontario; Broken Hill, New South Wales.
*Treatment.* Any dilute acid apart from nitric may be used as a cleaning agent.

## Carbides

**Moissanite SiC**
Probably the only natural occurrence of moissanite is that in the Diablo Canyon meteorite in Arizona, where it is associated with tiny diamonds. It occurs in small green hexagonal plates. Data for the artificial material, carborundum, are as follows: H 9.5; SG 3.1; RI 2.6–2.7

The following are found only in meteorites:
**osbornite TiN**
**cohenite $Fe_3C$**
**schreibersite $(Fe, Ni)_3P$**

## Sulphides, Selenides, Tellurides, Arsenides, Antimonides and Bismuthides

**Chalcocite $Cu_2S$**
Chalcocite crystallizes in the orthorhombic system, sometimes forming pseudo-hexagonal twins. It is more frequently found massive. A cubic modification occurs at temperatures over

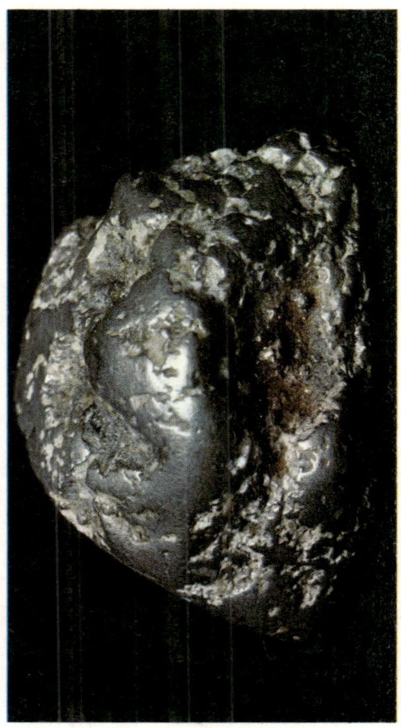

*Far left: Meteoritic iron from Henbury, Australia. Most specimens of iron are meteoritic; in terrestrial rocks iron is usually found as grains*

*Left: Native platinum. This specimen weighs 105 gm and was found in Siberia*

*Right: Chalcocite from Cornwall*

*Far right: Bornite from Carn Brea, Cornwall*

91 °C. The colour is grey, tarnishing to black; the lustre is metallic and the streak black. H 2.5–3.0; SG 5.5–5.8
*Occurrence.* Chalcocite is found with native copper or with cuprite, usually occurring in secondary sulphide zones.
*Localities.* Fine crystals of chalcocite occur in the St. Just, St. Ives, Camborne and Redruth areas of Cornwall, England; very fine crystals are found at Bristol, Connecticut; large quantities from Montana, Nevada and California.

**Digenite $Cu_{1.5-1.9}S$**
Digenite crystallizes in the cubic system in blue or black masses with a submetallic lustre. H 2.5–3; SG 5.6
*Occurrence.* Occurs in copper ore deposits.
*Localities.* From Butte, Montana; South-West Africa; Sweden; Kennecott, Alaska.

**Covelline CuS**
Covelline crystallizes in the hexagonal crystal system, forming hexagonal plates. However, massive forms, often foliated, are more common. There is a perfect basal cleavage; the colour is dark blue with a purple iridescent tarnish. If the plates are sufficiently thin they may be translucent. The lustre is metallic and the streak dark grey to black. H 1.5–2.0; SG 4.6–4.8
*Occurrence.* Covelline occurs in copper veins, associated with chalcopyrite, bornite (from which it may be distinguished by its perfect cleavage), and chalcocite.
*Localities.* Fine crystals from the Calabona mine, Alghero, Sardinia; other localities are Chile, Bolivia, Argentine and Peru. It is also found at Butte, Montana.

**Berzelianite $Cu_2Se$**
Berzelianite crystallizes in the cubic system although a non-cubic phase appears to exist. It is found in thin dendritic crusts, silver-white in colour, with a metallic lustre, tarnishing to grey. H 2; SG 6.71

*Major Localities.* Found with copper minerals at the Skrikerum mine, Kalmar, Sweden and from the Harz Mountains, Germany.

**Umangite $Cu_3Se_2$**
Umangite crystallizes in the orthorhombic system as masses or grains coloured blue to black with a tinge of red. The lustre is metallic and the streak black. H 3; SG 6.4
*Localities.* Occurs in a pink calcite as veins, in association with berzelianite and other minerals, at Lake Athabasca, Saskatchewan; from Sierra de Umango, La Rioja, Argentina; Harz Mountains, Germany; from the copper mine at Skrikerum, Sweden.

**Klockmannite CuSe**
Klockmannite crystallizes in the hexagonal system as granular aggregates coloured grey to black. There is a perfect cleavage. H about 2; SG 6.0

*Localities.* Occurs in uranium ores at Lake Athabasca, Saskatchewan; Skrikerum, Sweden; Harz Mountains, W. Germany; etc.

**Rickardite**
Rickardite, a copper telluride of uncertain composition, crystallizes in the tetragonal system as compact purple masses, which lose brightness on exposure to light. The streak is red. H 3.5; SG 7.5
*Occurrence.* Occurs with tellurides in veins bearing gold and quartz.
*Localities.* From Gunnison Co., Colorado; Arizona; USSR; San Salvador; South Africa; Japan; etc.

**Lautite CuAsS**
Lautite crystallizes in the orthorhombic system as tabular crystals or as radiating granular masses coloured grey or black with a tinge of red. H 3.5; SG 4.9
*Occurrence.* Occurs with other sulphides in veins with native arsenic.
*Localities.* From Lauta, Germany; Ste. Marie-aux-Mines, Alsace, France.

**Bornite $Cu_5FeS_4$**
Bornite crystallizes in the cubic system and is usually massive, though some cubic and rhombdodecahedral crystals are found; twins may occur. The colour is reddish-brown but an iridescent tarnish quickly develops which is purple in colour; the name 'peacock ore' is derived from this tarnish. The lustre is metallic and the streak a pale grey-black. H 3; SG 4.9–5.4
*Occurrence.* Bornite is found in hydrothermal veins with chalcopyrite and chalcocite. It may also occur as a primary mineral in igneous rocks and pegmatite veins.
*Localities.* Fine crystals are found in the Redruth area of Cornwall, England and in the copper ores of Montecatini, Tuscany, Italy. Fine-coloured specimens are found at Androta, Malagasy Republic. It is the principal ore of some Chilean copper mines and also occurs at Butte, Montana.
*Treatment.* No steps are normally taken to remove the tarnish, which is considered desirable; clean with water.

*Right: The copper sulphide covelline. It is rarely found as single crystals, and is usually encountered in masses like this one from Sardinia*

*Far right: This specimen of covelline from Sardinia shows the lamellar (thin, platy) structure typical of the mineral*

*Left: Crystals of chalcopyrite, a copper-iron sulphide. They appear tetrahedral but their true form is bisphenoidal. They come from Cornwall*

*Below left: Pyrite. These crystals are pentagonal dodecahedra*

*Below right: Acanthite from Saxony. This is the stable form of silver sulphide at normal temperatures*

**Chalcopyrite $CuFeS_2$**
The most important ore of copper, chalcopyrite crystallizes in the tetragonal system, often forming crystals resembling tetrahedra. Massive forms are common and various types of twinning occur. An alternative name is copper pyrite. The colour is brass-yellow with an iridescent tarnish; the lustre is metallic and the streak greenish-black. It is less hard and is a deeper yellow than iron pyrite, and it is harder than gold. Fracture uneven, sometimes conchoidal. H 3.5–4.0; SG 4.1–4.3
*Occurrence.* Occurs as a primary mineral in igneous rocks and in hydrothermal vein deposits with pyrite, sphalerite and other minerals. It also occurs in pegmatites and contact metamorphic deposits.
*Localities.* Chalcopyrite deposits occur in many localities. Important sulphide copper deposits in which chalcopyrite is the chief mineral are found in the USA in the states of Arizona, Montana, Nevada, New Mexico and California. Very fine crystals are found in Chester Co., Pennsylvania. In Europe good crystals occur in Westphalia and at Ste. Marie-aux-Mines, Alsace. Chalcopyrite may also be found at St. Agnes, Cornwall and in Devon.
*Treatment.* Cyanide solutions may remove the black coating often found. Hydrochloric acid may sometimes induce an iridescent coating. Distilled water should be used for cleaning.

**Cubanite $CuFe_2S_3$**
Sometimes known as chalmersite, cubanite crystallizes in the orthorhombic crystal system forming thin elongated prisms, vertically striated. Twinning is common. The colour is brass-yellow and the mineral is strongly magnetic. There is a metallic lustre. H 3.5; SG 4.1
*Occurrence.* Cubanite is found with copper ores and with gold.
*Localities.* From Barracanao, Cuba and from the Morro Velho gold mine, Minas Gerais, Brazil.
*Treatment.* As for chalcopyrite.

**Acanthite and Argentite $Ag_2S$**
*Acanthite* is the low-temperature monoclinic modification of $Ag_2S$; most natural silver sulphide specimens are acanthite pseudomorphous after argentite, which is the high-temperature cubic modification. Acanthite forms slender prismatic crystals which are sectile. The colour is iron-black. SG 7.2–7.3
*Argentite* forms octahedra or cubes, frequently in arborescent or reticulated groups; it is found massive and as a coating. The colour and streak are grey to black; the lustre is metallic and shining, and there is a frequent alteration of the surface to a black sulphide. H 2.0–2.5; SG 7.20–7.36
*Localities.* Acanthite is found at Jachymov, Czechoslovakia, and at Freiberg, E. Germany. It also occurs at Georgetown, Colorado and in Chihuahua and Zacatecas, Mexico. Argentite is the most important primary mineral of silver and occurs in hydrothermal veins with pyrargyrite, proustite and native silver. It may also occur as a product of silver sulphides that have been attacked by weather. It occurs at Jachymov, Czechoslovakia; Freiberg, E. Germany; Andreasberg, Harz Mountains, Germany; Liskeard, Cornwall; it is common in the silver mines of Mexico, especially in Guanajuato and Zacatecas and at Arizpe, Sonora. It is found with copper ores at Butte, Montana and in the silver districts of Colorado and Nevada.
*Treatment.* Both minerals darken when exposed to bright light. This coating may be removed ultrasonically. Clean with water.

**Aguilarite $Ag_4SSe$**
Aguilarite is polymorphous, though the high- and low-temperature forms are not distinguished by separate names. The high-temperature form crystallizes in the cubic system, forming skeleton dodecahedral crystals which are sectile. The colour is black, and lustre metallic. H 2.5; SG 7.58
*Localities.* Aguilarite is found with silver at Guanajuato, Mexico.
*Treatment.* Clean with water.

**Hessite $Ag_2Te$**
Hessite is polymorphous though the high- and low-temperature forms do not possess distinguishing names. It crystallizes in the monoclinic system and is usually found massive. The colour is grey and lustre metallic; the material may be sectile. When gold is contained the mineral graduates towards petzite. H 2.5–3.0; SG 8.3–8.4
*Occurrence.* Found with silver and gold.
*Localities.* Altai Mountains, USSR; Coquimbo, Chile; Colorado; San Sebastian and Jalisco, Mexico.
*Treatment.* Should be cleaned with water or alternatively with dilute hydrochloric acid.

**Empressite**
Empressite, a silver telluride of varying composition, crystallizes in the orthorhombic system, although some authorities have noted hexagonal forms. It occurs as yellow granular masses with a grey to black streak. H 3.5; SG 7.6
*Localities.* Occurs with galena and tellurium at the Empress Josephine mine, Kerber Creek, Colorado.

**Stromeyerite AgCuS**
Stromeyerite crystallizes in the orthorhombic system as pseudohexagonal prisms or as compact masses coloured dark grey with a blue tarnish; the streak is steel grey. H 2.5–3; SG 6.2
*Localities.* Occurs in Colorado as a major ore of silver; also from British Columbia; Mexico; Chile; Germany; USSR; Tasmania; and also at some other localities.

Above: Petzite from Kalgoorlie, Australia

Above right: Calaverite from Cripple Creek, Colorado

**Jalpaite $Ag_3CuS_2$**
Jalpaite crystallizes in the tetragonal system as foliated masses coloured grey but tarnishing to dark grey or yellow. The streak is black. H 2.5; SG 6.8
*Localities.* Occurs with chalcopyrite at Jalpa, Mexico; also from Příbram, Czechoslovakia; and Colorado.

**Eucairite AgCuSe**
Eucairite crystallizes in the orthorhombic system as granular masses or as films on calcite. The colour is silver-white or grey tarnishing to light yellow. H 2.5; SG 7.6–7.8
*Localities.* Occurs in basalt at Lake Athabasca, Saskatchewan; in quartz and calcite at Skrikerum, Sweden; and in a copper ore at Sierra de Umango, La Rioja, Argentina.

**Sternbergite $AgFe_2S_3$**
Sometimes known as flexible silver ore, sternbergite crystallizes in the orthorhombic crystal system forming fan-like aggregates; twinning may also occur. The individual crystals take the form of thin laminae which are flexible. There is a perfect cleavage. The colour is brown with a black streak and a metallic lustre. H 1.0–1.5; SG 4.2
*Frieseite* is a mixture of sternbergite and pyrite; and it is thought that *argyropyrite* may be identical in composition with sternbergite or argentopyrite.
*Occurrence.* Sternbergite occurs in silver mines with pyrargyrite and stephanite.
*Localities.* From Jachymov, Czechoslovakia; Freiberg, E. Germany; Colorado and California.
*Treatment.* Clean with water.

**Argentopyrite $AgFe_2S_3$**
Argentopyrite crystallizes in the orthorhombic system as pseudohexagonal crystals coloured white or grey tarnishing to brown, blue, green or purple. H 4; SG 4.2
*Localities.* Occurs with arsenic and proustite at Freiberg, E. Germany; Jachymov, Czechoslovakia.

**Calaverite $AuTe_2$**
Calaverite contains some silver and crystallizes in the monoclinic system, forming thin prisms striated parallel to their length. Massive forms also occur. The colour is white, often tinged with yellow; the lustre is metallic. Calaverite may be distinguished from sylvanite by its lower silver content, but this can only be established by chemical tests. H 2.5; SG 9.0
*Occurrence.* In vein deposits, with native gold and other minerals.
*Localities.* Found in Western Australia at Kalgoorlie; in the Cripple Creek district, Teller Co., Colorado and in Calaveras Co., California.
*Treatment.* Clean with water.

**Krennerite $AuTe_2$**
Krennerite crystallizes in the orthorhombic system as prismatic crystals with a perfect cleavage. The colour is pale yellow or white with a metallic lustre. H 3; SG 8.6
*Occurrence.* Occurs in low-temperature veins with calaverite at Cripple Creek, Teller Co., Colorado; also from Kalgoorlie, Western Australia; and from other localities.

**Petzite $Ag_3AuTe_2$**
Petzite contains three parts of silver to one of gold and crystallizes in the cubic crystal system, in which it forms granular masses. It is grey to black and may tarnish to the latter colour. Its lustre is metallic. Petzite graduates toward hessite (q.v.) which is silver telluride, $Ag_2Te$. It is brittle and somewhat sectile. H 2.5–3; SG 8.7–9.0
*Occurrence.* In vein deposits with tellurides.
*Localities.* Petzite is found at Kalgoorlie, Western Australia and in Calaveras County, California.
*Treatment.* It may be cleaned in dilute acids avoiding nitric acid.

**Sylvanite $AgAuTe_4$**
An ore of gold, sylvanite is a telluride of gold and silver. It crystallizes in the monoclinic system, commonly as twins, which are arborescent and resemble writing; also as bladed and columnar crystals and as granular masses. It is steel-grey in colour and streak and has a brilliant metallic lustre and perfect cleavage. H 1.5–2.0; SG 7.9–8.3
*Occurrence.* Sylvanite occurs in gold-bearing veins and is usually associated with igneous rocks.
*Localities.* Found in Romania and at Kalgoorlie in Western Australia. Also found in the mines at Carson Hill, Calaveras County, California.
*Treatment.* Surface alteration takes place on exposure to strong light. Any acid apart from nitric acid or aqua regia can be used as a cleaning agent.

Right: Sylvanite crystals. Sylvanite is a telluride of gold and silver

*Above: Red blende (sphalerite) from Wales*

*Left: Blende from Switzerland. These crystals show 'spinel twinning'; that is, crystals interpenetrate each other, the whole resembling a spinel crystal*

**Blende ZnS**

Blende, also called sphalerite, is an important ore of zinc and has also been used, despite its softness and easy cleavage, as a gemstone. The mineral crystallizes in the cubic system, common forms being tetrahedra, dodecahedra and cubes. Polysynthetic twinning is common. There is a perfect dodecahedral cleavage and a nearly adamantine lustre. The colour is usually yellow to yellow-brown or black, but red and colourless examples may also be found. The streak is brownish to yellow. Some specimens may exhibit triboluminescence. Blende is the stable form of ZnS below 1020°C; wurtzite (q.v.) the stable form at higher temperatures. H 3.5–4; SG 3.9–4.1; RI 2.37–2.42; dispersion 0.156

*Varieties.* Marmatite contains up to 20% iron; pribramite contains some cadmium. Blende forms veins in limestone or occurs as concretions.

*Occurrence.* Blende is found in areas of contact metamorphism where intrusive igneous material has introduced sulphides into adjacent rocks. Limestones or dolomites frequently contain ores formed by replacement. Blende is found in veins and is frequently found associated with galena, pyrite, calcite and dolomite.

*Localities.* Fine gem-quality material is found at Picos de Europa, Santander, Spain and also from Joplin, Missouri; the St. Agnes area of Cornwall provides material; the most important economic deposits are in Missouri, Oklahoma and Kansas, and from the Bou-Beker area in Morocco.

*Treatment.* Calcite encrustation may be removed with dilute hydrochloric acid though prolonged application may dull bright surfaces.

*Fashioning. Uses:* faceting or cabochons; *cleavage*: perfect, dodecahedral; brittle; *cutting angles*: crown 30°–40°, pavilion 37°–40°; *heat sensitivity*: low.

*Right: This crystal of cinnabar from Almaden, Spain, shows pinacoidal (top) and rhombohedral (side) faces*

*Below right: Cinnabar in its commoner form of a granular mass*

**Wurtzite ZnS**
Wurtzite crystallizes in the hexagonal system as hemimorphic pyramidal crystals or as crusts or fibrous masses. The colour is brown or orange to black with a brown streak. May fluoresce orange under ultra-violet light. H 3.5–4; SG 4.0–4.1
*Occurrence.* Occurs in hydrothermal veins with blende; sometimes in sedimentary deposits.
*Localities.* From England; Peru; USA; Czechoslovakia; etc.

**Greenockite CdS**
Greenockite is an ore of cadmium. It crystallizes in the hexagonal crystal system in hemimorphic pyramidal crystals with a distinct cleavage. The colour is honey or orange-yellow and the streak may be the same colour, or a brick-red. The lustre is resinous. H 3.0–3.5; SG 4.9–5.0; RI (when transparent) 2.50, 2.52
*Occurrence.* Greenockite is associated, often as a coating, with zinc minerals, and particularly blende.
*Localities.* Good crystals may be found at Bishopton, Renfrewshire, Scotland; at Příbram, Czechoslovakia; at Franklin, New Jersey and in Missouri.
*Treatment.* May be cleaned with any acid apart from hydrochloric.

**Cinnabar HgS**
Cinnabar is the only common ore of mercury and crystallizes in the hexagonal system, forming rhombohedral or thick tabular crystals; penetration twins are common. Most cinnabar, however, is found as compact granular masses. There is a perfect prismatic cleavage. It is cochineal-red with a tendency to brown; the lustre is close to metallic and the streak is vermilion. H 2–2.5; SG 8.0–8.2; RI 2.91–3.27
*Occurrence.* Cinnabar is found in fractures, often in sedimentary rocks. In many cases it occurs in areas associated with volcanic activity, and also in the vicinity of hot springs.
*Localities.* From Mt. Avala near Belgrade, Yugoslavia. Good crystals are found at Moschellandsberg (Landsberg) in W. Germany. The most important economic deposit is at Almaden, Ciudad Real, Spain. In California cinnabar is found in the Coast Range. Some large transparent red crystals come from China.
*Treatment.* Cinnabar may tarnish when exposed to strong light. Can be cleaned with cold concentrated citric acid.
*Fashioning. Uses:* faceting or cabochons; *cleavage:* perfect prismatic; sectile; *cutting angles:* crown 30°–40°, pavilion 37°–40°; *heat sensitivity:* high.

*Right: The cadmium sulphide greenockite is usually found as a coating as in this specimen*

**Metacinnabarite HgS**
An ore of mercury, metacinnabarite belongs to the cubic crystal system. It forms tetrahedral crystals, although these are rare; it is more usually found massive. The colour and streak are black, and the lustre is metallic. H 3; SG 7.7
*Occurrence.* Found in the upper portions of mercury deposits.
*Localities.* From Idria, Italy; the Bedington mine near Knoxville, California; and at other places in the same state.
*Treatment.* May be cleaned with dilute acids.

**Tiemannite HgSe**
Tiemannite crystallizes in the cubic system as tetrahedra or as masses coloured grey with a tinge of purple. The streak is black. H 2.5; SG 8.2–8.3
*Localities.* Occurs with baryte and calcite with manganese in a limestone at Piute Co., Utah; Harz Mountains, Germany.

**Coloradoite HgTe**
Coloradoite crystallizes in the cubic system as black granular masses. H 2.5; SG 8.1–8.6
*Localities.* Occurs in telluride ores in Colorado; also from California and Kalgoorlie, Western Australia.

**Galena PbS**
The most important ore of lead, also containing silver, galena crystallizes in well-shaped crystals of the cubic system, most commonly in cubes, though octahedra are also found. It may also form skeleton crystals and contact and interpenetrant twins. There is a perfect cleavage. The colour is lead grey and the

streak similar; the lustre is metallic. H 2.5–2.75; SG 7.4–7.6
*Occurrence.* Galena is formed by hydrothermal reaction and is found in beds and veins, usually in eruptive rocks and in association with sphalerite, silver ores, quartz and calcite. It also occurs in contact metamorphic deposits, and particularly as replacement deposits in dolomites or limestones.
*Localities.* Galena is found with silver in Czechoslovakia; from Freiberg and the Harz Mountains, Germany; Truro and Liskeard in Cornwall, and from Missouri and Wisconsin.
*Treatment.* Calcite covering may be removed with dilute acetic acid.

**Clausthalite PbSe**
Clausthalite crystallizes in the cubic system as masses coloured lead-grey with a tinge of blue; some surfaces may show black with red or brown spots. H 2.5–3; SG 8.1–8.2
*Localities.* Occurs with selenides at Lake Athabasca, Saskatchewan; Harz Mountains, Germany; Falun, Sweden.

**Altaite PbTe**
Altaite crystallizes in the cubic system, as cubes or octahedra, but is usually found massive. It is white, with a metallic lustre, but possesses a yellowish tinge which tarnishes to a bronze colour. There is a perfect cubic cleavage and a black streak. H 2.0–3.0; SG 8.16
*Occurrence.* Found with hessite.
*Localities.* Altai Mountains, Siberia, USSR; Coquimbo, Chile; California and other areas of the United States.
*Treatment.* May be cleaned with any acid apart from nitric.

**Realgar AsS**
Realgar crystallizes in the monoclinic crystal system and is found as red or orange-yellow short prismatic crystals with vertical striations and a resinous lustre. The streak is orange to orange-red. H 1.5–2.0; SG 3.56
*Occurrence.* Realgar is found with ores of silver and lead.
*Localities.* Fine crystals occur in dolomite in Valais, Switzerland; also in the USA: and in Japan.
*Treatment.* Realgar alters to orpiment and finally crumbles to powder on prolonged exposure to light. It should therefore be kept in a container impervious to light. May be cleaned with water.

**Orpiment $As_2S_3$**
Orpiment, which is also known as yellow arsenic, is used as a pigment. It crystallizes in the monoclinic system. Crystals are small and the material is more commonly found massive, with a lemon-yellow colour and a pearly to resinous lustre. There is a perfect cleavage and the streak is pale yellow. H 1.5–2.0; SG 3.4–3.5
*Occurrence.* Frequently found with realgar. Results from the alteration of arsenic and some silver minerals.
*Localities.* Fibrous masses are found at Moldava, Romania and also in Kurdistan and near Salonika, Greece. Good quality crystals are found at Mercur, Utah and the mineral is also found as a

*Above: Crystals of galena occurring as cubes from Joplin, Missouri. Octahedra are also found*

*Left: The arsenic trisulphide orpiment usually occurs massive. This specimen is from Pakistan*

*Above: Prismatic crystals of stibnite, the commonest antimony mineral. From Victoria, Australia*

hot-spring deposit at Steamboat Springs, Nevada. Large workable deposits are found in Turkey, Iran and in Georgia, USSR.
*Treatment.* Dilute acetic acid is probably the most satisfactory medium for removing calcite encrustations, since orpiment is readily attacked by most acids. Its softness makes the use of sharp tools unwise.

**Stibnite $Sb_2S_3$**
Stibnite is the most important ore of antimony. It crystallizes in the orthorhombic system as prismatic crystals with vertical striations and, in some cases, with numerous well-developed faces. It may also be found massive or in radiating groups of columnar crystals. It is lead-grey in colour and in streak; there is a perfect cleavage and a metallic lustre which is very brilliant on freshly broken surfaces. Crystals may tarnish to black and may contain silver or gold. H 2.0; SG 4.52–4.62
*Occurrence.* Stibnite is most commonly found in veins with quartz, frequently in granitic rocks. It may also be found as beds in schists and in hot-spring deposits.
*Localities.* Fine crystals have been found at the Ichinokawa mines, Shikoku, Japan, and at Wolfsburg, Germany. Major economic deposits are in Honan Province, China, in Algeria and in Mexico.
*Treatment.* Best cleaning agent is water. Soaps and detergents should be avoided. Lustre dulls after exposure to strong light.

**Metastibnite $Sb_2S_3$**
This is the amorphous form of *stibnite,* with the same chemical composition. It is brick-red in colour with a sub-metallic lustre and has been found with cinnabar and arsenic sulphide on siliceous sinter at Steamboat Springs, Nevada.
*Treatment.* As for stibnite, the best cleaning agent is water, without the addition of soaps or detergents.

**Bismuthinite $Bi_2S_3$**
An ore of bismuth, bismuthinite sometimes contains added copper and iron. It is lead-grey in colour and streak with a metallic lustre, and crystallizes in the orthorhombic system as acicular crystals, though the material is far more commonly found massive. It has a perfect cleavage and may be sectile. H 2.0; SG 6.7–6.8
*Occurrence.* Most commonly found associated with igneous rocks and in

*Right: These acicular (needle-shaped) crystals of bismuthinite are rare; the mineral is more commonly found in masses. From Carn Brea, Cornwall*

tourmaline-bearing copper deposits and tourmaline-quartz veins.
*Localities.* Found in Bolivia, Cornwall, and with chrysoberyl at Haddam, Connecticut.
*Treatment.* It is fairly resistant to acids, but concentrated nitric should be avoided.

**Guanajuatite $Bi_2(Se, S)_3$**
Guanajuatite is the orthorhombic phase of bismuth selenide; the trigonal phase is paraguanajuatite. It forms bluish-grey acicular crystals and is also found massive. The lustre is metallic. H 2.5–3.5; SG 6.25–6.98
*Occurrence.* Found in the mines at Guanajuato, Mexico, associated with bismuth and pyrite; and also in the Harz Mountains, Germany, in calcite veins.
*Treatment.* May be cleaned with dilute acids.

**Tetradymite $Bi_2Te_2S$**
Tetradymite crystallizes in the hexagonal crystal system, forming small crystals sometimes bladed but more commonly massive. The colour is pale grey and the lustre metallic. There is a perfect cleavage. H 1.5–2.0; SG 7.2–7.6
*Occurrence.* Commonly found in gold-bearing quartz veins and in surface deposits formed by the action of hot water on igneous rocks.
*Localities.* Found in Czechoslovakia and Norway; in Bolivia; in California and Colorado in the United States; and in Canada.

**Joseite $Bi_3Te(Se, S)$**
Grunlingite and oruetite appear to be similar in composition to joseite.
*Localities.* From Minas Gerais, Brazil.

**Molybdenite $MoS_2$**
An important ore of molybdenum, molybdenite crystallizes in the hexagonal crystal system as tabular hexagonal prisms which taper and show horizontal striations. Granular and massive forms may also be encountered. The colour is lead-grey and the streak bluish-grey on paper and greenish-grey on porcelain. It is sectile and has a metallic lustre. It may feel greasy; it differs from graphite in its streak on paper. H 1.0–1.5; SG 4.7–5.0
*Occurrence.* Molybdenite is found in pneumatolytic contact deposits and is associated with cassiterite, scheelite, and wolframite; it may also be found in pegmatites and in quartz veins in association with granite.
*Localities.* Good quality specimens are found at Raade, Norway, at Blue Hill, Maine and in Colorado. There are several Canadian localities.
*Treatment.* Iron stains removable with oxalic acid.

**Tungstenite $WS_2$**
Tungstenite crystallizes in the hexagonal system as masses or scales coloured grey. H 2.5; SG 7.7
*Localities.* Occurs in limestone at the Emma mine, Salt Lake Co., Utah.

**Alabandite MnS**
Alabandite crystallizes in the cubic system and is usually found granular massive. The colour is black and the streak green; it has a metallic lustre. There is a perfect cleavage. H 3.5–4.0; SG 3.93–4.04
*Occurrence.* In ore veins with sphalerite and other sulphides.
*Localities.* Alabanda, Asia Minor; Morococha, Peru; Tombstone, Arizona.
*Treatment.* If necessary may be cleaned with water. It is liable to oxidize if stored in a moist atmosphere and may undergo surface alteration on exposure to strong light.

**Hauerite $MnS_2$**
Related to pyrite, hauerite is manganese disulphide and crystallizes in the cubic crystal system; although it is most commonly found massive, octahedral or pyritohedral crystals may occur. It is brown in colour with a metallic lustre and a brownish-red streak. H 4.0; SG 3.46
*Occurrence.* Found in association with gypsum and sulphur, probably deposited from manganese and sulphur-bearing water.
*Localities.* It is found in clay at the Destricello mine near Raddusa in Italy.
*Treatment.* Use any dilute acid apart from hydrochloric as a cleaning agent.

*Left: A rosette of pyrrhotine, an iron sulphide. From Chiuzbaia, Romania*

*Below left: This tapering hexagonal prism of molybdenite from Pontiac, Canada, shows a metallic lustre*

**Pyrrhotine FeS**
An alternative name for this ferrous sulphide is magnetic pyrite although its magnetic powers vary in intensity. It has a varying sulphur content. Crystallizing in the hexagonal crystal system, it is usually found massive, although tabular crystals or pyramidal ones with horizontal striations may occur. Its colour is bronze-yellow to copper-red and the streak is dark-grey to black. Crystals tarnish easily and have a metallic lustre. As pyrrhotine often includes nickel, its main importance is as an ore of that metal. H 3.5–4.5; SG 4.58–4.64
*Occurrence.* Associated with basic igneous rocks such as gabbro and often found with pyrite and magnetite. It may also be found in contact metamorphic

*Below: A crystal of hauerite displaying a combination of forms, in this case the cube and octahedron. From Sicily*

*Right: Pyrite crystal from Traversella, Italy*

*Far right: Pyrite from Blackdene, Durham, showing globular form*

*Below right: Arsenopyrite from Panasqueira, Portugal*

deposits. Some metamorphic limestones include pyrrhotine.
*Localities.* Large crystal groups are found in Carinthia, Austria; in Trentino, Italy; and in Norway and Sweden. The nickel-bearing variety is found in large workable quantities at Sudbury, Ontario.
*Treatment.* Iron stains may be removed with oxalic acid, and calcite by judicious use of hydrochloric acid. Careful washing must follow to ensure that all traces of acid are removed.

**Pyrite $FeS_2$**
Pyrite is very often confused with gold, which it somewhat resembles. Gold and copper are found in pyrite and the mineral is mined both as a source of these metals and also for its sulphur. It crystallizes in the cubic system as cubes, which are striated on each face, the striations being at right angles to each other on adjacent faces, due to oscillation between this form and that of the pyritohedron. Pyrite is also found massive. The streak is greenish-black. It displays a metallic lustre and may be distinguished from gold by its far lower specific gravity and from chalcopyrite by a paler colour and greater hardness. It may display triboluminescence. H 6.0–6.5; SG 4.95–5.10
*Occurrence.* Pyrite is a common constituent of many rock-types and is sometimes associated with coal. It usually occurs as small individual crystals but may display a radiating structure when found in concretions.
*Localities.* Pyrite is of world-wide occurrence; fine crystals are found in Germany and the St. Gotthard region of Switzerland. Pyritohedra are found in the island of Elba. In England good crystals have been found in the Liskeard, St. Just and St. Ives areas of Cornwall. Peru, Bolivia, Chile, Brazil, Japan and Mexico also provide excellent material.
*Treatment.* Remove iron stains with oxalic acid.
*Fashioning. Uses:* cabochons or faceting; *cleavage*: indistinct to cubic and octahedral faces; brittle and sensitive to shock; *cutting angles*: variable, to suit requirements; *heat sensitivity*: fairly high.

**Marcasite $FeS_2$**
It should be noted that what is known as marcasite in the jewellery trade is in fact pyrite (q.v.). Marcasite has an identical chemical composition, but crystallizes in the orthorhombic crystal system. The crystals are commonly tabular or pyramidal; it is also found massive and may display a wide variety of shapes such as reniform and globular. The colour is a bronze-yellow and this may deepen on exposure to light. The streak is greyish or brownish-black and the lustre metallic. It may be distinguished from pyrite by its lower SG and by its differing crystal forms; the colour is also paler. H 6.0–6.5; SG 4.85–4.90
*Occurrence.* Marcasite is associated with galena, sphalerite, calcite and dolomite in replacement deposits in limestones; also in druses of ore veins.
*Localities.* The Karlovy Vary area of Czechoslovakia supplies crystals of a spear-like shape. It is also found in the Kentish chalk marl between Folkestone and Dover. A stalactitic form is found at Galena, Illinois.
*Treatment.* Marcasite is a fairly unstable mineral and is liable to disintegrate with the formation of ferrous sulphate and sulphuric acid. It should not be cleaned.
*Fashioning. Uses*: cabochons or faceting; *cleavage*: poor, prismatic; brittle; *cutting angles*: variable, to suit requirements; *heat sensitivity*: fairly high.

**Löllingite $FeAs_2$**
Löllingite (or loellingite) is a diarsenide of iron, but passes into $Fe_3As_4$, which is leucopyrite; it is also close to arsenopyrite and safflorite $CoAs_2$. It is a member of the orthorhombic crystal system and is normally found massive, coloured silver-white to steel-grey to black. H 5.0–5.5; SG 7.0–7.4
*Occurrence.* Löllingite occurs in veins and is associated with calcite, silver, cobalt and gold ores. It is deposited from solution at medium temperatures.
*Localities.* The classic locality from which the name is taken is Lölling, near Hüttenberg, Carinthia, Austria; other localities are the Harz Mountains, Saxony and Silesia in Germany, and Poland.
*Treatment.* Hydrochloric acid may be used to remove calcite covering that is sometimes found.

**Arsenopyrite FeAsS**
An ore of arsenic, arsenopyrite is sometimes known as mispickel. Sometimes

*Above right: The iron disulphide marcasite from Cornwall. The name derives from the Arabic word used for pyrite*

*Right: Cobaltite on chalcopyrite, from Sweden*

part of the iron is replaced by cobalt (up to 12%); the name given to the mineral of this composition is danaite. Arsenopyrite crystallizes in the monoclinic crystal system and forms twins, which may be trillings or cruciform; the crystals themselves are prismatic, sometimes vertically flattened. Granular forms are also found. The colour is white inclining to grey and the streak greyish-black. There is a cleavage and the lustre is metallic. H 5.5–6.0; SG 5.9–6.2
*Occurrence.* Arsenopyrite is often associated with gold and also with tin and tungsten in pneumatolytic deposits; it is also associated with silver ores and with quartz in veins deposited by hot waters. It may occur in a disseminated form in limestones and serpentinites.
*Localities.* Arsenopyrite is found in the silver mines at Freiberg, E. Germany; in crystals from the Binnental, Valais, Switzerland; fine crystals from Franconia, New Hampshire. It is also found at Franklin, New Jersey. Large masses found in quartz veins at Deloro, Hastings County, Ontario.
*Treatment.* Unaffected by hydrochloric acid, which may be used to remove adhering minerals.

**Gudmundite FeSbS**
Gudmundite crystallizes in the monoclinic system as prismatic crystals, often twinned and coloured grey. H about 6; SG 6.7
*Occurrence.* Occurs in sulphide deposits.
*Localities.* From Sweden; Norway; Yellowknife, Northwest Territories; etc.

**Linnaeite $Co_3S_4$**
Linnaeite crystallizes in the cubic system as octahedra or as granular masses. The colour is grey, tarnishing to red or violet. H 4.5–5.5; SG 4.8–5.0
*Occurrence.* Occurs in hydrothermal veins with other sulphides.
*Localities.* From Siegen, Germany; Katanga, Zaire; Maryland, California; and other localities.

**Safflorite (Co, Fe)$As_2$**
Safflorite crystallizes in the orthorhombic and monoclinic systems as fibrous masses coloured white tarnishing to grey. The streak is grey to black. H 4.5–5; SG 7.2
*Occurrence.* Occurs with minerals containing cobalt or nickel in vein deposits.
*Localities.* From Great Bear Lake, Ontario; Sweden; Germany; etc.

**Smaltite (Co, Ni) $As_{2-3}$**
Smaltite is closely related to skutterudite. It is an ore of cobalt, crystallizing in the cubic crystal system as massive granular forms. It is tin-white inclining to grey, with a metallic lustre and a greyish-black streak. It is not possible to sharply differentiate between the species skutterudite and chloanthite since they grade into one another with the increase/decrease of cobalt/nickel. H 5.5–6.0; SG 5.7–6.8
*Occurrence.* In veins with ores of silver and cobalt; associated minerals include sphalerite, galena and sometimes bismuth.
*Localities.* From Czechoslovakia, where it is found embedded in calcite and from copper-bearing schists at Hesse-Nassau, W. Germany; a large deposit is located at Cobalt, Ontario.
*Treatment.* May undergo alteration in moist atmosphere. Adhering minerals may be removed with the aid of hydrochloric acid.

*Above: Acicular millerite crystals from Westwald, Germany. The crystals can also be found in radiating groups*

*Left: Skutterudite in calcite from Morocco. Skutterudite is part of a series which also includes smaltite and chloanthite*

**Skutterudite (Co, Ni) $As_3$**
An ore of cobalt, skutterudite is close to smaltite, $CoAs_2$, and to chloanthite, $NiAs_2$. It crystallizes in the cubic crystal system, usually in massive form. It is white inclining to grey with a metallic lustre, and may sometimes be iridescent. The streak is greyish-black. H 6.0; SG 6.5–6.9
*Occurrence.* Skutterudite usually occurs in veins with other cobalt and nickel minerals.
*Localities.* Found in New Jersey at Franklin. A large deposit is located at Cobalt, Ontario. The name comes from the classic locality at Skutterud, Norway.
*Treatment.* Adhering minerals removable with hydrochloric acid.

**Cobaltite CoAsS**
Cobaltite crystallizes in the cubic system as cubes, octahedra, pyritohedra and combinations of cube and pyritohedron. Faces are striated and there is a perfect cleavage. The colour is white with a brilliant metallic lustre and a grey streak. H 5.5; SG 6.3
*Occurrence.* Occurs in hydrothermal veins.
*Localities.* From Boulder, Colorado; Idaho; Nevada, California; Cobalt, Ontario; Sonora, Mexico; Sweden; England; etc.

**Carrollite $CuCo_2S_4$**
Carrollite crystallizes in the cubic system as octahedra and is also found as granular masses. The colour is grey tarnishing to red or violet. H 4.5–5.5; SG 4.5–4.8
*Occurrence.* Occurs in hydrothermal veins with other sulphides.
*Localities.* From Carroll Co., Maryland; Sweden.

**Glaucodot (Co, Fe) AsS**
A sulpharsenide of cobalt and iron, glaucodot crystallizes in the orthorhombic system in rhombic crystals or in massive form. The colour is grey to white and the lustre metallic. H 5.0; SG 5.90–6.01
*Occurrence.* With other cobalt minerals; frequently found intergrown with cobaltite.
*Localities.* Good crystals from Hakansbö, Vastmanland, Sweden; from Skutterud, Norway; and from the silver veins at Cobalt, Ontario.
*Treatment.* Clean with water.

**Millerite NiS**
Millerite is an ore of nickel. It is a member of the trigonal crystal system and is found as very slender crystals often in radiating groups; it may also occur as

*Right: Niccolite in its usual form of a crystalline aggregate*

*Far right, above: Typical form of the nickel arsenate rammelsbergite from Schneeberg, East Germany*

*Below right: Breithauptite with ullmannite in calcite*

*Far right, below: Another example of ullmannite*

tufted coatings. There is a perfect cleavage and the colour is brass-yellow with a greenish-black streak and metallic lustre. The crystals may develop a grey iridescent tarnish. H 3.0–3.5; SG 5.3–5.6
*Occurrence.* Millerite occurs with other nickel minerals and sometimes with coal; it has also been found associated with serpentinites and in meteoritic iron.
*Localities.* Millerite has been found with nickel, cobalt and silver ores in Czechoslovakia; with iron ores in Westphalia, W. Germany; very fine hair-like crystals from Merthyr Tydfil, Mid Glamorgan, Wales; with a green chrome-bearing garnet at Orford, Ontario.
*Treatment.* The thin crystals should only be cleaned, if at all, in alcohol. They are very easily matted and may also be attacked by acids.

**Polydymite $Ni_3S_4$**
Polydymite crystallizes in the cubic system as octahedra or granular masses. The colour is grey tarnishing to red or violet. H 4.5–5.5; SG 4.5–4.8
*Occurrence.* Occurs in hydrothermal veins.
*Localities.* From Siegen, Westphalia, Germany.

**Melonite $NiTe_2$**
Melonite crystallizes in the hexagonal system as lamellae with a perfect cleavage and is reddish-brown in colour with a dark grey streak. H 1–1.5; SG 7.7
*Occurrence.* Occurs in hydrothermal veins with other tellurides, also with gold and quartz.
*Localities.* From Calaveras Co., California; Canada; South Australia; USSR.

**Maucherite $Ni_{11}As_8$**
Maucherite crystallizes in the tetragonal system as tabular crystals or as fibrous masses. The colour is grey tinged with red with a dark grey streak. H 5; SG 7.9
*Localities.* With nickel minerals at Sudbury, Ontario; also from Germany and Malaga, Spain.

**Niccolite NiAs**
An ore of nickel, niccolite is sometimes known as copper nickel. It is a member of the hexagonal crystal system although crystals are rare; it is usually found massive. Reniform or columnar shapes are sometimes found. It is pale copper-red with a pale-brown to black streak. It has a metallic lustre. Some iron and cobalt is found in niccolite and in some cases the arsenic is partly replaced by antimony; this brings it closer to breithauptite, NiSb. H 5–5.5; SG 7.8
*Occurrence.* Niccolite is found associated with native silver and silver-arsenic minerals.
*Localities.* It is found at Franklin, New Jersey; Styria, Austria; and Saxony and Thuringia, E. Germany. It is found with silver and cobalt ores at Cobalt, Ontario.
*Treatment.* Dilute hydrochloric acid may be used to remove calcite encrustations.

**Rammelsbergite $NiAs_2$**
Rammelsbergite is a member of the orthorhombic crystal system; it is usually found massive. The colour is white with a reddish tinge; the lustre is metallic. H 5.5–6.0; SG 6.9–7.2
*Occurrence.* Often found associated with quartz and pyrite and with other nickel minerals.
*Localities.* Lölling, Carinthia, Austria; in the silver veins, Cobalt, Ontario.
*Treatment.* A coating of green annabergite may develop in a moist atmosphere.

**Gersdorffite NiAsS**
Gersdorffite crystallizes in the cubic system; often massive. Iron and cobalt may replace some of the nickel. The colour is white to grey, and the lustre metallic. H 5.5; SG 5.6–6.2
*Occurrence.* Often in veins with siderite and other iron minerals.
*Localities.* Lobenstein, E. Germany; Sudbury, Ontario.
*Treatment.* If necessary, any dilute acid apart from nitric may be used as a cleaning agent.

**Breithauptite NiSb**
Breithauptite is a mineral that crystallizes in the hexagonal system as prismatic crystals but is more commonly found massive. The colour is light red with a metallic lustre; the streak is reddish-brown. H 5.5; SG 7.5–8.2
*Occurrence.* Associated with native silver and silver ores, also with silver-arsenic minerals (cf niccolite).
*Localities.* St. Andreasberg, Harz Mountains, Germany; Cobalt, Ontario.
*Treatment.* Encrustations removable with hydrochloric acid.

**Ullmannite NiSbS**
Ullmannite, a member of the cobaltite family, usually contains some arsenic. It crystallizes in the cubic crystal system; usually massive. When crystals do occur they may be pyritohedra or tetrahedra. The colour is grey to white with a metallic lustre. H 5.0–5.5; SG 6.2–6.7
*Occurrence.* Occurs in veins, often with iron minerals, and sometimes with sphalerite and galena.
*Localities.* Found at Lölling, near Hüttenberg, Carinthia, Austria; from Sardinia and France; from Brancepeth Colliery, Co. Durham, and from Gunnison Co., Colorado.
*Treatment.* Cleaned with water.

**Pentlandite $(Fe, Ni)_9S_8$**
Pentlandite is a sulphide of iron and nickel. It occurs in massive form and is a member of the cubic crystal system. It is a light bronze-yellow in colour, with a metallic lustre, and shows a light

brown streak. H 3.5–4.0; SG 5.0
*Occurrence.* Usually found intergrown with pyrrhotine and associated with millerite, pyrite, chalcopyrite and niccolite.
*Localities.* Occurs with chalcopyrite in Norway and with pyrrhotine in the Sudbury district of Ontario; San Diego Co., California.
*Treatment.* Clean with any dilute acid.

**Bravoite (Fe, Ni)$S_2$**
Bravoite is closely related to pyrite but may contain up to 20% nickel. It crystallizes in the cubic system, though it is commonly only found as small fragments or grains. It is pale yellow with a reddish tarnish. H 5.5–6.0; SG 4.6
*Localities.* Bravoite is found in the vanadium ores at Minas Ragra, Peru; Derbyshire; Spain; Germany; Colorado.
*Treatment.* Clean with dilute acid.

**Kermesite $Sb_2S_2O$**
Alternative names for this oxysulphide of antimony are red antimony, purple blende and antimony blende. Kermesite is a member of the monoclinic or triclinic crystal system. It occurs as tufts of crystals of a cherry-red colour with a perfect cleavage and adamantine lustre; the streak is brownish-red. H 1.0–1.5; SG 4.5–4.6
*Occurrence.* Occurs as an alteration product of stibnite and is commonly associated with other secondary antimony minerals.
*Localities.* Kermesite is found in Czechoslovakia, north-west of Bratislava; south-east of Constantine in Algeria; in Wolfe County, Quebec and in Nova Scotia; at Sonora, Mexico.
*Treatment.* As it loses water in dry atmospheres, store in a closed container.

## Sulpho-Salts

**Tennantite $Cu_3AsS_3$ or $Cu_{12}As_4S_{13}$**
Tennantite is related to tetrahedrite. It is a member of the cubic crystal system and forms dodecahedral crystals; alternatively it may be found massive. The colour is black to grey, with a metallic lustre, and the streak black, brown or dark red. H 3.0–4.5; SG 4.59–4.75
*Occurrence.* Often with silver or zinc.
*Localities.* The variety from Cornwall (Wheal Jewel) contains copper and iron; an argentiferous form, known as fredericite, occurs in Sweden at Falun. The variety binnite is found in the Binnental, Valais, Switzerland; this variety contains up to 14% silver. Sandbergerite is the zinc-bearing variety and is found at Morococha, Peru.

**Tetrahedrite $Cu_{12}Sb_4S_{13}$**
Tetrahedrite is a member of the cubic crystal system in which it forms tetrahedral crystals, often twinned; also found massive. The colour is grey to black; the streak is similar but may also incline to red or brown. The lustre is metallic. Arsenic is usually present and this brings the mineral close to tennantite. H 3–4.5; SG 4.4–5.1

*Above: Tetrahedra of tetrahedrite partly covered by a layer of chalcopyrite. This particular form is called a triakistetrahedron. From the Harz Mountains of Germany*

*Left: Tennantite crystals. This mineral is associated with tetrahedrite in a series. The well-shaped crystals shown here are from Idaho Springs, Colorado*

*Above: Pyrargyrite with amethyst from Guanajuato, Mexico*

*Right: Two proustite crystals from Chanarcillo, Chile. The adamantine lustre is clear*

*Far right: Tabular pseudo hexagonal crystals of stephanite from East Germany*

*Occurrence.* Commonly found in copper or silver veins or in contact-metamorphic deposits. Common associates include chalcopyrite, bornite, sphalerite, galena and the ruby silvers.
*Localities.* Very fine crystals have been found in Romania at Cavnic (Kapnikbanya); an argentiferous form has been found at St. Andreasberg in the Harz Mountains, Germany; fine specimens come from the copper and tin mines in Cornwall, in particular the Herodsfoot mine near Liskeard.
*Treatment.* Clean with water.

**Chalcostibite $CuSbS_2$**
Chalcostibite crystallizes in the orthorhombic system as prismatic crystals or as granular masses. There is a perfect cleavage. H 3–4; SG 4.8–5.0
*Localities.* Occurs with quartz and sulphides at Oruro, Bolivia; Harz Mountains, Germany; Granada, Spain.

**Emplectite $CuBiS_2$**
Emplectite crystallizes in the orthorhombic system as prismatic crystals with a perfect cleavage. The colour is grey or white. H 2; SG 6.3–6.5
*Occurrence.* Occurs with chalcopyrite in veins.
*Localities.* From Colorado; Chile; Saxony, Germany; etc.

**Wittichenite $Cu_3BiS_3$**
Wittichenite crystallizes in the orthorhombic system as prismatic crystals or as masses. The colour is grey or white, tarnishing to yellow; the streak is black. H 2–3; SG 6.2
*Localities.* Occurs with enargite at Butte, Montana; Wittichen and Baden, Germany; Peru; Japan.

**Smithite $AgAsS_2$**
Smithite crystallizes in the monoclinic system as red tabular crystals with a red streak. H 1.5–2.0; SG 4.9
*Occurrence.* Occurs in dolomite with sphalerite and pyrite.
*Localities.* From the Binnental, Valais, Switzerland.

**Proustite $Ag_3AsS_3$**
An alternative name for this silver-bearing mineral is ruby silver ore (cf pyrargyrite). Belonging to the hexagonal crystal system, it is found as acute rhombohedral or scalenohedral crystals; massive forms also occur. There is a distinct cleavage and the colour is scarlet with a similarly coloured streak. The lustre is adamantine and the mineral suffers surface alteration when exposed to light. H 2.0–2.5; SG 5.57–5.64; RI (when transparent) 3.0, 2.7
*Occurrence.* Proustite is found in the upper portions of silver veins with galena and sphalerite.
*Localities.* Jachymov, Czechoslovakia; fine crystals from Ste. Marie-aux-Mines, Alsace, France; from the Dolores mine, Chanarcillo, and from Atacama, Chile; silver-bearing districts in USA; W. Germany.
*Treatment.* Silvery coating forms on surface on exposure to light; removable by gentle wiping, preferably with cotton.
*Fashioning. Uses:* faceting or cabochons; *cleavage:* distinct, rhombohedral; brittle; *cutting angles:* crown 30°–40°, pavilion 37°–40°; *heat sensitivity:* high, dop with cold-setting cement.

**Xanthoconite $Ag_3AsS_3$**
Xanthoconite crystallizes in the monoclinic system as tabular crystals or as reniform masses. The colour is yellow, red or orange with an orange-yellow streak. H 2–3; SG 5.5
*Occurrence.* Occurs in hydrothermal veins with other silver minerals.
*Localities.* From Ste. Marie-aux-Mines, Alsace, France; Chanarcillo, Chile; Freiberg, E. Germany; Czechoslovakia.

**Miargyrite $AgSbS_2$**
Miargyrite crystallizes in the monoclinic system as complex crystals; also massive. The colour is black to grey, but deep-red in thin section. The streak is cherry-red and the lustre metallic. H 2.0–2.5; SG 5.10–5.30
*Occurrence.* Associated with silver and antimony ores. Found in hydrothermal vein deposits formed at low temperatures with other silver sulpho-salts.
*Localities.* From Příbram, Czechoslovakia; Chile, Bolivia; Silver City, Idaho.
*Treatment.* Surface darkens on exposure to strong light.

**Pyrargyrite $Ag_3SbS_3$**
Pyrargyrite crystallizes in prismatic crystals of the hexagonal crystal system and may also be found massive. Multiple twins are common. The colour is black to greyish-black by reflected light and deep red by transmitted light through thin section. The streak is purple-red. There is a distinct cleavage and the lustre is metallic to adamantine. H 2.5; SG 5.77–5.86
*Occurrence.* Pyrargyrite is found in the upper portions of silver veins; associated minerals include galena and sphalerite.
*Localities.* It is found with proustite at Atacama, Chile; from Příbram, Czechoslovakia; in the silver-bearing areas of the Rocky Mountains, including the Silver City area of Colorado; Harz Mountains, Germany.
*Treatment.* As for proustite.

**Stephanite $Ag_5SbS_4$**
Sometimes known as brittle silver ore, stephanite crystallizes in the orthorhombic crystal system as short prismatic or tabular crystals; pseudo-hexagonal twins are common and the crystal faces are sometimes obliquely striated. The

colour and streak are black, and the lustre metallic. H 2.0–2.5; SG 6.2–6.3
*Occurrence.* Occurring in silver deposits, stephanite is associated with other silver minerals and with galena and blende.
*Localities.* From Přibram, Czechoslovakia; Atacama, Chile; and Cornwall. An economically important deposit is located at Comstock Lode, Nevada; Andreasberg, Harz Mts., Germany.
*Treatment.* Exposure to strong light causes a dark coating to form which can be removed ultrasonically.

**Polybasite $Ag_{16}Sb_2S_{11}$**
Polybasite belongs to the monoclinic crystal system, in which it crystallizes as six-sided tabular prisms; twins are also found. The colour and streak is black and the lustre metallic; in thin section the colour is cherry-red. May contain up to 13% copper. H 2.0–3.0; SG 6.0–6.2
*Occurrence.* Found in silver veins; and is associated with silver and lead sulpho-salts, and with quartz and baryte.
*Localities.* Přibram, Czechoslovakia; Atacama, Chile; the silver mines of Colorado and Nevada; Las Chiapas, Sonora, Mexico.
*Treatment.* Dark surface alteration may be removed ultrasonically.

**Matildite $AgBiS_2$**
Matildite crystallizes in the hexagonal crystal system as slender prismatic crystals. Crystals, however, are rare, the mineral more often being found massive. The colour is grey and the lustre metallic. H 2.5; SG 6.9
*Occurrence.* Found with silver ores.
*Localities.* From the Matilda mine, Morococha, Peru; Cobalt, Ontario; Inyo Co., California; Boise Co., Idaho.

**Nagyagite $Pb_5Au\ (Te, Sb)_4\ S_{5-8}$**
A telluride and sulphide of antimony, lead and gold, with $Sb_2S_3$ replacing some PbS. It crystallizes in the tetragonal system as tabular crystals and is also found as granular masses. The colour and streak are grey to black and

Left: Crystals of nagyagite from Transylvania, Romania

there is a perfect cleavage. The lustre is metallic. H 1.0–1.5; SG 7.4
*Occurrence.* In hydrothermal vein deposits associated with native gold.
*Localities.* From Sacarambu (formerly Nagy-Ag), Romania; also from Colorado; Kalgoorlie, Western Australia.

**Hutchinsonite**
**$(Tl, Pb)_2\ (Cu, Ag)As_5S_{10}$**
Hutchinsonite is a member of the orthorhombic crystal system, in which it forms flattened rhombic prisms with a good cleavage. The colour is scarlet to red, and the lustre is adamantine. There is a high birefringence. H 1.5–2.0; SG 4.6
*Localities.* Found in dolomite from the Binnental, Valais, Switzerland; Quiruvilca, Peru.

**Sartorite $PbAs_2S_4$**
Sartorite crystallizes in the orthorhombic crystal system as slender striated crystals of a dark-grey colour and metallic lustre. H 3.0; SG 5.4
*Localities.* In dolomite from the Binnental, Valais, Switzerland.

**Jordanite $(Pb, Tl)_{13}\ As_7S_{23}$**
Jordanite is isomorphous with geocronite. It is a member of the monoclinic crystal system and forms pseudo-hexagonal twins. It is grey in colour, with a metallic lustre and a black streak. H 3.0; SG 5.5–6.4
*Occurrence.* In cavities in dolomite.
*Localities.* Found in the Binnental, Valais, Switzerland.

**Zinkenite $Pb_6Sb_{14}S_{27}$**
Zinkenite crystallizes in the hexagonal system, as crystals resembling hexagonal forms through twinning. Massive forms are more commonly found. The colour and streak are steel-grey and the lustre metallic. H 3.0–3.5; SG 5.12–5.35
*Occurrence.* Occurs with quartz and with other sulpho-salts.
*Localities.* From Wolfsburg in the Harz Mountains, Germany; a silver-bearing variety from Dundas, Tasmania; from Nevada and Colorado; Bolivia; British Columbia.
*Treatment.* Clean fibrous forms in alcohol.

**Boulangerite $Pb_5Sb_4S_{11}$**
Boulangerite crystallizes in the monoclinic crystal system, in which it may either form tabular prismatic crystals or occur massive. The colour is bluish lead-grey and the lustre metallic; there are two directions of cleavage and the streak is reddish-brown. H 2.5–3.0; SG 5.7–6.3
*Occurrence.* Found in ore veins with lead sulpho-salts, galena and pyrite. It may also be found associated with quartz and dolomite.
*Localities.* From Přibram, Czechoslovakia; fine crystals from Sala, Vastmanland, Sweden; also from Nevada and Washington State.

**Geocronite $Pb_5SbAsS_8$**
Isomorphous with jordanite, geocronite is a member of the monoclinic system and is usually found massive granular; it is lead-grey or white and has a metallic lustre. H 2.0–3.0; SG 6.4

Below left: Crystals of meneghinite from Bottino, Italy

*Occurrence.* Often found as nodules in galena.
*Localities.* From Sala, Vastmanland, Sweden: Meredo, Asturias, Spain; Val di Castello, Tuscany, Italy; called kilbrickenite, from Co. Clare, Ireland.

**Cannizzarite**
This is a lead bismuth sulphide, but the exact chemical formula has not yet been determined It is a bladed mineral with a metallic lustre found in fumaroles on Vulcano, Lipari Islands, Sicily, Italy. H not known; SG 6.7

**Meneghinite $Pb_{13}Sb_7S_{23}$**
Meneghinite crystallizes in the orthorhombic system as slender prismatic crystals; it is also found massive. The colour is black to grey, and the lustre metallic. H 2.5; SG 6.34–6.43
*Occurrence.* Associated with galena, sphalerite etc.
*Localities.* Bottino, Italy; Marble Lake, Frontenac County, Ontario; Santa Cruz, California.

Left: A good example of jordanite from the Binnental, Valais, Switzerland. The light-coloured mineral is dolomite

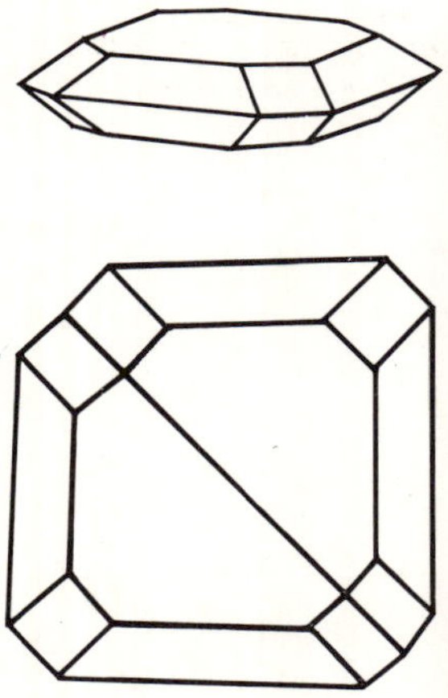

Top: Bournonite from Czechoslovakia. This crystal shows twinning like that depicted in the diagram

Above right: Bournonite crystals on the iron carbonate siderite. From Huttenberg, Austria

**Bournonite $CuPbSbS_3$**
Sometimes known as cog-wheel ore from its appearance, or endellionite from its original Cornish location, bournonite crystallizes in the orthorhombic crystal system, frequently as twins, which by repetition form crosses and wheel shapes. The colour and streak are grey and there is a brilliant metallic lustre. H 2.5–3.0; SG 5.7–5.9
*Occurrence.* Bournonite occurs in veins with galena, sphalerite, etc; also with other sulpho-salts.
*Localities.* Large crystals are found at Neudorf in the Harz Mountains, Germany; from Wheal Boys, Endellion, Cornwall, where it was originally found by Count Bournon. It is also found in Arizona and Nevada.

**Dufrenoysite $Pb_2As_2S_5$**
Dufrenoysite crystallizes in the monoclinic system as tabular crystals with a perfect cleavage and grey in colour. The streak is reddish-brown. H 3; SG 5.5
*Localities.* Occurs in dolomite at the Binnental, Valais, Switzerland; also from Dundas, Tasmania; and from some other localities.

**Aikinite $CuPbBiS_3$**
Aikinite crystallizes in the orthorhombic system as prismatic crystals, or as masses. The colour is black or grey, with a streak of similar colour. H 2.5; SG 7.1
*Localities.* Occurs with galena, gold and quartz at Beresovsk, USSR; from Utah, Idaho; France; Mexico.

**Owyheeite $Ag_2Pb_5Sb_6S_{15}$**
An alternative name for this mineral is silver jamesonite. It is a member of the orthorhombic crystal system, in which it may either occur as acicular crystals or massive. There is a cleavage and the colour is steel-grey to silver-white, with a metallic lustre; there is a yellowish tarnish. The streak is reddish-brown. H 2.5; SG 6.2–6.5
*Occurrence.* In quartz veins.
*Localities.* Poorman mine, Silver City district, Owyhee County, Idaho.

**Freieslebenite $Ag_5Pb_3Sb_5S_{12}$**
Freieslebenite is a member of the monoclinic crystal system, in which it forms prismatic crystals. The colour is light-grey to silver-white and it may also be found as a dark grey, resembling lead. The streak is of a similar colour and the lustre is metallic. H 2–2.5; SG 6.2–6.4
*Occurrence.* Found with silver ores including argentite.
*Localities.* From Freiberg, E. Germany; near Guadalajara, Spain; Gunnison Co., Colorado.

**Berthierite $FeSb_2S_4$**
Berthierite crystallizes in the orthorhombic system as prismatic crystals or as masses with a grey colour tarnishing to dark brown. The streak is dark brown to grey. H 3; SG 4.6
*Occurrence.* Occurs with stibnite and quartz in veins.
*Localities.* From England; France; Germany; Czechoslovakia; Colorado; New Brunswick.

**Jamesonite $Pb_4FeSb_6S_{14}$**
Sometimes known as grey antimony, jamesonite is a member of the monoclinic crystal system and forms acicular crystals; it is also found massive with a fibrous texture. The colour is grey and the streak greyish-black. The lustre is metallic and there is a perfect cleavage. H 2.0–3.0; SG 5.5–6.0
*Occurrence.* Jamesonite is found in ore veins with other lead sulpho-salts, galena, pyrite and calcite.
*Localities.* Found at Endellion in Cornwall; Mount Bischoff, Tasmania; and at the antimony mines in Arkansas and South Dakota.
*Treatment.* Gentle washing in distilled water is the best method of cleaning.

**Stannite $Cu_2FeSnS_4$**
Sometimes called tin pyrite or bell-

metal ore, stannite is a sulphostannate of copper, iron and sometimes zinc. Traces of germanium may also be found. Bolivianite is a synonym. It crystallizes in the tetragonal crystal system and crystals appear pseudotetrahedral through twinning. Massive forms are also found. It is grey to black with a similar streak; the lustre is metallic. H 3.5; SG 4.3–4.5
*Occurrence.* Occurs in tin-bearing veins with cassiterite, tetrahedrite and pyrite.
*Localities.* From Cinvald, Czechoslovakia; Cornwall, at Wheal Rock near St. Agnes; Oruro, Bolivia; Black Hills of South Dakota.

**Teallite $PbSnS_2$**
Teallite is found in thin flexible folia of the orthorhombic crystal system. It is black to grey with a metallic lustre. There is a black streak and a perfect cleavage. H 1.0–2.0; SG 6.4
*Occurrence.* With silver minerals and in tin veins.
*Localities.* Himmelsfürst mine, Freiberg, E. Germany; Santa Rosa, Antequera, Bolivia.

**Cylindrite $Pb_3Sn_4Sb_2S_{14}$**
Cylindrite crystallizes in the orthorhombic system, occurring in cylindrical forms which separate under pressure into shells or leaves. It is black to grey with a metallic lustre. H 2.5; SG 5.4
*Occurrence.* Occurs with pyrite and blende.
*Localities.* From Poopó, Oruro, Bolivia.

**Germanite $Cu_3(Ge, Ga, Fe, Zn)(As, S)_4$**
Germanite contains 6–10% germanium and up to 2% gallium. It is a member of the cubic crystal system, although it is most commonly found massive. The colour is dark reddish-grey with a metallic lustre. H 4.0; SG 4.46–4.59
*Localities.* Intergrown with tennantite and pyrite at Tsumeb, South-West Africa.

**Argyrodite $Ag_8GeS_6$**
Argyrodite often contains tin, grading towards canfieldite. It is a member of the cubic crystal system and forms octahedra and dodecahedra, although these crystals are often minute. Crystals may be twinned; also occurs massive. The colour is grey but turns to red and violet after exposure to air. H 2.5; SG 6.1–6.3
*Occurrence.* With silver minerals.
*Localities.* From the Himmelsfürst mines, Freiberg, E. Germany and from Bolivia.

**Enargite $Cu_3AsS_4$**
An ore of copper and arsenic, dimorphous with luzonite, enargite is a member of the orthorhombic crystal system, in which it forms small crystals with vertically striated prismatic faces; star-shaped trillings and massive forms are also found. The colour is grey to black with a similar streak; there is a perfect cleavage and the lustre is metallic. H 3.0; SG 4.43–4.45
*Occurrence.* An uncommon mineral found in primary deposits and associated with bornite, pyrite, sphalerite, quartz and baryte, among other minerals.
*Localities.* An important deposit at Bor, Yugoslavia; large masses from Morococha, Peru; at Butte, Montana and from Colorado. Famatinite is closely linked with enargite with the formula $Cu_3SbS_4$, and is found at the Sierra de Famatina, La Rioja, Argentina; luzonite is found at Luzon Island, Philippines. Also related is epigenite, of probable formula $(Cu, Fe)_5AsS_6$. It is thought to belong to the orthorhombic system and crystallizes in short prisms; found at Wittichen, near Baden, Germany.
*Treatment.* Dun-black coating is not removable.

**Famatinite $Cu_3SbS_4$**
Famatinite crystallizes in the tetragonal system as granular masses coloured deep pink or brown with a black streak. H 3.5; SG 4.6
*Occurrence.* Occurs in copper deposits.
*Localities.* From Famatina, Argentina; Nevada; Sonora, Mexico; Japan; etc.

Left: Octahedral crystals of cuprite from Cornwall

## Oxides and Hydroxides

**Lithiophorite $(Al, Li)MnO_2(OH)_2$**
Lithiophorite crystallizes in the monoclinic system as botryoidal masses coloured blue to black and with a perfect cleavage. The streak is dark grey to black. H 3; SG 3.1–3.4
*Localities.* Occurs at Schneeberg, E. Germany; South Africa; Virginia and Arizona.

**Cuprite $Cu_2O$**
An ore of copper, and now sometimes cut as a gemstone, cuprite is sometimes

Above left: Small striated enargite crystals from Mexico

Far left: Stannite with cubic pyrite crystals from Oruro, Bolivia

Left: These crystals of argyrodite from Saxony display mamillary habit

*Right: A superb trilling of chrysoberyl from Brazil. The apparent hexagonal form is due to grouping of orthorhombic crystals. This is called pseudo-hexagonal twinning.*

*Right, centre: Typical crystals of psilomelane showing dendritic form. From the Restormel mine, Cornwall*

called red copper ore. It is a member of the cubic crystal system, in which it forms octahedra, dodecahedra and cubes; it may also be found massive. It is cochineal-red with a brownish-red streak and an adamantine lustre. H 3.5–4.0; SG 5.8–6.1
*Occurrence.* Formed by the oxidation and alteration of copper sulphide deposits and associated with native copper, malachite and azurite.
*Localities.* Ekaterinburg, USSR; St. Day, Cornwall; Broken Hill, New South Wales; South-West Africa (gem quality).
*Treatment.* Exposure to strong light causes surface film to form.
*Fashioning. Uses*: faceting; *cleavage*: octahedral, interrupted; brittle; *cutting angles*: no information available; the faceted stones are usually shallow to help reduce the deep colour; *heat sensitivity*: low.

**Crednerite $CuMnO_2$**
Crednerite crystallizes in the monoclinic system as coatings or as thin black plates with a brownish-black streak. H 4; SG 5.3
*Localities.* Occurs with cerussite at Higher Pitts, Mendip Hills, England; etc.

**Bromellite BeO**
Bromellite is a member of the hexagonal crystal system and forms prismatic crystals. It is white in colour. It has been manufactured for commercial use. H 9.0; SG 3.0; RI 1.719, 1.733
*Occurrence.* With swedenborgite at Långban, Värmland, Sweden.
*Treatment.* Should be cleaned with water only.

**Chrysoberyl $BeAl_2O_4$**
A notable gem material, chrysoberyl includes the varieties alexandrite and cymophane (cat's-eye) as well as an attractive yellow-green stone. It crystallizes in the orthorhombic system, often forming pseudo-hexagonal twins or trillings. The lustre is vitreous. The double refraction is 0.009 and there is strong pleochroism; in the alexandrite variety this gives the pleochroic colours red, orange-yellow and green. The presence of chromium, which in alexandrite gives the red and green (so balanced in the absorption spectrum that the colour seen depends on the nature of the incident light—red in tungsten light and green by daylight), can be detected with the spectroscope. The chromium replaces the aluminium, which may also be replaced by ferric iron; this shows in the absorption spectrum as a sharp band at 4,440 Å. The cymophane variety contains a multitude of microscopic channels which reflect light when the stone is cut as a cabochon with the perpendicular to the surface at right angles to them. H 8.5; SG 3.50–3.84; RI 1.747, 1.748, 1.757
*Occurrence.* In granites, pegmatites and schists; also from sands and gravels.
*Localities.* Ural Mountains, USSR (alexandrites); Sri Lanka gem gravels (all varieties); Minas Gerais, Brazil (yellow-green and alexandrite); Malagasy Republic (yellow-green); Somabula Forest, Rhodesia (alexandrite); Mogok, Burma (colourless and green varieties).

*Treatment.* Any dilute acid may be used as a cleaning agent.
*Fashioning. Uses*: faceting or cabochons; *cleavage*: distinct // to the brachydome; brittle; *cutting angles*: crown 40°, pavilion 40°; *pleochroism*: strong in deep colours; *heat sensitivity*: very low.

**Taaffeite $BeMgAl_4O_8$**
Originally thought to be spinel, this pale mauve mineral, with a vitreous lustre, was found to be birefringent by Count Taaffe of Dublin in 1945. It contains a trace of iron. The system was found by X-ray diffraction to be hexagonal and the mineral a member of the trapezohedral class. H 8.0–8.5; SG 3.61; RI 1.721–1.723, and 1.717–1.718
*Localities.* Sri Lanka gem gravels; also

*Right: Octahedra of blue spinel from Franklin, New Jersey*

China, from banded sediments in association with fluorite.
*Fashioning. Uses*: faceting; *cleavage*: not known; *cutting angles*: crown 40°, pavilion 40°; *pleochroism*: weak; *heat sensitivity*: not known. Taaffeite is treated as for spinel by native cutters.

**Periclase MgO**
Periclase crystallizes in the cubic system as cubes or octahedra; also forms grains. It is colourless, with a vitreous lustre, and has a good cleavage. Periclase has been synthesized and may very occasionally be used as a gem. H 5.5; SG 3.56–3.58; RI 1.74
*Occurrence.* In contact-metamorphosed limestones.
*Localities.* Mte. Somma, Mt. Vesuvius, Italy; Nordmark, Värmland, Sweden.
*Treatment.* Bright surfaces may dull in moist atmosphere.
*Fashioning. Uses:* faceting or cabochons; *cleavage:* distinct cubic; tough; *cutting angles:* crown 40°, pavilion 40°; *heat sensitivity:* low.

**Spinel $MgAl_2O_4$**
Spinel is a member of the cubic crystal system, in which it forms octahedra, which occasionally show dodecahedral truncations. Cubes are also found. The colour depends on the variety but for gem use the red is much the most favoured. This variety owes its red colour to chromium; it is distinguished from ruby by the specific gravity. The lustre is vitreous. Blue, violet, black and green colours may also be found. Although a colourless variety is sometimes quoted, it is not found naturally; a seemingly colourless stone is likely to have a tinge of colour, which is not immediately detectable. Spinel has been synthesized by both the Verneuil and flux-melt methods, the products frequently being used as gems. The Verneuil flame-fusion material may be distinguished by its higher SG and refractive index, brought about by an excess of alumina over that found in the natural stones. H 8; SG 3.58 (red variety: other colours may be higher); 3.62 (Verneuil synthetic); RI 1.718 (natural); 1.728 (Verneuil synthetic).
*Occurrence.* Frequently from gem gravels or embedded in limestone or dolomite.
*Major Localities.* Mogok, Burma; Sri Lanka; various localities in the USA.
*Treatment.* Clean with any dilute acid.
*Fashioning. Uses*: faceting or cabochons; *cleavage*: imperfect octahedral; *cutting angles*: crown 40°, pavilion 40°; *heat sensitivity*: very low.

**Psilomelane**
A manganese oxide with water and barium, psilomelane is sometimes given the formula $Ba\,Mn^{2+}\,Mn_8^{4+}\,O_{16}\,(OH)_4$, but strictly speaking it is a mixture of no fixed composition. It is an ore of manganese and is found massive, botryoidal, reniform and sometimes stalactitic. The colour is black to grey and the streak brownish-black. The lustre is submetallic. H 5.0–7.0; SG 6.4
*Occurrence.* Associated with pyrolusite often in alternating layers and frequently found in laterite deposits.
*Localities.* Schneeberg, E. Germany; Lanlivery, Cornwall; Ouro Preto, Minas Gerais, Brazil; in Lake Superior hematite deposits, Michigan.
*Treatment.* Clean with oxalic acid.
*Fashioning. Uses*: cabochons, tumbling, faceting, intaglios, etc.; *cleavage*: none; *cutting angles*: variable to suit requirements; *heat sensitivity*: low.

**Zincite ZnO**
An ore of zinc, zincite is occasionally cut as a gem. It is deep red with a tinge of yellow and an orange-yellow streak. The lustre is sub-adamantine. It crystallizes in the hexagonal system, though it is usually found massive or as grains. There is a perfect cleavage. The red colour is caused by the manganese content. H 4.0–4.5; SG 5.43–5.70; RI 2.013; 2.029
*Localities.* With franklinite and willemite at Franklin, Sussex County, New Jersey.

**Franklinite**
**$(Zn, Mn, Fe^{2+})\,(Fe^{3+}, Mn^{3+})_2O_4$**
An ore of zinc, franklinite is predominantly $ZnFe_2O_4$. It forms octahedra in the cubic system or may be found massive and granular. The colour is black and the streak reddish-brown or black. H 5.5–6.5; SG 5.07–5.22; RI 2.36 (in very thin section).
*Occurrence.* From ores in Precambrian limestones; associated with willemite, zincite and calcite.

Left: A crystal of franklinite, named after its locality, Franklin, New Jersey

*Localities.* Franklin, Sussex County, New Jersey.
*Treatment.* Calcite coating removable with HCl.

**Corundum $Al_2O_3$**
Celebrated for its varieties ruby and blue sapphire, corundum is aluminium oxide, with $Cr_2O_3$ substituting for the alumina in ruby, and $Fe_2O_3$ substituting similarly in sapphire of various colours; in blue sapphires titanium is present in addition to iron. The mineral is a member of the hexagonal crystal system, forming tabular prisms with rhombohedra in the case of ruby, and hexagonal bipyramids in the case of sapphire,

*Above left: A crystal of ruby, a variety of corundum, in green zoisite from Tanzania*

*Left: A rare mineral only known from Franklin, New Jersey, zincite. It has sometimes been faceted*

*Right: In this crystal of quartz from Italy the apparent pyramid faces at the top are really two rhombohedra. Note also the horizontal striation of the prism faces*

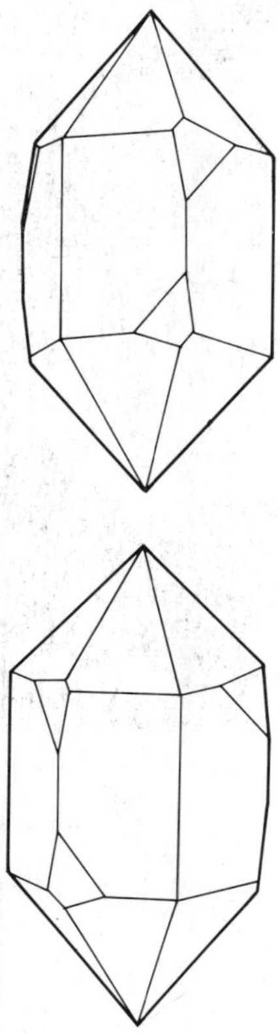

*Below: Left-handed and right-handed forms of quartz. These are sometimes combined in a single twinned crystal*

particularly the Sri Lanka specimens; much material is found water-worn. Lamellar twinning is common and parting may take place parallel to the lamellae; there is no cleavage. The lustre is vitreous. Dichroism is marked, ruby showing crimson and orange-red, blue sapphire showing dark and light blue. Asterism is quite common and is due to reflection of light from crystals of rutile arranged at right angles to the vertical crystal axis. The presence of chromium may be detected by the spectroscope; the absorption spectrum differs from that shown by red spinel in that two or three lines are present in the blue. H 9; SG 3.99; RI 1.76; 1.77, with a double refraction of 0.008.
*Occurrence.* As an accessory mineral in dolomites, limestones, gneisses or mica schists. Associated minerals include spinel and tourmaline as well as other aluminium minerals.
*Localities.* The finest rubies come from Mogok, Upper Burma; this area also produces good quality sapphires. The Sri Lanka gem gravels produce rubies which tend to pink and verge into pink sapphire; parti-coloured stones also found in this region. Good quality rubies and sapphires come from Cambodia and Thailand; the rubies, owing to their iron content, are rather darker than the Burmese stones. Also from Montana (sapphire); from Central and East Africa (ruby and sapphire), particularly Tanzania, where blue sapphire is of good quality. Fine yellows come from Australia and Sri Lanka; greens from Australia, especially from the Anakie area, Queensland.
*Treatment.* Any acid can be used as a cleaning agent.
*Fashioning. Uses*: faceting, cabochons, intaglios, carvings, etc.; *cleavage*: none; planes of parting exist: 1) perfect // to basal pinacoid, 2) prominent, pyramidal; brittle; *cutting angles*: crown 40°, pavilion 40°; *dichroism*: strong in deeply coloured stones; *heat sensitivity*: low, but overheating during faceting and polishing may induce cracks along facet edges.

### Diaspore AlO.OH

Diaspore is the alpha-phase of AlO.OH and forms flattened prismatic crystals of the orthorhombic crystal system; it may also be found granular massive or stalactitic. The colour is white or greenish-grey, with a brilliant lustre. When observed, pleochroism is dark violet and faint yellow. The gamma phase of this material is boehmite. H 6.5–7.0; SG 3.3–3.5
*Occurrence.* As for corundum (see preceding entry).
*Localities.* In a granular limestone near Ekaterinburg, Ural Mountains, USSR; in dolomite at Campolungo, St. Gotthard, Switzerland; mangandiaspore, the dark-red manganese-bearing variety, from Postmasburg, South Africa; in the emery mines, Chester, Massachusetts.

### Gibbsite $Al(OH)_3$

Gibbsite is also known by the alternative name of hydrargillite. It is a member of the monoclinic crystal system, in which it forms tabular hexagonal crystals; it is also found as concretions or stalactitic. There is a perfect cleavage and the colour varies from white to reddish or greenish-white. The lustre is pearly. When breathed on the mineral may give the smell of wet clay. Some specimens may be transparent. H 2.5–3.5; SG 2.3–2.4
*Occurrence.* Gibbsite is formed from the alteration of aluminium-bearing minerals. It is frequently present together with bauxite.
*Localities.* Crystalline gibbsite from the Ural Mountains, USSR; with natrolite in the Langesundfiord, Norway; Ouro Preto, Minas Gerais, Brazil; the stalactitic form is found at Richmond, Massachusetts.

### Quartz $SiO_2$

There are a number of polymorphs of silica, that which is known as quartz being thermally stable below 573°C. High quartz is stable between 573°–870°C. Above this temperature the stable polymorph is tridymite and this retains stability up to 1470°C. Cristobalite is the polymorph stable above this temperature up to its melting point at 1723°C. Liquid silica, when cooled below 1720°C, can form a glass (silica-glass, lechatelierite), which, if heated over 1000°C, devitrifies and forms cristobalite as a stable or metastable phase. Keatite is a metastable form of silica, which has been synthesized at temperatures between 380°C and 585°C; coesite

*Left: Quartz from Bolzano, Italy*

*Below: The so-called Japan twinning of quartz in which two crystals join at nearly 90°. The striation of the prism faces is prominent*

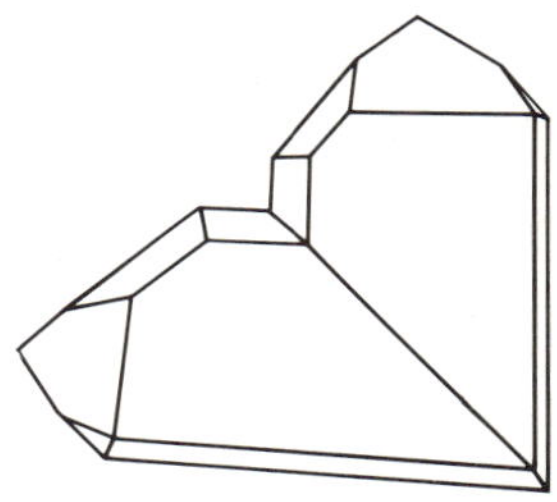

and stishovite are high-pressure polymorphs, which can exist metastably at ordinary temperatures and pressures.

Quartz is one of the most commonly occurring minerals and crystallizes in the hexagonal system; it is a member of the trigonal trapezohedral class. This class possesses the property of enantiomorphism; that is, the atoms of silica are arranged helically along the axes of reference. Crystals are described as being left- or right-handed. If a crystal is right-handed, there is a trigonal pyramid in the upper right corner of the prism face below the positive rhombohedron, and if there are any striations they slope to the right. Left-handed crystals show opposite relations.

The habit of quartz is most commonly the prism with positive and negative rhombohedra. Twinning is virtually universal although it is not usually observable in the external form of the crystal. Quartz is piezoelectric; that is, when it is subjected to mechanical stress it develops electric charges on the surface. Conversely, when it is subjected to an electric charge it shows mechanical strain. It is also pyroelectric; that is, it develops an electric charge on the surface as a result of a change of temperature. Quartz rotates the plane of polarization of light travelling parallel to the c-axis either to the right or left. H 7; SG 2.65; RI 1.544, 1.553

*Varieties.* Varieties of quartz include citrine (yellow); amethyst (violet to purple); rock crystal (colourless); smoky quartz (smoky brown to black); rose quartz (pink), usually but not invariably found massive; blue quartz, which is found as grains in some metamorphic and igneous rocks. Finer-grained varieties include chalcedony, which may be varied in colour; sard, light brown to reddish-brown; carnelian, uniform reddish-brown; moss agate, grey or bluish chalcedony with dark dendritic inclusions, often of an iron compound; agate, a chalcedonic variety in which successive layers differ in colour and translucency; chrysoprase, an apple-green nickel-coloured variety of chalcedony; plasma, a green microgranular quartz; bloodstone, which is greenish with red flecks of iron oxide or red jasper; flint and chert, the distinction between the two being indefinite; jasper, a massive fine-grained quartz with large amounts of additional material, in particular iron oxide, variable in colour but most commonly dark-red to yellow. Inclusions of rutile and tourmaline are common and specimens are known as rutilated or tourmalinated quartz. Star-stones and cat's-eyes are fairly common.

*Occurrence.* Silicon constitutes 27.7% by weight of the Earth's crust and is the second most abundant element after oxygen. Quartz is an important rock-forming mineral and occurs in many ways, though most of the best-developed crystals occur in granite pegmatites and may be deposited by hydrothermal action in granular form as a replacement of pre-existing rocks.

*Localities.* Very fine quartz crystals come from the St. Gotthard area of Switzerland and from Bourg d'Oisans, Isère, France; this locality is notable for twin crystals. In England, Cleator Moor in Cumbria furnishes good crystals; fine agates come from Brazil and formerly from Idar-Oberstein, Germany; small well-formed crystals occur in Herkimer County, New York State.

Fine amethyst is found in the Sverdlovsk area of the Ural Mountains, USSR; at Idar-Oberstein, Germany; Brazil;

*Right: Smoky quartz from the St. Gotthard, Switzerland*

Uruguay; India, where geodes are found in the Deccan. Rock crystal is widely distributed but good specimens come from the St. Gotthard area of Switzerland and from Brazil; rose quartz is found in Rio Grande do Norte at the Alto Feio; in the Malagasy Republic and India and in South-West Africa and South Africa; tiger's-eye comes from South Africa; citrine from Brazil; agates and the non-transparent quartzes particularly from Brazil, South Africa and India.

*Treatment.* Quartz may be cleaned in warm hydrochloric or other acids; hydrofluoric acid should be avoided as should rapid cooling, which may crack the material. Some quartz may be heated to give different colours. Much citrine is obtained by heating amethyst and some green transparent quartz is also obtained in this way.

*Fashioning. Uses*: faceting, cabochons, tumbling, carving, intaglios, etc; *cleavage*: indistinct, conchoidal fracture; brittle in crystalline varieties and tough in some cryptocrystalline varieties; *cutting angles*: crown 40°–50°, pavilion 43°; *dichroism*: strong in deeply coloured varieties of crystalline material; *heat sensitivity*: very low.

**Opal $SiO_2 . nH_2O$**

Opal is amorphous and contains up to 10% water. It is found massive, sometimes reniform or stalactitic; frequently pseudomorphous after other minerals, shells or wood. It has a vitreous lustre.

*Right: Amethyst crystals from Bolzano, Italy, displaying parallel growth*

*Left: Opal from Queensland, Australia*

*Far left: Fire opal from Zimapan, Mexico*

The colour may be milky-white with a play of spectral colour, or grey to black with a similar play of colour. These varieties are known as white and black opal respectively. The spectral colour is a result of diffraction of light from minute quartz spheroids, which are regularly stacked. Another variety has a red to orange body colour, sometimes with spectral colour in addition, which is called fire opal. Water opal has a clear colourless body with spectral colours apparently suspended in it. Opal without a red body-colour and without a play of colour is called common opal or potch. Most common opal is grey or black, although a green form, perhaps coloured by nickel, is also found. Boulder opal is brown and may sometimes display spectral colour.

H 5.5–6.5; SG 1.9–2.3; RI 1.43, 1.45

*Occurrence.* Opal is deposited at low temperatures from water containing silica and occurs with many types of rock. It fills seams and fissures of igneous rock, occurs in mineral veins, and may be deposited from hot springs. Boulder opal is found in sandstone as veins, or as concretions made of shells of sandstone and a hard siliceous clay, with opal between them or filling the centre.

*Localities.* Opal has been found in the area of Cervenica, Czechoslovakia; the fire opal occurs in a trachyte porphyry at Zimapan, Hidalgo, Mexico and the water opal comes from San Luis Potosi in the same country. Some opal is found in Honduras and Guatemala. The finest opals come from Australia where the black opals are found at Lightning Ridge, north-west New South Wales; fine white opals come from the fields at Coober Pedy, and Andamooka in South Australia; boulder opal is found in Queensland. In the USA opal, often pseudomorphous after wood, is found in the Virgin Valley area of Nevada. Recently white opal has been found in the state of Piaui, Brazil.

*Treatment.* Clean with water, which must not contain any dirt or colouring matter.

*Fashioning. Uses*: faceting or cabochons; *cleavage*: none, conchoidal fracture; *cutting angles*: crown 40°–50°, pavilion 43°, table facet often slightly

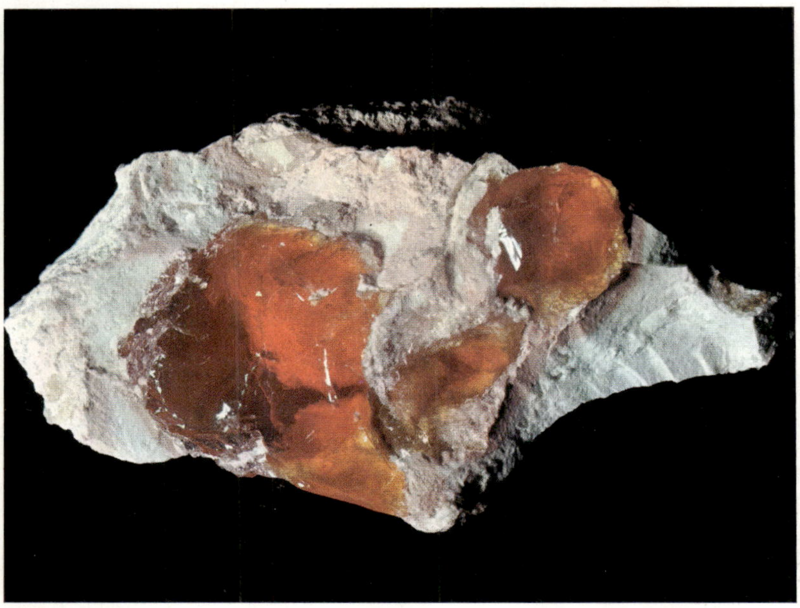

*Far left: Clear masses of fire opal from Mexico*

*Left: Queensland opal*

*Right: Fine geniculate (knee-shaped) rutile crystal from Brazil*

*Far right: Another habit of rutile. These are acicular crystals in quartz from Brazil. Rutile completely enclosed by quartz is sometimes called Venus' hair stone*

domed; *heat sensitivity*: high, care should be taken when dopping and polishing.

**Rutile $TiO_2$**

Rutile, anatase and brookite are polymorphs of $TiO_2$. Rutile crystallizes in the tetragonal system, forming prismatic crystals terminated by bipyramids; twins are found which are sometimes geniculate, or knee-shaped. The colour is reddish-brown to black, the streak pale brown and the lustre adamantine. There is an uneven fracture. H 6–6.5; SG 4.2–4.4; RI 2.62, 2.90 (synthetic rutile). The birefringence is 0.287 and the dispersion about 0.3.

*Occurrence.* Rutile is found as an accessory mineral in igneous rocks and in gneiss, mica schist, granular limestone and dolomite. It may be secondary in origin, occurring as an alteration of mica or sphene. It is found as acicular crystals penetrating quartz (rutilated quartz).

*Localities.* Rutile is found south-west of Graz, Austria; in the St. Gotthard area, Switzerland; from Minas Gerais, Brazil; Waterbury, Vermont; North Carolina; and Graves' Mountain, Georgia. Fine crystals of rutilated quartz from Val Travetsch, Switzerland and from Alexander County, North Carolina.

*Treatment.* Silicate coatings may be removed with hydrofluoric acid, and iron stains with oxalic acid.

*Fashioning. Uses*: faceting; *cleavage*: distinct, prismatic (1st and 2nd order); *cutting angles*: crown 30°–40°, pavilion 37°–40°; *heat sensitivity*: low.

**Anatase $TiO_2$**

Sometimes known as octahedrite, anatase, with rutile and brookite, is a polymorph of $TiO_2$. It forms bipyramidal crystals of the tetragonal system and is also found tabular. It may be yellow, blue, brown or black in colour, with a white streak. The lustre is adamantine to metallic, the latter when the mineral is black and opaque. The fracture is subconchoidal and there is a perfect cleavage. H 5.5–6.0; SG 3.8–4.0

*Occurrence.* Anatase is found as an accessory mineral in igneous and meta-

*Far right: Prismatic anatase from Binnental, Switzerland. Anatase and rutile, which are tetragonal, form a series with brookite, which is orthorhombic*

*Right: This crystal of anatase from Bourg d'Oisans, France, at first sight seems to be an octahedron but is in fact a bipyramid*

morphic rocks, and is derived from the alteration of other titanium minerals. It is associated with quartz, hematite, apatite, sphene and other minerals.
*Localities.* Anatase occurs as fine crystals in the area of Bourg d'Oisans, Isère, France; in the Binnental, Valais, Switzerland; and in chlorite near Tavistock, Devon. It is also found at Somerville, Massachusetts, and as blue crystals in Beaver Creek, Colorado.
*Treatment.* Iron stains may be removed with oxalic acid.

**Brookite $TiO_2$**
Brookite, rutile and anatase are polymorphs of $TiO_2$. Brookite crystallizes in the orthorhombic system, in platy or tabular crystals. The colour is reddish-brown to black, the streak white and the lustre metallic to adamantine. The cleavage is poor and the fracture uneven. H 5.5–6.0; SG 3.9–4.2
*Occurrence.* Brookite is found as an accessory mineral in igneous and metamorphic rocks and in hydrothermal veins.
*Localities.* Brookite occurs in the gold placers of the Urals, USSR, and at St. Gotthard, Switzerland. It is found on quartz with chalcopyrite and galena at Ellenville, Ulster County, New York and in thick black crystals at Magnet Cove, near Hot Springs, Arkansas.
*Treatment.* Clean with water or dilute acids.

**Perovskite $CaTiO_3$**
Perovskite crystallizes in pseudocubic forms of the orthorhombic system, forming cubes with irregularly distributed faces; these are striated parallel to the edges and are probably penetration twins. It may also be found in reniform masses showing small cubes. The colour ranges from pale yellow, through orange, to greyish-black; the streak is colourless to grey. There is an imperfect cleavage and the lustre is metallic-adamantine. H 5.5; SG 4.0
*Occurrence.* Perovskite is found in chlorite, talc or serpentinous rocks, or as an accessory constituent of melilite, nepheline or leucite basalts.
*Localities.* Found in a chlorite slate in the Urals, USSR; in the neighbourhood of the Findelen glacier, Zermatt, Switzerland; Val d'Aosta, Piedmont, Italy.
*Treatment.* Perovskite should be cleaned with dilute acids or water.

Left: *Brookite on albite from Switzerland*

*Far left: Brown anatase from the Binnental, Switzerland*

*Below left: The calcium titanate perovskite. It often looks cubic but the crystal system is orthorhombic. This specimen is from Achmatovsk, USSR*

**Ilmenite $FeTiO_3$**
Ilmenite contains up to about 6% $Fe_2O_3$ and crystallizes in the hexagonal system in thick tabular crystals. Massive compact forms are common and twinning on the basal pinacoid is frequently found. The colour is black, the lustre metallic, and the streak black to brownish-red. There is a basal parting; the fracture is conchoidal. H 5–6; SG 4.5–5.0
*Occurrence.* Ilmenite occurs as an accessory mineral in igneous rocks, including gabbro and diorite. It may occur in quartz veins and in pegmatites in association with hematite and chalcopyrite. It is found concentrated in alluvial sands with magnetite, rutile and monazite.

*Far left: Another crystal of perovskite showing interpenetration*

*Left: Brown perovskite from Val Malenco, Italy*

*Right: Minium from Broken Hill, New South Wales, showing the scaly habit*

*Below right: Prismatic cassiterite from La Villeder, France. It shows the mineral's characteristic high lustre*

*Localities.* Found in the Ilmen mountains in the Urals, USSR; in the Binnental, Switzerland; and as small crystals near Bourg d'Oisans, Isère, France. Fine crystals are found in New York State at Warwick, Amity and Monroe; also with magnetite deposits in the Adirondack region of the same state. Ilmenite in the form of sand is found at Menaccan, Cornwall.

**Baddeleyite $ZrO_2$**
Baddeleyite crystallizes in the monoclinic system forming tabular crystals with a nearly perfect cleavage. It is yellow, brown to black or colourless, and has a greasy lustre. Baddeleyite contains some hafnium. H 6.5; SG 5.5–6.0
*Localities.* Found in the diamond sands at Minas Gerais, Brazil, as rolled pebbles. From Sri Lanka and from Mte. Somma, Mt. Vesuvius, Italy; also near Bozeman, Montana.
*Treatment.* Clean with dilute acids.

**Cassiterite $SnO_2$**
Cassiterite or tinstone crystallizes in the tetragonal system, forming pyramidal or short prismatic crystals. It is also found massive and granular. The colour is reddish-brown to black; it may also be yellow. The streak is white or grey and the lustre adamantine. The fracture is uneven. H 6–7; SG 6.8–7.1; RI 1.9, 2.1; dispersion 0.071, birefringence 0.096
*Occurrence.* Cassiterite is the principal ore of tin and occurs in high-temperature hydrothermal veins and pegmatites in or near granites. It is associated with wolframite, topaz, quartz, tourmaline and other minerals. 'Stream tin', weathered cassiterite, is found in alluvial deposits. It may range from a fine powder through sand-sized grains to rounded pebbles. 'Wood tin' has a fibrous structure, displaying concentric bands and resembling wood.
*Localities.* Large veins of tin ores existed in Cornwall but the most accessible have now been worked out. The classic localities for specimens are St. Agnes, Callington, Camborne, St. Just and St. Austell. At Wheal Coates, near St. Agnes, pseudomorphs after feldspar are found. Other localities include northwest Czechoslovakia; Villeder, France, where fine twin crystals are found, and the Lake Ladoga area of Finland. There are important deposits in Malaysia and in New South Wales; in Bolivia near La Paz, Oruro and Potosi, and in Mexico from the states of Durango, Guanajuato and Jalisco. Small deposits occur in the USA, in the Santa Ana Mountains, California. Good material comes from Arandis, South-West Africa.
*Treatment.* Bolivian crystals are sometimes encrusted with a clay-like material, which can be removed by scraping, or with a sharp knife. Clean with dilute acid.
*Fashioning. Uses*: faceting or cabochons; *cleavage*: imperfect, prismatic (2nd order); *cutting angles*: crown 30°–40°, pavilion 37°–40°; *heat sensitivity*: very low.

**Massicot** and **Litharge PbO**
Massicot is the orthorhombic and litharge the tetragonal phase of PbO; massicot is yellow and litharge yellow-orange. The material is found earthy or scaly massive. Study of some crystals shows that the centre of crystal plates is massicot while the borders are litharge. Massicot is optically positive and litharge negative. Massicot: H 2; SG 9.6; litharge: H 2; SG 9.3
*Occurrence.* Both minerals are of secondary origin, associated with galena and other minerals.
*Localities.* Massicot and litharge are found at Freiberg, E. Germany; Sardinia and Colorado.
*Treatment.* Both minerals are attacked by acids and should be cleaned with water only.

**Minium $Pb_3O_4$**
Minium, sometimes called red lead, crystallizes in the tetragonal system and is found as crystalline scales of a vivid red mixed with yellow, with a greasy lustre. The streak is orange-yellow. More commonly seen as an artificial mineral made by heating litharge or massicot in air. H 2–3; SG 8.9–9.2
*Occurrence.* Minium is of secondary origin and occurs from the alteration of galena or cerussite.
*Localities.* Minium is found in the Altai Mountains, USSR; from the Eifel region of Germany; from Broken Hill, New South Wales and with native lead at the Jay Gould mine, Idaho.
*Treatment.* Clean with water.

**Plattnerite $PbO_2$**
Plattnerite crystallizes in the tetragonal system, and is usually found massive, though prismatic crystals sometimes occur. It is iron black with a chestnut-brown streak and a submetallic lustre. H 5–5.5; SG 9.40
*Localities.* Plattnerite is found with lead minerals at Leadhills, Lanarkshire, and at Wanlockhead, Dumfries and Galloway; and at Shoshone County, Idaho.
*Treatment.* Easily attacked by acids; clean with water.

**Quenselite $PbMnO_2 . OH$**
Crystallizing in the monoclinic crystal system, quenselite has a perfect basal cleavage. It is pitch-black with a metallic lustre and a brownish-grey streak. H 2.5; SG 6.8
*Localities.* Found at Långban, Värmland, Sweden.

**Cesarolite $PbMn_3O_7 . H_2O$**
Cesarolite forms cellular masses, steel-grey in colour. H 4.5; SG 5.2
*Localities.* Found at Sidi-Amer-ben-Salen, Tunisia.

**Magnetoplumbite $(Pb, Mn)_2Fe_6O_{11}$**
Magnetoplumbite crystallizes in the hexagonal system, forming pyramidal crystals. It is black with a dark-brown streak and possesses a good basal cleavage. It is strongly magnetic. H 6; SG 5.5
*Localities.* Magnetoplumbite is found associated with manganophyllite and

*Left: Chromite nodules from the USSR*

kentrolite at Långban, Värmland, Sweden.
*Treatment.* Clean with water.

**Navajoite $V_2O_5 . 3H_2O$**
Navajoite probably crystallizes in the monoclinic system. It is found in fibrous aggregates, dark-brown in colour.
*Localities.* Found with vanadium minerals in Utah, Arizona and Colorado.

**Arsenolite $As_2O_3$**
Arsenolite is the cubic phase of $As_2O_3$ and forms octahedra; it is sometimes found as crusts. There is an octahedral cleavage. The colour is white, with a vitreous lustre, and the mineral is in fact sometimes called white arsenic. H 1.5; SG 3.7
*Occurrence.* Arsenolite is a mineral of secondary origin associated with other arsenic minerals.
*Localities.* Found at Jachymov, Czechoslovakia; at the Amargosa mine, California, and as crystals with enargite in the Alps.
*Treatment.* As the mineral is slightly water-soluble and is affected by acids it has to be handled with care.

**Claudetite $As_2O_3$**
Claudetite is the monoclinic phase of $As_2O_3$ and forms thin plates with a perfect cleavage. The colour is white. The lustre is vitreous to pearly. H 2.5; SG 3.8–4.1
*Occurrence.* Claudetite is of secondary origin and is usually a sublimation product of mine fires.
*Localities.* Claudetite is found at Schmöllnitz, Czechoslovakia and at San Domingos, Algarve, Portugal; Decazeville, France.

**Senarmontite $Sb_2O_3$**
Senarmontite is the cubic phase of $Sb_2O_3$. It is found as octahedra or as crusts, but more commonly massive. It is colourless to grey, and has a resinous lustre. H 2; SG 5.3
*Occurrence.* Senarmontite is formed by the oxidation of stibnite and other antimony minerals.
*Localities.* Found in octahedral crystals and massive at the mine of Djebel-Haminate, Constantine, Algeria; Wolfe Co., Quebec.
*Treatment.* Clean with water.

**Valentinite $Sb_2O_3$**
Valentinite is the orthorhombic phase of $Sb_2O_3$ and occurs as prismatic crystals with a perfect cleavage. The colour is white and the lustre adamantine. H 2.5–3.0; SG 5.7
*Occurrence.* Valentinite is an oxidation product of antimony minerals.
*Localities.* Found at Příbram, Czechoslovakia; near Freiberg, E. Germany; at the Sensa mine, near Constantine, Algeria, and from South Ham, Wolfe Co., Quebec.
*Treatment.* Clean with water.

**Stibiconite $Sb_3O_6(OH)$**
Stibiconite is usually amorphous and massive in form. Its crystals are sometimes assigned to the cubic system. Some antimony is replaced by calcium. The colour is pale yellow to yellowish-white. It is partly isotropic and partly birefringent. H 3–7; SG 3.3–5.5
*Occurrence.* Stibiconite is an alteration product of antimony minerals.
*Localities.* Found at Goldkronach, in the Fichtelgebirge, W. Germany; Altar, Sonora, Mexico; the Empire district, Nevada; Australia.
*Treatment.* Avoid acids; clean ultrasonically; a white coating sometimes encountered is also stibiconite and is not removable.

**Bismite $Bi_2O_3$**
Bismite is the monoclinic alpha-phase of $Bi_2O_3$ and is straw-yellow in colour; its lustre is subadamantine. The cubic phase of $Bi_2O_3$ is sillenite. H 4.5; SG 8.64–9.22
*Occurrence.* Bismite results from the oxidation of other bismuth compounds.
*Localities.* Found with gold at Beresovsk, near Ekaterinburg, Ural Mountains, USSR; Schneeberg, E. Germany; Bolivia; California; New Mexico.

**Chromite $FeCr_2O_4$**
Chromite is the only ore of chromium and often includes some magnesium and aluminium. It crystallizes in the cubic system, forming octahedra, but massive forms are much more common. The colour is black to brownish-black and the streak dark brown. The lustre is metallic and the fracture uneven. H 5.5; SG 4.1–5.1
*Occurrence.* Chromite is an accessory mineral in igneous rocks such as peridotite and serpentinite.
*Localities.* Found in the Ural Mountains, USSR; from Styria, Austria and Zabkovke, Poland; as crystals from the Isle of Unst, Shetlands; from Selukwe, Rhodesia; and from North Carolina and California.
*Treatment.* Clean with dilute acids.

**Tungstite $WO_3 . H_2O$**
Found as powdery coatings, tungstite crystallizes in the orthorhombic system. The colour is yellow to yellowish-green. H 1–2; SG 5.5
*Occurrence.* Tungstite is a secondary mineral found with wolframite.
*Localities.* Found at Salmo, British

*Below left: Tungstite in massive form from Bolivia*

*Below: The octahedral form of senarmontite is clearly shown in this group of crystals from Algeria*

*Right: Becquerelite from Zaire. Many other uranium-bearing minerals are bright yellow*

Columbia; from Cornwall; Connecticut; and Bolivia.
*Treatment.* May be cleaned with dilute acids.

**Hydrotungstite $H_2WO_4 . H_2O$**
This mineral, crystallizing in the monoclinic system, is dark green to yellowish-grey. It is found in Cornwall, New Zealand, Bolivia, etc., as an alteration product of wolframite or scheelite.

**Uraninite $UO_2$**
Uraninite is an important ore of uranium and the source of radium. Well-known by its alternative name of pitchblende, it crystallizes in the cubic system, though crystals are rare. The mineral is usually found massive botryoidal and is brown to black with a brownish-black to grey streak. The lustre is submetallic and greasy, resembling pitch and the fracture is conchoidal to uneven. It is radioactive. The presence of various oxidation and decay products makes the composition very variable. The name uraninite is normally applied to the crystals; pitchblende to the massive material. H 5–6; SG 6.5–8.5 (massive material); 7.5–10.0 (crystals).
*Occurrence.* Crystalline material occurs in granite pegmatites associated with tourmaline, monazite and zircon. The massive forms are usually found as crusts in high-temperature hydrothermal veins in association with cassiterite, pyrite, chalcopyrite and galena. It may appear in alluvial deposits.
*Localities.* From Příbram and Jachymov, Czechoslovakia; various localities in Cornwall; Tanzania; feldspar quarries at Middletown, Connecticut; mica mines at Mitchell, North Carolina; Great Bear Lake, Canada; Shaba, Zaire; Rum Jungle, Northern Territory, Australia.
*Treatment.* Clean in dilute HCl.

*Right: Uraninite from Zaire. This mineral is radioactive*

**Becquerelite $CaU_6O_{19} . 11H_2O$**
Becquerelite crystallizes in minute crystals of the orthorhombic system; twinning is common. The colour is brownish-yellow and there is a perfect cleavage and a resinous lustre. It is radioactive. H 2.5; SG 5.1
*Localities.* Found with curite, soddyite, anglesite and uraninite at Kasolo, Zaire. The variety schoepite is from the same locality ($UO_3 . 2H_2O$), as is ianthinite, at present regarded as $UO_2 . 5UO_3 . 10H_2O$. It crystallizes in the orthorhombic system and forms acicular crystals, coloured violet-black with alteration to yellow on the edges. The streak is brown-violet.

**Davidite**
**$(Fe^{2+}, Ce, U)_2(Ti, Fe^{3+}, V, Cr)_5O_{12}$**
Davidite crystallizes in the hexagonal system but is usually found massive; it is black with a metallic lustre. It is radioactive. H 6; SG 4.5
*Localities.* Davidite is found at Radium Hill, Australia; and Tete, Mozambique.
*Treatment.* Alteration coatings cannot be removed. Clean with dilute acid.

**Brannerite (U, Ca, Ce) (Ti, Fe)$O_{16}$**
Brannerite crystallizes in the monoclinic system as prismatic crystals or as granular masses. The colour is black and the streak dark greenish-brown. H 4.5; SG 4.5–5.4
*Occurrence.* Found chiefly as a primary mineral in pegmatites; also found in gold placers.
*Localities.* From Stanley Basin, Idaho; Bou-Azzer, Morocco; Cordoba, Spain.
*Treatment.* Clean with water.

**Fourmarierite $PbU_4O_{13} . 4H_2O$**
Fourmarierite crystallizes in the orthorhombic crystal system, forming tabular crystals. The colour is red and the lustre adamantine. H 3–4; SG 6.0
*Occurrence.* Occurs as an alteration product of uraninite.
*Localities.* Found at Shinkolobwe, Shaba, Zaire.
*Treatment.* Clean with water.

**Curite $Pb_2U_5O_{17} . 4H_2O$**
Curite crystallizes in the orthorhombic

system, often forming minute brownish needles. The colour is reddish-brown to deep yellow by transmitted light and the lustre is adamantine. The streak is orange. It is strongly radioactive. H 4–5; SG 7.1
*Localities.* Found with other uranium minerals at Kasolo, Shaba, Zaire; Puy-de-Dôme, France.

**Clarkeite $(Na, K, Pb)_2 U_2O_7 . nH_2O$**
Clarkeite forms massive coatings, dark brown in colour, surrounding uraninite, of which it is an alteration product. Found at Spruce Pine, North Carolina. H 4.0–4.5; SG 6.3

**Gummite**
A general term for secondary uranium oxide. Much material described as gummite is curite.

**Uranosphaerite $Bi_2U_2O_9 . 3H_2O$**
Uranosphaerite crystallizes in the orthorhombic system forming semi-globular aggregates. The colour is orange-yellow to brick-red, and the lustre greasy. There is a distinct cleavage. H 2–3; SG 6.3
*Localities.* From Neustädtel, south of Schneeberg, E. Germany.

**Tellurite $TeO_2$**
Tellurite crystallizes in the orthorhombic system, forming slender prismatic crystals. The colour is white to yellow and the lustre subadamantine; there is a perfect cleavage. H 2; SG 5.9
*Occurrence.* Tellurite is an oxidation product of tellurides and of native tellurium.
*Localities.* Found at Sacarambu, Romania; Boulder County, Colorado; Nye County, Nevada.
*Treatment.* Readily attacked by most acids; clean with water.

**Manganosite MnO**
Manganosite crystallizes in the cubic system forming octahedra with a cubic cleavage. The colour is emerald-green, becoming black on exposure to light. The streak is brown and lustre vitreous. H 5–6; SG 5.1
*Localities.* Found at Långban, Värmland, Sweden; Franklin, New Jersey.
*Treatment.* Clean with water.

**Pyrochroite $Mn(OH)_2$**
Pyrochroite crystallizes in the hexagonal system and is usually found foliated. The colour is white, with a pearly lustre, but darkens on exposure to light. There is a perfect basal cleavage. H 2.5; SG 3.2
*Occurrence.* Found associated with haussmannite.
*Localities.* Långban, Värmland, Sweden; Franklin, New Jersey.
*Treatment.* Clean with water.

**Haussmannite $Mn_3O_4$**
Haussmannite may contain up to 7% FeO and up to 8% ZnO. It crystallizes in the tetragonal system, forming bipyramids; twinning is frequent. Massive forms with granular structure are often found. There is a cleavage; the colour is brownish-black, the streak chestnut-brown and the lustre is submetallic. H 5–5.5; SG 4.8
*Occurrence.* Found in veins associated with acid igneous rocks.
*Localities.* From Långban, Värmland, Sweden; Ouro Preto, Minas Gerais, Brazil; with psilomelane in the Batesville district, Arkansas.
*Treatment.* Clean with water.

**Pyrolusite $MnO_2$**
Pyrolusite crystallizes in the tetragonal system, sometimes forming dendritic coatings along joints or bedding planes in sedimentary rocks. It is found in many forms including divergent fibrous masses, although crystals are rare. The colour is black to bluish steel-grey and the streak is black. The lustre is metallic to dull, and the fracture is uneven or splintery. H 1–2 (massive material), 6–6.5 (crystals); SG 4.5–7.9
*Occurrence.* As a secondary mineral from the alteration of manganese-bearing minerals.
*Locations.* From Czechoslovakia; Lanlivery, Cornwall, central provinces of India; important deposits associated

*Above: Bright yellow prismatic tellurite crystals*

*Left, centre: Pyrolusite crystals from Restormel, Cornwall. This example shows the rather rare individual crystals*

*Left: Pyrochroite from Gwynedd, Wales*

*Right: Manganite. The radiating habit of manganite aggregates is well shown by this example from the Harz Mountains of Germany*

*Above: Octahedra of magnetite from the Binnental, Switzerland*

with psilomelane and brucite from Minas Gerais, Brazil, where there are high-grade manganese deposits; with the hematite ores of the Lake Superior region and from Colorado; from Hants County, Nova Scotia.

**Ramsdellite $MnO_2$**
Ramsdellite crystallizes in the orthorhombic system forming black tubular crystals, but these are less commonly found than the granular massive forms. The colour is black and the lustre metallic. H 3; SG 4.4
*Occurrence.* Found with other manganese minerals including pyrolusite and psilomelane.
*Localities.* Ramsdellite occurs at Horni Blatna, Czechoslovakia; in Minnesota, California and Montana.
*Treatment.* Clean with water.

**Manganite MnO(OH)**
Manganite crystallizes in the monoclinic system and is pseudo-orthorhombic. The crystals are prismatic and striated, often occurring as radiating aggregates. Twinning is common. The colour is dark-grey to black and the streak reddish-brown to black. The lustre is submetallic and there is a perfect cleavage. H 4; SG 4.2–4.4
*Occurrence.* Manganite, an ore of manganese, occurs in deposits precipitated from water under oxidizing conditions and is associated with pyrolusite and baryte. It may also occur in low-temperature hydrothermal veins in association with granitic rocks.
*Localities.* Manganite is found crystallized at the Botallack mine, St. Just, Cornwall; at Egremont, Cumbria, and at Exeter, Devon. It is found in the Lake Superior iron district, USA and in Nova Scotia. It is also found in the Harz Mountains, Germany.
*Treatment.* Black coating may be removed ultrasonically. Clean with water.

**Wad**
Wad may consist of one or more hydrous manganese oxides occurring in the oxidized zone of ore deposits. Minerals included in the mixture, not separately described, may include lithiophorite, lampadite, lubeckite, wackenrodite, rabdionite, asbolane, kakochlor. Wad often consists merely of pyrolusite and/or psilomelane. It is really a field term. Wad is amorphous and is stalactitic or massive reniform, often in earthy masses. The colour is black to brownish-black and the streak black. The lustre is earthy. SG 2.8–4.4

**Bixbyite $(Mn, Fe)_2O_3$**
Bixbyite is the cubic phase of manganese-iron oxide. It forms black crystals with a metallic lustre, which are often cubes modified by the octahedron. H 6–6.5; SG 4.9
*Occurrence.* Occurs with topaz in cavities in rhyolite.
*Localities.* From the Thomas Range, Utah; Ribas, Gerona, Spain; Valle de las Plumas, northern Patagonia, Argentina.
*Treatment.* May be cleaned with dilute acids.

**Jacobsite $(Mn, Fe, Mg)(Fe, Mn)_2O_4$**
Jacobsite contains MgO up to 10%, $Fe^{2+}$:$Mn^{2+}$ up to 1% and $Mn^{3+}$:$Fe^{3+}$ up to 0.45%. It crystallizes in the cubic system forming distorted octahedra. The fracture is conchoidal and the colour black with a reddish-brown streak. It is magnetic. H 6; SG 4.7
*Localities.* Found in Värmland, Sweden; and in Bulgaria.
*Treatment.* Clean with water.

**Magnetite $Fe_3O_4$**
Magnetite crystallizes in the cubic system and forms octahedra, rhombdodecahedra and granular masses. Twinning on the octahedron is common. It is strongly magnetic. The colour and streak are black and the lustre metallic. The fracture is uneven. H 5.5–6.5; SG 5.2
*Occurrence.* Magnetite is found in igne-

ous rocks as an accessory mineral, also in contact and regionally metamorphosed rocks, and occurs in high-temperature mineral veins. It is frequently associated with corundum in emery deposits.

*Localities.* The name may be taken from Magnesia, Greece; the largest deposits known are at Norrbotten, northern Sweden; other deposits are in Värmland and Vastmanland; Ural Mountains, USSR; as twinned octahedra in the Zillertal, Austria and the Binnental, Valais, Switzerland; fine crystals are found at Port Henry, New York and from Fiormeza, Cuba.

*Treatment.* Clean with dilute acid or water.

**Hematite $Fe_2O_3$**

Hematite crystallizes in the hexagonal system forming tabular or rhombohedral crystals, sometimes showing curved or striated rhombohedral faces. It may also be found columnar, laminated or massive

in mamillary or botryoidal forms. Penetration twinning is found on the basal pinacoid. The colour is grey to black; for massive and earthy material dull brownish red. The streak is red to reddish-brown. The fracture is uneven and the lustre metallic. H 5–6; SG 4.9–5.3

*Occurrence.* Hematite is the most important ore of iron. It occurs as an accessory mineral in igneous rocks and hydrothermal veins, and also in sedimentary rocks where it may be of primary origin. It may occur as a secondary mineral, being precipitated from iron-bearing water.

*Localities.* Hematite is very widely distributed. The most important locations are along the shores of Lake Superior, USA; fine crystals are found at St. Gotthard, Switzerland; Mt. Vesuvius Italy; the Isle of Elba; Cleator Moor, Cumbria; and Minas Gerais, Brazil.

*Treatment.* Clean in dilute hydrochloric acid.

*Fashioning. Uses:* faceting, cabochons, beads, intaglios, etc; *cleavage:* none, but basal and prismatic parting due to twinning, splintery; *cutting angles:* variable, to suit requirements; *heat sensitivity:* very low.

**Goethite FeO.(OH)**

Goethite is the alpha-phase of FeO.OH and crystallizes in the orthorhombic system. It occurs as vertically striated prisms, often flattened into scales, and also forms fibrous masses. Reniform and stalactitic forms with a radiated concentric structure are found. There is a perfect cleavage. The colour is yellow through red to blackish-brown and the streak brownish-yellow. The fracture is uneven and the lustre sub-adamantine. H 5–5.5; SG 3.3–4.3

*Occurrence.* Goethite is found with quartz and limonite. It is an alteration product of iron-bearing minerals.

*Localities.* Good crystals come from the

*Above: Fine banded hematite crystals. These are less common than the massive forms. This example is from the island of Elba*

*Left: Hematite. This rosette formation is called 'iron rose'*

*Far left: A fine single crystal of hematite*

*Left: Another good example of an octahedron of magnetite from the Binnental*

*Right: Fine crystals of goethite displaying stalagmitic habit. From Nassau, Germany*

*Below right: Halite crystal. This bluish-white colour is typical of the mineral*

Botallack mine, St. Just, Cornwall, and from Lostwithiel and Lanlivery in the same county. It is common in the Lake Superior hematite deposits and in the Pike's Peak region of Colorado.
*Treatment.* Clean with dilute hydrochloric acid.

**Lepidocrocite FeO.OH**
Lepidocrocite is the gamma-phase of FeO.OH and crystallizes in the orthorhombic system, forming scaly or fibrous aggregates, red to reddish-brown in colour. There is a perfect cleavage and an orange streak. H 5; SG 4.1
*Occurrence.* Like goethite, it is found with quartz and limonite.
*Treatment.* Clean with dilute hydrochloric acid.

**Limonite**
Limonite is a generic term for mixed oxides or hydroxides of iron. It has a yellowish-brown streak and a vitreous lustre. The colour and lack of cleavage distinguish it from goethite. Much so-called ferric oxide described as limonite is in fact goethite.

**Magnesioferrite (Mg, Fe)$Fe_2O_4$**
Magnesioferrite crystallizes in the cubic system commonly forming octahedra. The colour and streak are black and the lustre is metallic. It is strongly magnetic. H 6–6.5; SG 4.5–4.6
*Occurrence.* Magnesioferrite results from the action of heated water-bearing vapours on magnesium and ferric chlorides and occurs in the vicinity of volcanic fumaroles.
*Localities.* Found on Mt. Vesuvius, Italy; Mt. Stromboli, Lipari Islands, Italy.
*Treatment.* Clean with dilute hydrochloric acid.

**Hercynite $FeAl_2O_4$**
A member of the spinel series, hercynite often contains some Mg or $Fe^{3+}$ or both. It crystallizes in the cubic system and is normally massive with a granular texture. The colour is black and the lustre vitreous. H 7.5–8; SG 3.9–4.2
*Occurrence.* Hercynite occurs in igneous rocks, often with corundum.
*Localities.* Found in Czechoslovakia at Pobezovice; from a gabbro at Lago di Poschiavo, Grisons, Switzerland; from tin drifts near Morrina, Tasmania; from near Erode, Coimbatore district, India.
*Treatment.* Clean with dilute acid.

**Heterogenite CoO.OH**
Heterogenite is hexagonal, occurring as globular or reniform masses with a vitreous lustre. Varieties closely linked are mindigite with 7–10% CuO, and trieuite with up to 20% CuO.
*Occurrence.* Found at Schneeberg, E. Germany and in northern Chile.

**Bunsenite NiO**
Bunsenite crystallizes in the cubic system, forming green octahedra with a vitreous lustre. H 5.5; SG 6.4–6.8
*Localities.* Found at Johanngeorgenstadt, E. Germany, with nickel and bismuth.
*Treatment.* Clean with water.

**Trevorite $NiFe_2O_4$**
Though it crystallizes in the cubic system, trevorite is found as black grains with a greenish tint. It gives a black streak. It is strongly magnetic. H 5; SG 5.1
*Localities.* Found in a talcose rock in the Transvaal, South Africa.

## Halides

**Villiaumite NaF**
Villiaumite crystallizes in the cubic system forming small carmine-coloured grains. The birefringence and pleochroism are exceptionally strong. H 2–2.5; SG 2.8
*Localities.* Found in a nepheline syenite from the Islands of Los, Guinea; Kola Peninsula, USSR; Mont St. Hilaire, Quebec.

**Halite NaCl**
Halite crystallizes in the cubic system, and is usually found as cubes sometimes displaying concave faces; also massive, granular to compact, to which form the term rock salt is applied. The mineral is colourless but may display shades of yellow, red or blue. The streak is white and the lustre vitreous. There is a perfect cleavage and the fracture is conchoical. Halite is water-soluble and tastes of salt. H 2.5; SG 2.1–2.2 (pure material 2.16).
*Occurrence.* Halite is found in sedimentary rocks and has a world-wide distribution. Salt deposits are formed by the drying up of brines, or sea water that has been enclosed. Halite beds are associated with gypsum, sylvine and anhydrite.
*Localities.* Large deposits are found in southern USSR; at Stassfurt, E. Germany; Agrigento, Sicily, Italy; Northwich, Cheshire; Algeria; Ethiopia; Punjab, India; Colombia; China.
*Treatment.* Clean with alcohol.

**Sylvine KCl**
Sylvine crystallizes in the cubic system and may show cubes or a combination of cube and octahedron; it is also found massive and compact. It is colourless or may display shades of yellow, blue or red; the streak is white and the lustre vitreous. The fracture is uneven. Has a more bitter taste than halite. H 2; SG 2.0
*Occurrence.* Sylvine occurs in beds with other evaporites.
*Localities.* Stassfurt, E. Germany; Kalush, USSR.
*Treatment.* Easily soluble in both water and acids. Should be stored in a sealed container. It cannot be cleaned.

**Nantokite CuCl**
Nantokite crystallizes in the cubic system in granular masses. The colour is white to grey and the lustre adamantine. H 2–2.5; SG 3.9–4.1
*Localities.* From Nantoko, Chile; Broken Hill, New South Wales, Australia.

**Atacamite $Cu_2Cl(OH)_3$**
Atacamite crystallizes in the orthorhombic system and forms slender prismatic crystals showing striations; tabular forms are also found. Also occurs as fibrous or granular masses. The colour is bright to dark green; the lustre is adamantine to vitreous and the streak apple-green. There is also a perfect cleavage. Paratacamite is the rhombohedral phase of $Cu_2Cl(OH)_3$. H 3–3.5; SG 3.8
*Occurrence.* Atacamite is found in the oxidized zones of copper deposits, associated with cuprite and malachite.
*Localities.* Found at Atacama, Chile; Wallaroo, South Australia; Vesuvius.
*Treatment.* Clean with distilled water.

**Marshite CuI**
Marshite crystallizes in the cubic system and may form tetrahedra. There is a dodecahedral cleavage. It has an adamantine lustre, and is colourless to pale yellow when fresh, becoming flesh pink to dark brownish-red on exposure. It fluoresces red in ultraviolet light. H 2.5; SG 5.6
*Localities.* From Broken Hill, New South Wales, Australia; Chile.
*Treatment.* Clean with water.

**Chlorargyrite AgCl**
Chlorargyrite, also known as cerargyrite, crystallizes in the cubic system, forming cubes. These, however, are rare, the mineral more commonly being found massive. There is a conchoidal fracture. It is colourless, becoming violet-brown on exposure to light; the lustre is resinous. It is sectile. H 1.5–2.5; SG 5.5–5.6
*Occurrence.* Chlorargyrite occurs as a secondary mineral in the oxidized zone of silver deposits, with native silver and cerussite.
*Localities.* Atacama, Chile; Broken Hill, New South Wales, Australia; Colorado, Idaho, Utah.

**Embolite Ag (Cl, Br)**
Embolite crystallizes in the cubic system and is usually found massive. The colour is greyish-green to yellowish-green and yellow; the lustre is resinous. H 2.5; SG 5.7
*Localities.* From Chañarcillo, Chile; Broken Hill, New South Wales.

**Miersite (Ag, Cu)I**
Miersite has more silver than copper, approaching a proportion of 4:1, which is the stability limit for the cubic phase at normal temperatures. It forms tetrahedra with a dodecahedral cleavage and is bright yellow. It is thought that cuproiodargyrite is a variety of miersite. H 2–3; SG 5.6
*Localities.* From Broken Hill, New South Wales; cuproiodargyrite from Huantajaya, Peru.

**Sellaite $MgF_2$**
Sellaite crystallizes in the tetragonal system and forms prismatic crystals with a vitreous lustre. There are two directions of perfect cleavage. Sellaite is colourless. H 5–6; SG 2.9–3.1
*Localities.* Found on moraines of the Gebroulaz glacier near Moutiers, Savoie, France; Mt. Vesuvius, Italy.

**Bischofite $MgCl_2.6H_2O$**
Bischofite crystallizes in the monoclinic system in granular or fibrous forms. It is colourless, with a vitreous lustre. H 1.5; SG 1.56
*Localities.* Found at Stassfurt, E. Germany.
*Treatment.* Decomposes in air; keep in sealed container.

*Above: Marshite crystals from Broken Hill, New South Wales*

*Left: Crystals of miersite from Broken Hill*

*Far left: Chlorargyrite crystals showing cubic form from Saxony, East Germany*

*Left: Slender crystals of atacamite from Sierra Gorda, Chile*

*Right: Yellow cubes of fluorite on galena. From Wheal Mary Ann, Cornwall*

*Below right: Crystals of fluorite displaying interpenetrant twinning, very characteristic of this mineral*

**Carnallite $KMgCl_3 . 6H_2O$**
Carnallite crystallizes in the orthorhombic system, forming pseudo-hexagonal crystals. It is more often found granular massive. The colour is white to yellow or reddish; the lustre is greasy and the fracture conchoidal. Carnallite has a bitter taste and is deliquescent. H 2.5; SG 1.6
*Occurrence.* Carnallite occurs in evaporite deposits with halite and sylvine.
*Localities.* From Stassfurt, E. Germany; and Beienrode, W. Germany.
*Treatment.* Store in sealed container.

**Tachhydrite $CaMg_2Cl_6 . 12H_2O$**
Tachhydrite crystallizes in the hexagonal system with a rhombohedral cleavage. The colour is honey to yellow and the lustre is vitreous. The mineral is found massive. H 2; SG 1.6
*Localities.* Found in salt deposits of northern Germany including Stassfurt, E. Germany.
*Treatment.* Deliquescent; store in a sealed container.

**Fluorite $CaF_2$**
Fluorite crystallizes in the cubic system forming cubes and, rarely, octahedra or rhombdodecahedra. There is a perfect octahedral cleavage. There is a wide variety of colour including pink, blue, green, purple, red, black and colourless. Individual specimens are often colour-zoned. Penetration twins are common. The streak is white and the lustre vitreous. The fracture is subconchoidal. Fluoresces under long-wave ultra-violet light. H 4; SG 3.2; RI 1.43
*Occurrence.* Fluorite is found in mineral veins, alone or as a gangue mineral with metallic ores. Associated minerals include quartz, baryte, calcite, celestine, dolomite, galena, sphalerite and topaz. Fluorite is worked for its properties as a flux in the smelting of iron.
*Yttrian fluorite* contains 15–20% $YtF_3$ and crystallizes in the cubic system, being found massive and earthy. The colour is violet through grey to reddish-brown and there is a cleavage. H 4–5; SG 3–4
*Localities.* Found in the lead veins of Northumberland; Cleator Moor, Cumbria; Weardale, Durham; Derbyshire, Cornwall and Devon; from the mining districts of E. Germany; as pink octahedra from St. Gotthard, Switzerland; from Hardin County, Illinois and Crystal Peak, Colorado. Yttrian fluorite found near Falun, Sweden and Sussex County, New York State.
*Treatment.* Calcite coatings removed with dilute HCl and iron stains with oxalic acid. It is heat-sensitive. Do not attempt to clean yttrian fluorite.
*Fashioning. Uses:* faceting, cabochons, carvings, intaglios, etc; *cleavage:* perfect octahedral; brittle; *cutting angles:* crown 40°–50°, pavilion 43°; *heat sensitivity:* very high.

**Chlorocalcite $KCaCl_3$**
Chlorocalcite crystallizes in the orthorhombic system with twinned pseudo-cubic crystals. The colour is white. H 2.5–3.0; SG 2.1
*Occurrence.* Found on Mt. Vesuvius as a sublimation product, in the form of white cubes or as an encrustation.
*Treatment.* Deliquescent. Store in sealed container.

*Above right: Octahedral fluorite from Piedmont, Italy*

*Right: Another example of interpenetrant fluorite twins*

**Jarlite $NaSr_3Al_3F_{16}$**
Jarlite crystallizes in the monoclinic system as very small crystals; the mineral is more commonly found massive. The colour is white, with a vitreous lustre. Meta-jarlite is high in Ca and Ba. H 4–4.5; SG 3.8–3.9
*Localities.* Found with cryolite at Ivigtut, Greenland.

**Calomel $Hg_2Cl_2$**
Calomel crystallizes in the tetragonal system, giving tabular or pyramidal crystals, which are often highly complex. The colour ranges from white through yellow to brown, and lustre is adamantine. The streak is pale yellowish-white. It fluoresces dark red under ultraviolet light. Found as a coating on other minerals, usually being deposited from hot solutions. It also occurs as a secondary mineral. It is associated with cinnabar. H 1–2; SG 6.4
*Localities.* Calomel is found at Moschellandsberg, W. Germany; near Příbram, Czechoslovakia; Almaden, Ciudad Real, Spain; Terlingua, Texas.
*Treatment.* May be cleaned with hydrochloric acid.

*Left: Matlockite. It takes its name from one of its localities, Matlock in Derbyshire*

*Far left: Crystals of a fragile mineral, thomsenolite from Ivigtut, Greenland*

**Cryolite $Na_3AlF_6$**
Cryolite crystallizes in the monoclinic system, being rarely found as pseudo-cubic crystals. Massive granular forms are more common. There is no cleavage, but a basal and prismatic parting; twinning is common. It is colourless to brown or reddish and the streak is white. The fracture is uneven. The lustre is greasy. H 2.5; SG 3
*Occurrence.* Cryolite occurs in a pegmatite associated with siderite, quartz, galena, sphalerite and fluorite.
*Localities.* Cryolite is found in Greenland, at Ivigtut.
*Treatment.* Clean in water.

**Cryolithionite $Li_3Na_3Al_2F_{12}$**
The crystal structure of cryolithionite is identical with that of the garnets; that is, it is a member of the cubic system. It forms colourless dodecahedral crystals with a vitreous lustre and a dodecahedral cleavage. H 2.5; SG 2.7
*Localities.* Cryolithionite occurs with cryolite in the Ilmen mountains in the Soviet Union.
*Treatment.* As for cryolite.

**Chiolite $Na_5Al_3F_{14}$**
Chiolite crystallizes in the tetragonal system and forms small pyramidal crystals; it is also found granular and massive. There is a perfect cleavage and the colour is white, with a vitreous lustre. H 3.5–4; SG 2.8–2.9
*Occurrence.* Found with cryolite in the Greenland deposit at Ivigtut.
*Treatment.* As for cryolite.

**Ralstonite $NaMgAl(F, OH)_6 . H_2O$**
Ralstonite crystallizes in the cubic crystal system forming octahedra, which are white with a vitreous lustre. There is an octahedral cleavage. H 4.5; SG 2.5
*Occurrence.* Found with cryolite at Ivigtut, Greenland.

**Thomsenolite $NaCaAlF_6 . H_2O$**
Thomsenolite crystallizes in the monoclinic system and the crystals may resemble cubes, although prismatic forms are also found. It is colourless with a pearly lustre. There is a perfect cleavage. H 2; SG 2.9
*Occurrence.* Occurs with cryolite at Ivigtut, Greenland.

**Pachnolite $NaCaAlF_6 . H_2O$**
Pachnolite crystallizes in the monoclinic system forming prismatic crystals and pseudo-orthorhombic crystals through twinning. It is colourless, with a vitreous lustre. H 3; SG 2.9
*Occurrence.* Found in Greenland as an alteration product of cryolite.

**Prosopite $CaAl_2(F, OH)_8$**
Prosopite crystallizes in the monoclinic system and is commonly found granular massive. The colour is white to grey, and the lustre is vitreous to dull. H 4.5; SG 2.8
*Localities.* Found in Altenberg, E. Germany; Pike's Peak, Colorado.

**Fluocerite $(Ce, La)F_3$**
Fluocerite crystallizes in the hexagonal system, forming thick hexagonal prisms. It is also found massive. There is a distinct cleavage. The colour is pale yellow, changing to yellowish or reddish brown; the lustre is vitreous. H 4.5–5; SG 6.1
*Occurrence.* Found in the granite at Pike's Peak, Colorado; from Falun, Sweden.

**Matlockite PbFCl**
Matlockite crystallizes in the tetragonal system forming tabular crystals. It is yellow to green, with an adamantine lustre. H 2–3; SG 7.2
*Localities.* Found with percylite at Challacolla, Chile and at Laurion, Greece.
*Treatment.* Clean with distilled water.

*Below: Another Greenland mineral, pachnolite. Here it shows the pseudo-orthorhombic crystals that arise through twinning*

*Right: Cotunnite aggregates from Vesuvius. The background material is lava*

**Cotunnite $PbCl_2$**
Cotunnite crystallizes in the orthorhombic system as acicular crystals and semicrystalline masses. There is a perfect cleavage. The lustre is adamantine to pearly, and the colour is white to yellow. H 2.5; SG 5.3–5.8
*Localities.* Found in the area of Mt. Vesuvius, Italy; Tarapaca, Chile.

**Laurionite PbClOH**
Laurionite crystallizes in the orthorhombic system, forming minute colourless prismatic crystals with a cleavage. H 2–3; SG 6.2
*Occurrence.* Found in lead slags with paralaurionite, penfieldite, matlockite, phosgenite, etc.
*Localities.* Laurion, Greece; Wheal Rose, Cornwall.

**Penfieldite $Pb_2Cl_3OH$**
Penfieldite crystallizes in the hexagonal system and forms hexagonal prismatic crystals with a cleavage. It is white with an adamantine lustre.
*Occurrence.* Occurs with fiedlerite in lead slags.
*Localities.* Laurion, Greece.

**Mendipite $Pb_3Cl_2O_2$**
Mendipite crystallizes in the orthorhombic system, forming fibrous or columnar masses, often radiated. Cleavage is perfect and the colour is white. The lustre is pearly to adamantine. H 2.5–3; SG 7–7.2
*Localities.* Found in the Mendip Hills, Somerset.
*Treatment.* Clean with distilled water.

**Lorettoite $Pb_7Cl_2O_6$**
Lorettoite crystallizes in the orthorhombic system and is found as masses of coarse fibres or blades. It has a perfect basal cleavage. The colour is honey-yellow and the lustre adamantine. H 3; SG 7.6
*Localities.* Loretto, Tennessee; a reddish form previously considered a separate mineral and called chubutite is found at Chubut, Argentina.

**Fiedlerite $Pb_3Cl_4(OH)_2$**
Fiedlerite crystallizes in the monoclinic system and forms tabular crystals with a cleavage. The colour is white, and the lustre adamantine. H 3.5; SG 5.8
*Occurrence.* From the lead slags at Laurion, Greece.

**Cumengéite $Pb_4Cu_4Cl_8(OH)_8 \cdot H_2O$**
Cumengéite crystallizes in the tetragonal system and occurs intimately associated with boléite, from which it is distinguished by its lighter shade of indigo-blue. H 2.5; SG 4.6
*Localities.* Found at Boléo, near Santa Rosalia, Baja California, Mexico.
*Treatment.* May be cleaned with water.

**Boléite $Pb_9Cu_8Ag_3Cl_{21}(OH)_{16} \cdot H_2O$**
Boléite crystallizes in the tetragonal system and forms pseudocubes through twinning. There is a perfect cleavage. The colour is indigo-blue and the lustre vitreous to pearly. H 3–3.5; SG 5.0
*Localities.* Occurs with copper and lead minerals, including cumengéite and pseudoboléite, at Boléo, Baja California, Mexico; Broken Hill, New South Wales.
*Pseudoboléite* is $Pb_5Cu_4Cl_{10}(OH)_8 \cdot 2H_2O$ and is found only in parallel growth with boléite and cumengéite.
*Diaboléite* is $Pb_2CuCl_2(OH)_4$ and is found with chloroxiphite embedded in mendipite from Higher Pitts, Somerset. It is a bright sky-blue and crystallizes in the tetragonal system; H 2.5; SG 5.4
*Treatment.* May be cleaned with water.

**Chloroxiphite $Pb_3CuCl_2O_2(OH)_2$**
Chloroxiphite crystallizes in the monoclinic system and occurs as elongated crystals with a perfect cleavage. The colour is dull olive-green and the lustre is resinous to adamantine. Strong pleochroism shown by cleavage plates, the colours being bright emerald-green and yellowish-brown. H 2.5; SG 6.7
*Localities.* Found embedded in mendipite in the Mendip Hills, Somerset.
*Treatment.* Clean with water.

**Hematophanite $Pb_4Fe_4O_9(OH, Cl)_2$**
Hematophanite crystallizes in the tetragonal system forming lamellar aggregates of thin plates. The colour is dark reddish-brown and the lustre submetallic. There is a cleavage parallel to the base. The streak is yellowish-red. H 2–3; SG 7.7
*Occurrence.* Occurs with plumboferrite, etc, at Jakobsberg, Värmland, Sweden.

**Bismoclite BiOCl**
Bismoclite occurs in white to yellowish-brown earthy masses.

*Below: A group of penfieldite crystals in a cavity. The mineral's adamantine lustre can be seen*

*Left: The pseudocubic form taken by boleite crystals can be clearly seen in these examples from Boleo, Mexico*

*Localities.* It is found in Australia, Bolivia, Nevada and Utah; in Italy with bismuthinite at Rio Marina, Elba.

**Scacchite $MnCl_2$**
An extremely rare mineral isomorphous with chloromagnesite and lawrencite. SG 2.9
*Occurrence.* Scacchite is found on Mt. Vesuvius as pale rose or colourless encrustations, associated with sylvine, hydrophyllite and lawrencite.

**Kempite $Mn_2Cl(OH)_3$**
Kempite crystallizes in the orthorhombic system forming minute prismatic crystals coloured emerald-green. H 3.5; SG 2.9
*Occurrence.* Found with pyrochroite, hausmannite and rhodochrosite in a manganese ore boulder, formerly existing near San José, California.

**Chloromanganokalite $K_4MnCl_6$**
Chloromanganokalite crystallizes in the hexagonal system, forming rhombohedral crystals in parallel aggregates. It is isomorphous with rinneite and is coloured yellow. H 2.5; SG 2.3
*Localities.* Found around the fumaroles of Mt. Vesuvius.
*Treatment.* Decomposes very easily; do not attempt to clean.

**Lawrencite $FeCl_2$**
Lawrencite is isostructural with chloromagnesite, and forms compact masses. SG 3.1
*Occurrence.* It is found in meteoritic iron at Ouifak, Greenland.

**Douglasite $K_2FeCl_4 . 2H_2O$**
Douglasite crystallizes in the monoclinic system and is found as green granular masses. This colour alters to a reddish-brown on exposure to air.
*Occurrence.* Douglasite is found at Douglashall, near Stassfurt, E. Germany.

**Erythrosiderite $K_2FeCl_5 . H_2O$**
Erythrosiderite crystallizes in the orthorhombic system and forms tabular or pseudo-octahedral crystals. The colour is red and the lustre vitreous. SG 2.3
*Localities.* Found on Mt. Vesuvius and Mt. Etna; also from Stassfurt in East Germany.
*Treatment.* Deliquescent. Do not attempt to clean.

**Rinneite $K_3NaFeCl_6$**
Rinneite crystallizes in the hexagonal system, forming coarse granular masses. It is colourless or rose-coloured, violet or yellow when fresh, altering to brown on exposure to air; its lustre is silky. H 3; SG 2.3
*Localities.* Found at Wolkramshausen, near Nordhausen, E. Germany.

**Ferruccite $NaBF_4$**
A rare mineral from the Mt. Vesuvius area, associated with avogadrite, malladrite and hieratite. SG 2.4

*Left: Kernite from Kern Co., California*

**Avogadrite $(K, Cs)BF_4$**
Avogadrite crystallizes in the orthorhombic system in 8-sided tabular crystals or as granular masses. The colour is snow-white. Hardness and cleavage have not been determined: SG 3.
*Occurrence.* Found as a sublimate around fumaroles on Vesuvius.

**Malladrite $Na_2SiF_6$**
Malladrite crystallizes in the hexagonal system, forming minute prisms sometimes pyramidally terminated. It is the low-temperature phase of $Na_2SiF_6$.
*Occurrence.* Associated with avogadrite and hieratite on Mt. Vesuvius.

**Hieratite $K_2SiF_6$**
Hieratite is the cubic high-temperature phase of $K_2SiF_6$.
*Localities.* It forms stalactitic concretions from the fumaroles of Mt. Vesuvius and from Mt. Vulcano, Lipari Islands.

**Camermanite $K_2SiF_6$**
Camermanite is the hexagonal low-temperature phase of $K_2SiF_6$, forming masses.
*Localities.* Mt. Vesuvius.

**Cryptohalite $(NH_4)_2SiF_6$**
Cryptohalite is the cubic, high-temperature phase and forms whitish-yellow encrustations. H 2.5
*Localities.* The crater of Mt. Vesuvius.

**Bararite $(NH_4)_2SiF_6$**
Bararite is the low-temperature hexagonal phase.
*Localities.* Mt. Vesuvius.

## Borates

**Sassolite $B(OH)_3$**
Sassolite crystallizes in the triclinic system, forming pseudo-hexagonal plates or, more commonly, small pearly scales. The colour is white and there is a perfect basal cleavage. H 1; SG 1.48
*Occurrence.* Found deposited from the gases of fumaroles and in hot springs.
*Localities.* Some lagoons in Tuscany, Italy; the crater of Mt. Vulcano, Lipari Islands.

**Kernite $Na_2B_4O_7 . 4H_2O$**
Kernite crystallizes in the monoclinic system with perfect cleavage. The colour is white and the lustre vitreous to pearly. H 3; SG 1.95
*Occurrence.* Found associated with ulexite in south-eastern Kern Co., California.
*Treatment.* Store in sealed container.

**Borax $Na_2B_4O_7 . 10H_2O$**
Borax crystallizes in the monoclinic system forming short prismatic crystals; it is also found massive. The colour is white, sometimes tinged with grey or blue; the streak is white. There is a perfect cleavage and the lustre is vitreous to resinous; the fracture is conchoidal. H 2–2.5; SG 1.7
*Occurrence.* Borax is precipitated by evaporation of salt lakes. Associated minerals include halite, sulphates, carbonates and other borates.
*Localities.* Borax occurs in the Death Valley area, California; Nevada; and in Kashmir and Tibet.

*Right: Hambergite from the Malagasy Republic. This mineral may sometimes be cut as a gemstone when it displays a very high birefringence*

*Below right: Another mineral from the Malagasy Republic, rhodizite*

*Treatment.* Leave crust; borax alters to tincalconite, $Na_2B_4O_7.5H_2O$, on exposure; this forms an opaque white layer, which thickens until the entire crystal disintegrates.

**Rhodizite $CsB_{12}Be_4Al_4O_{28}$**
Rhodizite crystallizes in the cubic system, forming white dodecahedra with a silky lustre. H 8; SG 3.4; RI 1.69
*Occurrence.* Rhodizite is found on red tourmaline from Ural Mts, USSR; from Antandrokomby and Manjakandriana in the Malagasy Republic.
*Treatment.* Usually so integrated with matrix that attempts to free it are useless and may spoil the crystal. May be cleaned with dilute acids.

**Hambergite $Be_2BO_3(OH)$**
Hambergite crystallizes in the orthorhombic system and forms greyish-white prismatic crystals with a vitreous lustre and a perfect cleavage. H 7.5; SG 2.3
*Occurrence.* Found in a pegmatite vein near Halgaraen, southern Norway; good crystals from south of Betafo, Imalo and Maharitra, Malagasy Republic.
*Treatment.* Remove iron stains with oxalic acid.

**Szajbelyite $MgBO_2OH$**
Szajbelyite crystallizes in the orthorhombic system forming small nodules, which are white outside, with a silky lustre and yellow within. H 3.5; SG 2.60
*Occurrence.* Found with boracite and sylvine at Aschersleben, Ilmen Mts, E. Germany; Rézbánya, Romania; with ludwigite from Lincoln Co., Nevada.

**Pinnoite $MgB_2O_4.3H_2O$**
Pinnoite crystallizes in the tetragonal system and is found as nodules which are radiating and fibrous. The colour is sulphur-yellow and the lustre vitreous. H 3–4; SG 2.2
*Occurrence.* Found at Stassfurt, E. Germany, in saline deposits with kainite and boracite.

**Kurnakovite $Mg_2B_6O_{11}.15H_2O$**
Kurnakovite crystallizes in the triclinic system forming compact masses which appear cubic and are white in colour, with a vitreous lustre. H 3; SG 1.8
*Occurrence.* Found with borates at Inder, Kazakhstan, USSR; also from Boron, California.

**Inderite $Mg_2B_6O_{11}.15H_2O$**
Inderite crystallizes in the monoclinic system forming nodular masses and, sometimes, striated prismatic crystals, which are white in colour and have a vitreous lustre. H 3; SG 1.8–1.9
*Localities.* From Inder, Kazakhstan, USSR; Boron, California.

**Kaliborite $HKMg_2B_{12}O_{21}.9H_2O$**
Kaliborite crystallizes in the monoclinic system and forms aggregates of crystals with perfect cleavage. The colour is colourless to white. The lustre is vitreous. H 4–5; SG 2.1
*Localities.* Found at Stassfurt, E. Germany; Inder, Kazakhstan, in the Soviet Union.

**Colemanite $Ca_2B_6O_{11}.5H_2O$**
Colemanite crystallizes in the monoclinic system forming short prismatic crystals or granular compact masses. There is a perfect cleavage and the lustre is vitreous to adamantine. The fracture is uneven to conchoidal. The colour is milky white, yellow or grey. H 4–4.5; SG 2.4
*Localities.* Found in Death Valley and Calico, California.
*Fashioning. Uses:* faceting or cabochons; *cleavage:* perfect clinopinacoidal; very brittle; *cutting angles:* crown 40°, pavilion 40°; *heat sensitivity:* low.

**Meyerhofferite $Ca_2B_6O_{11}.7H_2O$**
Meyerhofferite crystallizes in the triclinic system and forms prismatic tabular crystals and fibrous masses. The colour is white and the lustre vitreous or fibrous. There is a cleavage. Inyoite alters to meyerhofferite. H 2; SG 2.1
*Occurrence.* Found with inyoite in Death Valley, California.

**Inyoite $Ca_2B_6O_{11}.13H_2O$**
Inyoite crystallizes in the monoclinic system forming tabular crystals with a cleavage. The colour is white, and the lustre vitreous. Alters to meyerhofferite. H 2; SG 1.8
*Occurrence.* From Death Valley, Inyo Co., California in association with colemanite.

*Right: Colemanite from San Bernardino Co., California, showing typical short prismatic crystals*

**Priceite $Ca_4B_{10}O_{19}.7H_2O$**
Priceite probably crystallizes in the triclinic system, forming microscopic rhomboidal plates with perfect cleavage or compact masses. The colour is snow-white. H 3–3.5; SG 2.4
*Localities.* Found in Curry Co., Oregon and Inyo Co., California.

**Ginorite $Ca_2B_{14}O_{23}.8H_2O$**
Ginorite is found as white fibrous masses. H 3.5; SG 2.0
*Localities.* Sasso Pisano, Italy.

**Ulexite $NaCaB_5O_9.8H_2O$**
Ulexite crystallizes in the triclinic system forming rounded masses of fine fibrous crystals, or parallel fibrous aggregates. The colour is white and the lustre silky. The mineral is transparent and print can sometimes be read along the length of the fibres, from which property the name 'television stone' is taken. H 2.5; SG 1.9–2
*Occurrence.* Ulexite is an evaporite mineral found in sedimentary rocks in borax deposits. It is accompanied by colemanite.
*Localities.* In the dry plains at Tarapaca, Chile; from Salinas de la Puna, Argentina; Esmeralda, Nevada; Death Valley, Desert Wells, Kern Co., and Los Angeles Co., California.
*Treatment.* Store in sealed containers with silica gel.

**Probertite $NaCaB_5O_9.5H_2O$**
Probertite crystallizes in the monoclinic system and forms radiating prismatic crystals. They are colourless and have a vitreous lustre. They possess a perfect cleavage. H 3.5; SG 2.1
*Occurrence.* Occurs in clay, borax or kernite in the Kramer district, Kern Co., California.

**Hydroboracite $CaMgB_6O_{11}.6H_2O$**
Hydroboracite crystallizes in the monoclinic system and forms fibrous foliated masses, which resemble gypsum. There is a perfect cleavage and the colour is white, with a vitreous to silky lustre. H 2; SG 2
*Localities.* Found at Stassfurt, E. Germany; and from the Ryan area, Inyo Co., California.

**Jeremejevite $Al_6B_5O_{15}(OH)_3$**
Jeremejevite, sometimes spelt jeremeyevite, crystallizes in the hexagonal system and forms prismatic pseudohexagonal crystals. These show both uniaxial and biaxial parts and are colourless to pale yellowish-brown, with a vitreous lustre. H 6.5; SG 3.2
*Localities.* Found at Mt. Soktuj, in the Adun-Chilon mountains, in Transbaikalia, USSR; also from South-West Africa. Quantities of facetable material have recently been discovered in this area.
*Treatment.* Clean with water or dilute acids.

**Sinhalite $MgAlBO_4$**
Sinhalite was discovered to be a separate mineral in 1951/52; it was long thought to be a brown variety of peridot. Sinhalite crystallizes in the orthorhombic system but little is yet known of the crystal morphology since much of the material was first noted as cut stones. The colour is dark greenish-brown, sometimes a golden yellow, with strong pleochroism. It has a vitreous lustre. It may be distinguished from peridot by an extra band in the absorption spectrum at 4630Å. H 6.5; SG 3.47–3.50
*Localities.* Found in Ceylon gem gravels, etc.
*Treatment.* Iron stains may be removed with oxalic acid but prolonged immersion should be avoided.
*Fashioning. Uses:* faceting or cabochons; *cleavage:* probably distinct macro- and brachypinacoidal; *cutting angles:* crown 40°, pavilion 40°; *pleochroism:* distinct; *heat sensitivity:* low.

Left: Fragments of jeremejevite. The vitreous lustre is very apparent

Left: Ulexite. Its fibrous nature is seen here in a specimen from Boron, California

**Warwickite $(Mg, Fe)_3TiB_2O_8$**
Warwickite, which may contain more magnesium than iron, crystallizes in the orthorhombic system as elongated prismatic crystals. The colour is dark brown to black, with a pearly lustre, and there is a cleavage. H 3–4; SG 3.3
*Localities.* Found at Warwick, Orange Co., New York State.

**Nordenskiöldine $CaSn_2O_6$**
Nordenskiöldine crystallizes in the hexagonal system, forming thin or thick tabular crystals or lens-like crystals; it is also found as parallel growths with calcite and other minerals. The colour is yellow or colourless; there is a perfect cleavage and the lustre is vitreous. H 5.5–6.0; SG 4.2
*Occurrence.* Found in an alkaline pegmatite with feldspar, zircon and other minerals on Arö island, Norway; with tourmaline, stannite and sulphides in marble at Arandis, South-West Africa.

**Sussexite $(Mn, Mg)BO_2(OH)$**
Sussexite contains more manganese than magnesium and may contain up to 3% zinc. It crystallizes in the orthorhombic system and forms veins or masses, which have a fibrous structure. The colour is white, pink or straw-yellow with a white streak and silky to earthy lustre. H 3–3.5; SG 3.3
*Occurrence.* Sussexite occurs with pyrochroite and other minerals at Franklin, New Jersey, where it is found in hydrothermal veins in franklinite; it is also found as veins in hematite at the Chicagon mine, Iron Co., Michigan and the Gonzen mine, Switzerland.

**Pinakiolite $(Mg, Mn^{2+})_2Mn^{3+}BO_5$**
Pinakiolite contains magnesium and manganese in the proportion 3:1 and crystallizes in the monoclinic system, forming thin tabular crystals; twinning is common. There is a good cleavage and the mineral is very brittle. The colour is black with a brilliant metallic lustre and the streak is brownish-grey. H 6; SG 3.8
*Occurrence.* Pinakiolite is found in a granular dolomite at Långban, Sweden.

*Above: Ludwigite in the form of radiating fibres, from Brosso, Italy*

**Ludwigite $(Mg, Fe^{2+})_2Fe^{3+}BO_5$**
Ludwigite crystallizes in the orthorhombic system forming fibrous granular masses or aggregates of needle-like crystals; prismatic crystals with rhombic cross-section are rare. There is a perfect cleavage and the colour is dark-green to black with a silky lustre. H 5; SG 3.8
*Occurrence.* Ludwigite is found as a high-temperature mineral in contact metamorphic deposits. It occurs in cassiterite ores and iron deposits.
*Localities.* Found with cassiterite in Kern Co., California; in magnetite skarn deposits in Norway; from Suan, Korea; and from other localities.

**Fluoborite $Mg_3BO_3(F, OH)_3$**
Fluoborite (nocerite) crystallizes in the hexagonal system and occurs as prismatic crystals, as compact fibrous masses or as divergent aggregates of prismatic crystals. The colour is white with a vitreous lustre; fibrous aggregates are silky. H 3.5; SG 2.9
*Occurrence.* Fluoborite is found as crystals in thermally metamorphosed impure limestones. It also occurs as veins in franklinite.
*Localities.* In limestones at Crestmore and with calcite near Ludlow, California; from Sterling Hill, New Jersey; from Broadford, Skye, etc.

**Boracite $Mg_3B_7O_{13}Cl$**
Alpha-boracite, the high-temperature form, is stable above 265° and crystallizes in the cubic system. Beta-boracite crystallizes in the orthorhombic system, and may be colourless, grey, yellow, green or bluish-green; crystals are pseudocubic and occur as cubes, dodecahedra, or octahedra. Fine-grained or fibrous masses also occur. The fracture is conchoidal and the lustre vitreous. H 7–7.5; SG 2.9
*Occurrence.* Boracite occurs in beds of gypsum, anhydrite and rock salt.
*Localities.* Found at Aislaby, Yorkshire; Luneville, France; the Choctaw salt dome, Iberville Parish, Louisiana; Otis, California; etc.
*Treatment.* Clean quickly in distilled water.

**Hilgardite $Ca_2B_5ClO_8(OH)_2$**
Hilgardite is dimorphous with parahilgardite and crystallizes in the monoclinic system, forming tabular crystals with hemimorphic habit. There is a perfect cleavage. The crystals are colourless with a vitreous lustre and are transparent. H 5; SG 2.7
*Occurrence.* Hilgardite occurs in salt domes, particularly the Choctaw dome, Iberville Parish, Louisiana.

**Lüneburgite $Mg_3(PO_4)_2B_2O_3 . 8H_2O$**
Lüneburgite crystallizes in the monoclinic system, forming minute pseudohexagonal tablets; it is also found as flattened masses with a fibrous structure. The colour is white to brown or green. H about 2; SG 2.0
*Occurrence.* Lüneburgite is found in clay with halite, sylvine and polyhalite. It has also been found in a guano deposit.
*Localities.* From Carlsbad, New Mexico and from parts of Texas; in Marl at Lüneburg, W. Germany; and in guano at Mejillones, Peru.

**Cahnite $Ca_2BAsO_4(OH)_4$**
Cahnite crystallizes in the tetragonal system and forms minute penetration twins with etched and rounded crystal faces. There is a perfect cleavage. The colour is white and the lustre vitreous. H 3; SG 3.1
*Occurrence.* Found with franklinite at Franklin, New Jersey and at some other localities.

**Seamanite $Mn_3PO_4BO_3 . 3H_2O$**
Seamanite crystallizes in the orthorhombic system and forms small acicular crystals which are pale yellow in colour. H 4; SG 3.1
*Occurrence.* Found in fractures cutting siliceous rock associated with sussexite and calcite at the Chicagon mine, Michigan.

**Sulphoborite $Mg_3SO_4B_2O_4(OH)_2 . 4H_2O$**
Sulphoborite crystallizes in the orthorhombic system and forms short to long colourless prismatic crystals. H 4–4.5; SG 2.4
*Occurrence.* Sulphoborite is found in salt deposits.
*Localities.* From Wittmar, Brunswick, W. Germany, and Westeregeln, E. Germany; the Inder Lake area, western Kazakhstan, USSR.

## Carbonates

**Thermonatrite $Na_2CO_3 . H_2O$**
Thermonatrite crystallizes in the orthorhombic system and forms crusts or efflorescences; it may also occur as clusters of platy needles. It is colourless to grey or yellow. Thermonatrite is sectile and the lustre is vitreous. H 1–1.5; SG 2.2
*Occurrence.* Found as a deposit from saline lakes, in association with fumaroles, and as an efflorescence on the soil in desert areas.
*Localities.* From Death Valley, California as an efflorescence; from Mt. Vesuvius; as a bedded deposit at the Gorodki oil field in the Kama region of the USSR; from the Sudan desert, etc.
*Treatment.* Store in a sealed container.

**Natron $Na_2CO_3 . 10H_2O$**
Natron crystallizes in the monoclinic system forming efflorescences and crusts; synthetic crystals have a tabular form. The crystals are colourless to yellow and are brittle with a vitreous lustre. H 1–1.5; SG 1.4
*Occurrence.* Natron is found in solution in soda lakes or as an efflorescence on lava.
*Localities.* From Wadi Natrum, Egypt;

*Right: Pirssonite from Searles Lake, California*

*Left: Malachite in botryoidal concretionary form from Zaire*

Mt. Vesuvius; Owens Lake, California.
*Treatment.* Store in a sealed container.

**Trona $Na_3H(CO_3)_2\ 2H_2O$**
Trona crystallizes in the monoclinic system and is commonly found massive, fibrous or columnar; crystals are elongated and flattened. The colour is greyish-white to pale yellow or brown; there is a perfect cleavage. The lustre is vitreous and glistening. H 2.5–3; SG 2.1
*Occurrence.* Trona occurs as a deposit in saline lakes or as an efflorescence on soil in dry, hot regions.
*Localities.* Occurs with borax at Searles Lake, and at Death Valley, California; also from Tibet, Mongolia and Iran, etc.
*Treatment.* Store in a sealed container.

**Nahcolite $NaHCO_3$**
Nahcolite crystallizes in the monoclinic system, forming concretionary masses which may be several feet in diameter; it may also occur as crystal aggregates or as elongated prismatic crystals. There is a perfect cleavage. The colour is white, but may be discoloured by impurities to grey or brown; it is transparent to translucent and the lustre is vitreous to resinous. H 2.5; SG 2.2
*Occurrence.* Nahcolite occurs in unweathered oil-shale of the Green River formation, north-west Colorado; in Searles Lake, California; from Egypt; and from Lake Magadi, Kenya; etc.
*Treatment.* Store in sealed container.

**Pirssonite $Na_2Ca(CO_3)_2.2H_2O$**
Pirssonite crystallizes in the orthorhombic system and forms short transparent prismatic crystals which may be colourless or grey. The lustre is vitreous. H 3–3.5; SG 2.3
*Occurrence.* Found in mud layers as euhedral crystals at Searles Lake, California; at Borax Lake, and as an efflorescence at Deep Spring Lake, California, and other localities.
*Treatment.* Store in a sealed container.

**Gaylussite $Na_2Ca(CO_3)_2.5H_2O$**
Gaylussite crystallizes in the monoclinic system and forms flattened, wedge-shaped elongated crystals with a perfect cleavage. The colour is white to yellow; the lustre is vitreous and the fracture conchoidal. H 2.5–3; SG 1.9
*Occurrence.* Gaylussite is found in lake deposits, particularly at Searles Lake and Deep Spring Lake, California; also from the eastern Gobi Desert, Mongolia; etc.
*Treatment.* Store in a sealed container.

**Malachite $Cu_2CO_3(OH)_2$**
Malachite crystallizes in the monoclinic system and is usually found massive as thick compact crusts with a botryoidal or mamillary surface and a fibrous and banded structure. It may also be stalactitic. When crystals are found they are small, acicular or prismatic with wedge-shaped terminations. There is a perfect cleavage. The colour is bright to dark green with a vitreous lustre. The streak is pale green. H 3.5–4; SG 4.0
*Occurrence.* Malachite occurs as a secondary mineral in the oxidation zone of copper deposits. It is associated with azurite and a variety combining the two is called azur-malachite.

*Right: Prismatic azurite crystals on a limonitic matrix. From Sardinia*

*Opposite page, upper: Prisms of calcite from Andreasberg in the Harz Mountains, West Germany*

*Opposite page, lower: Parallel growth of calcite in scalenohedral form. From Korsnäs, Finland*

*Below right: An encrustation of acicular artinite crystals from Val Malenco, Sondrio, Italy*

*Below: A fine prismatic crystal of azurite from Tsumeb, South-West Africa*

*Localities.* Malachite is found in the Ural Mountains; in Zaire; at Tsumeb, South-West Africa; at Broken Hill, New South Wales; at Bisbee, Arizona; and at Liskeard, Cornwall.
*Treatment.* Wash with distilled water, especially if cracked. Add ammonia until a blue precipitate forms and then add more water. The specimen can be allowed to soak for one hour and then should be soaked in distilled water. The water can be removed after several hours by soaking in wood alcohol and allowing to dry. Do not carry out this process if azurite is present.
*Fashioning. Uses:* cabochons, carvings, tumbling, beads, etc; *cleavage:* perfect pinacoidal in crystals (rare), parting easily in fibre directions in massive material; *heat sensitivity:* high, so the mineral should be treated with care.

**Azurite $Cu_3(CO_3)_2(OH)_2$**
Sometimes called blue malachite, azurite crystallizes in the monoclinic system forming massive specimens, nodular concretions, films and stains and, more rarely, tabular or short prismatic crystals. The colour is light to dark blue with a vitreous lustre and a blue streak; commonly associated with malachite to form the variety azur-malachite. H 3.5–4; SG 3.7
*Occurrence.* Found as a secondary mineral in the oxidation zone of copper deposits associated with malachite.
*Locations.* As for malachite; particularly fine crystals are found near Tsumeb, South-West Africa.
*Treatment.* Clean with distilled water.
*Fashioning. Uses:* faceting or cabochons; *cleavage:* perfect interrupted // to the clinodome; *cutting angles:* crown 40°, pavilion 40°; *heat sensitivity:* high in transparent faceting-quality crystals.

**Magnesite $MgCO_3$**
Magnesite crystallizes in the hexagonal system and is commonly found massive, compact, coarse- to fine-grained, lamellar or fibrous. Crystals, which are rare, may be rhombohedral, prismatic, tabular or scalenohedral. There is a perfect cleavage and the fracture is conchoidal. The colour is white to grey and may be yellowish-brown; the lustre is vitreous. The streak is white. Some specimens may be transparent. H 3.5–4.5; SG 3.0–3.1
*Occurrence.* Magnesite occurs as an alteration product of magnesium-rich rocks or as beds in metamorphic rocks. It may also occur as a gangue mineral in hydrothermal ore veins or in sedimentary deposits.
*Locations.* Found in Oberdorf, Austria, in fine crystals and as very fine crystals at Serra das Eguas, Bahia, Brazil. Large deposits occur in California and in Nevada. Cuttable crystals have been found at Bom Jesus dos Meiras, Brazil, and many other localities.
*Treatment.* Liquids best avoided, because of porosity.

**Artinite $Mg_2CO_3(OH)_2.3H_2O$**
Artinite crystallizes in the monoclinic system and forms crusts of acicular crystals or fibrous aggregates. There is a perfect cleavage and a high degree of brittleness. The colour is white and the lustre is vitreous or silky; the crystals may be transparent. H 2.5; SG 2.0
*Occurrence.* Found with hydromagnesite and other magnesium-bearing minerals coating surfaces in serpentinized ultrabasic rocks.
*Localities.* Fine specimens from the Aosta Valley, Italy; radiating fibrous aggregates from San Benito Co., California; sprays of acicular crystals from Long Island, New York; etc.
*Treatment.* Soil removed by a quick immersion in alcohol.

**Hydromagnesite $Mg_4(CO_3)_3(OH)_2.3H_2O$**
Hydromagnesite crystallizes in the monoclinic system and forms acicular or bladed crystals; sometimes, in large examples, they are vertically striated. It also occurs in crusts and massive forms. Twinning is common. The colour is white and crystals are transparent. The lustre is vitreous. There is a perfect cleavage. H 3.5; SG 2.2
*Occurrence.* Hydromagnesite is found as an alteration of serpentinite or other magnesian rocks.
*Localities.* Found as excellent crystals in the chromite deposits of Iran; from British Columbia; with artinite on Long Island, New York; from California; etc.

**Calcite $CaCO_3$**
Calcite crystallizes in the hexagonal system and forms a wide variety of crystals. The commonest forms are the scalenohedron and the rhombohedron; it may also be found massive, granular or stalactitic. Twinning is common and there is a perfect cleavage. The colour is white and various shades of grey, yellow, brown, red, green, blue and black may result from impurities. The lustre is vitreous to pearly. It is transparent to translucent with a whitish-grey streak. H 3; SG 2.7; RI 1.48, 1.65; dispersion very high.
*Occurrence.* Calcite is one of the commonest of minerals and occurs as the chief constituent in limestones. It may also be found as a component of other sedimentary and metamorphic rocks. It may be found in pegmatites and as a gangue mineral in ore deposits. It occurs as stalactites and stalagmites in caves and in geodes and concretions.
*Localities.* Fine specimens are found in Cumbria, Durham and Cornwall; Tsumeb, South West Africa; with copper on the Keweenaw Peninsula, Michigan; in the lead-zinc regions of Wisconsin and Illinois; etc.
*Treatment.* Clean if necessary with distilled water.
*Fashioning. Uses:* faceting, cabochons, tumbling, carvings, etc; *cleavage:* perfect rhombohedral in crystalline varieties; *cutting angles:* crown 40°–50°, pavilion 43°; *heat sensitivity:* high.

**Aragonite $CaCO_3$**
Dimorphous with calcite, aragonite crystallizes in the orthorhombic system forming acicular crystals elongated along the c-axis; often twinned; also in fibrous, columnar, stalactitic and micro-

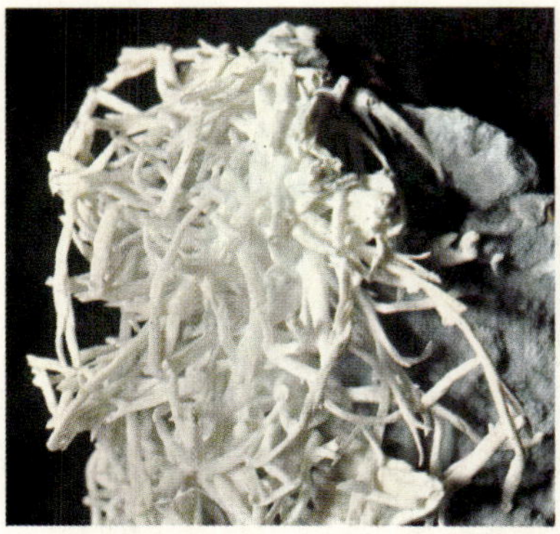

*Right: Flos ferri, a form of aragonite*

*Far right: Interpenetrating twins of aragonite*

*Below right: The pseudo-hexagonal form of aragonite, well shown in these fine crystals from Agrigento, Italy*

crystalline forms. There is a distinct cleavage. The colour is white, yellowish, green or blue, and there is some degree of transparency. The lustre is vitreous. H 3.5–4; SG 2.9

*Occurrence.* Aragonite occurs in low-temperature deposits, especially in limestone caves and in the vicinity of hot springs. It may be found in the oxidized zone of ore deposits and in some sedimentary rocks. Secreted by marine organisms.

*Localities.* Fine specimens from Cumbria, where they occur as aggregates of acicular crystals; from Carinthia, Austria; transparent crystals from Horschenz, Czechoslovakia; lead- and zinc-bearing varieties from Tsumeb, South West Africa; from Wind Cave, Custer Co., South Dakota; from the Magdalena district, Socorro Co., New Mexico; etc.

*Treatment.* Clean with distilled water.

*Fashioning. Uses:* faceting, cabochons, carvings; *cleavage:* distinct brachypinacoidal; brittle; *cutting angles:* crown 40°, pavilion 40°; *pleochroism:* weak; *heat sensitivity:* fairly high.

**Dolomite $CaMg(CO_3)_2$**

Dolomite crystallizes in the hexagonal system and forms simple rhombohedra; it may also be found as prismatic crystals terminated by rhombohedra; as twins; crystal aggregates; and massive, granular. There is a perfect cleavage. The colour is white, grey, through pink to pale brown, and the lustre is vitreous. RI 1.67, 1.50; H 3.5–4; SG 2.8

*Occurrence.* Dolomite occurs as strata formed in a number of different ways; in hydrothermal vein deposits, in veins in serpentinite and in altered basic igneous rocks containing magnesium.

*Localities.* Fine crystals from Switzerland and Italy; from Lockport, New York; in quartz geodes at Keokuk, Iowa; St. Eustache, Quebec; Guanajuato, Mexico.

*Right: Dolomite crystals with hematite and quartz*

*Treatment.* Clean if necessary with distilled water.

**Huntite $CaMg_3(CO_3)_4$**

Huntite crystallizes in the hexagonal system and forms compact masses resembling chalk; these are fibrous. The colour is white and the lustre earthy. H very soft; SG 2.6

*Occurrence.* Found in caverns where the country rock is rich in magnesium.

*Localities.* From Grotte de la Clamouse, Hérault, France; Dorog, Hungary; along the Trucial Coast; Carlsbad Caverns, New Mexico; etc.

**Strontianite $SrCO_3$**

Strontianite crystallizes in the orthorhombic system in prismatic crystals, which may be acicular; it is more frequently found massive, fibrous or concretionary. Twinning is frequent. The colour is white, grey, yellowish or brown, greenish or reddish, transparent to translucent. The lustre is vitreous. H 3.5; SG 3.7

*Occurrence.* Strontianite occurs as a

*Left: Smithsonite crystals from Berg Aukas, Grootfontein, South-West Africa*

*Far left: Characteristic dipyramidal crystals of witherite with horizontal striation of the faces clearly shown*

*Far left, lower: Strontianite from Thuringia*

*Below left: The rhombohedral form of smithsonite can be seen in these crystals from Chessy, France*

low-temperature mineral in veins and geodes in limestone, or in sulphide vein deposits as a gangue mineral.
*Localities.* Fine crystals from the Austrian Tyrol; Westphalia; Strontian, Strathclyde, Scotland; Strontium Hills, San Bernardino Co., California; etc.
*Treatment.* Clean with distilled water.

**Witherite $BaCO_3$**
Witherite crystallizes in the orthorhombic system and crystals are always twinned, forming pseudohexagonal dipyramids; faces are horizontally striated; massive and granular forms are also found. The colour is white to grey, sometimes tinged with yellow, green or brown. The mineral is transparent to translucent with a vitreous lustre. It phosphoresces blue under short-wave UV. H 3–3.5; SG 4.2
*Occurrence.* Found as a low-temperature mineral in hydrothermal vein deposits.
*Localities.* Very fine crystals from Northumberland, Cumbria and Durham; from the Minerva mine, Rosiclare, Illinois with fluorite and calcite; etc.
*Treatment.* Clean with distilled water.

**Alstonite $BaCa(CO_3)_2$**
Alstonite crystallizes in the orthorhombic system. It is dimorphous with barytocalcite and forms pseudohexagonal prisms. The colour is white, grey, or pink with a vitreous lustre. H 4–4.5; SG 3.6
*Occurrence.* Occurs as a low-temperature mineral in hydrothermal veins.
*Localities.* From the Brownley Hill mine, Alston, Cumbria; New Brancepeth, Durham; Hexham, Northumberland.

**Barytocalcite $BaCa(CO_3)_2$**
Dimorphous with alstonite, barytocalcite crystallizes in the monoclinic system; forms short to long prismatic crystals with striations; massive forms are also found. There is a perfect cleavage. The colour is white, grey, yellowish or greenish with a vitreous lustre. H 4; SG 3.6
*Occurrence.* Barytocalcite occurs associated with calcite, baryte and fluorite in veins in limestone from Alston Moor, Cumbria; also from Långban, Sweden.
*Treatment.* Clean with distilled water.

**Smithsonite $ZnCO_3$**
Smithsonite crystallizes in the hexagonal system and is found as rhombohedral crystals with curved faces or as scalenohedra; commonly botryoidal, reniform or stalactitic, massive, granular or as crusts. The colour may range from white, grey and pale yellow to deep yellow, pale to bright apple green, bluish green and blue, deep pink to purple and brown. The streak is white and the lustre vitreous to pearly. H 4–4.5; SG 4.3–4.4
*Occurrence.* Smithsonite occurs as a secondary mineral in the oxidized zone of ore deposits; as a replacement of calcareous rocks near ore deposits and sometimes as a secondary mineral derived from sphalerite in pegmatites.
*Localities.* Found at the Kabwe mine, Zambia, as fine transparent crystals; pink, white and grey crystals from Tsumeb, South West Africa; botryoidal encrustations from Kelly, Socorro Co., New Mexico; in pegmatite with hemimorphite and other minerals from Tin Mountain mine, South Dakota; as yellow banded crusts in lead mines at Yellville, Marion Co., Arkansas; Laurion, Greece; etc.
*Treatment.* Clean with distilled water.
*Fashioning. Uses:* faceting (rare), cabochons, beads, carvings, etc; *cleavage:* perfect rhombohedral, massive types separate easily between growth layers; brittle; *cutting angles:* crown 40°, pavilion 40°; *heat sensitivity:* low.

*Above: Concretionary form of hydrozincite from Powys, Wales*

*Above right: Dawsonite crystals from Monte Amiata, Italy*

**Hydrozincite $Zn_5(CO_3)_2(OH)_6$**
Hydrozincite crystallizes in the monoclinic system, and is found as compact masses, or as crusts, stalactites and reniform masses. Crystals are flattened and elongated, tapering to a sharp point. The colour is white, grey and pale pink, yellow and brown. The lustre is pearly if crystalline, dull to silky when massive. There is a perfect cleavage. H 2–2.5; SG 3.5–3.8
*Occurrence.* Hydrozincite is found as a secondary mineral formed by the alteration of sphalerite in the oxidation zone of ore deposits. It may also be found in pegmatites.
*Localities.* Found at Santander, Spain; Constantine, Algeria; Goodsprings, Nevada; Tin Mountain mine, Custer Co., South Dakota; Franklin, New Jersey; blade-like crystals from Mapimi, Mexico; and many other localities.
*Treatment.* Clean with distilled water.

**Rosasite $(Cu, Zn)_2CO_3(OH)_2$**
Rosasite crystallizes in the monoclinic system as botryoidal or mamillary crusts with a fibrous structure; crusts of microscopic crystals are sometimes found. The Cu to Zn ratio is near 3:2. The colour is bluish-green, green or sky-blue. H about 4.5; SG 4.0–4.2
*Occurrence.* Rosasite occurs as a secondary mineral in the oxidation zone of zinc-copper-lead deposits.
*Localities.* Found at the Rosas mine, Sulcis, Sardinia; with smithsonite and hemimorphite at Cerro Gordo, Inyo Co., California; with aurichalcite at Kelly, Socorro Co., New Mexico.
*Treatment.* Clean with distilled water.

**Aurichalcite $(Zn, Cu)_5(CO_3)_2(OH)_6$**
Aurichalcite has a Cu:Zn ratio of about 2:5. It crystallizes in the orthorhombic system and forms acicular crystals; more commonly tufted aggregates or encrustations. It may also be found granular, columnar or laminated. There is a perfect cleavage and the mineral is very brittle. The colour is pale green to greenish-blue, transparent. The lustre is silky to pearly. H 1–2; SG 3.9
*Occurrence.* Aurichalcite is found as a secondary mineral in oxidized zinc-copper deposits and sometimes in pegmatites.
*Localities.* Found at Laurion, Greece; Sardinia; Tin Mountain mine, South Dakota; very fine specimens from Mapimi, Durango, Mexico; etc.
*Treatment.* Clean with distilled water.

**Loseyite $(Zn, Mn)_7(CO_3)_2(OH)_{10}$**
Loseyite crystallizes in the monoclinic system forming radiating bundles of crystals coloured bluish-white to brown. H about 3; SG 3.2
*Occurrence.* Loseyite is found in small veins in massive ore with calcite, at Franklin, New Jersey.
*Treatment.* Clean with water.

**Otavite $CdCO_3$**
Otavite crystallizes in the hexagonal system, forming crusts of minute rhombohedral crystals coloured white to yellow-brown or reddish, with an adamantine lustre. H not determined; SG 4.9
*Occurrence.* Otavite occurs as a secondary mineral associated with smithsonite, azurite and malachite at Tsumeb, South West Africa.
*Treatment.* Do not attempt to clean.

**Dawsonite $NaAlCO_3(OH)_2$**
Dawsonite crystallizes in the orthorhombic system and is found as radial encrustations of acicular crystals. There is a perfect cleavage. The colour is white, transparent. The lustre is vitreous or silky. H 3; SG 2.4
*Occurrence.* Found as a low-temperature mineral in shale of the Green River formation, western Colorado; fine microscopic crystals from St. Michel, Quebec; in saline soils at Olduvai Gorge, Tanzania; etc.
*Treatment.* Do not attempt to clean.

**Hydrotalcite $Mg_6Al_2CO_3(OH)_{16}.4H_2O$**
Hydrotalcite crystallizes in the hexagonal system and is dimorphous with manasseite. It is found massive, foliated, or lamellar with a perfect cleavage. It is greasy to the touch. The colour is white, transparent; white streak. H 2; SG 2.0

*Far right: Aurichalcite from Yanga-Koubanza, Zaire, showing the acicular form of the individual crystals*

*Right: Rosasite as an encrustation, from Sardinia*

*Localities.* Found with serpentine at Nordmark and Snarum, Norway; Vernon, New Jersey; etc.

**Manasseite**
**$Mg_6Al_2CO_3(OH)_{16} \cdot 4H_2O$**
Dimorphous with hydrotalcite, manasseite crystallizes in the hexagonal system, forming massive foliated bodies. It has a perfect cleavage and a greasy feel. The colour may be white, grey or pale blue with a pearly lustre. H 2; SG 2
*Localities.* Associated with serpentine at Amity, New York; Nordmark and Snarum, Norway.

**Dundasite $PbAl_2(CO_3)_2(OH)_4 \cdot 2H_2O$**
Dundasite crystallizes in the orthorhombic system forming small round aggregates of radiating crystals and matted crusts. There is a perfect cleavage. The colour is white transparent and the lustre is vitreous to silky. H 2; SG 3.4
*Occurrence.* Dundasite is found as a secondary mineral in the oxidation zone of lead deposits.
*Localities.* Found with crocoite in the Adelaide Proprietary mine, Dundas, Tasmania, from Wensley, Derbyshire and Trefriw, Gwynedd, Wales; etc.

**Lanthanite $(La, Ce)_2(CO_3)_3 \cdot 8H_2O$**
Lanthanite crystallizes in the orthorhombic system and is found as scales, plates or thick tabular crystals. Twinning occurs. The colour is white, yellowish, pinkish, transparent. The lustre is pearly. H 2.5–3; SG 2.6–2.7
*Occurrence.* Found in oxidized zinc ores at Bethlehem, Lehigh Co., Pennsylvania; on cerite at Bastnaes, Sweden; etc.

**Calkinsite $(La, Ce)_2(CO_3)_3 \cdot 4H_2O$**
Calkinsite crystallizes in the orthorhombic system as yellow platy crystals with a perfect cleavage. Twinning is common. H about 2.5; SG 3.2
*Localities.* Occurs with barite and goethite in burbankite, Hill Co., Montana.

**Tengerite**
Tengerite is perhaps two distinct species: $BeYtCO_3(OH)_3 \cdot H_2O$ with the Yt including some Ce, etc; or $CaYt_3(CO_3)_4(OH)_3 \cdot 3H_2O$.
*Occurrence.* It occurs as crystalline powdery coatings and as fibrous mamillary crusts, a dull white in colour. H not measured; SG 3.1
*Localities.* Found on gadolinite at Clear Creek Canyon, Jefferson Co., Colorado; on melanocerite at the Cardiff uranium mine, Wilberforce, Ontario; etc.

**Cerussite $PbCO_3$**
Cerussite crystallizes in the orthorhombic system and forms crystals of varying habit; single crystals are usually tabular and elongated along the c-axis; clusters of crystals, reticulated masses and aggregates are also found. It may occur massive, granular or stalactitic. The colour ranges from transparent white to smoky and blue-green; the lustre is adamantine or submetallic and the streak colourless to white. H 3–3.5; SG 6.5
*Occurrence.* Cerussite is a secondary mineral in the oxidation zone of ore deposits and is associated with other secondary lead minerals.

*Left: Hydrotalcite from Snarum, Norway*

*Localities.* From Leadhills, Strathclyde; Tsumeb, South West Africa; Broken Hill, New South Wales; chatoyant material from the Mammoth mine, Pinal County, Arizona; etc.
*Fashioning. Uses:* faceting or cabochons; *cleavage:* distinct prismatic; very brittle; *cutting angles:* crown 40°, pavilion 40°; *heat sensitivity:* high.

**Hydrocerussite $Pb_3(CO_3)_2(OH)_2$**
Hydrocerussite crystallizes in the hexagonal system forming thick to thin tabular crystals with a hexagonal outline; steep pyramidal crystals are also found. There is a perfect cleavage. The colour is white or grey, transparent. The lustre is adamantine. H 3.5; SG 6.8
*Occurrence.* Found as a secondary mineral in oxidized ores, associated with cerussite, dioptase and boléite at the Mammoth mine, Tiger, Arizona; from the Mendip Hills, Somerset; Laurion, Greece; Altai Mts., USSR.

**Bismutite $(BiO)_2CO_3$**
Bismutite crystallizes in the tetragonal (orthorhombic) system, forming massive

*Below: Prismatic cerussite crystals from Tsumeb, South-West Africa*

*Right: The compact form of stichtite from Bou Azzer, Morocco*

*Below right: An exceptionally well formed crystal of liebigite from Utah*

bodies or fibrous crusts; lamellar aggregates are also found. The colour is yellow to brown, or greenish, grey or black. Some green or blue comes from associated copper minerals. The lustre is vitreous to pearly. H 2.5–3.5; SG 6.1–7.7 (a synthetic form was 8.1).
*Occurrence.* Found as a secondary mineral in the oxidized zone of veins and pegmatites which contain primary bismuth minerals.
*Localities.* From St. Just and Redruth, Cornwall; Colorado, Arizona and New Mexico; Bolivia, Australia; Malagasy Republic; etc.

**Beyerite $Ca(BiO)_2(CO_3)_2$**
Sometimes with lead replacing some calcium, beyerite crystallizes in the tetragonal system as thin rectangular flattened plates or as compact earthy masses. The colour is white to bright yellow, or greyish-green with a vitreous lustre. H 2–3; SG 6.5
*Localities.* Found as a secondary mineral with bismutite; as crystals in bismutite cavities near Wickenburg, Arizona; also from Schneeberg, E. Germany; etc.

**Stichtite $Mg_6Cr_2CO_3(OH)_{16}.4H_2O$**
Stichtite crystallizes in the hexagonal system and is dimorphous with barbertonite. It is found lamellar and foliated or in micaceous scales; the colour is lilac to rose-pink. There is a perfect cleavage. The streak is white to lilac and the lustre waxy. H 1.5–2; SG 2.1
*Occurrence.* Found in serpentinite rocks with chromite a common associate.
*Localities.* From Dundas, Tasmania; Barberton district, Transvaal; Black Lake, Quebec.

**Barbertonite**
**$Mg_6Cr_2CO_3(OH)_{16}.4H_2O$**
Dimorphous with stichtite, barbertonite crystallizes in the hexagonal system, forming twisted masses of fibres, or as flattened plates with a perfect cleavage. The colour is lilac to rose-pink, translucent with a pearly lustre. The streak is white to pale lilac. H 1.5–2; SG 2.1
*Occurrence.* Found in serpentinite rock with stichtite and chromite.
*Localities.* From Cunningsburgh, Scotland; Dundas, Tasmania; Barberton, Transvaal.

**Rutherfordine $UO_2CO_3$**
Rutherfordine crystallizes in the orthorhombic system forming thin single crystals or microscopic fibrous aggregates; there is a perfect cleavage. The colour is white, pale yellow to orange or brown; yellowish-green colours also occur. H not measured; SG 5.7
*Localities.* Found with becquerelite and masuyite from Shinkolobwe, Zaire; in a pegmatite resulting from the alteration of uraninite at Morogoro, Tanzania; from the Beryl Mountain pegmatite, New Hampshire; and from Newry, Maine; etc.

**Sharpite $(UO_2)(CO_3).H_2O$**
Sharpite apparently crystallizes in the orthorhombic system, though this is not certain; it is found as crusts of radiating fibres, greenish-yellow in colour. H about 2.5; SG at least 3.3
*Localities.* Found with uranophane, curite, becquerelite and masuyite at Shinkolobwe, Zaire; from Krüth, Haut-Rhin, France, with uraninite.

**Bayleyite $Mg_2UO_2(CO_3)_3.18H_2O$**
Bayleyite crystallizes in the monoclinic system forming short prismatic crystals or crusts. The colour is yellow becoming yellowish-white on exposure. Lustre vitreous. H not determined; SG 2.0
*Localities.* Bayleyite is found as a secondary mineral, which is water-soluble, at the Hillside mine, Bagdad, Arizona; as an efflorescence with epsomite and gypsum at Azegour, Morocco.

**Liebigite $Ca_2U(CO_3)_4.10H_2O$**
Liebigite crystallizes in the orthorhombic system and is usually found as granular or scaly crusts; crystals are short prismatic with rounded edges. The colour is green to yellowish-green, transparent, with a vitreous lustre. H 2.5–3; SG 2.4
*Localities.* Found at Wheal Basset, Cornwall; Jachymov, Czechoslovakia, as an efflorescence on mine walls; and in the oxidized zone of uraninite veins; from Utah and New Mexico.

**Andersonite**
**$Na_2CaUO_2(CO_3)_3.6H_2O$**
Andersonite crystallizes in the hexagonal system forming thick crusts; crystals may be pseudocubic. The colour is bright yellow-green, transparent to translucent with a vitreous lustre. H 2.5; SG 2.8
*Localities.* Occurs as a secondary mineral associated with bayleyite, gypsum and other minerals on mine walls at Bagdad, Arizona; as an efflorescence with liebigite from Jim Thorpe, Pennsylvania.

**Swartzite $CaMgUO_2(CO_3)_3.12H_2O$**
Swartzite crystallizes in the monoclinic system and forms crusts of bright green prismatic crystals which turn yellowish-white on dehydration. H not measured; SG 2.3
*Localities.* Found as an efflorescence on mine walls at the Hillside mine, Yavapai Co., Arizona, with bayleyite and other minerals.

**Rhodochrosite $MnCO_3$**
Rhodochrosite crystallizes in the hexagonal system and is commonly found massive, granular; it may also occur stalactitic or as rhombohedral crystals. There is a perfect cleavage. The colour is pale pink to deep red and may be orange or brown; the lustre is vitreous and the material may be transparent. H 3.5–4; SG 3.7
*Occurrence.* Occurs as a gangue mineral in hydrothermal ore veins or in high-temperature contact metasomatic deposits and as a secondary mineral in manganese deposits; occasionally in pegmatites.
*Localities.* Fine scalenohedra from Hotazel, Kuruman, South Africa; from Catamarca province, Argentina, where stalactitic aggregates are found; pink groups from Butte, Montana; from the Harz Mountains, Germany, and from Magdalena, Sonora, Mexico.
*Treatment.* May be cleaned with dilute hydrochloric acid; white coating formed after weathering cannot be removed.
*Fashioning. Uses:* faceting, cabochons, tumbling, beads, etc; *cleavage:* perfect rhombohedral, massive types may sep-

arate between growth layers; brittle; *cutting angles;* crown 40°, pavilion 40°; *heat sensitivity:* moderate, sensitive to shock.

**Manganosiderite (Mn, Fe)$CO_3$**
Manganosiderite crystallizes in the hexagonal system and is isomorphous with rhodochrosite. It is considered to be a variety of that mineral.

**Siderite $FeCO_3$**
Siderite crystallizes in the hexagonal system and is commonly found massive, granular. Crystals are rhombohedral, scalenohedral or tabular. Botryoidal and globular forms also occur. There is a perfect cleavage. The colour is pale yellow, grey, through browns, greens, reds and sometimes nearly colourless. The lustre is vitreous and the streak white. H 3.5–4.5; SG 3.9
*Occurrence.* Siderite is found in bedded sedimentary deposits and as a gangue mineral in hydrothermal ore veins; it occurs in basaltic igneous rocks and sometimes in pegmatites.
*Localities.* Found at Bodmin, St. Austell, Camborne, Lanlivery and Redruth, Cornwall; Příbram, Czechoslovakia; fine crystals from Val Taevetsch, Grisons, Switzerland; Broken Hill, New South Wales; Morro Velho gold mine, Ouro Preto, Minas Gerais, Brazil; etc.

**Pyroaurite**
**$Mg_6Fe_2CO_3(OH)_{16}.4H_2O$**
Pyroaurite crystallizes in the hexagonal system and is dimorphous with sjögrenite. Crystals are thin to thick tabular; fibrous forms are also found. There is a perfect cleavage. The colour is yellow to brownish-white, silver-white, greenish or colourless; the lustre is vitreous to pearly. H 2.5; SG 2.1
*Occurrence.* Found in serpentinite or as a low-temperature hydrothermal vein mineral.
*Localities.* From a dolomitic rock at Rutherglen, Ontario; also from Half-Grunay, north of Fetlar, in the Shetland Islands.

*Left: Pyroaurite on calcite from Långban, Sweden*

*Left, above: Rhodochrosite from Cavnic, Romania*

*Left: Rhombohedral crystals of rhodochrosite from the Sweet Home mine, Colorado*

**Sjögrenite**
**$Mg_6Fe_2CO_3(OH)_{16}.4H_2O$**
Sjögrenite crystallizes in the hexagonal system and is dimorphous with pyroaurite. Crystals are thin plates with a perfect cleavage, white, yellow or brownish in colour. The lustre is vitreous or waxy, transparent or translucent. H 2.5; SG 2.1
*Localities.* Occurs as a low-temperature hydrothermal mineral with calcite and pyroaurite at Långban, Sweden.

**Brugnatellite**
**$Mg_6FeCO_3(OH)_{13}.4H_2O$**
Brugnatellite crystallizes in the hexagonal system forming foliated masses of small flakes with a perfect cleavage. The colour is flesh-pink to yellowish or brownish-white. The lustre is pearly and the streak white. H about 2; SG 2.1
*Localities.* Occurs as crusts in hydrothermally altered serpentinites and as an alteration product of melilite at Iron Hill, Gunnison County, Colorado; found also in Piedmont, Italy.

**Ankerite Ca(Mg, Fe)$(CO_3)_2$**
Ankerite has over 10% iron and often contains some manganese. It crystallizes in the hexagonal system forming simple rhombohedral or massive, granular forms. There is a perfect cleavage. The colour is white, grey, yellow to brown with a vitreous to pearly lustre. H 3.5–4; SG 2.9
*Localities.* Occurs at Oldham, near Manchester; at Erzberg, Austria; as a gangue mineral at the Homestake gold mine, Lead, South Dakota; in sulphide veins in the Cour d'Alene region, Idaho; etc.

**Cobaltocalcite $CoCO_3$**
Cobaltocalcite crystallizes in the hexagonal system forming small spherical masses with radiated structure, or crusts. Crystals rare. The colour is rose-red, altering to grey-brown or black. The lustre is vitreous to waxy. H 4; SG 4.1
*Localities.* Occurs in the cobalt-nickel veins at Schneeberg, E. Germany; fine specimens from Shaba, Zaire; and from other localities.

*Right: Octahedron of northupite from California*

**Zaratite $Ni_3CO_3(OH)_4 \cdot 4H_2O$**
Zaratite, sometimes called emerald nickel, crystallizes in the cubic system forming compact masses and mamillary encrustations coloured emerald green. The lustre is greasy. H 3.5; SG 2.5–2.6
*Occurrence.* Found as a secondary mineral in serpentinites and basic igneous rocks, often associated with chromite and sometimes as an alteration of millerite or meteoritic iron.
*Localities.* From the Shetland Islands; India; Australia; the Coast Range counties of California; etc.

**Northupite $Na_3Mg(CO_3)_2Cl$**
Northupite crystallizes in the cubic system forming octahedral crystals, which are colourless, yellow or grey to brown. They are transparent with a vitreous lustre. H 3.5–4; SG 2.3
*Localities.* Found associated with galena, galeite and other minerals at Searles Lake, San Bernardino Co., California (this locality yields fine octahedra); and at other localities.

**Parisite $Ca(Ce, La)_2(CO_3)_3F_2$**
Parisite crystallizes in the hexagonal system and forms double hexagonal pyramids and sometimes rhombohedra. The colour is brown or brownish-yellow, transparent. The lustre is vitreous or resinous. H 4.5; SG 4.3
*Localities.* Occurs in carbonaceous shale beds in the Muzo emerald deposit, Colombia; in pegmatite pipes in riebeckite-aegirine-granite at Quincy, Massachusetts; and also from a number of other localities.

**Phosgenite $Pb_2CO_3Cl_2$**
Phosgenite crystallizes in the tetragonal system forming long to short prismatic crystals; massive granular forms are also found. The colour is colourless, white, yellow, brown and sometimes greenish or pinkish; the lustre is adamantine and the streak white. H 2–3; SG 6.1
*Occurrence.* Phosgenite occurs as a secondary mineral in the oxidation zone of lead deposits and is commonly associated with other secondary lead minerals.
*Localities.* From Matlock, Derbyshire; Tarnow, Poland; Monteponi, Sicily, as fine crystals; as acicular crystals in quartz at the Silver Sprout mine, Inyo Co., California; as large masses at the

*Right: Phosgenite crystal from Monteponi, Sardinia. Prism and pyramid forms can be clearly seen*

Terrible mine, Custer Co., Colorado; and at other localities.

**Caledonite $Cu_2Pb_5(SO_4)_3CO_3(OH)_6$**
Caledonite crystallizes in the orthorhombic system forming small elongated prismatic crystals usually in divergent groups; also found as coatings and massive. There is a perfect cleavage. The colour is dark blue to bluish-green, transparent, with a greenish-blue or bluish-white streak. The lustre is vitreous to resinous. H 2.5–3; SG 5.6
*Occurrence.* Found in the oxidation zone of copper-lead deposits.
*Localities.* From Leadhills, Strathclyde, Scotland; very fine blue crystals from the Mammoth mine, Tiger, Arizona; with linarite at the Wonder prospect, California; etc.

Left: Caledonite from the Mammoth mine, Tiger Co., Arizona

**Leadhillite $Pb_4SO_4(CO_3)_2(OH)_2$**
Leadhillite crystallizes in the monoclinic system and is dimorphous with susannite. Crystals are pseudohexagonal and massive; granular forms also occur; contact twins are found. There is a perfect cleavage. The colour ranges from colourless to white, grey, yellowish, pale green to blue; transparent to translucent. The lustre is resinous to adamantine. H 2.5–3; SG 6.5
*Occurrence.* Found in the oxidized zone of lead deposits as a secondary mineral associated with cerussite, lanarkite, galena, etc.
*Localities.* From Leadhills, Strathclyde, Scotland; Wanlockhead, Dumfries and Galloway also in Scotland; Tsumeb, South West Africa; the Mammoth mine, Tiger, Arizona; etc.

*Left: Phosgenite, showing several prism faces and a pinacoid (the upper horizontal face). From Monteponi, Sardinia*

**Susannite $Pb_4SO_4(CO_3)_2(OH)_2$**
Dimorphous with leadhillite, susannite is the high-temperature variety. It crystallizes in the hexagonal system forming rhombohedral crystals; there is a perfect cleavage. It is colourless to greenish or yellowish and the lustre is adamantine to resinous. H 2.5–3; SG 6.5
*Occurrence.* Occurs as a secondary mineral in the oxidation zones of lead deposits.
*Localities.* From Leadhills, Strathclyde; Mammoth mine, Tiger, Arizona; etc.

**Wherryite $Pb_4Cu(SO_4)_2CO_3(Cl, OH)_2O$**
Wherryite crystallizes in the monoclinic system in massive granular forms; fibrous aggregates of acicular crystals are also found. The colour is light green, yellow, or bright yellowish-green and the lustre is vitreous. H not measured; SG 6.4
*Localities.* Found in a vug at the Mammoth mine, Tiger, Arizona with chrysocolla, leadhillite and other minerals.

**Schrökingerite $NaCa_3UO_2SO_4(CO_3)_3F.10H_2O$**
Schrökingerite crystallizes in the orthorhombic system as pseudohexagonal plates or as crusts or globular aggregates. There is a perfect cleavage and the colour is between green and yellow. The lustre is vitreous to pearly. H 2.5; SG 2.5
*Occurrence.* Found as a secondary mineral often of recent formation.
*Localities.* From gypsum-bearing clays in Lost Creek, Sweetwater Co., Wyoming; Jachymov, Czechoslovakia; La Soberania mine, San Isidro, Mendoza, Argentina.

**Hanksite $Na_{22}K(SO_4)_9(CO_3)_2Cl$**
Hanksite crystallizes in the hexagonal system as tabular to prismatic crystals often showing interpenetrant twinning. It is colourless to grey, yellow or almost black, with a vitreous lustre. The streak is white. Saline taste. H 3–3.5; SG 2.5
*Occurrence.* Found with halite and other minerals in saline beds.
*Localities.* From the borax areas of Death Valley, California and the saline beds of Searles Lake in the same state.

## Nitrates

**Nitratine $NaNO_3$**
Often called soda-nitre, nitratine crystallizes in the hexagonal system forming crusts. Twinning is common and there is a perfect cleavage. The colour is colourless or white, discoloured grey or yellowish, transparent. The lustre is vitreous. H 1.5–2; SG 2.2
*Occurrence.* Occurs as an efflorescence in hot dry regions.
*Localities.* From Nevada, New Mexico, California; Peru; Bolivia; etc.

**Nitre $KNO_3$**
Nitre crystallizes in the orthorhombic system and occurs as thin crusts; also massive granular. It is colourless or white, discoloured by impurities. The lustre is vitreous. H 2; SG 2.1
*Occurrence.* Occurs as an efflorescence on soil or in caves.
*Localities.* From northern Chile; Bolivia; Italy; USSR; Kentucky, New Mexico; etc.

**Gerhardtite $Cu_2NO_3(OH)_3$**
Gerhardtite crystallizes in the orthorhombic system forming thick tabular crystals with a perfect cleavage. The colour is emerald green and the streak light green. H 2; SG 3.4
*Occurrence.* Occurs as a secondary mineral in the oxidation zone of copper deposits.
*Localities.* From Shaba, Zaire; with cuprite at the United Verde mine, Jerome, Arizona.

**Nitrocalcite $Ca(NO_3)_2.4H_2O$**
Nitrocalcite crystallizes in the monoclinic system. Its colour is white or grey. H soft; SG 1.9
*Occurrence.* It occurs as an efflorescence on soil or in limestone caverns and on calcareous rocks.
*Localities.* From France, Spain and Hungary; Arizona; California; etc.

*Above right: Nitrocalcite from the McDonnell Range, Australia*

*Right: Nitratine from Tarapaca, Chile*

**Buttgenbachite $Cu_{19}Cl_4(NO_3)_2(OH)_{32}.2$ or $3H_2O$**
Buttgenbachite crystallizes in the hexagonal system as acicular crystals, radiated sprays and felt-like aggregates. The colour is deep blue and the lustre vitreous. H 3; SG 3.4
*Localities.* Found as a secondary mineral at Likasi, Shaba, Zaire.

**Darapskite $Na_3NO_3SO_4.H_2O$**
Darapskite crystallizes in the monoclinic system, forming long prismatic crystals; occurs also as platy or granular material. Twinning is common. The crystals are colourless, transparent and the lustre is vitreous. H about 2.5; SG 2.2
*Localities.* From the nitrate deposits of Atacama, Chile, and other places.

## Silicates

### OLIVINE GROUP
A general name for the series from forsterite ($Mg_2SiO_4$) to fayalite ($Fe_2SiO_4$). The gem variety is peridot.

**Forsterite $Mg_2SiO_4$**
Forsterite crystallizes in the orthorhombic system forming thick tabular crystals with vertical striations and wedge-shaped terminations. Massive forms are also found. The colour is green, pale yellow or white and the lustre is vitreous. The streak is colourless. H 7; SG 3.2
*Occurrence.* Forsterite occurs in basic and ultrabasic igneous rocks and thermally metamorphosed impure dolomitic limestones.
*Localities.* From Germany; Sweden; Norway; USSR; San Bernardino Co., California; etc.
*Treatment.* Remove iron stains with oxalic acid.

**Hortonolite $(Fe, Mg)_2SiO_4$**
Hortonolite crystallizes in the orthorhombic system and is usually massive, granular. Crystals are thick tabular. The colour is light green to brown with a greasy lustre and colourless streak. H 7; SG 3.8
*Localities.* Found in dolerite and gabbro; Monroe, Orange Co., New York; Greenland; Transvaal; and from some other localities.
*Treatment.* Clean with distilled water.

**Peridot $(Mg, Fe)_2SiO_4$**
Peridot forms prismatic crystals, often flattened; masses or grains. There is a distinct cleavage. The colour is green to brown with a colourless or yellowish streak and vitreous lustre. H 6.5–7; SG 3.2–3.3; RI 1.63, 1.69; double refraction 0.038
*Occurrence.* Occurs in igneous rocks such as basalt or gabbro, or as a metamorphic product of sedimentary rocks containing silica and magnesium, such as impure dolomites. May occur as crystals in meteoritic iron.
*Localities.* Found on the Island of Zabarjad in the Red Sea; Burma; Hawaii (this variety may contain some chromium); Arizona; the Eifel region of W. Germany; Minas Gerais, Brazil.
*Fashioning. Uses*: faceting, cabochons, tumbling, beads, etc; *cleavage*: distinct brachypinacoidal; *cutting angles*:

*Left: Darapskite with nitratine from Chile*

*Below left: Fine crystals of chondrodite from a classic locality, the Tilly Foster mine, New York*

crown 40°, pavilion 40°; *pleochroism*: distinct; *heat sensitivity*: low.

**Fayalite $Fe_2SiO_4$**
Fayalite crystallizes in the orthorhombic system as thick tabular crystals, sometimes with wedge-shaped terminations; usually found massive. The colour is greenish-yellow, yellow or brown with a colourless streak; the lustre is vitreous. H 7; SG 4.3
*Occurrence.* Occurs in acid and alkaline volcanic and plutonic rocks; metamorphosed iron-rich sediments.
*Localities.* From Sweden; France; Salt Lake Crater, Oahu, Hawaii; and numerous other localities.
*Treatment.* Remove iron stains with oxalic acid.

**Monticellite $MgCaSiO_4$**
Monticellite crystallizes in the orthorhombic system forming prismatic crystals; it is more commonly found massive granular or as disseminated grains. The colour is colourless, grey or greenish with a vitreous lustre. H 5.5; SG 3.0–3.2
*Occurrence.* Occurs as a metamorphic or metasomatic mineral; also from ultrabasic rocks.
*Localities.* From Crestmore, Riverside Co., California; Italy; USSR; Zaire; and other localities.

**Tephroite $Mn_2SiO_4$**
Tephroite crystallizes in the orthorhombic system, forming short prismatic crystals or compact masses. The colour is grey, olive-green, flesh red or reddish-brown. The lustre is greasy. H 6; SG 4.1
*Occurrence.* Occurs in iron-manganese ore deposits; sometimes in metamorphic rocks derived from sediments rich in manganese.
*Localities.* From Franklin, New Jersey; Treburland mine, Cornwall; Långban, Sweden; and from a variety of other localities.
*Treatment.* Clean with distilled water.

**Glaucochroite $CaMnSiO_4$**
Glaucochroite crystallizes in the orthorhombic system as long prismatic crystals, sometimes in aggregates. The colour is bluish-grey, pink or white. The lustre is vitreous. Twinning is common. H 6; SG 3.4
*Localities.* Found with willemite and franklinite at Franklin, New Jersey.
*Treatment.* Clean with distilled water.

## HUMITE GROUP

The members of the humite group have the same ratio of unit cell dimensions b:c, but the a:c and a:b ratios alter from norbergite to clinohumite. The composition of the group can be given as $Mg(OH, F)_2 . nMg_2SiO_4$

**Norbergite $Mg_3SiO_4(F, OH)_2$**
Norbergite crystallizes in the orthorhombic system, often as grains. The colour is orange-yellow to brown, the lustre is vitreous. H 6–6.5; SG 3.2
*Occurrence.* Occurs in contact zones in limestone or dolomite.
*Localities.* From Franklin, New Jersey; Norberg, Västmanland, Sweden; etc.
*Treatment.* Clean with distilled water.

**Chondrodite $Mg_5Si_2O_8(F, OH)_2$**
Chondrodite crystallizes in the monoclinic system as crystals of varied habit or in masses, often with lamellar twinning. The colour is yellow, red or brown, with a vitreous lustre. H 6–6.5; SG 3.1–3.2
*Occurrence.* Occurs in contact zones in limestone or dolomite.
*Localities.* Pargas, Finland; Tilly Foster iron mine, Brewster, New York State; Riverside Co., California; etc.
*Treatment.* Clean with distilled water.

**Humite $Mg_7Si_3O_{12}(F, OH)_2$**
Humite crystallizes in the orthorhombic system as small crystals, which may be white, yellow, dark orange or brown; they have a vitreous lustre. H 6; SG 3.2–3.3
*Occurrence.* Occurs in contact zones in limestone or dolomite or in veins.
*Localities.* From Finland; Värmland, Sweden; Tilly Foster iron mine, Brewster, New York State; and other places.
*Treatment.* Clean with distilled water.

*Below: Crystals of humite with brown biotite from Mt Somma, Italy*

*Right: Five small almandine garnets. Their trapezohedral form can just be discerned*

**Clinohumite $Mg_9Si_4O_{16}(F, OH)_2$**
Clinohumite crystallizes in the monoclinic system, forming crystals which often show lamellar twinning. The colour is white, yellow or brown, with a vitreous lustre. H 6; SG 3.2–3.3
*Occurrence.* Occurs in contact zones in dolomite, in veins or talc schist.
*Localities.* From Pargas, Finland: Llanos de Juanar, Malaga, Spain; Tilly Foster iron mine, Brewster, New York State; and elsewhere.
*Treatment.* Clean with distilled water.

## HELVINE GROUP

Three minerals with the composition $R_4Be_3Si_3O_{12}S$, R being manganese in helvine, iron in danalite and zinc in genthelvite.

**Helvine $Mn_4Be_3Si_3O_{12}S$**
Helvine crystallizes in the cubic system as tetrahedra or rounded aggregates. The colour is reddish-brown, yellow or green, with a vitreous lustre. H 6; SG 3.1–3.3

*Right: A pyrope garnet embedded in matrix*

*Occurrence.* Occurs in granite pegmatites, skarns, hydrothermal veins, etc.
*Localities.* From Pala, San Diego Co., California; Mont St. Hilaire, Quebec, Canada; Brazil; Norway; and other localities.
*Treatment.* Clean with distilled water.

**Danalite $Fe_4Be_3Si_3O_{12}S$**
Danalite crystallizes in the cubic system as octahedra or dodecahedra and in granular masses. The lustre is vitreous. The colour is grey, lemon yellow, red or brown. H 5.5–6; SG 3.3–3.4
*Occurrence.* Occurs in granite pegmatites, contact-metasomatic deposits and hydrothermal veins.
*Localities.* From Redruth, Cornwall; Sweden; USSR; Carroll Co., New Hampshire; etc.
*Treatment.* Clean with distilled water.

**Genthelvite $Zn_4Be_3Si_3O_{12}S$**
Genthelvite crystallizes in the cubic system as tetrahedra or as rounded aggregates. The colour is white, yellow, emerald-green, purple, pink or brown to black, with a vitreous lustre. H 6–6.5; SG 3.6
*Localities.* Occurs with analcime in carbonatite at Mont St. Hilaire, Quebec; Kola Peninsula, USSR; etc.
*Treatment.* Clean with distilled water.

## GARNET GROUP

The garnets can be described by the general formula $X_3Y_2Si_3O_{12}$, in which X may be Ca, Mg, Mn, or $Fe^{2+}$ and Y may be Al, $Fe^{3+}$ or Cr. There is a considerable amount of atomic substitution in the garnets; they are therefore often described in terms of pure end members, of which the principal ones are as follows:

| | |
|---|---|
| pyrope | $Mg_3Al_2Si_3O_{12}$ |
| almandine | $Fe_3Al_2Si_3O_{12}$ |
| spessartine | $Mn_3Al_2Si_3O_{12}$ |
| grossular | $Ca_3Al_2Si_3O_{12}$ |
| uvarovite | $Ca_3Cr_2Si_3O_{12}$ |
| andradite | $Ca_3Fe_2Si_3O_{12}$ |

The first three and the second three form two separate groups with almost continuous substitution within each, but with very little substitution between them. All garnets crystallize in the cubic system. Although sometimes found in igneous rocks they are common in metamorphic rocks.

**Pyrope $Mg_3Al_2Si_3O_{12}$**
Pyrope crystallizes in the cubic system, forming dodecahedra or trapezohedra or combinations; more frequently found as pebbles or grains. It has a vitreous lustre; its colour is pink to purplish-red or crimson; some specimens may appear almost black. Chromium may be present and such stones are bright red. H 7–7.5; SG 3.5–3.8; RI 1.73–1.76
*Occurrence.* Occurs in peridotites or in serpentinites. An associate of diamond in the peridoitites of South Africa.
*Localities.* From South Africa; Queensland and New South Wales; Czechoslovakia; Madras, India.
*Treatment.* Clean with dilute acid.
*Fashioning. Uses*: faceting, cabochons, beads; *cleavage*: none, but a plane of parting exists // to dodecahedron; brittle; *cutting angles*: crown 40°, pavilion 40°, angles reduced in very deeply coloured material; *heat sensitivity*: fairly high, but unaffected by normal dopping temperatures.

**Almandine $Fe_3Al_2Si_3O_{12}$**
Almandine crystallizes in the cubic system forming dodecahedra or trapezohedra. Compact or granular masses are also found. The colour is deep red or brownish-black. The lustre is resinous and the streak white. H 7–7.5; SG 4.1–4.3; RI 1.83
*Occurrence.* Occurs in schists, gneiss and other metamorphic rocks. Also contact zones and alluvial deposits.
*Localities.* From India; Sri Lanka; Tanzania; Australia; Brazil; Malagasy Republic; North Creek, New York State. A star garnet is found in Idaho and elsewhere.
*Treatment.* Clean with dilute acid.
*Fashioning. Uses*: faceting, cabochons, beads, tumbling, etc; *cleavage*: none, but a plane of parting exists // to the dodecahedron; brittle; *cutting angles*: crown 40°, pavilion 40°; *heat sensitivity*: fairly high, but unaffected by normal dopping temperatures.

**Spessartine $Mn_3Al_2Si_3O_{12}$**
Spessartine crystallizes in the cubic system as dodecahedra or trapezohedra or in combination. Faces are often striated. Massive and granular forms also occur. The colour may be orange, orange-red, reddish-brown or brown. The streak is white and the lustre vitreous. H 7–7.5; SG 3.8–4.2; RI 1.8
*Occurrence.* Occurs in granite pegmatites, schists or quartzites.
*Localities.* Fine crystals from San Diego Co., California; Rutherford Mine, Amelia, Virginia; Malagasy Republic; etc.
*Treatment.* Clean with dilute acid.
*Fashioning. Uses*: faceting or cabochons; *cleavage*: none, but a plane of parting exists // to the dodecahedron; brittle; *cutting angles*: crown 40°, pavilion 40°; *heat sensitivity*: fairly high, but unaffected by normal dopping temperatures.

*Left: The manganese aluminium garnet spessartine, from San Diego Co., California. The white mineral is feldspar*

**Grossular $Ca_3Al_2Si_3O_{12}$**
Grossular crystallizes in the cubic system, forming dodecahedra or trapezohedra, or combinations. Massive and granular forms are found. The colour may be bright emerald-green, lime green, yellow, red, reddish-brown, orange, white, grey or black. Some varieties are transparent. The streak is white and the lustre resinous. H 6.5–7; SG 3.4–3.6; RI 1.73, 1.75
*Occurrence.* Occurs in metamorphosed impure calcareous rocks, particularly in contact zones; associated minerals include idocrase, calcite and diopside; it may also occur in schists.
*Localities.* A vanadium-bearing variety from Kenya has been named tsavorite; an opaque green variety is sometimes called Transvaal jade; hessonite from Sri Lanka; Brazil; Tanzania; some green stones from Pakistan; yellow material from Elba; Zermatt, Switzerland; etc.
*Treatment.* Clean with dilute acid.
*Fashioning. Uses*: faceting, cabochons, beads, carvings, tumbling, etc; *cleavage*: none, but a plane of parting exists // to the dodecahedron; brittle, except in the massive hydrogrossular or 'Transvaal jade' type which is very tough; *cutting angles*: crown 40°, pavilion 40°; *heat sensitivity*: fairly high, but unaffected by normal dopping temperatures.

**Uvarovite $Ca_3Cr_2Si_3O_{12}$**
Uvarovite crystallizes in the cubic system as dodecahedra or trapezohedra, or in combination; dodecahedral faces often striated; massive, coarse granular forms found. The colour is emerald green with a white streak and a vitreous lustre. H 6.5–7; SG 3.4–3.8; RI 1.86
*Occurrence.* Occurs with chromite in serpentinite, in skarn deposits and metamorphosed limestones.
*Localities.* Found with chromite at Bisert, Urals, USSR; fine crystals from Outokumpu, Finland; with diopside at Orford, Quebec; chromite deposits in northern California; etc.
*Treatment.* Remove calcite with dilute hydrochloric acid.

**Andradite $Ca_3Fe_2(SiO_4)_3$**
Andradite crystallizes in the cubic system, forming dodecahedra or trapezohedra or combinations. Massive forms also found. The colour may be yellow (topazolite); emerald-green (demantoid); black (melanite) and various shades of the above. The lustre is vitreous to resinous. H 6.5–7; SG 3.7–4.1; RI 1.89
*Occurrence.* Demantoid and topazolite occur in chlorite schist and serpentinite; melanite in alkaline igneous rocks. Also from metamorphosed limestones or contact zones.
*Localities.* Demantoid from the Ala Valley, Piedmont, Italy; the Ural Mountains, USSR; melanite from San Benito Co., California; Franklin, New Jersey; etc.
*Treatment.* Clean with dilute acid.
*Fashioning. Uses*: faceting or cabochons; *cleavage*: none, but may have a plane of parting // to the dodecahedron; brittle; *cutting angles*: crown 40°, pavilion 40°; *heat sensitivity*: fairly high, but unaffected by normal dopping.

Left: A dark variety of andradite from Oravita, Romania

Far left: Uvarovite, the calcium-chromium garnet. It is normally found only in small crystals like these from the Ural Mountains of the USSR

**EPIDOTE GROUP**
Minerals in this group are silicates of calcium, aluminium and ferric iron with some replacement by ferrous iron and magnesium.

**Zoisite $Ca_2Al_3Si_3O_{12}(OH)$**
Zoisite crystallizes in the orthorhombic system forming striated prismatic crystals or massive granular forms. There is a perfect cleavage. The colour is grey, white, pink (thulite); colourless to blue or purple (tanzanite); brown or green. There is a vitreous lustre. H 6.5–7; SG 3.3; RI 1.68, 1.72
*Occurrence.* Occurs in regionally metamorphosed rocks including calcareous schists, basic igneous rocks and metamorphosed impure limestones and dolomites. Also from quartz veins and pegmatites.
*Localities.* From Tanzania (tanzanite); Nevada and California; east Greenland (thulite); Italy; Mexico; Finland; etc. A green zoisite with embedded ruby crystals, from Tanzania, has been named anyolite.
*Treatment.* Clean with dilute acid.

Left: The demantoid variety of andradite. It owes its colour to chromium. These crystals, with chrysotile asbestos, are from Val Malenco, Italy

Opposite page: The hessonite variety of grossular garnet from the Ala Valley, Piedmont, Italy. Here the two forms of rhombdodecahedron and icositetrahedron are combined. The green crystals are diopside and the bluish lamellae are chlorite

*Fashioning. Uses*: faceting (tanzanite), cabochons, beads, carvings, tumbling, etc (thulite); *cleavage*: perfect, brachypinacoidal; brittle; *cutting angles*: crown 40°, pavilion 40°; *pleochroism*: strong; *heat sensitivity*: fairly low, unaffected by normal dopping temperatures, but excessive heat may cause tanzanite to change colour; *mechanical sensitivity*: high; tanzanite should never be cleaned in an ultrasonic cleaner.

**Clinozoisite $Ca_2Al_3Si_3O_{12}OH$**
Clinozoisite crystallizes in the monoclinic system forming prismatic crystals, often deeply striated and acicular; more commonly found as granular or fibrous masses. There is a perfect cleavage. It is colourless, yellow, green or pink; there is a vitreous lustre. The streak is colourless. H 6.5; SG 3.2
*Occurrence.* Occurs in regionally metamorphosed igneous and sedimentary rocks or as an alteration product of plagioclase feldspars.
*Localities.* From Sonora, Mexico; Switzerland; Austria; Italy; California; and other localities.
*Treatment.* Clinozoisite should be cleaned with dilute acid.

**Allanite**
**$(Ca, Fe^{2+})_2(R, Al, Fe^{3+})_3Si_3O_{12}OH$**
Allanite crystallizes in the monoclinic system as compact masses or grains; crystals are tabular but may be long prismatic. Polysynthetic twinning is common. The colour is brown to black and there is a resinous lustre. H 5–6; SG 3.9–4.0
*Occurrence.* Occurs in granites, granite pegmatites or gneiss.
*Localities.* From Canada; Norway; Germany; USSR; California; and elsewhere.

**Hancockite**
**$(Pb, Ca, Sr)_2(Al, Fe)_3Si_3O_{12}OH$**
Hancockite crystallizes in the monoclinic system as aggregates or compact masses. There is a perfect cleavage. The colour is yellowish-brown, and the lustre is vitreous. H 6–7; SG 4.0
*Localities.* Occurs with garnet and biotite at Franklin, New Jersey.

**Piemontite**
**$Ca_2(Al, Fe, Mn^{3+})_3Si_3O_{12}OH$**
Piemontite crystallizes in the monoclinic system, commonly forming coarse-grained masses; crystals are prismatic, acicular. There is a perfect cleavage. The colour is reddish-brown to black or may be a lighter red or yellow; there is a vitreous lustre. H 6; SG 3.4–3.5
*Occurrence.* Occurs in schists, or manganese ore deposits.
*Localities.* From a sericite schist at Piemonte, Italy; Nordmark, Värmland, Sweden; in a quartz schist at Black Peak, northwest Otago, New Zealand; Glen Coe, Highland, Scotland; Riverside Co., California; Annapolis, Missouri; etc.
*Treatment.* Clean with dilute acid.

**Epidote $Ca_2(Al, Fe)_3Si_3O_{12}OH$**
Epidote crystallizes in the monoclinic system as prismatic crystals deeply striated or as granular masses. There is a perfect cleavage. The colour is yellowish to brownish-green or black, and the lustre is vitreous. The streak is grey. H 6–7; SG 3.3–3.5; RI 1.74–1.76

*Above: Allanite crystals from Ontario, Canada*

*Right: Clinozoisite from Amborompotsy, Malagasy Republic. Clinozoisite is sometimes faceted though the material shown is opaque*

*Above: Fine monoclinic prisms of epidote from Traversella, Italy*

*Occurrence.* Occurs in regionally metamorphosed igneous and sedimentary rocks and as an alteration of plagioclase feldspars.
*Localities.* From the Ala Valley, Piedmont, Italy; fine crystals from the Untersulzbachtal, Salzburg, Austria; Malagasy Republic; USSR; Japan; Australia; Riverside and San Diego Counties, California; Prince of Wales Island, Alaska; Brazil; a chromium-bearing variety, tawmawite, occurs at Tawmaw, Burma, and at Outokumpu, Finland. The variety withamite contains some manganese; fouqueite contains up to 6% iron and up to 4% ferrous iron.
*Treatment.* Clean with dilute acid.
*Fashioning. Uses*: faceting or cabochons; *cleavage*: perfect // to basal pinacoid, imperfect // to orthopinacoid; brittle; *cutting angles*: crown 40°, pavilion 40°; *pleochroism*: strong; *heat sensitivity*: fairly low.

## MELILITE GROUP

The melilite group has the end-members gehlenite and akermanite.

### Gehlenite $Ca_2Al_2SiO_7$

Gehlenite crystallizes in the tetragonal system, forming short prismatic crystals but being more commonly found massive and granular. The colour is grey, green to brown, yellow or colourless, with a resinous lustre. H 5–6; SG 3.0
*Occurrence.* Occurs in calcium-rich basic eruptive rocks, thermally metamorphosed impure limestones and furnace slags.
*Localities.* From Durango, Mexico; USSR; Italy; Riverside Co., California; and other localities.
*Treatment.* Clean with dilute acid.

### Melilite
### $(Ca, Na)_2[(Mg, Fe^{+2}, Al, Si)_3O_7]$

Melilite crystallizes in the tetragonal system as thin tabular crystals or lamellar aggregates with a distinct cleavage. It is colourless, green, brown or yellow. H 5–6; SG 3.0
*Occurrence.* Occurs in certain basic igneous rocks, and in thermally metamorphosed limestones.
*Localities.* From Julianehaab, Greenland; Langesundfjord, Norway; and many other places.
*Treatment.* Clean with dilute acid.

### Akermanite $Ca_2(MgSi_2O_7)$

Akermanite, a member of the melilite group, crystallizes in the tetragonal system as prismatic crystals or as

*Left: Gehlenite from Val di Fassa, Italy*

*Right: Fine diopside crystal from the Ala Valley, Piedmont, Italy. The red crystals are hessonite*

granular masses. It is grey, brown, green or colourless with a vitreous or resinous lustre. H 5–6; SG 2.9
*Occurrence.* From rocks rich in calcium and in thermally metamorphosed limestones; also from slags.
*Localities.* As for gehlenite.

**PYROXENE GROUP**
The pyroxenes are an important group of rock-forming minerals found in many igneous and metamorphic rocks. They conform to the general formula $X_2Si_2O_6$ in which X is usually Ca, Mg, Fe, Li, Ti, Al or Na. There are two principal groups. The ortho-pyroxenes crystallize in the orthorhombic crystal system and contain very little calcium; the commonest are hypersthene and bronzite. The clino-pyroxenes are monoclinic and contain Ca, Na, Al, $Fe^{3+}$, or Li; they include augite, pigeonite, diopside, jadeite, aegirine and spodumene. The pyroxenes are characterised by having two cleavages intersecting almost at 90°.

**Enstatite $MgSiO_3$**
Enstatite crystallizes in the orthorhombic system, usually being found massive, sometimes fibrous or lamellar; crystals are prismatic. It is colourless, yellowish, green, emerald-green (a chrome-bearing variety); and brown, with a vitreous lustre. The streak is grey. H 5–6; SG 3.2–3.4
*Occurrence.* Enstatite occurs in basic or ultrabasic igneous rocks; in thermally metamorphosed rocks and in meteorites.
*Localities.* From the Harz Mountains and the Eifel region of Germany; the chrome variety from South Africa, where it is associated with diamond; from Colorado, Montana and other states of the USA; etc.
*Treatment.* Clean with dilute acid.
*Fashioning. Uses:* faceting or cabochons; *cleavage*: easy prismatic; *cutting angles*; crown 40°, pavilion 40°; *pleochroism*: distinct; *heat sensitivity*: low.

*Below: Enstatite. It may be found sufficiently transparent to facet. This opaque crystal is from Odegardens, Norway*

**Clinoenstatite $MgSiO_3$**
Dimorphous with enstatite, clinoenstatite crystallizes in the monoclinic system, with short prismatic or tabular crystals; massive, lamellar forms are also found. It may be colourless, yellowish to brown or greenish with a vitreous lustre. H 5–6; SG 3.1
*Localities.* Found in some igneous rocks and in meteorites, and also in a porphyritic volcanic rock from Vogelkop, West Irian, Indonesia.
*Treatment.* Clinoenstatite should be cleaned with dilute acid.

**Diopside $MgCaSi_2O_6$**
Diopside crystallizes in the monoclinic system forming short prismatic crystals; massive, lamellar or granular forms are also found. The colour is colourless, white, grey, pale to dark green, yellowish to reddish-brown. The lustre is vitreous and the streak white or grey. Some ferrous oxide is included in addition to the composition given. H 5.5–6.5; SG 3.2–3.3; RI 1.66, 1.72
*Occurrence.* Occurs in calcium-rich metamorphic rocks, also in some basic and ultrabasic rocks, sometimes in meteorites.
*Localities.* From Sweden; Switzerland; Italy; USSR; South Africa, Malagasy Republic; Burma; California; Montana; etc.
*Treatment.* Clean with dilute acid.
*Fashioning. Uses*: faceting or cabochons; *cleavage*: perfect prismatic; *cutting angles*: crown 40°, pavilion 40°; *pleochroism*: distinct; *heat sensitivity*: very low.

**Aegirine (Acmite) $NaFe^{3+}Si_2O_6$**
Aegirine crystallizes in the monoclinic system as long prismatic crystals with vertical striations, as tufts or aggregates of minute fibres. Twinning is common. The colour is dark green to black (the aegirine variety); reddish-brown (acmite). Lustre resinous; streak pale yellowish-grey. H 6; SG 3.5–3.6
*Occurrence.* Occurs in alkaline rocks such as syenites and also in metamorphic rocks.
*Localities.* From Mont St. Hilaire, Quebec; Greenland; Norway; Nigeria; Kenya; Scotland; etc.

**Spodumene $LiAlSi_2O_6$**
Spodumene crystallizes in the monoclinic system as prismatic crystals, flattened and vertically striated; cleavable masses also found and cleavage is perfect. It may be colourless, yellow, green, emerald-green (hiddenite), pink (kunzite). The lustre is vitreous and the streak white. May fluoresce under ultraviolet light. H 6.5–7.5; SG 3.0–3.2; RI 1.65, 1.68
*Occurrence.* Occurs in granite pegmatites with quartz, feldspar and muscovite.
*Localities.* Minas Gerais, Brazil; hiddenite, coloured by chromium, from Stony Point, North Carolina; kunzite from California; Afghanistan; Malagasy Republic; etc.
*Treatment.* Clean with dilute acid.
*Fashioning. Uses*: faceting or cabochons; *cleavage*: perfect prismatic; brittle; *cutting angles*: crown 40°, pavilion 40°; *pleochroism*: strong in deep colours; *heat sensitivity*: fairly high.

*Left: The lilac-pink kunzite variety of spodumene is frequently faceted. This crystal is from Pala, San Diego Co., California*

*Far left: Aegirine crystal from Magnet Cove, Arkansas*

**Hypersthene (Mg, Fe)$SiO_3$**
Hypersthene crystallizes in the orthorhombic system rarely forming short prismatic crystals; lamellar masses are more commonly found. The colour is brownish-green to black with a pearly or silky lustre. The streak is brownish-grey. Varieties include: bronzite, with 10–30 mols per cent of $FeSiO_3$; eulite, with 70–90 mols of $FeSiO_3$; and ferrohypersthene, with 10–30 mols per cent of $MgSiO_3$. H 5–6; SG 3.4–3.8
*Occurrence.* Occurs in basic igneous rocks and some metamorphic rocks; also from meteorites.
*Localities.* From Bodenmais, and the Eifel region, W. Germany; with labradorite on the Island of St. Paul, Labrador, Canada; California, Arizona, Colorado; etc.
*Treatment.* Clean with dilute acid.

**Clinohypersthene (Mg, Fe)$SiO_3$**
Clinohypersthene has 20–50 mols per cent $FeSiO_3$ and crystallizes in the monoclinic system. The habit is massive and the colour green to brown; H 5–6; SG 3.2–3.5
*Localities.* Occurs mainly in meteorites; from Broken Hill, New South Wales; Bon Accord quarry, Transvaal, South Africa.
*Treatment.* Clean with dilute acid.

**Hedenbergite $CaFeSi_2O_6$**
Hedenbergite crystallizes in the monoclinic system and is usually found massive; lamellar; crystals are short prismatic. Twinning is common. The colour is brownish to greyish-green or black with a white or grey streak. There is a vitreous lustre. Ferrohedenbergite has more iron than calcium. H 6; SG 3.5
*Occurrence.* Occurs in limestone contact zones, iron-rich metamorphic rocks and in granites.
*Localities.* From California; Arizona; Colorado; Sweden; etc.
*Treatment.* Clean with dilute acid.

**Pigeonite**
**(Mg, $Fe^{2+}$, Ca)(Mg, $Fe^{2+}$)[$Si_2O_6$]**
Pigeonite crystallizes in the monoclinic system, usually occuring as grains or micro-phenocrysts. Crystals are short prismatic. The colour is brown to light purple or greenish to black. H 6; SG 3.3–3.4
*Occurrence.* Occurs in volcanic rocks, particularly in andesite and dacite.
*Localities.* From Pigeon Point, Minnesota, and numerous other localities.
*Treatment.* Clean with dilute acid.

**Jadeite $NaAlSi_2O_6$**
Jadeite crystallizes in the monoclinic system, and, with nephrite, is one of the minerals to which the generic name jade

*Left: Radiating fibrous crystals of hedenbergite from Tuscany, Italy*

is given. It forms fine to coarse granular masses or alluvial boulders; crystals are rare but may be small elongated prismatic. The fracture is splintery and the mineral is very tough. The colour may vary from a translucent emerald-green (Imperial jade) to pale green, mauve, white, brown, yellow or grey. The lustre is vitreous, and the streak is colourless. Chloromelanite is a dark-green variety with black veining; maw-sit-sit is of similar appearance. H 6.5–7; SG 3.3; RI 1.66

*Occurrence.* Occurs in serpentinites derived from olivine rock in Burma; from cherts in California (San Benito and Contra Costa counties); Tibet; Mexico; New Zealand; perhaps from Yunnan, China; etc.

*Treatment.* Clean with dilute acid.

*Fashioning. Uses*: cabochons, carvings, beads, etc, very rarely faceted; *cleavage*: poor prismatic; tough; *heat sensitivity*: low.

**Augite**
**$(Ca, Na)(Mg, Fe, Al)(Si, Al)_2O_6$**

Augite crystallizes in the monoclinic system as short prismatic crystals or as compact masses or grains. Twinning is common. The colour is brown, purple or black with a greyish-green streak. The lustre is vitreous. Varieties include titanaugite and fassaite, rich in calcium oxide. H 5.5–6; SG 3.2–3.5

*Occurrence.* Of widespread occurrence in basic and ultrabasic igneous rocks and in some metamorphic rocks.

*Right: Tremolite from Bagat, Ontario*

*Below right: Bustamite from Broken Hill, New South Wales*

*Above right: Augite from Ariccia, Italy*

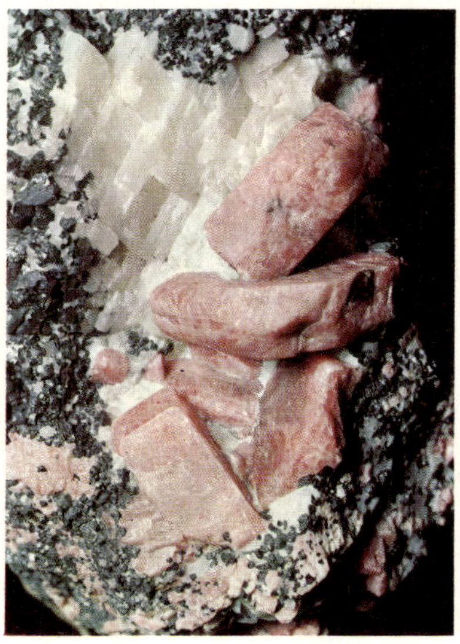

*Right: Rhodonite. These crystals are too opaque to facet although the material does occur in transparent specimens*

*Localities.* From Trentino, Italy; Czechoslovakia; Germany; South-West Africa; California; Montana; etc.

*Treatment.* Remove iron stains with oxalic acid.

## PYROXENOID GROUP

Certain minerals that are chemically similar to the pyroxenes but have a slightly different atomic structure are classified as 'pyroxenoids'.

**Rhodonite $MnSiO_3$**

Rhodonite crystallizes in the triclinic system, commonly being found massive; crystals are tabular with a perfect cleavage. The colour is pink to rose red, veined by black alteration products; the lustre is vitreous. H 5.5–6.5; SG 3.5–3.7; RI 1.71, 1.75

*Occurrence.* Occurs in manganese-bearing ore bodies formed by hydrothermal processes.

*Localities.* Fine crystals from Franklin, New Jersey; good crystals in galena from Broken Hill, New South Wales; also from USSR; South Africa; India; Japan; etc.

*Treatment.* Rhodonite should be cleaned with distilled water.

*Fashioning. Uses*: faceting, cabochons, tumbling, carving, beads, etc; *cleavage*: perfect prismatic, massive types tough; *cutting angles*: crown 40°, pavilion 40°; *pleochroism*: distinct in transparent material; *heat sensitivity*: low, crystalline material very sensitive to shock.

**Bustamite $(Ca, Mn)Si_2O_6$**

Bustamite crystallizes in the triclinic system, commonly being found massive; crystals are tabular with rounded edges. There is a perfect cleavage. The colour is pale pink to brownish-red; the lustre is vitreous. H 5.5–6.5; SG 3.3–3.4

*Occurrence.* Occurs in manganese-bearing ore bodies usually formed by metasomatic processes.

*Localities.* From Franklin, New Jersey.

*Treatment.* Clean with dilute acetic acid.

## AMPHIBOLE GROUP

The amphiboles are a group of hydrous silicates of considerable chemical com-

*Left: Fibrous crystals of tremolite from St. Gotthard, Switzerland. The large white crystals are feldspar*

*Below left: Anthophyllite from Moravia*

**Richterite**
**$(Na, K)_2(Mg, Mn, Ca)_6Si_8O_{22}(OH)_2$**
Richterite crystallizes in the monoclinic system forming long prismatic crystals with lamellar twinning and a perfect cleavage. The colour is brown, yellow, dark brownish-red or pale to dark green; there is a vitreous lustre. H 5–6; SG 2.9–3.1
*Occurrence.* From contact-metasomatic deposits, some alkaline igneous rocks and thermally metamorphosed limestones.
*Localities.* Leucite Hills, Wyoming; Burma; Malagasy Republic; etc.
*Treatment.* Clean with distilled water.

**Grunerite $(Fe, Mg)_7Si_8O_{22}(OH)_2$**
Grunerite crystallizes in the monoclinic system in fibrous lamellar radiating forms, commonly twinned. The colour is grey, dark green or brown. The lustre is silky. H 5–6; SG 3.4–3.6
*Occurrence.* In contact or regionally metamorphosed iron-rich rocks.
*Localities.* From Scotland; Arizona; South Africa; etc.
*Treatment.* Clean with dilute acid.

**Anthophyllite**
**$(Mg, Fe)_7Si_8O_{22}(OH)_2$**
Anthophyllite crystallizes in the orthorhombic system, being found massive, fibrous or lamellar; crystals are prismatic. There is a perfect cleavage. The colour is white to green or brown with a grey or colourless streak, and the lustre is vitreous. H 5.5–6; SG 2.8–3.5

*Below: Prominent green crystals of actinolite*

plexity because of the extensive atomic substitution that takes place. They are characterized by having two cleavages, which intersect at 120°. They are widely distributed in igneous and metamorphic rocks. The commoner amphiboles include anthophyllite, cummingtonite, grunerite, tremolite, actinolite, hornblende, glaucophane, riebeckite and arfvedsonite.

**Tremolite $Ca_2Mg_5Si_8O_{22}(OH)_2$**
Tremolite crystallizes in the monoclinic system forming long, bladed crystals; more often found as fibrous aggregates, often radiated. Twinning is common. The colour is colourless, white, grey, pale green, pink or brown. The lustre is vitreous. H 5–6; SG 2.9–3.2
*Occurrence.* Occurs in contact and regionally metamorphosed dolomites or low-grade ultrabasic rocks.
*Localities.* Italy; Switzerland; Ontario; California; Arizona; and in various other localities.
*Treatment.* Tremolite should be cleaned with dilute acid.

**Actinolite**
**$Ca_2(Mg, Fe)_5Si_8O_{22}(OH)_2$**
Actinolite crystallizes in the monoclinic system, usually forming fibrous or columnar aggregates, often radiated; crystals are long, bladed. The lustre is vitreous. The colour is green and a variety of shades are known; black is also found. H 5–6; SG 3.0–3.4
*Occurrence.* Occurs in contact and regionally metamorphosed dolomites, magnesian limestones and ultrabasic rocks.
*Localities.* The variety nephrite (one form of jade) is found in Alaska; British Columbia; New Zealand; Siberia; and California. The variety byssolite is found in Pennsylvania and Virginia, amongst other places.
*Fashioning. Uses*: faceting or cabochons; *cleavage*: highly perfect, prismatic; very brittle; *cutting angles*: crown 40°, pavilion 40°; *pleochroism*: distinct, increasing with iron content; *heat sensitivity*: fairly high, but unaffected by normal dopping temperatures; *mechanical sensitivity*: very high, treat with care.

*Occurrence.* Occurs in metamorphic rocks, including schists and gneisses; also metasomatic rocks.
*Localities.* From California; Arizona; Colorado; Norway; Italy; etc.
*Treatment.* Iron stains can be removed with oxalic acid.

**Cummingtonite**
**$(Mg, Fe)_7Si_8O_{22}(OH)_2$**
Cummingtonite usually contains a ratio of iron to magnesium of 3:2 or more. It crystallizes in the monoclinic system and is fibrous or lamellar with simple or lamellar twinning common. The colour is dark to greyish-green or brown with a silky lustre. H 5–6; SG 3.1–3.4
*Occurrence.* Occurs in contact or regionally metamorphosed rocks.
*Localities.* Homestake gold mine, Lead, Lawrence Co., South Dakota; Scotland; Sweden; etc.
*Treatment.* Clean with dilute acid.

**Arfvedsonite**
**$Na_3(Mg, Fe^{2+})_4Al[Si_8O_{22}](OH, F)_2$**
Arfvedsonite crystallizes in the monoclinic system in long prismatic crystals or prismatic aggregates. There is a perfect cleavage and lamellar twinning is common. The colour is greenish-black and the streak dark bluish-grey; the lustre is vitreous. H 5–6; SG 3.3–3.5
*Occurrence.* Occurs in plutonic alkali igneous rocks, such as nepheline syenite.
*Localities.* From Julianehaab, Greenland; Norway; Finland; USSR; Boulder Co., Colorado; etc.
*Treatment.* Clean with dilute acid.

**Gedrite**
**$(Mg, Fe^{2+}, Al)_7(Si, Al)_8O_{22}(OH)_2$**
Gedrite crystallizes in the orthorhombic system as fibrous masses; it has a perfect cleavage. The colour is white, greenish, brownish or yellow, with a vitreous or silky lustre. The streak is grey. H 5.5–6; SG 3.1–3.5
*Occurrence.* Occurs in metamorphic rocks.
*Localities.* From Greenland; Finland; North Carolina; Japan; Australia; etc.
*Treatment.* Clean with dilute acid.

**Glaucophane**
**$Na_2(Mg, Fe^{2+})_3Al_2Si_8O_{22}(OH)_2$**
Glaucophane crystallizes in the monoclinic system as fibrous masses; individual crystals are prismatic. There is a perfect cleavage and the colour is grey to bluish-black. The streak is bluish-grey, and the lustre is vitreous. H 6; SG 3.0–3.1
*Occurrence.* Occurs in crystalline schists with minerals such as jadeite, lawsonite and pumpellyite.
*Localities.* From Zermatt, Switzerland; Coast Range, California; etc.
*Treatment.* Clean with dilute acid.

*Above right: Cummingtonite with biotite mica from Cummington, Massachusetts*

*Right: Dark crystals of hornblende with oligoclase feldspar from Arendal, Norway*

**Crossite $Na_2(Mg, Fe^{2+})_3(Fe^{3+}, Al)_2Si_8O_{22}(OH)_2$**
Crossite crystallizes in the monoclinic system forming fibrous masses; it has a perfect cleavage. The colour is blue-grey. H 6; SG 3.1
*Occurrence.* Occurs in crystalline schists.
*Localities.* From the Coast Ranges, California; etc.

**Hastingsite $NaCa_2(Fe, Mg, Al)_5(Al_2Si_6)O_{22}(OH)_2$**
Hastingsite crystallizes in the monoclinic system as prismatic crystals or compact masses. There is a perfect cleavage. The colour is dark green to black, with a vitreous lustre. H 5–6; SG 3.2–3.6
*Occurrence.* Of widespread occurrence in igneous and metamorphic rocks.
*Localities.* From Hastings Co., Ontario; Riverside Co., California; and many other localities.
*Treatment.* Clean crossite with distilled water.

**Riebeckite**
**$Na_2Fe_3^{2+}Fe_2^{3+}Si_8O_{22}(OH)_2$**
Riebeckite crystallizes in the monoclinic system forming long prismatic crystals with striations parallel to the long direction; also massive fibrous (crocidolite), columnar or granular. There is a perfect cleavage. The colour is dark blue to black with a vitreous or silky (crocidolite) lustre. H 5; SG 3.3
*Occurrence.* Occurs in alkali granites and rhyolites, trachytes, syenites, bedded ironstones and regionally metamorphosed schists.
*Localities.* From St. Peter's Dome, El Paso Co., Colorado; Cumberland Hill, Rhode Island; Scotland; South Africa; Zambia; Malagasy Republic; and other localities.

**Katophorite**
**$Na_2Ca(Fe^{3+}, Al)_5(AlSi_7)O_{22}(OH)_2$**
Katophorite, sometimes known as taramite, crystallizes in the monoclinic system as prismatic crystals with a perfect cleavage. The colour is rose-red to brownish-black, with a vitreous lustre. H 5; SG 3.3–3.5
*Occurrence.* Occurs in basic alkaline rocks.
*Localities.* From Oslo, Norway; Ukraine, USSR; and elsewhere.
*Treatment.* Clean katophorite with dilute acid.

**Hornblende $(Ca, Na, K)_{2-3}(Mg, Fe^{2+}, Fe^{3+}, Al)_5(Si, Al)_8O_{22}(OH)_2$**
Hornblende crystallizes in the monoclinic system as prismatic crystals or as compact masses. Twinning is common. There is a perfect cleavage. The colour is green, brown to black, with a vitreous lustre. H 5–6; SG 3.0–3.3

*Left: Lamellae of muscovite from Branchville, Connecticut*

*Occurrence.* Occurs in many igneous and metamorphic rocks.
*Localities.* From many localities, including Mt. Vesuvius, Italy; USSR; Finland; Great Britain; Australia; California; New York State.
*Treatment.* Hornblende should be cleaned with dilute acid.

**Eckermannite**
**$Na_3(Mg, Li)_4(Al, Fe)Si_8O_{22}(OH, F)_2$**
Eckermannite crystallizes in the monoclinic system as long prismatic crystals or aggregates with a vitreous lustre. Lamellar twinning is found and there is a perfect cleavage. The colour is dark blue or green. H 5–6; SG 3.0–3.1
*Occurrence.* Occurs in nepheline syenites as well as in other rocks that are alkali-rich.
*Localities.* From Tawmaw, Burma; Boulder Co., Colorado; and from other localities.
*Treatment.* Eckermannite should be cleaned with distilled water.

## MICA GROUP

The micas crystallize in the monoclinic system, frequently as pseudohexagonal prisms with a perfect basal cleavage. All the micas contain hydroxyl (OH). Generally those species with a darker colour contain iron and magnesium while lighter species contain aluminium. Lithium, barium, chromium and manganese are sometimes present.
Apart from the minerals described here, the mica group includes anandite, celadonite, ephesite, hendricksite and polylithionite. The vermiculite group consists of altered micas that still show typical micaceous cleavage.

**Paragonite $NaAl_3Si_3O_{10}(OH)_2$**
Paragonite crystallizes in the monoclinic system in massive compact forms or scales. There is a perfect cleavage and the colour is pale yellow or colourless. The lustre is pearly. H 2.5; SG 2.7–2.9
*Occurrence.* Occurs in schists, gneisses, quartz veins and sediments.
*Localities.* From Monte Campione, Switzerland; Piedmont, Italy; Leadville, Colorado.
*Treatment.* Remove iron stains with oxalic acid

**Muscovite $KAl_3Si_3O_{10}(OH)_2$**
Muscovite is one of the commonest of the micas. It crystallizes in the monoclinic system as tabular crystals; more commonly it is lamellar or compact massive. Twinning is common and there is a perfect cleavage. Colours may be white, grey, yellow, green, brown, red or violet, and the lustre is vitreous or pearly. The streak is colourless. Varieties include hydromuscovite with a higher OH and lower K, or K and Al; phengite, which is higher in Si with low $H_2O$, or with (Fe, Mg) replacing some Al; mariposite, which contains more Si and up to 1 per cent $Cr_2O_3$; fuchsite, which contains up to 5 per cent $Cr_2O_3$; and sericite, which is scaly and occurs in fibrous aggregates. H 2.5–4.0; SG 2.7–2.8
*Occurrence.* Occurs in granites, pegmatites, schists and gneisses or in sediments.
*Localities.* Widespread occurrence; very large crystals from Custer, South Dakota; also from Sweden; Switzerland; USSR; India; etc.
*Treatment.* Muscovite should be cleaned with dilute acid.

**Illite**
**$K_{1-1.5}Al_4[Si_{7-6.5}Al_{1-1.5}O_{20}](OH)_4$**
The name illite has been given to micaceous clays in general and also to a mineral with the composition of muscovite or hydromuscovite, but giving a poor x-ray diffraction pattern.
*Treatment.* Clean with distilled water.

**Margarite $CaAl_4Si_2O_{10}(OH)_2$**
Margarite crystallizes in the monoclinic system in platy aggregates with brittle laminae. There is a perfect cleavage. The colour is grey, pink, yellow or green with a colourless streak. The lustre is pearly. H 3.5–4.5; SG 3.0–3.1
*Occurrence.* Occurs with corundum in metamorphic emery deposits and with staurolite in chlorite and mica schists.
*Localities.* From Italy; Greece; Austria; California; etc.
*Treatment.* Clean with dilute acid.

**Phlogopite $KMg_3AlSi_3O_{10}(OH)_2$**
Phlogopite crystallizes in the monoclinic and hexagonal systems as prismatic crystals, plates or scales. Twinning is common and there is a perfect cleavage. Thin laminae are flexible. The

*Left: Margarite from Makares, Greece. The platy nature of the mineral is well shown by these specimens*

*Above: A fine crystal of phlogopite from a classic US locality, Franklin, New Jersey*

*Above right: Rose-coloured lepidolite from Moravia*

colour is yellow to brown or red to green, or white to colourless. The lustre is pearly. The streak is colourless. Phlogopite may show asterism. Its varieties include: hydrophlogopite; natronphlogopite; bariumphlogopite; manganphlogopite; fluorphlogopite. H 2–2.5; SG 2.7–2.9
*Occurrence.* Occurs in metamorphic limestones and ultrabasic igneous rocks.
*Localities.* Sweden; Italy; India; USA; and other localities.
*Treatment.* Clean with dilute acid.

**Clintonite**
**$Ca(Mg, Al)_3(Al, Si)O_{10}(OH)_2$**
Clintonite crystallizes in the monoclinic system as tabular pseudohexagonal crystals; also as foliated or lamellar masses. There is a perfect cleavage. It is colourless, yellowish, greenish, reddish-brown or copper-red, with a vitreous or pearly lustre. The streak may be colourless, yellowish or greenish. H 3.5 and 6, according to direction; SG 3.0–3.1
*Occurrence.* Occurs with calcite and other minerals in crystalline limestones.
*Localities.* From Riverside Co., California; the Pargas area of Finland; southern Urals, USSR; etc.
*Treatment.* Clean with dilute acid.

**Roscoelite**
**$K(V, Al, Mg)(Al, Si_3)O_{10}(OH)_2$**
Roscoelite crystallizes in the monoclinic system as minute scales. There is a perfect cleavage and the colour is brown to greenish-brown. There is a pearly lustre. H 2.5; SG 3.0
*Localities.* Occurs with native gold with which it may be intermingled at Granite Creek, El Dorado Co., California; Kalgoorlie, Western Australia.

**Glauconite $(K, Na)(Al, Fe^{3+}, Mg)_2$-$(Al, Si)_4O_{10}(OH)_2$**
Glauconite crystallizes in the monoclinic system as aggregates of platelets with a perfect cleavage, and dull lustre. It is yellowish-green in colour. H 2; SG 2.4–2.9
*Occurrence.* Occurs in greensands, impure limestones and many rocks of marine origin.
*Localities.* From France; USSR; India; and many other localities.
*Treatment.* Clean with dilute acid.

**Biotite**
**$K(Mg, Fe)_3(Al, Fe)Si_3O_{10}(OH, F)_2$**
Biotite crystallizes in the monoclinic and trigonal systems, forming massive scaly aggregates, or disseminated; it has a perfect cleavage and twinning occurs. The colour is brown, reddish-brown or green, with a metallic to vitreous lustre. The streak is colourless. H 2.5–3 (on cleavage surfaces); SG 2.7–3.4
*Occurrence.* Occurs in granites, pegmatites, gneisses, schists and other rocks. Varieties include lepidomelane, manganophyllite and siderophyllite.
*Localities.* From Mt. Vesuvius, Italy; Arendal, Norway; Sweden; USSR; Japan; California; Colorado; and very many other localities.
*Treatment.* Clean with dilute acid.

**Tainiolite $KMg_2LiSi_4O_{10}(OH, F)_2$**
Tainiolite crystallizes in the monoclinic system as pseudohexagonal tabular crystals and as scales or aggregates. There is a perfect cleavage. The colour is either brown or colourless. H 2.5–3; SG 2.8–2.9
*Occurrence.* Occurs in nepheline-syenite pegmatites with natrolite and other minerals.
*Localities.* From Lovozero Massif, Kola Peninsula, USSR; Greenland; Magnet Cove, Arkansas.
*Treatment.* Clean with dilute acid.

**Lepidolite**
**$K(Li, Al)_3(Si, Al)_4O_{10}(F, OH)_2$**
Lepidolite crystallizes in the monoclinic system as cleavable masses or scaly aggregates; crystals are tabular. The cleavage is a perfect one. The mineral's colour is pink to purple, colourless or white. There is a pearly lustre. The streak is colourless. H 2.5–3.0; SG 2.8–3.3
*Occurrence.* Occurs in granite pegmatites with spodumene and amblygonite; sometimes from tin veins.
*Localities.* From Brazil; Mozambique; Malagasy Republic; Pala area, San Diego Co., California; and elsewhere.
*Treatment.* Clean with dilute acid.
*Fashioning. Uses*: carvings, cabochons,

*Far right: A thin section of biotite shown between crossed polarizers*

*Right: Biotite from Langesundfjord, Norway*

faceting (rare); *cleavage*: perfect basal; *cutting angles*: crown 40°–50°, pavilion 43°; *pleochroism*: weak to distinct; *heat sensitivity*: low.

**Zinnwaldite**
**$K(Li, Al, Fe)_3(Al, Si)_4O_{10}(OH, F)_2$**
Zinnwaldite crystallizes in the monoclinic system as prismatic crystals or scales with a vitreous or pearly lustre. There is a perfect cleavage. The colour is grey, green or brown. H 2.5–4; SG 2.9–3.3
*Occurrence.* Occurs principally in granite pegmatites and high-temperature quartz veins.
*Localities.* From Cornwall; Saxony, E. Germany; San Diego Co., California and other localities.
*Treatment.* Clean with dilute acid.

**CHLORITE GROUP**
Minerals of the chlorite group are frequently green and crystallize in the monoclinic system. There is a basal cleavage similar to that in the micas. Chlorites are aluminium silicates with ferrous iron, magnesium and water. Apart from the minerals described here the chlorites include prochlorite, moravite, cronstedtite, and stilpnomelane.

**Pennantite**
**$(Mn, Al)_6(Si, Al)_4O_{10}(OH)_8$**
Pennantite crystallizes in the monoclinic system as masses or tiny flakes; there is a perfect cleavage; it is orange in colour. H 2–3; SG 3.0
*Localties.* Occurs with spessartine, banalsite, etc, at the manganese mine at Benallt, Gwynedd, Wales.

**Daphnite**
**$(Mg, Fe)_3(Fe, Al)_3(Si, Al)_4O_{10}(OH)_8$**
Daphnite crystallizes in the monoclinic system as spherical or botryoidal aggregates. There is a perfect cleavage. The colour is dark green, and there is a pearly lustre. H 2–3; SG 3.2
*Localities.* With quartz and arsenopyrite at Penzance, Cornwall; etc.
*Treatment.* Clean with dilute water.

**Amesite**
**$(Mg, Fe^{2+})_4Al_4Si_2O_{10}(OH)_8$**
Amesite crystallizes in the hexagonal system forming hexagonal plates in foliated aggregates. There is a perfect cleavage and the colour is pale green, with a pearly lustre. H 2.5–3; SG 2.8
*Localities.* Occurs with corundophilite and magnetite at Chester, Massachusetts; and elsewhere.
*Treatment.* Clean with distilled water.

**Corundophilite**
**$(Mg, Fe, Al)_6(Si, Al)_4O_{10}(OH)_8$**
Corundophilite crystallizes in the triclinic system as granular or foliated masses; it has a perfect cleavage. The colour is dark green, and the lustre is pearly. H 2–3; SG 2.8
*Localities.* Occurs with magnetite at Chester, Massachusetts; etc.
*Treatment.* Clean with distilled water.

**Ripidolite**
**$(Mg, Fe, Al)_6(Si, Al)_4O_{10}(OH)_8$**
Ripidolite crystallizes in the monoclinic system as tabular crystals; more commonly as granular or scaly masses. There is a perfect cleavage. The colour is dark green with a colourless or pale green streak. The lustre is pearly. H 2–3; SG 2.9–3.1
*Occurrence.* Occurs in schists, sometimes in ore veins.
*Localities.* From the tin veins of Cornwall; Malagasy Republic; New Zealand; and elsewhere.
*Treatment.* Clean ripidolite with distilled water.

**Delessite** **$(Mg, Fe^{2+}, Fe^{3+}, Al)_6(Si, Al)_4O_{10}(O, OH)_8$**
Delessite crystallizes in the monoclinic system as foliated or granular masses; it has a perfect cleavage. The colour is black tinged with green. It has a streak that is olive-green in colour. H 2–3; SG 2.7
*Localities.* Occurs at the diabase quarry at Somerville, Massachusetts.
*Treatment.* Clean delessite with distilled water.

*Left: Amesite crystals from Saranovskoje, USSR*

*Below left: Crystals of zinnwaldite from the original locality, Zinnwald, Czechoslovakia*

*Bottom left: Ripidolite from Rauris, Austria*

*Right: Clinochlore from the Tilly Foster mine, New York*

**Chamosite**
**$(Mg, Fe^{2+})_3Fe^{3+}_3(AlSi_3)O_{10}(OH)_8$**
Chamosite crystallizes in the monoclinic and hexagonal systems forming compact masses. The colour is greenish to black. H about 3; SG 3.0–3.4
*Occurrence.* Found in sedimentary ironstones and in some clay deposits.
*Localities.* From Chamoson, Valais, Switzerland; Czechoslovakia; etc.
*Treatment.* Clean with distilled water.

**Thuringite**
**$(Fe^{2+}, Fe^{3+}, Mg)_6(Al, Si)_4O_{10}(OH)_8$**
Thuringite crystallizes in the monoclinic system as scaly aggregates; it has a perfect cleavage. The colour is olive green to brown, and the lustre is pearly. H 2–3; SG 3.0–3.3
*Occurrence.* Occurs with iron ores in metamorphic rocks.
*Localities.* From Thüringer Wald, E. Germany; South Africa; Lake Superior, Michigan; etc.
*Treatment.* Clean with distilled water.

**Clinochlore**
**$(Mg, Fe^{2+}, Al)_6(Si, Al)_4O_{10}(OH)_8$**
Clinochlore crystallizes in the monoclinic system as foliated masses or as tabular crystals with a hexagonal cross-section. There is a perfect cleavage. The colour is white, yellow, colourless, deep green or olive green with a colourless to greenish-white streak. There is a pearly lustre. Varieties include leuchtenbergite, chromeclinochlore and kochubeite. H 2–2.5; SG 2.6–3.0
*Occurrence.* Occurs in schists and other metamorphic rocks or as an alteration of hydrothermal minerals in igneous rocks.
*Localities.* From Italy; Austria; Switzerland; California; Colorado; etc.
*Treatment.* Clean with distilled water.

**Brunsvigite**
**$(Fe^{2+}, Mg, Al)_6(Si, Al)_4O_{10}(OH)_8$**
Brunsvigite crystallizes in the monoclinic system as foliated masses or radiating spherical aggregates; crystals are hexagonal tabular and very small. There is a perfect cleavage. The colour is yellow or dark green with a pearly lustre. H about 2; SG 3.0–3.1
*Localities.* Occurs in veins in granite in the Mourne Mountains, N. Ireland; and elsewhere.
*Treatment.* Clean with distilled water.

**Penninite**
**$(Mg, Fe, Al)_6(Si, Al)_4O_{10}(OH)_8$**
Penninite crystallizes in the monoclinic system as thick tabular crystals, or compact masses. There is a perfect cleavage. The colour is emerald or olive green, white or yellow. There is a vitreous or pearly lustre. H 2–2.5; SG 2.6–2.8
*Occurrence.* Occurs with serpentine or in schists.
*Localities.* From the Ala Valley, Piedmont, Italy; Zermatt, Switzerland; etc.
*Treatment.* Clean with distilled water.

**Sudoite**
**$(Al, Fe, Mg)_{4-5}(Si, Al)_4O_{10}(OH)_8$**
Sudoite crystallizes in the monoclinic system as fine-grained masses; it has a perfect cleavage and is white in colour. H not measured; SG 2.6
*Localities.* Occurs in hematite ore at Negaunee, Michigan; etc.
*Treatment.* Clean with distilled water.

**Diabantite**
**$(Mg, Fe^{2+}, Al)_6(Si, Al)_4O_{10}(OH)_8$**
Diabantite crystallizes in the monoclinic system as compact fibrous masses coloured dark green and with a perfect cleavage. H 2–2.5; SG 2.8–2.9
*Localities.* Occurs in dolerite at Farmington Hills, Connecticut; Germany; etc.
*Treatment.* Clean with distilled water.

**Nimite**
**$(Ni, Mg, Fe, Al)_6(AlSi_3)O_{10}(OH)_8$**
Nimite crystallizes in the monoclinic system as very small irregular veins in talc. The colour is yellowish-green. H 3; SG 3.2
*Localities.* From the area of the Scotia talc mine, Barberton Mountain, Transvaal, South Africa.
*Treatment.* Clean with distilled water.

**SERPENTINE GROUP**
Closely related to the chlorites are the serpentines, which are fibrous or lamellar. They are usually monoclinic. Other members of the group apart from those described below are marmolite, picrolite, garnierite, iddingsite, etc.

*Right: Fibrous chrysotile in an altered serpentine from Silesia, Poland*

*Below: Penninite in tabular form from Zermatt, Switzerland*

**Chrysotile $Mg_3Si_2O_5(OH)_4$**
Chrysotile crystallizes in the monoclinic system, forming fibrous masses. The fibres are flexible and easily separated. The colour is white, grey, green to brown with a silky lustre. H 2.5; SG 2.5
*Occurrence.* Occurs as compact veins in serpentinite rock.
*Localities.* From Italy; USSR; Rhodesia; in the United States it is found in the Coast Ranges and Sierra Nevada, California; etc.

alteration product of serpentine or magnesite.
*Localities.* Fine nodular masses from Eskisehir, Turkey; also from Spain, Greece, Morocco; California and Arizona; and elsewhere.
*Treatment.* Clean with distilled water.

*Left: Crystals of antigorite from Sverdlovsk, USSR*

## KAOLINITE GROUP

These clay minerals, also known as kandites, form scales or plates with angles of 60° and 120°. They usually occur as earthy masses. Apart from kaolinite and dickite, described here, the group includes nacrite and halloysite.

**Dickite $Al_2Si_2O_5(OH)_4$**
Dickite crystallizes in the monoclinic system, forming thin tabular crystals, sometimes pseudohexagonal, or platelets; clay-like massive forms are the commonest, plastic when moist. There is a perfect cleavage. Usually colourless, may be tinted yellow or brown; it has a dull lustre. H 2–2.5; SG 2.6

**Antigorite $Mg_3Si_2O_5(OH)_4$**
Antigorite crystallizes in the monoclinic system and is usually massive and very fine-grained; lamellar and foliated forms are also common; crystals are flaky and very small. There is a perfect cleavage. The colour is white, yellow, green, bluish-green and brownish-red with a white streak and resinous lustre. The term bowenite is used somewhat indiscriminately to describe a translucent greenish serpentine. It is sometimes used as a jade simulant. H 2.5–3.5; SG 2.6
*Occurrence.* Found mixed with chrysotile in serpentinites.
*Localities.* Val Antigorio, Italy (this material is not mixed with chrysotile); Switzerland; California; Utah and other states of the USA; etc. Bowenite is found at Smithfield, Rhode Island, the South Island of New Zealand and elsewhere.
*Treatment.* Clean with dilute acid.

**Talc $Mg_3Si_4O_{10}(OH)_2$**
Sometimes known as steatite, talc crystallizes in the monoclinic system, usually massive and fine-grained or as foliated or fibrous masses; crystals are thin tabular. There is a perfect cleavage. The colour is pale to dark green, white, grey or brown with a white streak and greasy lustre. H 1; SG 2.5–2.8
*Occurrence.* Talc is a secondary mineral formed by the hydrothermal alteration of ultrabasic rocks or the thermal metamorphism of siliceous dolomites.
*Localities.* Found near the Lizard, Cornwall; Shetland Islands; the Zillertal, Austrian Tyrol; Barberton, Transvaal, South Africa; California, Vermont, Pennsylvania and other states; etc.
*Treatment.* Clean with dilute acid.

**Sepiolite $Mg_3Si_4O_{11}.5H_2O$**
Sometimes known as meerschaum, sepiolite crystallizes in the orthorhombic system forming fine fibrous masses or compact nodules. The colour may be white or grey, yellowish or blue-green to red. Dry porous masses float on water. H 2–2.5; SG about 2
*Occurrence.* Sepiolite occurs as an

*Above left: Foliated talc crystals from the USA*

*Left: Grey sepiolite from Anatolia, Turkey*

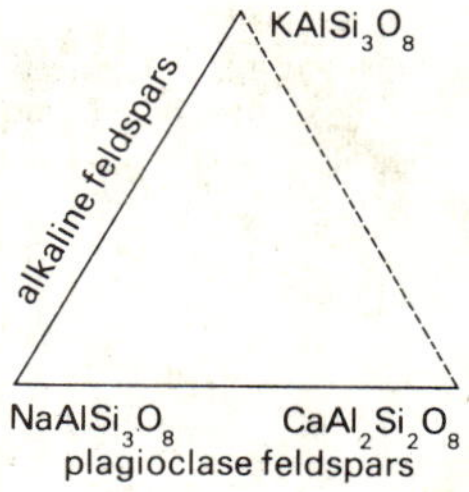


*Above: The feldspars*

*Above right: Microcline just falls within the triclinic crystal system. This crystal is from a classic American locality, Pikes Peak, Colorado*

*Opposite page: These crystals of orthoclase show Manebach twinning and are accompanied by quartz. From Baveno, Italy*

*Below: Twinned albite crystals from Schmirn, Austria*

*Occurrence.* Occurs hydrothermally with quartz and sulphides in ore deposits.
*Localities.* From Anglesey; Boulder Co., Colorado; Shokozan, Japan; etc.
*Treatment.* Clean with distilled water.

**Kaolinite $Al_2Si_2O_5(OH)_4$**
Kaolinite crystallizes in the triclinic system as thin hexagonal plates or compact masses. There is a perfect cleavage. The colour is white, colourless, with tints of yellow, blue, red or brown; the lustre is dull. H 2–2.5; SG 2.6
*Occurrence.* Occurs as a clay mineral formed by the weathering or hydrothermal alteration of feldspars and aluminous silicates.
*Localities.* From St. Austell, Cornwall; California; Utah; etc.
*Treatment.* Clean with distilled water.

## MONTMORILLONITE GROUP

Also known as smectites, these clay minerals have the general formula $(\frac{1}{2}Ca, Na)_{0.7}(Al, Mg, Fe)_4(Si, Al)_8O_{20}(OH)_4.nH_2O$.

**Montmorillonite $(Na, Ca)_{0.33}(Al, Mg)_2Si_4O_{10}(OH)_2.nH_2O$**
Montmorillonite crystallizes in the monoclinic system in clay-like massive forms; crystals have a perfect cleavage. The colours are white, grey, yellowish, greenish and pink and the lustre is dull. H 1–2; SG 2–3
*Occurrence.* Occurs as the principal constituent of bentonite clay deposits; also found in soils, sedimentary and metamorphic rocks.
*Localities.* France; Italy; USA; and other localities.
*Treatment.* Clean with distilled water.

**Sauconite $Na_{0.33}Zn_3(Si, Al)_4O_{10}(OH)_2.4H_2O$**
Sauconite crystallizes in the monoclinic system as very fine-grained masses or micaceous plates forming laminated masses. The colour is reddish-brown or brownish-yellow, with a dull lustre. H 1–2; SG not measured.
*Localities.* Occurs in the Leadville district, Lake Co., Colorado; Saucon Valley, Pennsylvania; etc.
*Treatment.* Clean with distilled water.

**Hectorite $Na_{0.33}(Mg, Li)_3Si_4O_{10}(F, OH)_2$**
Hectorite crystallizes in the monoclinic system as fine-grained masses, white in colour, with a dull lustre. There is a perfect cleavage. H 1–2; SG 2–3
*Localities.* In bentonite at Hector, San Bernardino Co., California.
*Treatment.* Clean with distilled water.

**Saponite $(Mg, Al, Fe)_3(Al, Si)_4O_{10}(OH)_2$**
Saponite crystallizes in the monoclinic system as fine-grained masses with a perfect cleavage. The colour is white or yellowish, grey, greenish, bluish or reddish, with a greasy lustre. H 1–2; SG 2.2–2.3
*Occurrence.* Occurs in cavities in basic volcanic rocks.
*Localities.* From Lake Superior; Canada; Transvaal; the variety cathkinite occurs at the Cathkin Hills, Glasgow.
*Treatment.* Clean with distilled water.

## VERMICULITE GROUP

This group, sometimes regarded as belonging to the smectites, has the general formula $(Mg, Fe, Al)_3(Al, Si)_4O_{10}(OH)_2.4H_2O$; varieties include copper vermiculite, jefferisite, vaalite, hydrovermiculite and nickel vermiculite.

## FELDSPAR GROUP

These are the most abundant minerals in the Earth's crust and are to be found in a wide variety of rocks. Their chemical composition can be expressed by the general formula $X(Al, Si)_4O_8$ in which X may be Ca, Na, K, or Ba. The barium feldspars are rare. The other feldspars can be considered as belonging to a three-component system; the three components are $KAlSi_3O_8$ (orthoclase, sanidine, or microcline), $NaAlSi_3O_8$ (albite) and $CaAl_2Si_2O_8$ (anorthite). There is a complete series of feldspars from pure potassium to pure sodium feldspar, the 'alkali feldspar series'. Similarly, there is every gradation between pure sodium feldspar and pure calcium feldspar, the 'plagioclase series'. The two series are shown diagramatically in the triangular diagram, which also indicates that there is no potassium-calcium series. The plagioclase series is arbitrarily subdivided according to the proportions of albite component present as follows:

- 'albite': 100–90 per cent albite;
- oligoclase: 90–70 per cent;
- andesine: 70–50 per cent;
- labradorite: 50–30 per cent;
- bytownite: 30–10 per cent;
- anorthite: 10–0 per cent.

**Albite $NaAlSi_3O_8$**
Albite crystallizes in the triclinic system as tabular or platy crystals. Usually massive, sometimes with curved laminae, twinning is common. There is a perfect cleavage. The colour is white to colourless, bluish, brown or reddish. The streak is white, and the lustre vitreous. H 6–6.5; SG 2.6
*Occurrence.* Common constituent of pegmatites, granites, andesite, syenite and other alkaline igneous rocks.
*Localities.* Of very common occurrence, albite is found as fine crystals in the Alps, for example, the St. Gotthard region; Bourg d'Oisans, Isère, France; Morro Velho gold mine, Minas Gerais, Brazil; Arizona; New Mexico; the variety of albite called cleavelandite is found at Amelia, Virginia; peristerite and pericline are other varieties.
*Treatment.* Clean with dilute acid.
*Fashioning. Uses*: faceting or cabochons; *cleavage*: perfect // to basal pinacoid, distinct brachypinacoidal; brittle; *cutting angles*: crown 40°–50°, pavilion 43°; *pleochroism*: weak; *heat sensitivity*: fairly high, but unaffected by normal dopping temperatures.

**Microcline $KAlSi_3O_8$**
Microcline is dimorphous with orthoclase. It crystallizes in the triclinic system in short prismatic crystals; there is a perfect cleavage. It may occur in tabular crystals or massive forms, which are the most common. Carlsbad, Manebach, Baveno and other forms of twinning are very common. The colour is white, grey, yellowish, green. There is a vitreous or pearly lustre. Amazonite and perthite are varieties. H 6–6.5; SG 2.5–2.6
*Occurrence.* Occurs in plutonic rocks such as granites and in pegmatites. From crystalline schists and sometimes from hydrothermal veins.
*Localities.* Rhodesia; Brazil; Mexico; Canada; Amelia, Virginia; Black Hills, South Dakota; etc.
*Treatment.* Clean with dilute acid.
*Fashioning. Uses*: cabochons, beads, carvings, tumbling; *cleavage*: perfect // to basal pinacoid, distinct brachypinacoidal; brittle; *heat sensitivity*: fairly high but unaffected by normal dopping temperatures.

**Orthoclase $KAlSi_3O_8$**
Orthoclase feldspar is dimorphous with microcline and crystallizes in the monoclinic system. It forms short prismatic crystals, but occurs more commonly as masses, which may be lamellar. Carlsbad, Baveno and Manebach twins are

*Right: Labradorescence is the name given to the play of colour shown by the feldspar labradorite. This crystal is from Labrador*

*Below left: Baveno twin of orthoclase from Baveno, Italy*

*Below right: Prismatic crystals of anorthite*

very common and there is a perfect cleavage. The colour is white, colourless, grey or yellowish. The streak is white and the lustre vitreous to pearly. H 6–6.5; SG 2.5–2.6
*Occurrence.* Occurs in igneous rocks such as pegmatites and granites, or in crystalline schists, ore veins and in sedimentary deposits.
*Localities.* From the Eifel region of W. Germany (the variety sanidine); Switzerland (adularia or moonstone); yellow transparent material from the pegmatites at Itrongay, Malagasy Republic; California, Oregon, etc; Baveno, Piedmont, Italy; Karlovy Vary, Czechoslovakia; St. Agnes, Cornwall. Moonstones from Sri Lanka, Burma and some other places.
*Treatment.* Clean with dilute acid.
*Fashioning. Uses*: cabochons, faceting, beads; *cleavage*: perfect // to basal pinacoid, distinct clinopinacoidal; brittle; *cutting angles*: crown 40°–50°, pavilion 43°; *pleochroism*: weak; *heat sensitivity*: fairly high, but unaffected by normal dopping temperatures.

**Anorthoclase (Na, K)$AlSi_3O_8$**
One of the alkali feldspars, anorthoclase crystallizes in the triclinic system forming short prismatic or tabular crystals, commonly twinned. Massive forms are more common and these may be lamellar. There is a perfect cleavage. The colour is white, colourless to yellowish, brown or red. The lustre is vitreous, and the streak is white. H 6–6.5; SG 2.5–2.6
*Occurrence.* Mainly in volcanic rocks.
*Localities.* From Pantelleria, Sicily; Kilimanjaro, E. Africa; Franklin, New Jersey; and many other localities.
*Treatment.* Clean with dilute acid.

**Anorthite $CaAl_2Si_2O_8$**
A member of the plagioclase feldspar group, anorthite crystallizes in the triclinic system, forming short prismatic crystals or lamellar, cleavable masses, frequently twinned according to the Manebach, Carlsbad or Baveno laws; albite and pericline twinning are most widespread. The colour is white to grey with a white streak and vitreous lustre. H 6–6.5; SG 2.7
*Occurrence.* Occurs as a rock-forming mineral in basic volcanic and plutonic rocks and in metamorphic rocks; also from meteorites.
*Localities.* Widespread occurrence, including Franklin, New Jersey; Mt. Vesuvius, Italy; etc.
*Treatment.* Clean with distilled water.

**Bytownite (Na, Ca)$Al_{1-2}Si_{3-2}O_8$**
Bytownite crystallizes in the triclinic system forming tabular crystals or cleavable compact masses. It is colourless, white or grey, with a vitreous lustre. Carlsbad, albite and pericline twinning is common. H 6–6.5; SG 2.7
*Occurrence.* Occurs as a rock-forming mineral in basic plutonic and volcanic rocks; also from meteorites.
*Localities.* From Scotland; Transvaal; Montana; etc.
*Treatment.* Clean with dilute acid.
*Fashioning. Uses*: faceting or cabochons; *cleavage*: perfect // to basal pinacoid, distinct brachypinacoidal; brittle; *cutting angles*: crown 40°–50°, pavilion 43°; *pleochroism*: weak; *heat sensitivity*: fairly high, but unaffected by normal dopping temperatures.

**Labradorite (Na, Ca)$Al_{1-2}Si_{3-2}O_8$**
Labradorite crystallizes in the triclinic system as tabular crystals; more commonly found massive, granular with a perfect cleavage and following Carlsbad, albite and pericline twinning laws. The colour is white or grey, often displaying a play of spectrum colour due to interference of light from lamellar twinning. H 6–6.5; SG 2.6–2.7
*Occurrence.* Occurs as a constituent of basic igneous and metamorphic rocks.
*Localities.* From eastern Labrador, Canada; Greenland; Sweden; California; South Dakota; etc.
*Treatment.* Clean with dilute acid.
*Fashioning. Uses*: faceting, cabochons, carvings, intaglios, tumbling, etc; *cleavage*: perfect // to basal pinacoid, distinct brachypinacoidal; brittle; *cutting angles*: crown 40°–50°, pavilion 43°; *pleochroism*: weak; *heat sensitivity*: fairly high, but unaffected by normal dopping.

**Andesine (Na, Ca)$Al_{1-2}Si_{3-2}O_8$**
Andesine crystallizes in the triclinic system as tabular crystals or cleavable masses following Carlsbad, albite or pericline twinning laws. The colour is white or grey, with a vitreous lustre. H 6–6.5; SG 2.6
*Occurrence.* Occurs as a rock-forming mineral in intermediate igneous rocks or in metamorphic rocks.
*Localities.* Greenland; Norway; etc.
*Treatment.* Clean with dilute acid.

*Left: A rough specimen of sunstone, a variety of oligoclase*

**Oligoclase (Na, Ca)$Al_{1-2}Si_{3-2}O_8$**
Oligoclase crystallizes in the triclinic system as cleavable masses obeying Carlsbad, albite or pericline twinning laws. Crystals are tabular. The colour is grey, greenish, yellow, brown or reddish, with a vitreous lustre. The variety sunstone shows brilliant reflections from inclusions. The streak is white. H 6–6.5; SG 2.6
*Occurrence.* Occurs in pegmatites, granites and syenites.
*Localities.* From Canada and Norway (the sunstone variety); California; New York State; Sweden; USSR; etc.
*Treatment.* Clean with dilute acid.
*Fashioning. Uses*: faceting, cabochons, carvings, intaglios, etc; *cleavage*: perfect // to basal pinacoid, distinct brachypinacoidal; brittle; *cutting angles*: crown 40°–50°, pavilion 43°; *pleochroism*: weak; *heat sensitivity*: fairly high, but unaffected by normal dopping.

**Celsian $BaAl_2Si_2O_8$**
Celsian crystallizes in the monoclinic system forming masses or short prismatic crystals with a perfect cleavage. Carlsbad, Manebach and Baveno twinning is common. The colour is colourless, white or yellow, and the lustre is vitreous. H 6–6.5; SG 3.1–3.4
*Occurrence.* Occurs in the contact zones of manganese deposits.
*Localities.* From Rhiw, Gwynedd, Wales; Santa Cruz Co., California; Italy; etc.
*Treatment.* Clean with distilled water.

**Paracelsian $BaAl_2Si_2O_8$**
Paracelsian crystallizes in the monoclinic system forming large well-formed crystals with multiple twinning. It is colourless and has a vitreous lustre. H 6; SG 3.3
*Localities.* Occurs in a band in shale and sandstone in a manganese mine at Rhiw, Gwynedd, Wales; etc.
*Treatment.* Clean with distilled water.

**Hyalophane**
**(K, Ba) (Al, Si)$_2$$Si_2O_8$**
Hyalophane crystallizes in the monoclinic system as prismatic crystals often displaying Carlsbad, Manebach or Baveno twinning. There is a perfect cleavage. The colour is white, colourless or yellow; the lustre is vitreous. H 6–6.5; SG 2.6–2.8
*Localities.* Occurs in manganese deposits at Otjosondu, South-West Africa; in gneiss at Broken Hill, New South Wales; etc.
*Treatment.* Clean with distilled water.

## FELDSPATHOID GROUP

These are a group of sodium and potassium aluminosilicates that have similar chemical compositions to the alkali feldspars but contain less silica. They occur in alkali-rich igneous rocks that are deficient in silica, and they never occur with quartz. They include leucite, nepheline, cancrinite, sodalite, haüyne, nosean and lazurite.

**Sodalite $Na_4Al_3Si_3O_{12}Cl$**
Sodalite crystallizes in the cubic system as dodecahedral crystals or as masses. The colour is light to dark blue or colour-

*Left: Sodalite from Dungannon, Ontario*

less; there is a vitreous lustre and a colourless streak. H 5.5–6; SG 2.1–2.4
*Occurrence.* Occurs in nepheline syenites, other silica-undersaturated igneous rocks and metasomatized calcareous rock.
*Localities.* From Bancroft, Ontario; Brazil; USSR; Burma; Italy; Montana; New Jersey; and many other localities.
*Treatment.* Clean with distilled water.
*Fashioning. Uses*: faceting, cabochons, carvings, beads, tumbling, etc; *cleavage*: distinct, dodecahedral; brittle; *cutting angles*: crown 40°–50°, pavilion 43°; *heat sensitivity*: low.

**Lazurite**
**$(Na, Ca)_8(Al, Si)_{12}O_{24}(S, SO_4)$**
Lazurite crystallizes in the cubic system as dodecahedra or as compact masses of a fine dark blue or greenish-blue. There is a dull lustre. The streak is bright blue. H 5–5.5; SG 2.3–2.4
*Occurrence.* Occurs in limestones as a mineral of contact metamorphism with calcite and pyrite. The mixture lapis lazuli contains lazurite.
*Localities.* From the Kokcha River valley, Badakshan, Afghanistan; the Andes of Chile; Mt. Vesuvius, Italy; San Bernardino Co., California; etc.

*Treatment.* Clean with distilled water.
*Fashioning. Uses*: cabochons, carvings, beads, tumbling, etc; *cleavage*: imperfect, dodecahedral; *heat sensitivity*: low.

**Nosean $Na_8Al_6Si_6O_{24}SO_4$**
Nosean crystallizes in the cubic system as dodecahedra; more commonly found as colourless, white, blue or grey granular masses. The lustre is vitreous. H 5.5; SG 2.3–2.4
*Occurrence.* Only in alkali-rich lavas.
*Localities.* The Laacher See, Germany; Cripple Creek, Colorado; Wolf Rock, Cornwall; etc.
*Treatment.* Clean with distilled water.

**Haüyne**
**$(Na, Ca)_{4-8}Al_6Si_6O_{24}(SO_4)_{1-2}$**
Haüyne crystallizes in the cubic system as dodecahedra or octahedra. They have a vitreous lustre, and the colour is nearly always blue, sometimes white. H 5.5–6; SG 2.4–2.5
*Occurrence.* In undersaturated lavas.
*Localities.* From the Laacher See, Germany; Cripple Creek, Colorado; etc.
*Treatment.* Clean with distilled water.
*Fashioning. Uses*: cabochons, beads, etc.; *cleavage*: distinct, dodecahedral; *heat sensitivity*: low.

*Right: Lazurite, one of the minerals that together form lapis lazuli. It is shown here with pyrite from Afghanistan*

*Opposite page: Radiating fibrous crystals of natrolite from Bolzano, Italy*

*Right: Prismatic striated crystal of davyne from Monte Somma, Italy*

**Cancrinite**
**$Na_6(Al_6Si_6O_{24})CaCO_3 . 2H_2O$**
Cancrinite crystallizes in the hexagonal system as masses or as prismatic crystals with a perfect cleavage. The colour is yellow, orange, pink, white or blue; the lustre is vitreous or pearly. H 5–6; SG 2.4–2.5
*Occurrence.* Occurs in alkaline igneous rocks and as an alteration product of nepheline.
*Localities.* From the Fen complex, southern Norway; Finland; India; USSR; Iron Hill, Gunnison Co., Colorado; etc.
*Treatment.* Clean with distilled water.

**Davyne $(Na, Ca, K)_8$-$Al_6Si_6O_{24}(Cl, SO_4, CO_3)_{2-3}$**
Davyne crystallizes in the hexagonal system as small prismatic crystals with vertical striations and a perfect cleavage. It is white or colourless, and has a vitreous lustre. H 6; SG 2.4–2.5
*Localities.* Occurs in leucite-rich lava at Mt. Somma, Italy.
*Treatment.* Clean with distilled water.

**Nepheline $NaAlSiO_4$**
Usually containing some potassium, nepheline crystallizes in the hexagonal system, forming prismatic crystals or compact masses or grains. Twinning is common. The colour is white, colourless, grey, dark green or brownish-red with a white streak. There is a vitreous or greasy lustre. H 5.5–6; SG 2.5–2.6
*Occurrence.* Occurs in alkaline plutonic rocks or in pegmatites in association with nepheline-syenites.
*Localities.* From Langesundfjord, Norway; Julianehaab, Greenland; Zaire; Transvaal, South Africa; etc.
*Treatment.* Clean with distilled water.

**Leucite $KAlSi_2O_6$**
Leucite belongs to the tetragonal system and forms pseudocubic crystals, often trapezohedral; the faces may be striated due to twinning. It also occurs as grains and in massive forms. It is white or grey with a colourless streak and a vitreous lustre. H 5.5–6; SG 2.4–2.5
*Occurrence.* In potassium-rich lavas.
*Localities.* From Italy (Vesuvius); the Eifel district of W. Germany; Erzgebirge, E. Germany; Leucite Hills, Wyoming; etc.
*Treatment.* Clean with distilled water.

**SCAPOLITE GROUP**
The theoretical end-members of the scapolite group are marialite, $Na_4Al_3Si_9O_{24}Cl$, and meionite, $Ca_4(Al_6Si_6O_{24})(SO_4, CO_3, Cl_2)$. These pure end-members do not occur naturally, however. A formula for the whole group could be given as $(Na, Ca, K)_4Al_3(Al, Si)_3Si_6O_{24}$-$(Cl, F, OH, CO_3, SO_4)$.

Specimens of gemstone quality are pink, white, colourless, violet or yellow; cat's eyes are common. Found in Burma, the Malagasy Republic, Brazil, etc; H 6; SG 2.6–2.7; RI 1.54–1.55, 1.55–1.58
*Fashioning. Uses*: faceting or cabochons; *cleavage*: distinct prismatic (1st and 2nd order); brittle; *cutting angles*: crown 40°–50°, pavilion 43°; *dichroism*: strong in deep colours; *heat sensitivity*: low.

**Marialite $Na_4Al_3Si_9O_{24}Cl$**
Marialite crystallizes in the tetragonal system as prismatic crystals or masses. The colour is white, colourless, grey, blue, green, yellow, pink or brown, with a vitreous lustre. The streak is colourless. H 5.5–6; SG 2.5–2.6
*Occurrence.* Occurs in regionally metamorphosed or altered igneous rocks.
*Localities.* From Ontario and Quebec; USSR; and other localities.

**Meionite**
**$Ca_4(Al_6Si_6O_{24})(SO_4, CO_3, Cl_2)$**
Meionite crystallizes in the tetragonal system as prismatic crystals or granular masses. The colour is white, colourless, grey, brown, yellow, pink or violet. The lustre is vitreous and the streak is colourless. H 5.5–6; SG 2.7
*Occurrence.* Occurs in regionally metamorphosed rocks and contact metamorphic aureoles.
*Localities.* From Italy, Finland and elsewhere.

**ZEOLITE GROUP**
Zeolites are silicates of aluminium that contain water that is driven off on heating. The water is removed continuously rather than in definite amounts at certain temperatures. When exposed to water vapour the material once more takes up water. Apart from the minerals described below, the group includes: epistilbite, laumontite, offretite, paulingite, pollucite, scolecite, viséite and wellsite.

**Natrolite $Na_2Al_2Si_3O_{10}.2H_2O$**
Natrolite crystallizes in the orthorhombic system, forming slender prismatic crystals vertically striated; commonly fibrous and radiating or compact massive. There is a perfect cleavage. It is colourless, white, yellowish or reddish, with a vitreous or greasy lustre. H 5–5.5; SG 2.2
*Occurrence.* Occurs in cavities in basalts or as an alteration product of nepheline or sodalite in nepheline syenites; also as an alteration product of plagioclase in aplites and dolerites.
*Localities.* From Mont St. Hilaire, Quebec; Greenland; Bishopton, Strathclyde, Scotland; near Belfast, N. Ireland; San Benito Co., California; etc.

*Above: Radiating fibrous crystals of ferrierite from Kamloops Lake, British Columbia*

*Above right: Radiating crystals of stilbite from Rio Grande do Sul, Brazil*

**Analcime $NaAlSi_2O_6 . H_2O$**
Analcime crystallizes in the cubic system as well formed trapezohedra or modified cubes; massive granular material also found. Lamellar twinning is common. The colour is white, yellowish, pink or greenish, and the lustre is vitreous. H 5–5.5; SG 2.2
*Occurrence.* Occurs in basalts and other igneous rocks; as an alteration product of nepheline; and in some sandstones.
*Localities.* From the Isle of Skye; Kilpatrick Hills, Strathclyde; Cowlitz Co., Washington; as well as from a number of other localities.

**Ferrierite**
**$(Na, K)_2MgAl_3Si_{15}O_{36}(OH) . 9H_2O$**
Ferrierite crystallizes in the orthorhombic system as thin tabular crystals, often in radiating groups. There is a perfect cleavage. The lustre is vitreous and the colour is white or colourless. H 3–3.5; SG 2.1
*Occurrence.* Occurs with chalcedony and opal in basalt seams, Kamloops Lake, Canada; etc.

**Mesolite**
**$Na_2Ca_2Al_6Si_9O_{30} . 8H_2O$**
Mesolite crystallizes in the monoclinic system forming groups of radiating crystals, which may be acicular. There is a perfect cleavage. The colour is white or colourless. The lustre is silky when fibrous. H 5; SG 2.3
*Occurrence.* Occurs in cavities in volcanic rocks with other zeolites.
*Localities.* From the Isle of Skye; Kilmacolm, Strathclyde, Scotland; Giant's Causeway, Moyle, N. Ireland; Kern Co., California; India; Australia; and from some other localities.

**Gonnardite**
**$Na_2CaAl_4Si_6O_{20} . 7H_2O$**
Gonnardite crystallizes in the orthorhombic system in fibrous masses. The colour is white with a silky lustre. H 4.5–5; SG 2.3
*Occurrence.* Occurs with thomsonite in basalt in Sicily; with wollastonite and pyrite at Crestmore, Riverside Co., California; etc.

*Right: A sheaf-like aggregate of stilbite crystals*

*Above: Gismondine, Ballyclare, Northern Ireland*

*Above left: Gmelinite from New Jersey*

**Levyne $NaCa_3Al_7Si_{11}O_{36} \cdot 15H_2O$**
Levyne crystallizes in the hexagonal system as thin tabular crystals or as aggregates, is colourless, grey, white or yellowish, with a vitreous lustre. H 4–4.5; SG 2.1–2.2
*Localities.* Occurs in basalt as fine crystals at Grant Co., Oregon; Glenarm, N. Ireland; etc.

**Gmelinite** near
**$(Na_2, Ca)Al_2Si_4O_{12} \cdot 6H_2O$**
Sometimes containing small amounts of potassium, gmelinite crystallizes in the hexagonal system as pyramidal crystals or rhombohedra. Vertical striations and penetration twinning are common. The colour is white, yellowish, reddish or pink, and the lustre is vitreous. H 4.5; SG 2.0–2.1
*Occurrence.* Occurs in basaltic lavas with other zeolites.
*Localities.* From Glenarm, N. Ireland; Faroe Islands; New Jersey; and some other localities.

**Faujasite**
**$(Na_2, Ca)Al_2Si_4O_{12} \cdot 6H_2O$**
Faujasite crystallizes in the cubic system as octahedra, commonly twinned. It is colourless or white and may be stained by impurities, thin sections are transparent. The lustre is vitreous. H 5; SG 1.9
*Occurrence.* Occurs with other zeolites at the St. Gotthard, Switzerland; with augite in the Kaiserstuhl, Baden, W. Germany.

**Stilbite $NaCa_2Al_5Si_{13}O_{36} \cdot 14H_2O$**
Stilbite crystallizes in the monoclinic system as cruciform penetration twins; as aggregates or in radiating forms. There is a perfect cleavage. It is white, grey, yellowish, pink, orange or brown, with a vitreous lustre. The streak is colourless. H 3.5–4; SG 2.1–2.2
*Occurrence.* Occurs in cavities in basalt or granite pegmatites; also from some hot spring deposits.
*Localities.* From the Isle of Skye, Kilmacolm, Strathclyde, and the Kilpatrick Hills, Scotland; Faroe Islands; Switzerland; San Diego Co., California; and from many other places.

**Gismondine $CaAl_2Si_2O_8 \cdot 4H_2O$**
Gismondine crystallizes in the monoclinic system as pseudotetragona bipyramids produced by twinning. The colour is white, colourless, grey or reddish, with a vitreous lustre. H 4.5; SG 2.2
*Localities.* Occurs in basaltic lavas in Ireland; Iceland; with chlorite in an altered granite from Queensland, Australia; etc.

**Chabazite $CaAl_2Si_4O_{12} \cdot 6H_2O$**
Chabazite crystallizes in the hexagonal system as rhombohedra which may resemble cubes, or as penetration twins. It is white, yellowish, pinkish or greenish with a colourless streak and a vitreous lustre. H 4–5; SG 2.0–2.1
*Occurrence.* Occurs in cavities in basalt with other zeolites, calcite and quartz. May also be found in schists and crystalline limestones.
*Localities.* From Kilmacolm, Strathclyde, Scotland; Giant's Causeway, Moyle, Ireland; Riverside Co., California; Bay of Fundy, Nova Scotia; Italy; Germany; USSR; Australia; etc.

**Thomsonite $NaCa_2Al_5Si_5O_{20} \cdot 6H_2O$**
Thomsonite crystallizes in the orthorhombic system as radiating or lamellar aggregates; crystals are acicular prismatic. There is a perfect cleavage. The colour is white, yellowish or pink and the streak is colourless. It has a vitreous lustre. Metathomsonite is a high-temperature polymorph. H 5–5.5; SG 2.2–2.4
*Occurrence.* Thomsonite occurs in cavities in basalt with other zeolites; also in some schists.
*Localities.* From the Kilpatrick Hills, Strathclyde and Bishopton, Scotland; Faroe Islands; Italy; Germany; Kern Co., California; etc.

**Phillipsite** near
**$(K_2, Na_2, Ca)Al_2Si_4O_{12} \cdot 4\frac{1}{2}H_2O$**
Phillipsite crystallizes in the monoclinic system as penetration twins or spherulites. It is white, colourless or reddish, with a vitreous lustre. H 4–4.5; SG 2.2
*Occurrence.* Occurs in cavities in basalt, saline lake deposits and as deposits from hot springs.

*Far left: Pseudocubes of chabazite from Bolzano, Italy*

*Left: Phillipsite from Iceland*

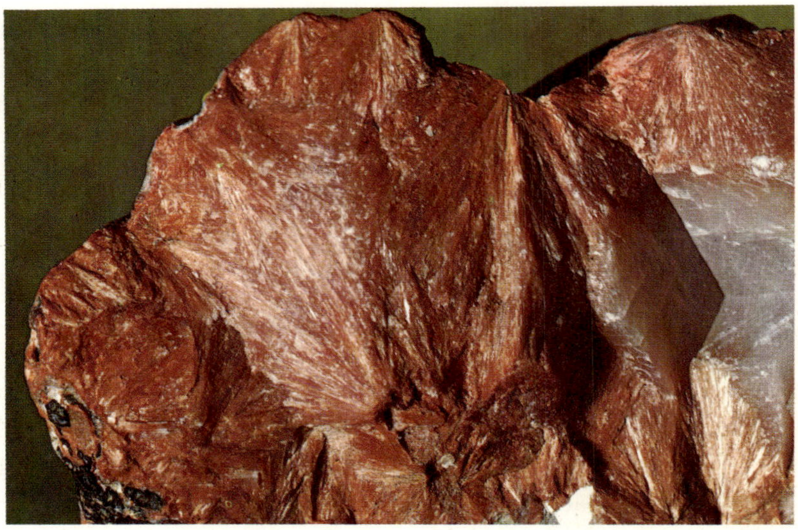

*Right: Fibrous aggregates of mordenite from the Val dei Zuccanti, Italy*

*Localities.* From Giant's Causeway, Moyle, N. Ireland; good crystals from Capo di Bove, Italy; from Idar-Oberstein, W. Germany; and from some other localities.

**Erionite**
**$(Ca, Na_2, K_2)_{1\text{-}5}Al_9Si_{27}O_{72}.27H_2O$**
Erionite crystallizes in the hexagonal system as fibrous masses resembling wool. The colour is white. H not measured; SG about 2.0
*Occurrence.* Occurs with opal in rhyolitic tuffs or in basalt.
*Localities.* From the Faroe Islands; Baker Co., Oregon; Nevada; South Dakota.

**Heulandite** **$(Na, Ca)_{4\text{-}6}Al_6\text{-}(Al, Si)_4Si_{26}O_{72}.24H_2O$**
Heulandite crystallizes in the monoclinic system as granular masses or trapezoidal crystals. There is a perfect cleavage. It is white, colourless, grey, yellow, pink, red or brown with a vitreous lustre and a colourless streak. H 3.5–4; SG 2.1–2.2
*Occurrence.* Occurs in cavities in basalt with other zeolites; sometimes in gneiss or sandstone.
*Localities.* From the Isle of Skye, Scotland; northern New Jersey; Switzerland; and elsewhere.

**Dachiardite** near
**$(Ca, K_2, Na_2)_3Al_4Si_{18}O_{45}.14H_2O$**
Dachiardite crystallizes in the monoclinic system forming twinned prismatic crystals with a perfect cleavage. It is colourless, with a vitreous lustre. H 4–4.5; SG 2.1–2.2
*Occurrence.* Occurs with other zeolites in pegmatite on Elba.

**Mordenite**
**$(Ca, Na_2, K_2)Al_2Si_{10}O_{24}.7H_2O$**
Mordenite crystallizes in the orthorhombic system, often as fibrous aggregates; crystals are prismatic, vertically striated. The colour is white, colourless or yellowish to pink, and the lustre is vitreous. H 4–5; SG 2.1
*Occurrence.* In cavities in igneous rocks.
*Localities.* From the Hoodoo Mts., Wyoming; Morden, Nova Scotia; and many other localities.

**Brewsterite**
**$(Sr, Ba, Ca)Al_2Si_6O_{16}.5H_2O$**
Brewsterite crystallizes in the monoclinic system as short prismatic crystals or as fibrous aggregates. Twinning is common and there is a perfect cleavage. The colour is white or colourless, with a vitreous lustre. H 5; SG 2.4
*Occurrence.* Occurs in cavities in basalt and in schists associated with calcite.
*Localities.* From Strontian, Highland, Scotland; Mendocino Co., California; etc.

**Edingtonite $BaAl_2Si_3O_{10}.4H_2O$**
Edingtonite crystallizes in the orthorhombic system as minute pyramidal crystals or in masses. There is a perfect cleavage. The colour is white, grey or pink, and the lustre is vitreous. H 4; SG 2.8
*Localities.* Occurs with harmotome and other zeolites in basic igneous rock at Old Kilpatrick, Strathclyde, Scotland; etc.

**Harmotome $BaAl_2Si_6O_{16}.6H_2O$**
Harmotome crystallizes in the monoclinic system as penetration twins or as radiating aggregates. The colour is white, colourless, grey, pink, yellow or brown with a white streak. There is a vitreous lustre. H 4.5; SG 2.4–2.5
*Occurrence.* Occurs in cavities in basalts and with manganese minerals.
*Localities.* From Old Kilpatrick, Strathclyde and Strontian, Highland, Scotland; Wales; Westchester Co., New York; and elsewhere.

## Other Silicates

**Dioptase $CuSiO_2(OH)_2$**
Dioptase crystallizes in the hexagonal system forming prismatic crystals, crystalline aggregates or massive forms. There is a perfect cleavage. The colour is emerald-green to bluish-green with a vitreous lustre and a pale greenish-blue streak. H 5; SG 3.2
*Occurrence.* Occurs in the oxidation zone of copper deposits.
*Localities.* From Altyn-Tube, Khirgiz Steppes, USSR; Shaba, Zaire; with calcite at Tsumeb, South-West Africa; Soda Lake Mountain, San Bernardino Co., California; associated with cerussite, orange wulfenite and other minerals at

*Far right: Dioptase from a classic locality, Renéville, Zaire. Crystals are sometimes sufficiently large to facet*

*Right: Harmotome from Strontian, Scotland*

*Above: Radiating columnar dioptase crystals from Mindouli, Zaire*

the Mammoth mine, Tiger, Arizona.
*Treatment.* Remove calcite with dilute acetic acid.
*Fashioning. Uses*: faceting or cabochons; *cleavage*: perfect and rhombohedral; fairly brittle; *cutting angles*: crown 40°, pavilion 40°; *dichroism*: weak; *heat sensitivity*: very low.

**Planchéite $Cu_8Si_8O_{22}(OH)_4 . H_2O$**
Planchéite crystallizes in the orthorhombic system forming fibrous radial aggregates. The colour is pale to dark blue. H 5.5; SG 3.6–3.8
*Occurrence.* Occurs as a secondary mineral in the oxidation zone of copper deposits with malachite and other secondary copper minerals.
*Localities.* From Shaba, Zaire; Table Mountain mine, Klondyke, Arizona.
*Treatment.* Clean with distilled water.

**Chrysocolla $Cu_2H_2Si_2O_5(OH)_4$**
Chrysocolla is thought to crystallize in the orthorhombic system; it is found as microscopic acicular crystals in radiating groups or as close-packed aggregates; it is more commonly found cryptocrystalline or botryoidal. The colour is blue to blue-green and may be brown to black. The lustre is vitreous or earthy. H 2–4; SG 2.0–2.4
*Occurrence.* Found in the oxidation zone of copper deposits.
*Localities.* From Liskeard, Cornwall; Roughten Gill, Cumbria; Shaba, Zaire; Pennsylvania and other states of the USA; etc.
*Treatment.* Clean with distilled water.

**Phenakite $Be_2SiO_4$**
Phenakite crystallizes in the hexagonal system and forms rhombohedral or prismatic crystals. Granular aggregates are found and radiating fibrous spherulites. Twinning is common. The colour is pale yellow through pink to brown, and colourless; the lustre is vitreous. H 7.5–8; SG 2.9–3.0; RI 1.65, 1.67
*Occurrence.* Found in pegmatites with topaz; in hydrothermal veins with quartz, cassiterite and beryl; in calcite veins with sulphides and in Alpine veins with adularia and hematite.
*Localities.* From the Takowaja River, Sverdlovsk, USSR; Minas Gerais, Brazil; France; Switzerland; Pala, San Diego Co., California; Pikes Peak, Colorado; etc.
*Treatment.* Remove iron stains with oxalic acid.
*Fashioning. Uses*: faceting or cabochons; *cleavage*: distinct and prismatic; *cutting angles*: crown 40°, pavilion 40°; *heat sensitivity*: very low.

**Bertrandite $Be_4Si_2O_7(OH)_2$**
Bertrandite crystallizes in the orthorhombic system forming thin tabular or prismatic crystals; it may be pseudomorphous after beryl. There is a perfect cleavage and twinning is common. It is colourless or pale yellow, transparent, with a vitreous lustre. H 6–7; SG 2.6
*Occurrence.* Occurs in granite pegma-

*Right: Wollastonite from Meldon, Devon*

*Below right: Radiating acicular crystals of pectolite. This fine specimen is from Weehawken, New Jersey*

*Bottom right: Gadolinite from Norway. The greasy lustre can be seen*

tites and pneumatolytic-hydrothermal veins with beryl, quartz and calcite.
*Localities.* From the Pala pegmatites, San Diego Co., California; Cornwall; Mica Creek, Mt. Isa, Queensland; etc.
*Treatment.* Clean with dilute acid.

**Eudidymite $NaBeSi_3O_7OH$**
Eudidymite is dimorphous with epididymite. It crystallizes in the monoclinic system forming tabular crystals or spherulites; twinning is common. There is a perfect cleavage. The colour is white or colourless and may be grey, yellow, blue or violet. The lustre is vitreous. H 6–7; SG 2.5
*Occurrence.* Occurs in nepheline-syenite pegmatites with albite, fluorite and other minerals.
*Localities.* From Greenland, Langesundfjord, Norway; Kola Peninsula, USSR.
*Treatment.* Clean with distilled water.

**Epididymite $NaBeSi_3O_7OH$**
Dimorphous with eudidymite, epididymite crystallizes in the orthorhombic system, forming tabular crystals with a perfect cleavage or spherulites, and with twinning frequent. It is white or colourless and may be shades of grey, blue, yellow or violet. The lustre is vitreous. H 6–7; SG 2.5
*Occurrence.* Occurs in nepheline-syenite pegmatites with fluorite, albite and other minerals.
*Localities.* From Greenland; Langesundfjord, Norway; Kola Peninsula, USSR.
*Treatment.* Clean with distilled water.

**Barylite $BaBe_2Si_2O_7$**
Barylite crystallizes in the orthorhombic system and forms thin tabular or prismatic crystals; massive forms or disseminated grains are also found. There is a perfect cleavage. The colour is white or bluish, transparent with a vitreous lustre. H 7; SG 4.0
*Occurrence.* Occurs with willemite and hedyphane in calcite veins at Franklin, New Jersey; fine crystals from Park Co., Colorado; etc.
*Treatment.* Clean with dilute acid.

**Gadolinite $Be_2FeY_2Si_2O_{10}$**
Gadolinite crystallizes in the monoclinic system, forming prismatic crystals or masses. The colour is black, greenish-black and sometimes light green. The lustre is vitreous to greasy and the streak greenish-grey. Other rare earths in small quantities may replace yttrium. H 6.5–7; SG 4.0–4.6
*Localities.* Found in granites and granite pegmatites, commonly with fluorite and allanite. From Sweden; Switzerland; Colorado, Arizona; etc.
*Treatment.* Clean with dilute acid; do not try to remove brown coating.

**Parawollastonite $CaSiO_3$**
Parawollastonite crystallizes in the monoclinic system and is the alpha-form of $CaSiO_3$. Crystals are tabular; fibrous masses are more commonly found. There is a perfect cleavage and twinning is common. The colour is white or grey, sometimes yellowish with a vitreous or pearly lustre. H 4.5–5; SG 2.9
*Occurrence.* Occurs in contacts of igneous intrusions in limestones and in limestone fragments ejected from volcanoes.
*Localities.* From Mt. Somma, Italy; Csiklova, Romania; Crestmore, Riverside Co., California.
*Treatment.* Clean with dilute acid.

**Wollastonite $CaSiO_3$**
The triclinic form of $CaSiO_3$, wollastonite forms tabular crystals but is more commonly found massive and fibrous. There is a perfect cleavage and twinning is common. The colour is white, grey or pale green with a vitreous or pearly lustre. H 4.5–5; SG 2.8–3.0
*Occurrence.* Occurs in metamorphosed limestones and in some alkaline igneous rocks.
*Localities.* From Norway; Finland; Inyo Co., California; etc.
*Treatment.* Clean with dilute acid.

**Okenite $CaSi_2O_4(OH)_2 . H_2O$**
Okenite crystallizes in the triclinic system and forms blade-shaped crystals; more commonly found as fibrous inter-

laced masses. There is a perfect cleavage and twinning occurs. The colour is white, sometimes tinged with yellow or blue. The lustre is vitreous or pearly. H 4.5–5; SG 2.2–2.3
*Occurrence.* Occurs in amygdales in basalt.
*Localities.* From Disco Island, Greenland; Faroe Islands; Chile; Syhadree Mts., Bombay.

*Left: Specimen of willemite fluorescing under short-wave ultraviolet light. The willemite is showing green; the pink mineral is calcite. From Franklin, New Jersey*

*Far left: The same specimen in normal light*

**Gyrolite $Ca_2Si_3O_7(OH)_2 . H_2O$**
Gyrolite crystallizes in the hexagonal system forming radiating lamellar masses or concretions. There is a perfect cleavage and the colour is white or colourless. H 3–4; SG 2.3–2.4
*Occurrence.* Occurs in crevices in rocks as a secondary mineral formed by the alteration of lime silicates.
*Localities.* From Fort Point, San Francisco Co., California, in association with apophyllite; from Collinward, near Belfast, N. Ireland; Isle of Skye; etc.
*Treatment.* Clean with distilled water.

**Tobermorite**
**near $Ca_5Si_6O_{16}(OH)_2 . 4H_2O$**
Tobermorite crystallizes in the orthorhombic system as fibrous or granular masses, or as plates. The colour is white or pinkish-white and the lustre is silky. Small amounts of sodium and potassium may replace calcium in the formula given, and small amounts of aluminium may replace silicon. Three distinct hydrates of similar composition appear to occur, called plombierite, tobermorite and riversideite respectively. H 2.5; SG 2.4
*Occurrence.* Pseudomorphous after wilkeite in association with calcite, monticellite and vesuvianite at Crestmore, Riverside Co., California: Tobermory, Isle of Mull, Scotland; etc.

**Xonotlite $Ca_3Si_3O_8(OH)_2$**
Xonotlite crystallizes in the monoclinic system forming acicular crystals; more commonly found massive, compact or fibrous. The colour is chalky white, colourless, pink or grey with a greasy lustre. H 6; SG 2.7
*Occurrence.* Occurs as veins in serpentine or in contact zones.
*Localities.* From Tetela de Xonotla, Mexico; Yauco, Puerto Rico; Riverside Co. and San Francisco Co., California.
*Treatment.* Clean with distilled water.

**Afwillite $Ca_3Si_2O_4(OH)_6$**
Afwillite crystallizes in the monoclinic system forming tabular crystals with a perfect cleavage and also massive forms. It is white or colourless. H 3; SG 2.6
*Localities.* Occurs in cracks in blocks of contact rock in Commercial Quarry, Crestmore, California; with calcite in a spurrite rock at Scawt Hill, Antrim, N. Ireland; at Dutoitspan diamond mine, Kimberley, South Africa in a dolerite inclusion in kimberlite.
*Treatment.* Clean with dilute acid.

**Pectolite $NaCa_2Si_3O_8OH$**
Pectolite crystallizes in the triclinic system forming aggregates of needle-like crystals, radiating and forming globular masses. There is a perfect cleavage and the colour is white. The lustre is silky. H 4.5–5; SG 2.7–2 8
*Occurrence.* Occurs in cavities in basaltic rocks, often with zeolites; also in lime-rich metamorphic rocks.
*Localities.* Paterson and Franklin New Jersey; Weardale, Durham and Ratho, near Edinburgh; etc.
*Treatment.* Can be cleaned ultrasonically.

**Merwinite $Ca_3Mg[Si_2O_8]$**
Merwinite crystallizes in the monoclinic system forming compact granular masses; the crystals have a perfect cleavage. It is colourless to pale green with a greasy lustre. H 6; SG 3.1
*Occurrence.* Occurs in contact zones with monticellite; spinel, etc.
*Localities.* From Scawt Hill, Antrim, N. Ireland; limestone quarries, Crestmore, Riverside Co., California.
*Treatment.* Clean with dilute acid

**Willemite $Zn_2SiO_4$**
Willemite crystallizes in the hexagonal system forming short hexagonal prismatic crystals or fibrous compact masses or grains. It is colourless, white, green, red, yellow, brown or grey with a colourless streak and resinous lustre. Intense yellowish-green fluorescence under ultra-violet light. Strong phosphorescence. H 5.5; SG 3.9–4.2
*Occurrence.* Occurs as an ore mineral.
*Localities.* Fine specimens from Franklin and Sterling Hill, New Jersey; also from Greenland; Zaire; Zambia; Tsumeb, South-West Africa; etc.
*Treatment.* Clean with distilled water.

**Hemimorphite $Zn_4Si_2O_7(OH)_2 . H_2O$**
Hemimorphite crystallizes in the orthorhombic system forming thin tabular crystals with vertical striations; hemimorphic development shown by doubly-terminated crystals; also found as fan-shaped aggregates and as masses, granular or stalactitic. There is a perfect cleavage. The colour is white or colourless, sometimes pale blue, greenish or grey. The lustre is silky and the streak colourless. H 4.5–5; SG 3 4–3.5
*Occurrence.* Occurs as a secondary mineral in the oxidized zone of ore deposits or in calcareous rocks; sometimes in pegmatites. Associated with galena, sphalerite, smithsonite etc.
*Localities.* From Roughten Gill, Cumbria (acicular crystals and mamillary crusts, of a fine green); Matlock, Derbyshire; Mapimi, Durango, Mexico; California; Nevada; etc.

**Hardystonite $Ca_2ZnSi_2O_7$**
Hardystonite crystallizes in the tetragonal system in granular masses coloured white, pink or brown. H 3–4; SG 3.4
*Localities.* Found with willemite, etc, at Franklin, New Jersey.

**Clinohedrite $CaZnSiO_3(OH)_2$**
Clinohedrite crystallizes in the monoclinic system, usually being found massive or as lamellar aggregates; crystals are prismatic, tabular or wedge-shaped. There is a perfect cleavage. It is white or colourless and may be amethystine. Orange fluorescence under short-wave UV. H 5.5; SG 3.2–3.3
*Localities.* Found with willemite, etc, at Franklin, New Jersey.
*Treatment.* Clean with distilled water.

**Larsenite $PbZnSiO_4$**
Larsenite crystallizes in the orthorhombic system forming slender prismatic crystals vertically striated. It is white with an adamantine lustre. H 3; SG 5.9
*Localities.* Found with willemite, etc, at Franklin, New Jersey.
*Treatment.* Clean with distilled water.

**Hodgkinsonite $MnZn_2SiO_5 . H_2O$**
Hodgkinsonite crystallizes in the monoclinic system forming acute pyramidal or stout prismatic crystals; massive forms also found. There is a perfect cleavage and the colour is bright pink to reddish-brown. The lustre is vitreous. H 4.5–5; SG 3.9
*Localities.* Found with willemite, etc, at Franklin, New Jersey.
*Treatment.* Clean with distilled water.

**Thortveitite $(Sc, Y)_2Si_2O_7$**
Thortveitite crystallizes in the monoclinic system forming prismatic crystals showing some distortion and commonly displaying twinning. The colour is grey-

*Above: Bright yellow monoclinic crystals of sphene from Bolzano, Italy. The crystals are wedge-shaped and the name sphene derives from the Greek for wedge*

ish-green with a streak of the same colour, while the lustre is vitreous. H 6–7; SG 3.5
*Occurrence.* Found in granite pegmatites rich in rare-earth elements.
*Localities.* From Iveland, Norway; Befanamo, Malagasy Republic; Ural Mts, USSR; Japan.
*Treatment.* Clean with distilled water.

**Thalenite $Y_2Si_2O_7$**
Thalenite crystallizes in the monoclinic system, usually forming compact masses; crystals are tabular or prismatic. The colour is flesh pink, brown or greenish. The lustre is greasy. H 6; SG 4.3–4.6
*Occurrence.* Found in granite pegmatites with fergusonite, magnetite, etc.
*Localities.* From Osterby, Sweden; Iizaka, Fukuoka Prefecture, Japan; Siberia; Snowflake feldspar mine, Teller Co., Colorado.
*Treatment.* Clean with distilled water.

**Cerite $(Ca, Mg)_2(RE)_8(SiO_4, FCO_3)_7(OH, H_2O)_3$**
(RE in the above formula is any rare earth.) Cerite crystallizes in the hexagonal system forming pseudo-octahedral crystals; more commonly found massive, granular. The colour is brown to cherry-red with a resinous lustre. H about 5.5; SG 4.7
*Localities.* Found with rare earths in veins at Mountain Pass, California; with fluorite and epidote in the Jamestown district, Boulder Co., Colorado; the Bastnaes mine, Riddarhyttan, Vastmanland, Sweden; Mt. Tenbazan, Korea.
*Treatment.* Clean with distilled water.

**Murmanite $Na_2(Ti, Nb)_2Si_2O_9 . H_2O$**
Murmanite crystallizes in the monoclinic system as aggregates of platy crystals with a perfect cleavage. The colour is lilac to bright pink; altered varieties are grey to brown or black. H 2–3; SG 2.7–2.8
*Localities.* From alkali pegmatites and nepheline-syenite with microcline, eudialyte etc; from Kola Peninsula, USSR.
*Treatment.* Clean with distilled water.

**Sphene $CaTiSiO_5$**
Sphene crystallizes in the monoclinic system, forming flattened wedge-shaped crystals; massive, compact and lamellar forms are also found. Lamellar varieties give a distinct parting. Sphene is colourless, brown, green, yellow, rose-red or black; parti-coloured varieties are known. The streak is white and the lustre adamantine to resinous. H 5–5.5; SG 3.4–3.5
*Occurrence.* Occurs as an accessory mineral in igneous rocks; in schists, gneisses and iron ore; also as a detrital mineral in sedimentary deposits.
*Localities.* Found at Schwarzenstein and Rotenkopf in the Zillertal, Austria; the Ala Valley, Piedmont, Italy; the Grisons, Switzerland, as fine crystals; Midongy, Malagasy Republic; from the Tilly Foster iron mine, Brewster, New York; a honey-yellow variety from Franklin, New Jersey; from Pino Solo, Baja California Norte, Mexico; etc.
*Treatment.* Clean with dilute acid.
*Fashioning. Uses*: faceting or cabochons; *cleavage*: distinct prismatic; *cutting angles*: crown 30°–40°, pavilion 37°–40°; *pleochroism*: strong in deep colours; *heat sensitivity*: very low.

**Lamprophyllite $Na_2(Sr, Ba)_2Ti_3(SiO_4)_4(OH, F)_2$**
Lamprophyllite crystallizes in the monoclinic and orthorhombic systems, forming tabular elongated crystals or needle-like aggregations. Polysynthetic twinning is found. The colour is golden to dark brown with a vitreous lustre. H 2–3; SG 3.4–3.5
*Occurrence.* Occurs in nepheline-syenites and associated pegmatites with microcline, eudialyte, etc.
*Localities.* From Langesundfjord, Norway; Bear Paw Mts., Montana; etc.

**Benitoite $BaTiSi_3O_9$**
Benitoite crystallizes in the hexagonal system forming pyramidal or tabular crystals somewhat flattened along the c-axis and with a triangular shape. The colour is blue, purple, pink, white or colourless and some crystals are parti-coloured. Blue fluorescence under short-wave ultraviolet light. The streak is colourless and the lustre vitreous. H 6–6.5; SG 3.6; RI 1.7, 1.8
*Localities.* Found with neptunite, natrolite and joaquinite in serpentine near the headwaters of the San Benito River, San Benito Co., California; from the Eocene sands of south-west Texas; etc.
*Treatment.* Clean with dilute acid.
*Fashioning. Uses*: faceting or cabochons; *cutting angles*: crown 40°, pavilion 40°; *dichroism*: strong; *heat sensitivity*: low.

*Right: Benitoite, commonly found only in California. The darker crystals are neptunite*

**Joaquinite $Ba_2NaCe_2Fe(Ti, Nb)_2Si_8O_{26}(OH, F)_2$**
Joaquinite crystallizes in the orthorhombic system forming small tabular crystals coloured honey-yellow to brown. The lustre is vitreous. H 5.5; SG 3.8
*Localities.* Found with neptunite, natrolite and benitoite near the headwaters of the San Benito River, San Benito Co., California.
*Treatment.* Clean with dilute acid.

**Chevkinite $(Ca, Ce)_4(Fe, Mg)_2(Ti, Fe)_3Si_4O_{22}$**
Chevkinite crystallizes in the monoclinic system forming slender prisms;

more commonly in irregular masses. The colour is dark reddish-brown to black. Lustre resinous. Varieties are perrierite (an oxidized variety) and thorchevkinite (thorium-bearing). H 5–6; SG 4.3–4.6
*Localities.* Found in pumice fragments from Cenozoic volcanoes in the western USA; from alkali pegmatites, Kola Peninsula, USSR.
*Treatment.* Clean with distilled water.

**Neptunite**
**$(Na, K)_2(Fe^{2+}, Mn)TiSi_4O_{12}$**
Neptunite crystallizes in the monoclinic system forming prismatic crystals with a square cross-section. There is a perfect cleavage and the colour is black; reddish brown from internal reflection. The streak is reddish-brown and the lustre vitreous. H 5–6; SG 3.1–3.2
*Localities.* Found with benitoite at the headwaters of the San Benito River, San Benito Co., California. A mangan-neptunite occurs at Mont St. Hilaire, Quebec, and on the Kola Peninsula, USSR.
*Treatment.* Clean with dilute acid.

**Astrophyllite**
**$(K, Na)_3(Fe, Mn)_7Ti_2Si_8O_{24}(O, OH)_7$**
Astrophyllite crystallizes in the triclinic system as bladed crystals in stellate groups with a perfect cleavage. The colour is bronze-yellow or golden-yellow with a submetallic lustre. H 3; SG 3.3–3.4
*Localities.* Occurs with quartz, feldspar, etc, at St. Peter's Dome, El Paso Co., Colorado; from nepheline-syenite at Mont St. Hilaire, Quebec; etc.
*Treatment.* Clean with distilled water.

*Left: The adamantine lustre of zircon can be seen in this crystal from Slatoust, USSR*

**Zircon $ZrSiO_4$**
Zircon crystallizes in the tetragonal system forming short prismatic crystals; often dipyramidal; metamict varieties with curved faces and edges or as sub-parallel aggregates. The colour may be red, brown, green, yellow or colourless with an adamantine lustre; metamict varieties have a greasy lustre. H 7.5; SG 4.6–4.7 (metamict 4.0); RI 1.92, 2.0; dispersion 0.038
*Occurrence.* Found as an accessory mineral in igneous rocks and in some metamorphic rocks. Also found as a detrital mineral in sedimentary deposits.
*Localities.* From Thailand; Sri Lanka (metamict varieties also from this locality); red variety from Expailly-St.-Marcel, France; Burma; Australia; St. Peter's Dome, El Paso Co., Colorado;

*Below: A superb group of benitoite crystals showing a well developed pyramidal habit*

*Right: Acicular crystals of the radioactive mineral sklodowskite from Shinkolobwe, Zaire*

*Below right: Braunite has a submetallic lustre, which can be seen in these crystals from Thuringia*

and numerous other localities.
*Treatment.* Clean with dilute acid.
*Fashioning. Uses*: faceting or cabochons; *cleavage*: imperfect prismatic; brittle; *cutting angles*: crown 40°, pavilion 40°; *dichroism*: distinct in some colours; *heat sensitivity*: very low.

**Catapleiite $(Na_2, Ca)ZrSi_3O_9.2H_2O$**
Catapleiite crystallizes in the hexagonal system as thin hexagonal plates or lamellar masses. Twinning is common and there is a perfect cleavage. The colour is light yellow to yellowish-brown or red; sometimes sky blue or colourless. The lustre is vitreous. H 5–6; SG 2.6–2.8
*Occurrence.* Found in alkaline rocks and pegmatites with feldspars, sphene, etc.
*Localities.* Mont St. Hilaire, Quebec; Langesundfjord, Norway; Malagasy Republic; Magnet Cove, Arkansas; etc.
*Treatment.* Clean with distilled water.

**Wadeite $K_2CaZrSi_4O_{12}$**
Wadeite crystallizes in the hexagonal system, forming prismatic crystals with a hexagonal cross-section. It is colourless, light pink or lilac, with an adamantine lustre. H 5–6; SG 3.1
*Occurrence.* Occurs in potassium-rich rocks with zeolites, leucite, apatite, etc.
*Localities.* From Kimberley, South Africa; Australia; Kola Peninsula, USSR.
*Treatment.* Clean with dilute acid.

**Thorite $ThSiO_4$**
Thorite crystallizes in the tetragonal system forming short prismatic crystals or reniform masses. The colour is brownish-yellow to orange, black or dark green. Resinous lustre. Varieties include hydrothorite, (a metamict hydrous thorite), calciothorite and freyalite, which contains cerium. H about 4.5; SG 4.1–6.7
*Occurrence.* Found as a primary mineral in pegmatites or metasomatized zones in impure limestones; hydrothermal veins and detrital deposits.
*Localities.* From Langesundfjord, Norway; Sicily; Batum, USSR; Henderson Co., North Carolina; etc.
*Treatment.* Clean with distilled water.

**Huttonite $ThSiO_4$**
Dimorphous with thorite, huttonite crystallizes in the monoclinic system forming anhedral grains coloured pale cream with an adamantine lustre. SG 7.1
*Localities.* Associated with scheelite and cassiterite from sands at Gillespie Beach, New Zealand.
*Treatment.* Clean with distilled water.

**Stokesite $CaSnSi_3O_9.2H_2O$**
Stokesite crystallizes in the orthorhombic system as pyramidal crystals. There is a perfect cleavage. It is colourless. H 6; SG 3.1
*Localities.* Occurs with axinite at Roscommon Cliff, St. Just, Cornwall.
*Treatment.* Clean with distilled water.

**Barysilite $MnPb_8(Si_2O_7)_3$**
Barysilite crystallizes in the hexagonal system and is found massive with a curved lamellar structure; the colour is white to pink and with a tarnish after exposure. H 3; SG 6.5–6.7
*Localities.* From Franklin, New Jersey.
*Treatment.* Clean with distilled water.

**Eulytine $Bi_4Si_3O_{12}$**
Eulytine crystallizes in the cubic system forming minute tetrahedral crystals or spheres. It is colourless to yellow or grey or dark brown. H 4.5; SG 6.6
*Localities.* Occurs as crystals on quartz at Johanngeorgenstadt, Schneeberg, E. Germany, in association with native bismuth.
*Treatment.* Clean with distilled water.

**Soddyite $(UO_2)_5Si_2O_9.6H_2O$**
Soddyite crystallizes in the orthorhombic system as bipyramidal crystals or as divergent clusters or otherwise as fibrous aggregates. There is a perfect cleavage. The colour is amber in small crystals, larger ones are canary yellow. The streak is pale yellow and the lustre is vitreous to resinous. H 3.5; SG 4.7
*Localities.* Occurs with uranophane as pseudomorphs after uraninite at the Ruggles pegmatite, Grafton Center, New Hampshire; from pegmatites at Norrabees south of the Orange river in Namaqualand, South Africa; from Shinkolobwe, Shaba, Zaire.
*Treatment.* Clean with distilled water.

**Cuprosklodowskite $Cu(UO_2)_2Si_2O_7.6H_2O$**
Cuprosklodowskite crystallizes in the triclinic system forming acicular crystals, stellate aggregates or silky coatings with a radial fibrous structure; they have a vitreous or silky lustre. The colour is pale to emerald green or a darker green. H 4; SG 3.8
*Occurrence.* Occurs as a secondary mineral from the alteration of primary copper minerals and uraninite.
*Localities.* From Shaba, Zaire, with sklodowskite, etc; Jachymov, Czechoslovakia; with dioptase from Amelal, Morocco; San Juan Co., Utah with brochantite; etc.

**Sklodowskite $Mg(UO_2)_2Si_2O_7.6H_2O$**
Sklodowskite crystallizes in the monoclinic system as prismatic acicular crystals or radial fibrous aggregates or granular masses. There is a perfect cleavage. The colour is pale to greenish yellow with a silky lustre. H 2–3; SG 3.6
*Localities.* Occurs as a secondary mineral with cuprosklodowskite at Kalongwe, Shaba, Zaire; also from New Haven mine, Crook Co., Wyoming; etc.

**Uranophane $Ca(UO_2)_2Si_2O_7.6H_2O$**
Uranophane crystallizes in the monoclinic system forming acicular to hair-like crystals and as radiated aggregates or tufts. There is a perfect cleavage. The colour is pale to lemon yellow, also amber to brown with a greasy lustre. It fluoresces weakly in ultraviolet light. H about 2.5; SG 3.8
*Occurrence.* Occurs in pegmatites as pseudomorphs after uraninite and in the oxidized zones of veins of uraninite.
*Localities.* Fine crystals from Shaba, Zaire; from the Hanosh mine, Grants district, New Mexico; Wölsendorf, E. Germany; and many other localities.

**Braunite $Mn^{2+}Mn_6^{3+}SiO_{12}$**
Braunite crystallizes in the tetragonal system as pyramidal striated crystals or as masses. There is a perfect cleavage. The colour is black to brown with a submetallic lustre. H 6–6.5; SG 4.7–4.8

*Occurrence.* Occurs in veins as a secondary mineral formed by weathering and associated with other manganese minerals.
*Localities.* From Panama; Norway; Sweden; Italy; etc.
*Treatment.* Clean with distilled water.

**Alleghanyite $Mn_5Si_2O_8(OH)_2$**
Sometimes containing titanium or fluorine, alleghanyite crystallizes in the monoclinic system forming plate-like crystals deeply striated by twinning; usually massive. The colour is brown or deep pink, and the lustre vitreous. H 5.5; SG 4.0
*Localities.* Occurs with franklinite and willemite at Franklin, New Jersey, etc.
*Treatment.* Clean with distilled water.

**Leucophoenicite $Mn_7Si_3O_{12}(OH)_2$**
Leucophoenicite crystallizes in the monoclinic system, usually found massive, granular. The colour is light to deep pink or purple to brown. The lustre is vitreous. H 5.5–6; SG 3.8
*Localities.* With willemite in hydrothermal veins at Franklin, New Jersey.
*Treatment.* Clean with distilled water.

**Bementite $Mn_8Si_6O_{15}(OH)_{10}$**
Bementite crystallizes in the monoclinic system; it is usually found massive, sometimes radiating or stalactitic. There is a perfect cleavage. The colour is brown to grey and darkens on exposure; the lustre is vitreous. H 6; SG 2.9–3.1
*Localities.* Occurs in primary manganese ore, notably from Franklin, New Jersey.
*Treatment.* Clean with distilled water.

*Left: Fibrous crystals of johannsenite from Recoaro, Italy*

**Johannsenite $CaMnSi_2O_6$**
Johannsenite crystallizes in the monoclinic system, usually being found massive or as radiating spherulitic aggregates of fibres and prisms; crystals are short prismatic. The colour is grey, green to brown or black, with a vitreous lustre. It is often stained black by manganese oxide. H 6; SG 3.4–3.5
*Occurrence.* Occurs in metasomatized limestones.
*Localities.* From Broken Hill, New South Wales, etc.
*Treatment.* Clean with distilled water.

**Babingtonite $Ca_2Fe^{2+}Fe^{3+}Si_5O_{14}OH$**
Babingtonite crystallizes in the triclinic system forming short prismatic or platy crystals with a perfect cleavage. The colour is greenish to brownish-black,

*Far left: Babingtonite on orthoclase feldspar. From Baveno, Italy*

*Left: A triclinic crystal of babingtonite. Here the basal pinacoid can be seen as the vertical face on the right. From Baveno, Italy*

*Right: The chiastolite variety of andalusite with cross shaped carbonaceous inclusions. From Bimbowrie, Australia*

with a vitreous lustre. H 5.5–6; SG 3.3
*Occurrence.* Occurs in cavities in granite and gneiss.
*Localities.* From Devon; Baveno, Piedmont, Italy; fine crystals from the Lane trap rock quarry, Westfield, Massachusetts, etc.
*Treatment.* Clean with dilute acid.

**Inesite $Ca_2Mn_7Si_{10}O_{28}(OH)_2 \cdot 5H_2O$**
Inesite crystallizes in the triclinic system. It forms prismatic or tabular crystals with a chisel-shape; also acicular radiating aggregates with a perfect cleavage. The colour is pink or orange, darkening to brown on exposure. H 5.5; SG 3.0
*Localities.* Occurs with rhodochrosite at Hale Creek mine, Trinity Co., California; with apophyllite at New Broken Hill mine, Australia; etc.
*Treatment.* Clean with distilled water.

**Pyroxmangite (Mn, Fe)$SiO_3$**
Pyroxmangite crystallizes in the triclinic system usually in massive forms or grains; crystals are tabular. There is a perfect cleavage. The colour is pale to rose pink or dark reddish-brown due to alteration; there is a vitreous lustre. H 5.5–6; SG 3.6–3.8
*Localities.* Occurs in metamorphic or metasomatic rocks with rhodochrosite, spessartine, etc; from Broken Hill, New South Wales; Iva, South Carolina; and other localities.
*Treatment.* Clean with dilute acid.

**Cronstedtite $Fe_2^{2+}Fe_2^{3+}SiO_5(OH)_4$**
Cronstedtite crystallizes in the monoclinic system forming 3- or 6-sided pyramids or fibrous forms. There is a perfect cleavage. The colour is greenish to brownish-black; thin plates are emerald green by transmitted light. The lustre is vitreous. The streak is dark olive green. H 3.5; SG 3.3–3.4
*Localities.* Occurs at Ouro Preto, Minas Gerais, Brazil; Truro, Cornwall; Příbram, Czechoslovakia; etc.
*Treatment.* Clean with distilled water.

**Chloropal $Na_{0.33}Fe_2^{3+}(Al, Si)_4O_{10}(OH)_2 \cdot nH_2O$**
Chloropal, sometimes known as nontronite, crystallizes in the monoclinic system, forming fine-grained masses with a perfect cleavage. The colour is yellow to olive green, with a waxy lustre. H1–2; SG 2.3
*Occurrence.* Occurs as an alteration product of volcanic glasses; in mineral veins with quartz and opal.
*Localities.* From France; Germany; Malagasy Republic; California; Utah; etc.
*Treatment.* Clean with distilled water.

**Ilvaite $CaFe_2^{2+}Fe^{3+}Si_2O_8(OH)$**
Ilvaite crystallizes in the orthorhombic system forming thick prismatic crystals

*Below: Ilvaite from Rio Marina, Elba*

*Left: Radiating pyrophyllite crystals from the Ural Mts, USSR*

**Pyrophyllite $Al_2Si_4O_{10}(OH)_2$**
Pyrophyllite crystallizes in the monoclinic system in elongated tabular crystals, which are often curved or distorted; usually foliated, radiating, lamellar or fibrous. There is a perfect cleavage; the laminae are flexible. Greasy feel. The colour is white to yellowish-blue to brownish-green. Lustre pearly. H 1–2; SG 2.6–2.9
*Occurrence.* Occurs in schistose rocks with andalusite, kyanite and sillimanite or in hydrothermal veins with quartz and mica.
*Localities.* From Minas Gerais, Brazil; San Bernardino Co., California; etc.
*Treatment.* Remove iron stains with oxalic acid.

**Allophane $Al_2SiO_5 . nH_2O$**
Crystal system undetermined. Various colours. H 2–3; SG 1.8
*Localities.* From fissures and cavities in ore veins or coal deposits, western USA; Wheal Hamblyn, Devon; etc.
*Treatment.* Clean with distilled water.

with diamond-shaped cross section and with vertical striations; also massive, compact or columnar. The colour is grey to black with a black streak (brownish or greenish) and a submetallic lustre. H 5.5–6; SG 3.8–4.1
*Occurrence.* As a contact-metasomatic mineral, and in iron, zinc and copper ore deposits.
*Localities.* From Laxey mine, South Mountain, Idaho; Julianehaab, Greenland; Rio Marinha and Capo Calamita, Isle of Elba; etc.
*Treatment.* Clean with distilled water.

**Andalusite $Al_2SiO_5$**
Andalusite crystallizes in the orthorhombic system, forming prismatic crystals with an almost square cross-section. Massive forms and fibrous aggregates also occur. It is trimorphous with sillimanite and kyanite. The colour is pink, reddish-brown or greenish with strong pleochroism. The variety chiastolite contains carbonaceous inclusions, which give a cruciform pattern in cross-section. The streak is colourless and the lustre vitreous. H 6.5–7.5; SG 3.1
*Occurrence.* Occurs in slates and pelitic schists in contact-metamorphic aureoles, also mica schists; sometimes in pegmatites. Associated minerals include sillimanite and kyanite.
*Localities.* From Brazil; Sri Lanka; Malagasy Republic; chiastolite from Rhodesia; California; Massachusetts; etc.
*Treatment.* Clean with dilute acid.
*Fashioning. Uses*: faceting or cabochons; *cleavage*: distinct to perfect prismatic; brittle; *cutting angles*: crown 40°, pavilion 40°; *pleochroism*: strong; *heat sensitivity*: low.

**Kyanite $Al_2SiO_5$**
Kyanite, which is trimorphous with andalusite and sillimanite, crystallizes in the triclinic system, forming long bladed crystals which may be twisted. Massive and fibrous forms also occur; lamellar twinning is frequent and there is a perfect cleavage. The colour is blue with white, green, yellow or pink, sometimes showing in the same crystal; the streak is colourless and the lustre vitreous. H 4–7.5 (varying with crystallographic direction); SG 3.5–3.6
*Occurrence.* Occurs in schists and gneisses or from granite pegmatites.
*Localities.* From the Ural Mts, USSR; the Tyrol, and Carinthia, Austria; Kenya; Zaire; Virginia, New York and North Carolina, etc.
*Treatment.* Remove iron stains with oxalic acid.
*Fashioning. Uses*: faceting or cabochons; *cleavage*: highly perfect pinacoidal; brittle; *cutting angles*: crown 40°, pavilion 40°; *pleochroism*: distinct; *heat sensitivity*: low.

**Sillimanite $Al_2SiO_5$**
Sillimanite, which is trimorphous with andalusite and kyanite, crystallizes in the orthorhombic system forming fibrous crystals, usually felted. Massive forms also occur. There is a perfect cleavage. The colour is colourless, grey to blue or yellowish. The streak is colourless, and there is a vitreous lustre. H 6.5–7.5; SG 3.2
*Occurrence.* Occurs in schists, gneisses and granites, associated with andalusite or corundum.
*Localities.* From Mogok, Burma; South Africa; Kenya; Boehls Butte, Idaho; Custer Co., South Dakota; and many other localities.
*Treatment.* Sillimanite should be cleaned with dilute acid.
*Fashioning. Uses*: faceting or cabochons; *cleavage*: highly perfect // to the brachypinacoid; *cutting angles*: crown 40°, pavilion 40°; *pleochroism*: weak to distinct; *heat sensitivity*: low.

**Mullite $Al_6Si_2O_{13}$**
Mullite crystallizes in the orthorhombic system forming colourless or pale pink prismatic crystals, with a vitreous lustre. H 6–7; SG 3.0–3.1
*Occurrence.* Occurs in fused argillaceous inclusions in Tertiary eruptive rocks on the island of Mull, Scotland; andalusite, sillimanite and kyanite transform to mullite on intense heating.
*Treatment.* Clean with dilute acid.

*Below: A fine crystal of kyanite from the Italian Alps. Kyanite is sometimes faceted*

**Petalite $LiAlSi_4O_{10}$**
Petalite crystallizes in the monoclinic system and is usually found massive; polysynthetic twinning common. There is a perfect cleavage. It is colourless, grey, yellow or white. The lustre is vitreous. H 6–6.5; SG 2.3–2.5; RI 1.50, 1.52
*Occurrence.* Occurs in granite pegmatites with quartz, lepidolite, etc.
*Localities.* From Elba; Sweden; USSR; Londonderry, Western Austrlia; South-West Africa; etc.
*Treatment.* Clean with dilute acid.
*Fashioning. Uses*: faceting or cabochons; *cleavage*: perfect clinopinacoidal; brittle; *cutting angles*: crown 40°–50°, pavilion 43°; *pleochroism*: weak; *heat sensitivity*: low.

**Eucryptite $LiAlSiO_4$**
Eucryptite crystallizes in the hexagonal system, usually in massive granular aggregates; it forms small, well-formed crystals. Colourless or white. Pink fluorescence under ultra-violet light. H 6.5; SG 2.6
*Occurrence.* Occurs with albite in New Hampshire and Connecticut; from pegmatite at the Harding mine, Dixon, New Mexico; Bikita, Rhodesia.
*Treatment.* Clean with distilled water.

**Cookeite $LiAl_4(Si, Al)_4O_{10}(OH)_8$**
Cookeite crystallizes in the monoclinic system as pseudohexagonal plates or curved radial scales. There is a perfect cleavage. Colour white, greenish, yellowish, pink or brown. Lustre pearly. H 2.5–3.5; SG 2.6–2.7
*Occurrence.* Occurs in lithium-rich granite pegmatites with tourmaline, albite, quartz, etc.
*Localities.* From Pala, San Diego Co., California; Londonderry, Western Australia; etc.
*Treatment.* Clean with distilled water.

**Holmquistite** near **$(Na, K, Ca)Li(Mg, Fe^{2+})_3Al_2Si_8O_{22}(OH)_2$**
Holmquistite crystallizes in the orthorhombic system, as slender prismatic crystals, often with vertical striations, or massive. There is a perfect cleavage. The colour is dark violet, and the lustre is vitreous. H 5–6; SG 3.1
*Occurrence.* Occurs where lithium-rich pegmatites come into contact with country rocks of basic composition; associates include quartz, biotite, tourmaline, and plagioclase feldspar.
*Localities.* From USSR; Utö, Sweden; Edison spodumene mine, Pennington Co., South Dakota; Hiddenite mine, Alexander Co., North Carolina; etc.
*Treatment.* Clean with distilled water.

**Bityite $CaLiAl_2(AlBeSi_2)O_{10}(OH)_2$**
Bityite crystallizes in the monoclinic system as thin tabular crystals, rosettes and micaceous aggregates with a perfect cleavage. It is white to yellow. H 5.5; SG 3.0
*Occurrence.* Occurs in lithium-rich pegmatites.
*Localities.* From Maharitra, Mt. Bity, Malagasy Republic in association with pink tourmaline and lepidolite; Londonderry, Western Australia.
*Treatment.* Clean with distilled water.

**Beryl $Be_3Al_2Si_6O_{18}$**
Beryl crystallizes in the hexagonal system as prismatic crystals, sometimes vertically striated and sometimes terminated by small pyramid faces. The cleavage is indistinct. The colour may be emerald-green (emerald); golden yellow (heliodor); yellow (yellow beryl); light blue to green (aquamarine); pink (morganite); colourless (goshenite); red (bixbite). The lustre is vitreous. H 7–8; SG 2.6–2.9; RI 1.56, 1.59; birefringence 0.006; synthetics with some exceptions, have lower SG and RI.
*Occurrence.* Occurs in granite pegmatites, biotite schists and pneumatolytic hydrothermal veins.
*Localities.* Emerald is found in Colombia, particularly at the mines of Muzo and Chivor; Brazil; India; Pakistan; Rhodesia; Australia; Mozambique; Austria; Zambia; USSR; North Carolina; Transvaal. Heliodor is found in South-West Africa; yellow beryl from Brazil and Malagasy Republic; aquamarine from Brazil, Mourne Mountains of Ireland, Malagasy Republic, USSR. Morganite is found in Brazil, Malagasy Republic, USSR, San Diego Co. in California. Goshenite comes from Goshen, Massachusetts; bixbite from the Thomas Mountains, Utah.
*Treatment.* Clean with dilute acid.
*Fashioning. Uses*: faceting, cabochons; carvings, beads, tumbling; *cleavage*: imperfect basal; brittle; *cutting angles*: crown 40°–50°, pavilion 43°; *dichroism*: distinct especially in deep colours; *heat sensitivity*: very low.

**Euclase $BeAlSiO_4OH$**
Euclase crystallizes in the monoclinic system, forming long prismatic crystals with a perfect cleavage. The colour may be green, blue or colourless; the lustre is vitreous. H 7.5; SG 3.0–3.1
*Occurrence.* May occur in granite pegmatites, mica schists or placer deposits.
*Localities.* Fine crystals from Minas Gerais, Brazil; also from Tanzania; the Ural Mts. of the USSR; Bavaria, W. Germany; etc.
*Treatment.* Clean with dilute acid.
*Fashioning. Uses*: faceting or cabochons; *cleavage*: perfect // to clinopinacoid; *cutting angles*: crown 40°, pavilion 40°; *pleochroism*: weak; *heat sensitivity*: very low.

**Bavenite $Ca_4(Be, Al)_4Si_9(O, OH)_{28}$**
Bavenite crystallizes in the orthorhombic system as prismatic crystals or fibrous aggregates with lamellar twinning. There is a perfect cleavage. The colour is white, greenish, pink or brown and the lustre is silky. The streak is white. H 5.5; SG 2.7
*Occurrence.* Occurs in granite pegmatites with beryl.
*Localities.* From Pala, San Diego Co., California; Rutherford mine, Amelia, Virginia; Baveno, Italy; etc.
*Treatment.* Clean with distilled water.

**Milarite $KCa_2AlBe_2(Si_{12}O_{30}).H_2O$**
Milarite crystallizes in the hexagonal system, forming prismatic crystals. The colour is pale green, yellow or colourless, and the lustre is vitreous. H 5–6;

*Left: Globular aggregates of platy bavenite on a background of orthoclase*

*Below: Milarite crystals from Switzerland. These are hexagonal prisms*

SG 2.4–2.6
*Occurrence.* Occurs in pegmatites and syenites or hydrothermal veins.
*Localities.* From the Valencia mine, Guanajuato, Mexico; St. Gotthard, Switzerland; Henneberg, East Germany; Kola Peninsula, USSR; Swakopmund, South-West Africa.
*Treatment.* Milarite should be cleaned with distilled water.

**Sapphirine $Mg_{3.5}Al_9Si_{1.5}O_{20}$**
Sapphirine crystallizes in the monoclinic system as tabular crystals; more commonly found as disseminated grains. The colour is pale blue or grey to green. H 7.5; SG 3.4–3.5
*Occurrence.* Occurs in aluminium or magnesium-rich metamorphic rocks with a low silicon content.
*Localities.* From Greenland; Malagasy Republic; India; Quebec; New York State; etc.
*Treatment.* Sapphirine should be cleaned with dilute acid.

**Sheridanite**
**$(Mg, Al)_6(Si, Al)_4O_{10}(OH)_8$**
Sheridanite crystallizes in the monoclinic system and is found massive or as scaly aggregates; there is a perfect cleavage. The colour is greenish, colourless or yellow and the lustre is pearly. H 2–3; SG 2.6–2.8
*Occurrence.* Occurs in schists.
*Localities.* From Sheridan Co., Wyoming; and other localities.
*Treatment.* Sheridanite should be cleaned with distilled water.

**Palygorskite**
**$(Mg, Al)_2Si_4O_{10}(OH).4H_2O$**
Palygorskite crystallizes in the monoclinic and orthorhombic systems, usually as thin flexible sheets composed of interlocking fibres. There is an easy cleavage. The colour is white or grey, and the lustre is dull. H very soft; SG 2.2
*Occurrence.* Occurs in hydrothermal veins or altered serpentinites or granites.
*Localities.* From the Shetland Islands; Metaline Falls, Washington; Morocco; etc.
*Treatment.* Palygorskite should be cleaned with distilled water.

**Lawsonite**
**$CaAl_2(Si_2O_7)(OH)_2.H_2O$**
Lawsonite crystallizes in the orthorhombic system as prismatic crystals or granular masses. There is a perfect cleavage and the colour is white, grey or pinkish with a white streak. There is a vitreous lustre. H 6; SG 3.0–3.1
*Occurrence.* Occurs in glaucophane schists.
*Localities.* From Santa Clara, Cuba; France; Italy; Coast Ranges of California; etc.
*Treatment.* Clean with dilute acid.

**Scolecite $CaAl_2Si_3O_{10}.3H_2O$**
Scolecite crystallizes in the monoclinic system as slender prismatic crystals or radiating fibrous masses. There is a perfect cleavage. The colour is white or colourless and the lustre silky. H 5; SG 2.2
*Occurrence.* Occurs in cavities in basalt or in schists.
*Localities.* From the Isle of Skye; Faroe Islands; Riverside Co., California; etc.
*Treatment.* Clean with distilled water.

*Left: Euclase. Most commonly found in Brazil, this crystal is from Tanzania*

*Opposite page: Hexagonal prism of aquamarine, a variety of beryl, from Brazil*

*Right: Laumontite with quartz from Berufjordur, Iceland*

*Below right: Epistilbite from Teigarhorn, Iceland. The radiating habit can easily be seen*

**Prehnite $Ca_2Al_2Si_3O_{10}(OH)_2$**
Prehnite crystallizes in the orthorhombic system, usually as compact granular masses or as botryoidal, stalactitic or reniform forms. Crystals are usually tabular or prismatic. The colour is pale or dark green, yellow or white, and the lustre is vitreous. The streak is colourless. Ferroprehnite is an iron-bearing variety. H 6–6.5; SG 2.9
*Occurrence.* Occurs as a secondary or hydrothermal mineral in basic igneous rocks or in granites and metamorphosed limestones.
*Localities.* In Scotland, from the Kilpatrick Hills, Strathclyde, Campsie Hills, Central Region and Corstorphine Hill, Edinburgh; Switzerland; France; Keweenaw Co., Michigan; etc.
*Fashioning. Uses*: faceting, cabochons, tumbling, beads, etc; *cleavage*: distinct basal, parting easily along fibre directions in massive material; *cutting angles*: crown 40°, pavilion 40°; *pleochroism*: weak; *heat sensitivity*: low.

**Laumontite $CaAl_2Si_4O_{12}.4H_2O$**
Laumontite crystallizes in the monoclinic system, forming square prisms or fibrous, columnar radiating masses. There is a perfect cleavage. The colour is white, grey, yellowish-pink or brown; there is a vitreous lustre. The mineral may become opaque and powdery on exposure to light. H 3–4; SG 2.2–2.4
*Occurrence.* Occurs in basalts, decomposed granites or in metallic vein deposits and metamorphic rocks.
*Localities.* From the Kilpatrick Hills and Kilmacolm, Strathclyde, Scotland; Montecatini, Tuscany, Italy; Pine Creek tungsten mine, Bishop, California; etc.

**Epistilbite $CaAl_2Si_6O_{16}.5H_2O$**
Epistilbite crystallizes in the monoclinic system, forming twinned prismatic crystals or radiated spherical aggregates. The twinning is interpenetrant cruciform; there is a perfect cleavage. The colour is white or pink, with a vitreous lustre. H 4; SG 2.2
*Occurrence.* Occurs in pegmatites with beryl at Bedford, New York; in basalt in Hawaii; from the Isle of Skye; etc.
*Treatment.* Clean with distilled water.

**Sarcolite $NaCa_4Al_3Si_5O_{19}$**
Sarcolite crystallizes in the tetragonal system in small crystals, flesh-pink in colour. Vitreous lustre. H 6; SG 2.9
*Localities.* From a volcanic rock on Mt. Vesuvius, Italy.
*Treatment.* Clean with distilled water.

**Cymrite $BaAlSi_3O_8OH$**
Cymrite crystallizes in the hexagonal system forming hexagonal prisms or fibrous masses. There is a perfect cleavage. It is colourless, dark green or brown with a satiny lustre. H 2–3; SG 3.4
*Occurrence.* Occurs at the Benallt manganese mine, Rhiw, Gwynedd, Wales; in copper deposits at Ruby Creek, Alaska; from San Benito Co., California.
*Treatment.* Clean with distilled water.

**Banalsite $Na_2BaAl_4Si_4O_{16}$**
Banalsite crystallizes in the orthorhombic system with a massive habit. The colour is white and the lustre vitreous. H 6; SG 3.0
*Localities.* Occurs in a manganese vein at Rhiw, Gwynedd, Wales.
*Treatment.* Clean with distilled water.

**Armenite $BaCa_2Al_6Si_8O_{28}.2H_2O$**
Armenite crystallizes in the hexagonal system as prismatic crystals coloured greyish-green, with a vitreous lustre. H 7.5; SG 2.8
*Localities.* Occurs with axinite, pyrrhotine and quartz from the silver-bearing calcite veins of the Armen mine, Kongsberg, Norway.
*Treatment.* Clean with distilled water.

**Carpholite $MnAl_2Si_2O_6(OH)_4$**
Carpholite crystallizes in the orthorhombic system as radiated tufts coloured yellow. There is a perfect cleavage. H 5–5.5; SG 2.9–3.0
*Localities.* Occurs near Neuville, Ardennes, Belgium; Harz Mts, Germany; Prilep, Macedonia, Yugoslavia; etc.
*Treatment.* Clean with dilute acid.

**Sursassite $Mn_5Al_4Si_5O_{21}.3H_2O$**
Sursassite crystallizes in the monoclinic system as fibrous masses coloured reddish-brown, with a silky lustre. H not measured; SG 3.3
*Localities.* Occurs with calcite and quartz in veins in iron-manganese ores near Woodstock, New Brunswick, Canada. Also from the manganese deposits at Val d'Err, Grisons, Switzerland.

**Ganophyllite $NaMn_3(Si, Al)_4O_{10}(OH)_4$**
Ganophyllite crystallizes in the monoclinic system as short prismatic or tabular crystals; rosettes or foliated forms are also found. There is a perfect cleavage. The colour is brown or brownish-yellow. H 4–4.5; SG 2.8–2.9
*Occurrence.* Occurs with baryte in manganese ores or with rhodonite, etc.
*Localities.* From manganese ores at Santa Clara Co., California; with rhodonite at Franklin, New Jersey; etc.
*Treatment.* Clean with distilled water.

**Ekmanite $(Fe, Mn, Mg)_6(Si, Al)_8$-$O_{20}(OH)_8.2H_2O$**
Ekmanite probably crystallizes in the orthorhombic system as foliated masses or as scales. There is a perfect cleavage.

*Left: Fine crystal of cordierite from Orijärvi, Finland. Cordierite is more frequently found as pebbles*

The colour is grey to black or green. H 2–2.5; SG 2.8
*Localities.* Occurs with pyrochroite in cavities in magnetite ore at Brunsjo, Sweden.
*Treatment.* Clean with distilled water.

**Stilpnomelane**
**$K(Fe, Mg, Al)_3Si_4O_{10}(OH)_2 . nH_2O$**
Stilpnomelane crystallizes in the triclinic system as thin foliated plates or coatings. There is a perfect cleavage and the colour is black to reddish-brown, sometimes dark green. The lustre is pearly. H 3–4; SG 2.5–2.9
*Occurrence.* Occurs in schists with chlorite, epidote and lawsonite; also in iron ore deposits.
*Localities.* From Canada; Greenland; USSR; Switzerland; Minnesota; Michigan; and many other places.
*Treatment.* Clean with distilled water.

**Cordierite $(Mg, Fe^{3+})_2Al_4Si_5O_{18}$**
Cordierite, sometimes called iolite, crystallizes in the orthorhombic system forming short prismatic crystals; it is more often found massive. Twinning is common. The colour is blue to brown or yellowish and sometimes strong pleochroism is displayed. There is a vitreous lustre. The streak is colourless. H 7–7.5; SG 2.5–2.8; RI 1.52–1.57
*Occurrence.* Occurs in thermally altered aluminium-rich rocks, gneisses, schists and pegmatites.
*Localities.* From Sri Lanka; Malagasy Republic; Guilford, Connecticut; and many other localities.
*Treatment.* Clean with dilute acid.
*Fashioning. Uses*: faceting, cabochons, beads, carvings, tumbling, etc.; *cleavage*: distinct brachypinacoidal: brittle; *cutting angles*: crown 40°–50°, pavilion 43°; *pleochroism*: strong; *heat sensitivity*: low.

**Staurolite**
**$(Fe, Mg)_2Al_9Si_4O_{23}(OH)$**
Staurolite crystallizes in the monoclinic system forming short prismatic crystals with cruciform twinning common. The colour is dark reddish-brown or yellowish with a resinous lustre. The streak is colourless or grey. H 7–7.5; SG 3.6–3.8
*Occurrence.* Occurs in mica schists with garnet, muscovite and kyanite.
*Localities.* Found in the Ticino, Switzerland; Brittany, France; Chesterfield, Hampshire Co., Massachusetts; and many other localities.
*Treatment.* Clean with dilute acid.
*Fashioning. Uses*: faceting or cabochons; *cleavage*: distinct brachypinacoidal; brittle; *cutting angles*: crown 40°, pavilion 40°; *pleochroism*: distinct; *heat sensitivity*: low.

**Chloritoid**
**$(Mg, Fe^{2+})_2Al_4Si_2O_{10}(OH)_4$**
Chloritoid crystallizes in the triclinic and monoclinic systems as pseudo-hexagonal tabular crystals; more commonly as foliated masses or as scales. Lamellar twinning is common and there is a perfect cleavage. It has a pearly lustre. The colour is dark grey or greenish to black. Closely related are sismondite

*Below left: Twinned crystals of staurolite from Antsirabe, Malagasy Republic. Staurolite is often called cross stone*

*Below: A staurolite crystal from the Italian Alps*

*Right: Chloritoid from Pregratten, Austria*

and ottrelite, and, reputedly, salmite and venasquite. H 6.5; SG 3.6
*Occurrence.* Occurs in phyllites, in mica schists or as a hydrothermal alteration product in lavas.
*Localities.* From the Tyrol, Austria; Deep River, North Carolina; Shetland Islands, Scotland; and many other localities.
*Treatment.* Clean with distilled water.

**Ferrocarpholite**
**$(Fe, Mg)Al_2Si_2O_6(OH)_4$**
Ferrocarpholite crystallizes in the orthorhombic system as prismatic crystals with a perfect cleavage. The colour is dark green. H 5.5; SG 3.0
*Localities.* Occurs with rutile and zircon in a quartz vein in the eastern Celebes; Calabria, Italy.
*Treatment.* Clean with distilled water.

**Yagiite**
**$(Na, K)_3Mg_4Al_6(Si, Al)_{12}O_{60}$**
Yagiite crystallizes in the hexagonal system and occurs as small grains in the Colomera iron meteorite.

**Pumpellyite**
**$Ca_2MgAl_2(SiO_4)(Si_2O_7)(OH)_2 . H_2O$**
Pumpellyite crystallizes in the monoclinic system as fibrous crystals or as flat plates. Twinning is common. The colour is green to brown, with a vitreous lustre. H 6; SG 3.2
*Occurrence.* Occurs in a wide range of igneous and metamorphic rocks.
*Localities.* In copper-bearing ores in Michigan; in glaucophane schists in California; from New Jersey; South Africa; Japan; USSR; Haiti; etc.
*Treatment.* Clean with distilled water.

**Idocrase**
**$Ca_{10}Mg_2Al_4(SiO_4)_5(Si_2O_7)_2(OH)_4$**
Sometimes known as vesuvianite, idocrase crystallizes in the tetragonal system as short prismatic crystals or as granular masses. The colour is greenish-yellow to brown, sometimes red, white or blue; the lustre is vitreous or resinous. The streak is white. Varieties include californite, which is translucent white or yellow; cyprine, which is blue and opaque; chrome-idocrase, bright green. H 6–7; SG 3.3–3.4; RI 1.71–1.73
*Occurrence.* Occurs in metamorphosed calcareous rocks and in veins in ultrabasic rocks.
*Localities.* From Mt. Vesuvius, Italy; Zermatt, Switzerland; Ala Valley, Piedmont, Italy; Lake Ladoga, Finland; Androscoggin Co., Maine; Franklin, New Jersey; Quebec and Ontario; USSR and elsewhere.
*Treatment.* Clean with distilled water.
*Fashioning. Uses*: faceting, cabochons, tumbling, etc; *cleavage*: indistinct prismatic; brittle; *cutting angles*: crown 40°, pavilion 40°; *dichroism*: fairly weak; *heat sensitivity*: low.

**Osumilite** **$(K, Na)(Mg, Fe^{2+})_2(Al, Fe^{3+})_3(Si, Al)_{12}O_{30} . H_2O$**
Osumilite crystallizes in the hexagonal system as short prismatic crystals, dark blue to black in colour, with a vitreous lustre. H not measured; SG 2.6
*Localities.* Occurs with feldspars and other minerals in andesite at MacKenzie Pass, Lane Co., Oregon; also from Sakkabira, Kagosima Prefecture, Kyushu, Japan.
*Treatment.* Clean with distilled water.

**Leucophane**
**$(Ca, Na)_2BeSi_2(O, F, OH)_7$**
Leucophane crystallizes in the orthorhombic system as pseudotetragonal crystals with twinning common; sometimes of penetration type. Also as spherules. There is a perfect cleavage and the colour is white to yellowish-green, with a vitreous lustre. H 4; SG 3.0
*Localities.* Occurs in nepheline–syenite pegmatites at Mont St. Hilaire, Quebec, Canada; Lovozero intrusion, Kola Peninsula, USSR; etc.
*Treatment.* Clean with dilute acid.

*Above right: A crystal of idocrase from Italy, showing prism and pyramid faces*

*Right: Idocrase crystals from Quetta, Baluchistan, Pakistan*

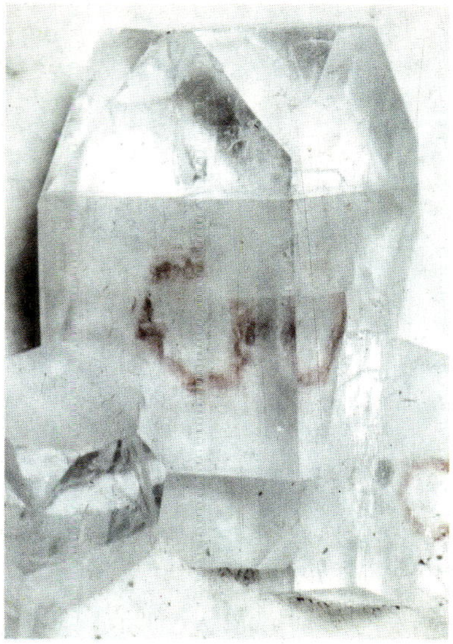

*Left: Apophyllite from Poona, India*

*Far left: Pseudocubic apophyllite. The crystal system is tetragonal. From Rio Grande do Sul, Brazil*

*Below left: Apophyllite crystals of tabular habit from Bolzano, Italy*

**Hsianghualite $Ca_3Li_2Be_3(SiO_4)_3F_2$**
Hsianghualite crystallizes in the cubic system as dodecahedral crystals or as granular masses. The colour is white, the lustre vitreous. H 6.5; SG 3.0
*Localities.* Occurs in phlogopite veins in metamorphosed limestone in Hunan Province, China.
*Treatment.* Clean with distilled water.

**Zeophyllite $Ca_4Si_3O_7(OH)_4F_2$**
Zeophyllite crystallizes in the triclinic system as plates or in spherical forms with a radiating foliated structure. There is a perfect cleavage. The colour is white. H 3; SG 2.7
*Localities.* Occurs with apophyllite in basalt at Alten Berg, Czechoslovakia.

**Cuspidine $Ca_4Si_2O_7(F, OH)_2$**
Cuspidine crystallizes in the monoclinic system as small spear-shaped crystals or as granular masses. Lamellar twinning occurs. The colour is white, grey, greenish or rose red, the lustre is vitreous. H 5–6; SG 2.8–3.0
*Localities.* In metamorphosed limestone at Crestmore, Riverside Co., California; with nasonite at Franklin, New Jersey; and at other localities.
*Treatment.* Clean with distilled water.

**Bultfonteinite $Ca_2SiO_2(OH, F)_4$**
Bultfonteinite crystallizes in the triclinic system as acicular crystals or in spherulitic masses. Twinning is common. The colour is pink or colourless. H 4.5; SG 2.7
*Localities.* Occurs with calcite and apophyllite at Bultfontein, Dutoitspan and Jagersfontein mines, Kimberley, South Africa.

**Apophyllite**
**$KCa_4Si_8O_{20}(F, OH).8H_2O$**
Apophyllite crystallizes in the tetragonal system as pseudocubic crystals or as granular masses. There is a perfect cleavage and the colour is white, grey or pale yellow, greenish or reddish. The lustre is vitreous or pearly and the streak is white. H 4.5–5; SG 2.3–2.4
*Occurrence.* Occurs in cavities in basalt, also in gneiss or limestone or as a low-temperature mineral in sulphide ores.

*Localities.* From the Isle of Skye, Scotland; Collinward, N. Ireland; Lake Superior copper mines, Michigan; Mexico; Brazil and elsewhere.
*Treatment.* Clean with distilled water.
*Fashioning. Uses*: faceting or cabochons; *cleavage*: highly perfect / / to basal pinacoid, perfect prismatic; brittle; *cutting angles*: crown 40°–50°, pavilion 43°; *pleochroism*: weak; *heat sensitivity*: fairly high, but unaffected by normal dopping temperatures.

**Combeite $Na_4Ca_3Si_6O_{16}(OH, F)_2$**
Combeite crystallizes in the hexagonal system as hexagonal prisms. They are colourless and have an SG of 2.8
*Localities.* Occurs with hornblende and other minerals in a nephelinite lava from Mt. Shaheru, Zaire.
*Treatment.* Clean with distilled water.

**Canasite $(Na, K)_5(Ca, Mn, Mg)_4(Si_2O_5)_5(OH, F)_3$**
Canasite crystallizes in the monoclinic system as grains with polysynthetic twinning and a perfect cleavage. The colour is greenish-yellow and the streak colourless. The lustre is vitreous. H not measured; SG 2.7
*Localities.* Occurs with lamprophyllite in pegmatite in the Khibina Tundra alkali massif, USSR.
*Treatment.* Clean with distilled water.

**Mosandrite**
**$(Na, Ca, Ce)_3Ti(SiO_4)_2F$**
Mosandrite crystallizes in the monoclinic system as long prismatic crystals with striations on the prism faces. Massive forms also encountered. Lamellar twinning occurs. The colour is yellowish-green to reddish-brown, with a vitreous lustre. H5; SG 2.9–3.5
*Occurrence.* Occurs in nepheline-syenites and associated pegmatites.
*Localities.* From Mont St. Hilaire, Quebec, Canada; Julianehaab, Greenland; Kola Peninsula, USSR; Transvaal, South Africa.
*Treatment.* Clean with distilled water.

**Hiortdahlite**
**$(Ca, Na)_{13}Zr_3Si_9(O, OH, F)_{33}$**
Hiortdahlite crystallizes in the triclinic system as flattened tabular crystals, often with polysynthetic twinning. The colour is light yellow to yellowish-brown, with a vitreous lustre. H 5.5; SG 3.3
*Occurrence.* Occurs in alkali rocks and pegmatites.
*Localities.* From Langesundfjord area, Norway; Mt. Somma, Italy; Iles de Los, Guinea; etc.
*Treatment.* Hiortdahlite should be cleaned with distilled water.

**Seidozerite**
**$Na_2(Zr, Ti, Mn)_2Si_2O_8F_2$**
Seidozerite crystallizes in the monoclinic system as radiating crystals or fibrous masses. There is a perfect cleavage. The colour is brownish-red, with a vitreous lustre. H 4–5; SG 3.5
*Localities.* Occurs in nepheline syenite pegmatites of the Louozero intrusion, Kola Peninsula, USSR.
*Treatment.* Seidozerite should be cleaned with distilled water.

**Rosenbuschite**
**$(Ca, Na)_3(Zr, Ti)Si_2O_8F$**
Rosenbuschite crystallizes in the triclinic system as fibrous masses. Crystals are prismatic, acicular, with a perfect cleavage and a silky lustre. The colour is grey or orange. H 5–6; SG 3.3
*Occurrence.* Occurs in nepheline-syenite deposits.

*Right: Prismatic topaz crystal showing prism and dome faces. From Siberia, USSR*

*Localities.* From the Kola Peninsula, USSR; Langesundfjord area, Norway; Red Hill, Moultonboro, New Hampshire.
*Treatment.* Clean with distilled water.

**Narsarsukite $Na_2(Ti, Fe)Si_4(O, F)_{11}$**
Narsarsukite crystallizes in the tetragonal system as prismatic crystals with a perfect cleavage. The colour is yellow, green, brown or colourless; the lustre is vitreous. H 6–7; SG 2.8
*Localities.* Occurs with quartz and aegirine in north-central Montana and in carbonatite at Mont St. Hilaire, Quebec, Canada; etc.
*Treatment.* Clean with distilled water.

**Sonolite $Mn_9(SiO_4)_4(OH, F)_2$**
Sonolite crystallizes in the monoclinic system as prismatic crystals or fine-grained masses. The colour is red or orange to brown. The lustre can be vitreous or dull. H 5.5; SG 3.8
*Localities.* Occurs with willemite, zincite, etc, at Franklin, New Jersey; and also in Japan.
*Treatment.* Clean with distilled water.

*Right: This is the most prized colour for topaz. The crystal shows prism and dome faces. From Brazil*

**Topaz $Al_2SiO_4(OH, F)_2$**
Topaz crystallizes in the orthorhombic system as prismatic crystals, often with well-developed terminations and a perfect cleavage; often found as water-worn pebbles. The colour is red, golden yellow, blue, brown, colourless or pink; there is a vitreous lustre. The streak is colourless. H 8; SG 3.4–3.5; RI 1.62–1.64
*Occurrence.* Occurs in pegmatites and quartz veins, contact zones and alluvial deposits.
*Localities.* From Minas Gerais, Brazil; Nigeria; San Diego Co., California; Rhodesia; Cornwall; Mourne Mts., Ireland; Urals, USSR; Burma; South-West Africa and elsewhere.
*Treatment.* Clean with dilute acid.
*Fashioning. Uses*: faceting, cabochons, tumbling, etc; *cleavage*: perfect // to basal pinacoid; brittle; *cutting angles*: crown 40°, pavilion 40°; *pleochroism*: distinct in deep colours; *heat sensitivity*: low.

**Leifite**
**$(NaH_3O)_2(Si, Al, Be, B)_7(O, F, OH)_{14}$**
Leifite crystallizes in the hexagonal system as striated colourless acicular crystals with a vitreous lustre. H 6; SG 2.6
*Localities.* Found in alkali pegmatites at Narsarsuk, Greenland.
*Treatment.* Clean with distilled water.

**Meliphane**
**$(Ca, Na)_2Be(Si, Al)_2(O, F)_7$**
Meliphane crystallizes in the tetragonal system as thin tabular crystals or lamellar aggregates with a vitreous lustre. There is a perfect cleavage. The colour is yellow or colourless. H 5–5.5; SG 3.0
*Localities.* Found in nepheline-syenite pegmatites at Julianehaab, Greenland; etc.
*Treatment.* Clean with distilled water.

**Götzenite**
**$(Ca, Na)_7(Ti, Al)_2Si_4O_{15}(F, OH)_3$**
Götzenite crystallizes in the triclinic system as colourless prismatic crystals. There is a perfect cleavage. H not measured; SG 3.1
*Localities.* Occurs in lava at Mt. Shaheru, Zaire.
*Treatment.* Clean with distilled water.

**Barytolamprophyllite**
**$Na_2(Ba, Sr)_2Ti_3(SiO_4)_4(OH, F)_2$**
Barytolamprophyllite crystallizes in the monoclinic system, and has a perfect cleavage. It is found as foliated aggregates and is dark brown. H2–3; SG 3.6
*Localities.* Occurs with nepheline, cancrinite, etc, in the Lovozero complex, Kola Peninsula, USSR.
*Treatment.* Clean with distilled water.

**Zunyite $Al_{13}Si_5O_{20}(OH, F)_{18}Cl$**
Zunyite crystallizes in the cubic system as tetrahedra or twinned octahedra. The colour is white or grey to pink, with a vitreous lustre. H 7; SG 2.8
*Occurrence.* Occurs in Colorado as a vein mineral or as an alteration product of feldspar, and at other localities.
*Treatment.* Clean with dilute acid.

**Pennaite**
Pennaite, a silicate and chloride of sodium, calcium, iron, manganese, titanium and zirconium, crystallizes in the monoclinic system as prismatic crystals with polysynthetic twinning. The colour is yellow to brown. H and SG not known.
*Localities.* Occurs with nepheline and other minerals on the Pocos de Caldas plateau, Brazil.
*Treatment.* Clean with distilled water.

**Beryllosodalite $Na_4BeAlSi_4O_{12}Cl$**
Beryllosodalite crystallizes in the tetragonal system as crypto-crystalline masses with a vitreous lustre. The colour is rose pink, bluish, greenish or white with a strong rose fluorescence under ultraviolet light. H about 4; SG 2.2
*Localities.* Occurs in pegmatites in the Kola Peninsula, USSR; and in a nepheline-syenite pegmatite at Tugtup agtakôrfia, Ilimaussaq, Greenland.
*Treatment.* Clean with distilled water.

**Tugtupite $Na_4BeAlSi_4O_{12}Cl$**
Tugtupite crystallizes in the tetragonal system in compact masses. The colour is pink or red with a bright red fluorescence under ultraviolet light. There is a vitreous lustre. H about 4; SG 2.3
*Localities.* Occurs in a nepheline-syenite pegmatite at Tugtup agtakôrfia, Ilimaussaq, Greenland.
*Treatment.* Clean with distilled water.
*Fashioning. Uses*: faceting or cabochons: *cutting angles*: crown 40°–50°, pavilion 43°; *dichroism*: distinct; *heat sensitivity*: low.

**Eudialyte $Na_4(Ca, Fe, Ce, Mn)_2ZrSi_6O_{17}(OH, Cl)_2$**
Eudialyte crystallizes in the hexagonal system as tabular crystals of trigonal habit with a vitreous lustre. The colour is yellow, brown or red with a colourless streak. Eucolite is a calcium-rich variety. H 5–5.5; SG 2.7–2.9
*Occurrence.* Occurs in nepheline-syenite deposits.
*Localities.* From Mont St. Hilaire, Quebec, Canada; Julianehaab, Greenland; Langesundfjord area, Norway; Kola Peninsula, USSR; Malagasy Republic; etc.
*Treatment.* Clean with distilled water.

**Nasonite $Ca_4Pb_6Si_6O_{21}Cl_2$**
Though nasonite crystallizes in the hexagonal system as prismatic crystals,

it more often occurs as granular masses. The colour is white and the lustre greasy. H 4; SG 5.5
*Localities.* Occurs with datolite, willemite and other minerals at Franklin, New Jersey; and also from Långban in Sweden.
*Treatment.* Clean with distilled water.

**Friedelite**
**$(Mn, Fe)_8Si_6O_{18}(OH, Cl)_4 . 3H_2O$**
Friedelite crystallizes in the hexagonal system as tabular crystals or lamellar aggregates; it has a perfect cleavage. The colour is pale pink to dark red or yellow, the lustre is vitreous. H 4–5; SG 3.0
*Localities.* Occurs with willemite and other minerals at Franklin, New Jersey; Adervielle, France; and at some other localities.
*Treatment.* Clean with distilled water.

*Left: Tilleyite from California*

**Pyrosmalite**
**$(Mn, Fe)_{14}Si_3O_7(OH, Cl)_6$**
Pyrosmalite crystallizes in the hexagonal system as hexagonal prisms or foliated masses. There is a perfect cleavage. The colour is dark green to pale brown, with a pearly lustre. H 4–4.5; SG 3.1–3.2
*Localities.* Occurs with calcite and pyroxene at Broken Hill, New South Wales; Nordmark and Dannemora, Sweden.
*Treatment.* Clean with distilled water.

**Manganpyrosmalite**
**$(Mn, Fe)_8Si_6O_{15}(OH, Cl)_{10}$**
Manganpyrosmalite crystallizes in the hexagonal system as granular masses; it has a perfect cleavage. The colour is brown, the lustre pearly. H 4.5; SG 3.1
*Localities.* Occurs with franklinite and other minerals at Franklin, New Jersey.
*Treatment.* Clean with distilled water.

**Muirite**
**$Ba_{10}Ca_2MnTiSi_{10}O_{30}(OH, Cl, F)_{10}$**
Muirite crystallizes in the tetragonal system as tetragonal crystals or as grains. The colour is orange, with a vitreous lustre. H 2.5; SG 3.8
*Localities.* Occurs in metamorphic rock in Fresno Co., California.
*Treatment.* Clean with distilled water.

**Tilleyite $Ca_5Si_2O_7(CO_3)_2$**
Tilleyite crystallizes in the monoclinic system as masses or grains with a perfect cleavage. The colour is white or colourless. H not known; SG 2.8
*Localities.* Occurs in thermally metamorphosed limestones at Carlingford, Ireland; Crestmore, Riverside Co., California.
*Treatment.* Clean with distilled water.

**Spurrite $Ca_5Si_2O_8CO_3$**
Spurrite crystallizes in the monoclinic system as granular masses with a vitreous lustre. The colour is grey or pale blue. H 5; SG 3.0
*Localities.* Occurs as a contact mineral at Scawt Hill, N. Ireland; and other localities.
*Treatment.* Store in a sealed container.

**Scawtite $Ca_7Si_6O_{18}(CO_3) . 2H_2O$**
Scawtite crystallizes in the monoclinic system as thin tabular crystals in

*Above left: Eudialyte in a specimen from the Kola Peninsula, USSR*

*Left: Pyrosmalite from Norway. The hexagonal prismatic form is clear*

*Above: Datolite crystals from New Jersey*

divergent groups or as grains. Colourless with a vitreous lustre. H 4.5–5; SG 2.7
*Localities.* Occurs at Scawt Hill, N. Ireland; and other localities.
*Treatment.* Clean with distilled water.

**Carletonite**
**$KNa_4Ca_4Si_8O_{18}(CO_3)_4(F, OH) . H_2O$**
Carletonite crystallizes in the tetragonal system as masses; it has a perfect cleavage. The colour is pink or blue; the lustre is vitreous to waxy. H 4–4.5; SG 2.4
*Localities.* Occurs with calcite, fluorite and other minerals at Mont St. Hilaire, Quebec, in a nepheline-syenite.

**Kainosite**
**$Ca_2(Ce, Y)_2(SiO_4)_3(CO_3) . H_2O$**
Kainosite (or cenosite) crystallizes in the orthorhombic system as prismatic or pseudotetragonal crystals with a vitreous lustre coloured yellow to brown, or light red to colourless. H 5–6; SG 3.3–3.6
*Localities.* Occurs in granite pegmatites at Cotopaxi, Colorado; at the uranium mine at Bancroft, Ontario; Val Curnera, Switzerland; and also from some other localities.
*Treatment.* Clean with distilled water.

**Manandonite**
**$LiAl_4(AlBSi_2O_{10})(OH)_8$**
Manandonite crystallizes in the monoclinic system as lamellar aggregates and crusts or plates. It has a perfect cleavage and is colourless. It has a pearly lustre. H about 2.5; SG 2.9
*Localities.* Occurs with tourmaline and other minerals in pegmatite at Mt. Bity, on the Manandona River in the Malagasy Republic.
*Treatment.* Clean with distilled water.

**Searlesite $NaBSi_2O_6 . H_2O$**
Searlesite crystallizes in the monoclinic system as prismatic crystals or radiating fibrous spherulites. There is a perfect cleavage. The colour is white or light brown. H not known, but soft; SG 2.4
*Localities.* Occurs in clay at Searles Lake, San Bernardino Co., California, and elsewhere in the US.
*Treatment.* Clean with distilled water.

**Reedmergnerite $NaBSi_3O_8$**
Reedmergnerite crystallizes in the triclinic system as colourless stubby prisms with a perfect cleavage and a vitreous lustre. H 6–6.5; SG 2.7
*Localities.* Occurs in unmetamorphosed dolomitic oil shales of the Green River formation in Utah.
*Treatment.* Clean with distilled water.

**Stillwellite (Ce, La, Ca)$BSiO_5$**
Stillwellite crystallizes in the hexagonal system as rhombohedral crystals or compact masses. The colour is light blue, brown or yellow, and the lustre is resinous. H not known; SG 4.6
*Localities.* Occurs with garnet and uraninite in Queensland, Australia: Langesundfjord area, Norway.
*Treatment.* Clean with distilled water.

**Danburite $CaB_2Si_2O_8$**
Danburite crystallizes in the orthorhombic system as prismatic crystals with diamond-shaped cross-section, vertically striated; also as granular masses. They are colourless, yellow, gold, pale pink or brown, with a vitreous lustre. The streak is colourless. H 7; SG 3.0; RI 1.63, 1.64
*Localities.* Occurs with feldspar in dolomite at Danbury, Fairfield Co., Connecticut; from Charcas, San Luis Potosi, Mexico; Uri, Switzerland; fine yellows from Mogok, Burma.
*Treatment.* Clean with distilled water.
*Fashioning. Uses*: faceting or cabochons; *cleavage*: none; *cutting angles*: crown 40°, pavilion 40°; *pleochroism*: weak; *heat sensitivity*: very low.

**Datolite $CaBSiO_4OH$**
Datolite crystallizes in the monoclinic system as short prismatic crystals or as granular masses. The colour is white, colourless, pale yellow, pale green or reddish-brown. There is a vitreous lustre. The streak is colourless. H 5–5.5; SG 2.8–3.0; RI 1.62, 1.67
*Occurrence.* Occurs in cavities in basic igneous rocks associated with prehnite and calcite; may also occur in metallic veins, in granites and in other rocks.
*Localities.* From Fife, Scotland; Norway; Italy; New Jersey; the copper area of Keweenaw, Michigan; Riverside and San Bernardino Counties, California; etc.
*Treatment.* Clean with distilled water.
*Fashioning. Uses*: faceting or cabochons; *cleavage*: not significant; brittle; *cutting angles*: crown 40°, pavilion 40°; *pleochroism*: weak; *heat sensitivity*: low.

**Bakerite**
**$Ca_4B_4(BO_4)(SiO_4)_3(OH)_3 . H_2O$**
Bakerite crystallizes in the monoclinic system as prismatic crystals and occurs in nodules and veins. The crystals are white or colourless, and have a vitreous lustre. H 4.5; SG 2.9
*Localities.* Occurs in an altered volcanic rock in Upper Baker Canyon, Death Valley, and elsewhere in California.
*Treatment.* Clean with distilled water.

**Howlite $Ca_2B_5SiO_9(OH)_5$**
Howlite crystallizes in the monoclinic system as tabular crystals or compact masses. The colour is white, though the mineral is frequently stained to imitate turquoise. It has a vitreous lustre. H 3.5; SG 2.4
*Localities.* Occurs with colemanite in Los Angeles Co., the Mohave desert, San Bernardino Co., and elsewhere in California; also in Nova Scotia.
*Treatment.* Clean with distilled water.
*Fashioning. Uses*: cabochons, tumbling, carving, intaglios, beads, etc; *cleavage*: none, quite tough; *heat sensitivity*: fairly low.

*Right: Fine crystals of axinite from Bourg d'Oisans, France. Axinite is strongly pleochroic*

*Left: Superb tourmaline crystals from Elba*

*Below left: Fine pink prismatic tourmaline crystals, showing the vertical striation of the prism faces*

**Harkerite** $Ca_{48}Mg_{16}Al_3(BO_3)_{13}$-$(CO_3)_{19}(SiO_4)_{14}(OH)_2Cl_2.2H_2O$
Harkerite crystallizes in the cubic system as colourless octahedra with a vitreous lustre. H not known; SG 2.9
*Localities.* Occurs at the contact of dolomitic limestone with Tertiary granite at Broadford, Isle of Skye, Scotland.
*Treatment.* Harkerite should be cleaned with distilled water.

**Cappelenite** $(Ba, Ca, Ce, Na)_3$-$(Y, Ce, La)_6(BO_3)_6Si_3O_9$
Cappelenite crystallizes in the hexagonal system as prismatic crystals coloured greenish-brown. H 6; SG 4.4
*Localities.* Occurs in a nepheline-syenite on an island in Langesundfjord, Norway.
*Treatment.* Cappelenite should be cleaned with distilled water.

**Dumortierite** $Al_7O_3(BO_3)(SiO_4)_3$
Dumortierite crystallizes in the orthorhombic system as granular or fibrous masses usually coloured blue to violet, or pink to brown. Their lustre is vitreous or dull. The streak is white. H 8.5; SG 3.4
*Occurrence.* Occurs in aluminium-rich metamorphic rocks and sometimes in pegmatites.
*Localities.* From the Malagasy Republic; Arizona, Colorado, California; and elsewhere.
*Treatment.* Remove iron stains with oxalic acid.
*Fashioning. Uses*: faceting (rare), cabochons, carvings, beads, tumbling, etc; *cleavage*: distinct macropinacoidal; *cutting angles*: crown 40°, pavilion 40°, (estimated); *pleochroism*: strong in transparent material, not significant in massive material; *heat sensitivity*: low.

**Holtite** $(Al, Sb, Ta)_7(B, Si)_4O_{18}$
Holtite crystallizes in the orthorhombic system as pseudohexagonal crystals; it forms pebbles and twinning occurs. The colour is brown or orange to green with a bright yellow fluorescence under longwave ultraviolet light. There is a vitreous lustre. H 8.5; SG 3.9
*Localities.* Occurs with tantalite at Greenbushes, Western Australia.
*Treatment.* Clean with distilled water.

**Painite** $Al_{20}Ca_4BSiO_{38}$
Painite crystallizes in the hexagonal system. The only specimen known is in the British Museum (Natural History), and this appears to be pseudo-orthorhombic. It is very dark red and has a vitreous lustre. H about 8; SG 4.0
*Localities.* From Mogok, Burma.
*Treatment.* Clean with distilled water.

**Leucosphenite** $BaNa_4Ti_2B_2Si_{10}O_{30}$
Leucosphenite crystallizes in the monoclinic system as tabular crystals with twinning common. The colour is white, colourless or pale blue. There is a vitreous lustre. H 6.5; SG 3.0
*Localities.* Occurs with shortite and analcime in the Green River formation, Wyoming and Utah; Mont St. Hilaire, Quebec; etc.
*Treatment.* Clean with dilute acid.

**Axinite**
$(Ca, Mn, Fe, Mg)_3Al_2BSi_4O_{15}(OH)$
Axinite's wedge-shaped tabular crystals belong to the triclinic system; the mineral also occurs in lamellar masses The colour is violet-brown or colourless to yellow, and the lustre is vitreous. The streak is colourless. Varieties include tinzenite, with more manganese than iron, and with calcium up to 1.5%; ferroaxinite, with more iron than manganese, and with calcium above 1.5%; and manganaxinite, with more manganese than iron, and with calcium above 1.5%. H 6.5–7; SG 3.3–3.4; RI 1.68, 1.69
*Occurrence.* In areas of contact metamorphism or metasomatism with calcite and quartz, etc.
*Localities.* From Baja California, Mexico; Bourg d'Oisans, Isère, France; Cornwall; tinzenite from Switzerland; fine yellow crystals, though very small, from Franklin, New Jersey; etc.
*Treatment.* Clean with dilute acid.
*Fashioning. Uses*: faceting or cabochons; *cleavage*: distinct brachypinacoidal; brittle; *cutting angles*: crown 40°, pavilion 40°; *pleochroism* strong; *heat sensitivity*: low.

**Kornerupine**
$Mg_3Al_6(Si, Al, B)_5O_{21}(OH)$
Kornerupine crystallizes in the orthorhombic system as prismatic crystals with a vitreous lustre. They may be dark green, emerald green, pink, yellow, brown colourless or black. H 6–7 SG 3.3–5.0; RI 1.66, 1.69
*Localities.* Occurs with quartz, orthoclase feldspar and other minerals at Lac Ste-Marie, Gatineau Co., Quebec; from Itrongay, Malagasy Republic, where it is found with zircon and spinel; a vanadium-coloured (apple-green) variety from Kenya; from the gem gravels of Sri Lanka; etc.
*Treatment.* Clean with dilute acid.
*Fashioning. Uses*: faceting or cabochons; *cleavage*: distinct to perfect prismatic; brittle; *cutting angles*: crown 40°, pavilion 40°; *pleochroism*: distinct; *heat sensitivity*: low.

**Tourmaline**
$(Na, Ca)(Li, Mg, Fe^{2+}, Al)_3$-$(Al, Fe^{3+})_6B_3Si_6O_{27}(O, OH, F)_4$
Tourmaline crystallizes in the hexagonal system as prismatic crystals with a 'rounded triangular' cross-section and vertically striated. They have a vitreous lustre. Colours include red (rubellite), blue (indicolite), yellow, brown, green, black, colourless or parti-coloured. H 7; SG 3.0–3.1; RI 1.62, 1.64; double refraction 0.018
*Occurrence.* Occurs in granite pegmatites and metamorphic rocks.
*Localities.* From San Diego Co., California; Sri Lanka; Brazil; Mozambique; Malagasy Republic; Maine; etc.
*Treatment.* Clean with dilute acid.
*Fashioning. Uses*: faceting, cabochons, carvings, beads, tumbling, etc; *cleavage*: not significant; brittle; *cutting angles*: crown 40°, pavilion 40°; *dichroism*: strong; *heat sensitivity*: fairly high, keep the stone cool during cutting or polishing.

**Homilite** $(Ca, Fe)_3B_2Si_2O_{10}$
Homilite crystallizes in the monoclinic system as brown or black tabular crystals. H 5; SG 3.4
*Localities.* Occurs on islands in the Langesundfjord, Norway.
*Treatment.* Clean with distilled water.

**Serendibite** $Ca_4(Mg, Fe, Al)_6$-$(Al, Fe)_9(Si, Al)_6B_3O_{40}$
Serendibite crystallizes in the triclinic system as granular masses coloured

*Right: Lomonosovite in a nepheline syenite*

various shades of blue and showing polysynthetic twinning. They have a vitreous lustre. H 6.5–7; SG 3.4
*Localities.* Occurs as a contact mineral in limestone from Crestmore, Riverside Co., California; Tanzania; Sri Lanka; etc.
*Treatment.* Serendibite should be cleaned with dilute acid.

**Grandidierite $(Mg, Fe)Al_3BSiO_9$**
Grandidierite crystallizes in the orthorhombic system as elongated crystals or as masses. There is a perfect cleavage. The colour is greenish-blue, the lustre vitreous. H 7.5; SG 2.9
*Localities.* Occurs in pegmatites in the Malagasy Republic.
*Treatment.* Grandidierite should be cleaned with dilute acid.

**Hyalotekite**
**$(Pb, Ca, Ba)_4BSi_6O_{17}(OH, F)$**
Hyalotekite probably crystallizes in the orthorhombic system as crystalline masses coloured white or grey, with a vitreous lustre. H 5–5.5; SG 3.8
*Localities.* Occurs with barylite at Långban, Sweden.
*Treatment.* Clean with distilled water.

**Melanocerite $Ce_4CaBSi_2O_{12}(OH)$**
Melanocerite crystallizes in the hexagonal system as rhombohedral crystals or compact masses. The colour is brown or black, the lustre is resinous. H 6; SG 4.1–4.2
*Localities.* Occurs in alkali pegmatites at the Cardiff uranium mine, Wilberforce, Ontario; Langesundfjord, Norway; and elsewhere.
*Treatment.* Melanocerite should be cleaned with distilled water.

**Tritomite $(Y, Ca, La, Fe)_5(Si, B, Al)_3(O, OH, F)_{13}$**
Tritomite crystallizes in the hexagonal system as compact masses or grains coloured dark green, reddish-brown or black. H 3.5–6.5; SG 3.0–3.4
*Localities.* Occurs with magnetite and zircon in a granite pegmatite in Sussex Co., New Jersey and associated with red apatite, diopside and purple fluorite at Cardiff, Ontario.
*Treatment.* Clean with distilled water.

**Kolbeckite $ScPO_4 . 2H_2O$**
Kolbeckite crystallizes in the orthorhombic system as prismatic crystals coloured yellow or blue or colourless. They have a vitreous lustre. H 5; SG 2.4
*Localities.* Occurs with wardite in altered variscite nodules at Fairfield, Utah, and with silver ore from Felsöbánya, Romania.
*Treatment.* Clean with distilled water.

**Viséite**
**$NaCa_5Al_{10}Si_3P_5O_{30}(OH,F)_{18} . 16H_2O$**
Viséite crystallizes in the cubic system in masses, white or bluish-white in colour. Vitreous lustre. H 3–4; SG 2.2
*Localities.* Occurs with delvauxite at Visé, Belgium.
*Treatment.* Clean with distilled water.

**Lomonosovite**
**$Na_8(Mn, Fe, Ca, Mg)Ti_3Si_4P_2O_{24}$**
Lomonosovite crystallizes in the triclinic system as laminated tabular crystals with a perfect cleavage. The colour is dark brown to black or reddish-violet, the lustre is vitreous. H 3–4; SG 3.1
*Localities.* Occurs with hackmanite and other minerals in pegmatites in syenite, Kola Peninsula, USSR.
*Treatment.* Clean with distilled water.

**Steenstrupine $CeNaMnSi_3O_9$**
Steenstrupine crystallizes in the hexagonal system as rhombohedral crystals or masses coloured reddish-brown or black. H 5; SG 3.1–3.6
*Localities.* Occurs in nepheline-sodalite syenite pegmatites at Julianehaab, Greenland; Kola Peninsula, USSR.
*Treatment.* Clean with distilled water.

**Britholite**
**$(Ca, Y)_5(SiO_4, PO_4)_3(OH, F)$**
Britholite crystallizes in the hexagonal system as hexagonal crystals black in colour, with an adamantine lustre. H 5; SG 4.2
*Localities.* Occurs in pegmatite in the Abukuma Range, Iisaka, Fukushima Prefecture, Japan, and in the USSR.
*Treatment.* Clean with distilled water.

**Wilkeite**
**$Ca_5(SiO_4, PO_4, SO_4)_3(O, OH, F)$**
Wilkeite crystallizes in the hexagonal system and forms masses or rounded crystals coloured pale pink or yellow. Vitreous lustre. H about 5; SG 3.1–3.2
*Localities.* Occurs in blue calcite in marble at Crestmore, Riverside Co., California, etc.
*Treatment.* Clean with distilled water.

**Ardennite**
**$Mn_5Al_5(As, V)O_4Si_5O_{20}(OH)_2 . 2H_2O$**
Ardennite crystallizes in the orthorhombic system as crystalline aggregates. It has a perfect cleavage. The colour is yellow to brown or black. H 6–7; SG 3.6
*Localities.* Occurs with calcite and cuprosklodowskite in a limestone at Grants, New Mexico; the Ardennes, Belgium; Madhya Pradesh, India; etc.
*Treatment.* Clean with distilled water.

**Macgovernite**
**$Mn_9Mg_4Zn_2As_2Si_2O_{17}(OH)_{14}$**
Macgovernite crystallizes in the hexagonal system, forming light- to reddish-brown granular masses with a pearly lustre. Cleavage perfect. H not known; SG 3.7
*Localities.* Occurs with franklinite and other minerals at Franklin, New Jersey.
*Treatment.* Macgovernite should be cleaned with distilled water.

**Schallerite**
**$(Mn, Fe)_8Si_6As(O, OH, Cl)_{26}$**
Schallerite crystallizes in the hexagonal system as reddish-brown granular masses, with a waxy or pearly lustre. H about 5; SG 3.3
*Localities.* Occurs with calcite and other minerals at Franklin, New Jersey.
*Treatment.* Clean with distilled water.

**Yeatmanite**
**$(Mn, Zn)_{13}Sb_2Si_4Zn_2O_{28}$**
Yeatmanite crystallizes in the triclinic system as brown pseudo-orthorhombic crystals with a perfect cleavage. H 4; SG 5.0
*Localities.* Occurs embedded in willemite at Franklin, New Jersey.
*Treatment.* Yeatmanite should be cleaned with distilled water.

**Langbanite $Mn_4^{2+}Mn_3^{3+}Sb^{5+}Si_2O_{24}$**
Langbanite crystallizes in the hexagonal system as prismatic crystals which are

Left: Murmanite from the Kola Peninsula, USSR, a classic mineral locality

black with a metallic lustre. H 6.5; SG 4.6–4.8
*Localities.* Occurs in ores at Langban, Sweden.
*Treatment.* Clean with distilled water.

**Chapmanite $Fe_2Sb(SiO_4)_2(OH)$**
Chapmanite crystallizes in the orthorhombic system as compact olive-green or deep yellow masses with a greenish-yellow streak. H up to 2.5; SG 3.6–3.7
*Localities.* Occurs with silver at the Keeley Mine, Cobalt, Ontario; from Durango, Mexico; with quartz at Braunsdorf, E. Germany.
*Treatment.* Clean with distilled water.

**Epistolite**
**$Na_2(Nb, Ti)_2Si_2O_9 . nH_2O$**
Epistolite crystallizes in the monoclinic system as rectangular plates with a perfect cleavage or as lamellar aggregates. The colour is white, grey, yellow or brown; the lustre is pearly. H 1–1.5; SG 2.6–2.8
*Localities.* Occurs in alkali pegmatites in the Julianehaab area, Greenland, and the Kola Peninsula, USSR.
*Treatment.* Clean with distilled water.

**Murmanite**
**$Na_2(Ti, Nb)_2Si_2O_9 . H_2O$**
Murmanite crystallizes in the monoclinic system as aggregates of platy crystals with a perfect cleavage and bright pink in colour. H 2–3; SG 2.7–2.8
*Localities.* Occurs in alkali pegmatites and nepheline-syenites, Kola Peninsula, USSR.
*Treatment.* Clean with distilled water.

**Fersmanite**
**$(Na, Ca)_2(Ti, Nb)Si(O, F)_6$**
Fersmanite crystallizes in the monoclinic system as pseudotetragonal crystals coloured light to dark brown with a white streak. They have a vitreous lustre. H 5–5.5; SG 3.4
*Localities.* Occurs in nepheline-syenite pegmatites, Kola Peninsula, USSR.
*Treatment.* Clean with distilled water.

**Nenadkevichite**
**$(Na, Ca)(Nb, Ti)Si_2O_7 . 2H_2O$**
Nenadkevichite probably crystallizes in the orthorhombic system and forms dark brown to rose-coloured masses. The streak is rose. H about 5; SG 2.8
*Localities.* Occurs in alkali pegmatites, Kola Peninsula, USSR.
*Treatment.* Clean with distilled water.

**Wöhlerite**
**$NaCa_2(Zr, Nb)Si_2O_8(O, OH, F)$**
Wöhlerite crystallizes in the monoclinic system as prismatic crystals or as grains. The colour is light to dark yellow or brown with a yellowish-white streak. H 5.5–6; SG 3–4
*Localities.* Occurs in alkali rocks and pegmatites in the Langesundfjord area, Norway; Kola Peninsula, USSR.
*Treatment.* Clean with distilled water.

Far left: Ardennite from the Ardennes, Belgium

Left: Wöhlerite from the Langesundfjord, Norway

*Right: Crystals of fergusonite in quartz from Itterby, Sweden*

**Låvenite**
**$(Na, Ca, Mn)_3(Zr, Ti, Fe)(SiO_4)_2F$**
Låvenite crystallizes in the monoclinic system as prismatic crystals with a perfect cleavage; sometimes as radial aggregates. It is colourless or light yellow to brown with a vitreous lustre. H 6; SG 3.5
*Localities.* Occurs in alkali rocks and pegmatites in the Langesundfjord area, Norway; Kola Peninsula, USSR; and in other localities.
*Treatment.* Clean with distilled water.

**Roeblingite**
**$Pb_2Ca_7Si_6O_{14}(OH)_{10}(SO_4)_2$**
Roeblingite crystallizes in the monoclinic system; cleavage is perfect. It forms compact white or pink masses with a dull lustre. H 3; SG 3.4
*Localities.* Occurs with garnet, axinite and other minerals at Franklin, New Jersey, and in Sweden.
*Treatment.* Clean with distilled water.

**Afghanite** **$(Na, Ca, K)_{12}$-$(Si, Al)_{16}O_{34}(Cl, SO_4, CO_3)_4 . H_2O$**
Afghanite crystallizes in the hexagonal system; it has a perfect cleavage. It forms blue masses. H 5.5–6; SG 2.5
*Localities.* Occurs in the lapis-lazuli mine at Sar-e-Sang, Badakshan, Afghanistan.
*Treatment.* Clean with distilled water.

**Thaumasite**
**$Ca_3Si(OH)_6(CO_3)(SO_4) . 12H_2O$**
Thaumasite crystallizes in the hexagonal system as compact white or colourless masses with a vitreous lustre. Crystals are acicular. H 3.5; SG 1.9
*Localities.* Occurs with spurrite at Crestmore, Riverside Co., California; Paterson, New Jersey; Långban, Sweden; etc.
*Treatment.* Clean with distilled water.

## Niobates and Tantalates

**Lueshite $NaNbO_3$**
Lueshite crystallizes in the orthorhombic system as cubes with striated faces. The colour is black. H 5.5; SG 4.4
*Localities.* Occurs on a yellow mica at Lueshe, Zaire.

**Rankamaite** **$(Na, K, Pb, Li)_3$-$(Ta, Nb, Al)_{11}(O, OH)_{30}$**
Rankamaite crystallizes in the orthorhombic system and is found as water-worn pebbles coloured white. H 3–4; SG 5.5
*Localities.* Occurs with simpsonite, cassiterite and other minerals at Mumba, Kivu, Zaire.
*Treatment.* Clean with distilled water.

**Microlite**
**$(Ca, Na, Fe)_2(Ta, Nb)_2(O, OH, F)_7$**
Microlite, a member of the pyrochlore group, crystallizes in the cubic system as octahedra or masses. The colour is pale yellow to reddish-brown, sometimes emerald-green; the lustre is vitreous. H 5–5.5; SG 4.3–5.7
*Occurrence.* Occurs in pegmatites with lepidolite and spodumene.
*Localities.* From Greenland; Norway; Malagasy Republic; fine crystals at the Rutherford mine, Amelia, Virginia; southern California; and elsewhere.
*Treatment.* Clean with dilute acid.
*Fashioning. Uses*: faceting or cabochons; *cutting angles*: crown 40°–50°, pavilion 37°–40°; *heat sensitivity*: low.

**Pandaite**
**$(Ba, Sr)_2(Nb, Ti)_2(O, OH)_7$**
Pandaite, a member of the pyrochlore group, crystallizes in the cubic system as small octahedra with cube faces also present. The colour is yellowish to light green or grey. H 4.5–5; SG 4.0
*Localities.* Occurs in a biotite-rich rock at Panda Hill, Tanzania.
*Treatment.* Clean with distilled water.

**Simpsonite $Al_4Ta_3O_{13}OH$**
Simpsonite crystallizes in the hexagonal system as tabular crystals or crystalline masses. The colour is yellow, brown or colourless; a yellow, blue or white fluorescence may be observed under ultra-violet light. There is a vitreous lustre. H 7–7.5; SG 5.9–6.8
*Occurrence.* Occurs in granite pegmatites.
*Localities.* From Rio Grande do Norte, Brazil; Kola Peninsula, USSR; the Mdara mine, Bikita, Rhodesia; and from some other localities.
*Treatment.* Clean with oxalic acid to remove iron stains.

**Thoreaulite $SnTa_2O_7$**
Thoreaulite crystallizes in the monoclinic system as prismatic crystals, sometimes with lamellar twinning. They have a perfect cleavage and an adamantine to resinous lustre. The colour is brown or yellow with a yellow or greenish streak. H 5.5–6; SG 7.6–7.9
*Occurrence.* Occurs in granite pegmatites.
*Localities.* From Maniema, Kivu, Zaire; Sebeia, Rwanda; USSR.
*Treatment.* Clean with distilled water.

**Stibiotantalite $Sb(Ta, Nb)O_4$**
Stibiotantalite crystallizes in the orthorhombic system as prismatic crystals sometimes with polysynthetic twinning. The colour is dark brown to yellowish-brown or red, and the lustre is vitreous. H 5–5.5; SG 7.3
*Localities.* Occurs with pink tourmaline, lepidolite, morganite and other minerals in a pegmatite at Mesa Grande, San Diego Co., California; fine crystals from the Muiane pegmatite, Ribaue-Alto Ligonha pegmatite, Mozambique; etc.
*Treatment.* Clean with dilute acid.
*Fashioning. Uses*: faceting or cabochons; *cleavage*: perfect, macropinacoidal; *cutting angles*: crown 30°–40°, pavilion 37°–40°; *heat sensitivity*: fairly high.

**Bismutotantalite**
**$(Bi, Sb)(Ta, Nb)O_4$**
Bismutotantalite crystallizes in the orthorhombic system as prismatic crystals; also found as water-worn pebbles. There is a perfect cleavage. The colour is brown to black with a yellow-brown streak; there is an adamantine lustre. H 5; SG 8.5
*Localities.* Occurs in pegmatites with tourmaline and cassiterite at Gamba Hill, south-west Uganda; as pebbles from Acari, Campina Grande, Brazil.
*Treatment.* Clean with dilute acid.

**Tantalite $(Fe, Mn)(Ta, Nb)_2O_6$**
Tantalite crystallizes in the orthorhombic system as tabular crystals or aggregates. The colour is black or brown with a reddish-brown streak and a metallic lustre. H 6–6.5; SG 8.2
*Occurrence.* Occurs in granite pegmatites with quartz, spodumene and other minerals.
*Localities.* From Canada; USSR; Rhodesia; Finland; South Dakota; etc.
*Treatment.* Clean with dilute acid.

**Columbite $(Fe, Mn)(Nb, Ta)_2O_6$**
Columbite crystallizes in the orthorhombic system as tabular crystals or as aggregates or compact masses. The colour is brown or black with a streak of the same colour, and the lustre is metallic. H 6; SG 5.1
*Occurrence.* Occurs in granite pegmatites.
*Localities.* From Canada; Brazil; Argentina; California; Virginia; and elsewhere.
*Treatment.* Clean with dilute acid.

**Tapiolite**
**$(Fe, Mn)(Ta, Nb)_2O_6$**
Tapiolite crystallizes in the tetragonal system as prismatic crystals with some polysynthetic twinning. The colour is black with a black or brown streak and there is a metallic lustre. H 6–6.5; SG 7.8
*Occurrence.* Occurs in granite pegmatites.
*Localities.* From Morocco; USSR; Western Australia; South Dakota; etc.
*Treatment.* Clean with dilute acid.

**Fergusonite**
**$(Y, Er, Ce, Fe)(Nb, Ta, Ti)O_4$**
Fergusonite crystallizes in the tetragonal system as prismatic crystals or as grains. They have a vitreous lustre. The colour is brown to black; the streak may be yellow, grey or brown. H 5.5–6.5; SG 5.4
*Occurrence.* Occurs in granite pegmatites.
*Localities.* From Greenland; USSR; San Diego Co., California.

**Pyrochlore**
**$(Na, Ca, U)_2(Nb, Ta, Ti)_2O_6(OH, F)$**
Pyrochlore crystallizes in the cubic system as octahedra or granular masses. The colour is yellow, red or brown, with a vitreous lustre. H 5–5.5; SG 4.5
*Occurrence.* Occurs in carbonatites, pegmatites and in nepheline-syenites.
*Localities.* From St. Peter's Dome, El Paso Co., Colorado; Oka, Quebec; the variety ellsworthite (containing uranium) from Hybla, Hastings Co., Ontario, and the variety hatchettolite, also with uranium, from the Woodcox mine in the same area. Good crystals from Mbeya, Tanzania, and elsewhere.
*Treatment.* Clean with dilute acid.

**Fersmite** **$(Ca, Ce, Na)(Nb, Ti, Fe, Al)_2(O, OH, F)_6$**
Fersmite crystallizes in the orthorhombic system as prismatic crystals with striations on the prism faces. The colour is dark brown or black with a greyish-brown streak; there is a resinous lustre. H 4–4.5; SG 4.7–4.8
*Localities.* Occurs in a marble in Ravalli Co., Montana; from pegmatites in the Central Urals, USSR.
*Treatment.* Clean with dilute acid.

**Polymignite**
**$(Ca, Fe, Y, Th)(Nb, Ti, Ta)O_4$**
Polymignite crystallizes in the orthorhombic system as prismatic crystals with vertical striations and a metallic lustre. The colour is black with a dark brown streak. H 6.5; SG 4.8
*Localities.* Occurs in a pegmatite at Fredriksvärn, Norway; Beverly, Massachusetts.
*Treatment.* Clean with dilute acid.

**Aeschynite**
**$(Y, Ca, Fe, Th)(Ti, Nb)_2(O, OH)_6$**
Aeschynite crystallizes in the orthorhombic system as prismatic crystals or compact masses. The colour is brown to black with a reddish-yellow streak and there is an adamantine lustre. H 5–6; SG 4.9
*Localities.* Occurs in pegmatites; also in placer deposits from the Malagasy Republic; Ural Mts, USSR; and some other localities.
*Treatment.* Clean with dilute acid.

**Betafite** **$(Ca, Fe, U)_{2-x}(Nb, Ti, Ta)_2O_6(OH, F)_{1-z}$**
Betafite, a member of the pyrochlore group, crystallizes in the cubic system as octahedra coloured black, brown, greenish or yellow, with a metallic lustre. H 3–5.5; SG 4.1
*Occurrence.* Occurs in pegmatites with zircon and other minerals.
*Localities.* From the Silver Crater mine, Bancroft, Ontario; the Malagasy Republic; Gunnison Co., Colorado; San Bernardino Co., California; and some other localities.
*Treatment.* Do not try to remove brown coating that occurs on specimens from the Malagasy Republic.

**Yttrotantalite $(Y, U, Fe)(Ta, Nb)O_4$**
Yttrotantalite crystallizes in the monoclinic system as prismatic crystals or compact masses coloured brown or black with a metallic or greasy lustre. H 5–5.5; SG 5.7
*Occurrence.* Occurs in pegmatites with gadolinite, mica and other minerals.
*Localities.* From Hattevick, Norway; Ytterby and Falun, Sweden.
*Treatment.* Clean with dilute acid.

**Euxenite** **$(Y, Er, Ce, La, U)(Nb, Ti, Ta)_2(O, OH)_6$**
Euxenite crystallizes in the orthorhombic system as prismatic crystals or compact masses. The colour is black tinged with brown or green, with a metallic lustre. The streak is yellow, brown or grey. H 5.5–6.5; SG 4.3–5.9
*Occurrence.* Occurs in granite pegmatites with rare-earth minerals.
*Localities.* From San Bernardino Co., California; Malagasy Republic; Brazil; etc.
*Treatment.* Do not try to remove brown coatings.
*Fashioning. Uses*: faceting or cabochons; *cleavage*: not significant; tough; *cutting angles*: crown 30°–40°, pavilion 37°–40°; *heat sensitivity*: low.

*Left: Euxenite from Ambatofotskyely, Malagasy Republic*

*Right: Crust of cornetite crystals from the Empire Nevada mine, Yerington, Nevada*

**Polycrase (Y, Er, Ce, La, U)-(Ti, Nb, Ta)$_2$(O, OH)$_6$**
Polycrase crystallizes in the orthorhombic system as prismatic crystals or compact masses. The colour is black with a grey, brown or yellow streak and a metallic lustre. H 5.5–6.5; SG 4.3–5.9
*Occurrence.* Occurs in granite pegmatites with other rare-earth minerals.
*Localities.* From Henderson Co., North Carolina; Canada; Brazil; USSR; etc.
*Treatment.* Do not try to remove brown coatings.

**Samarskite**
**(Fe, Y, U)$_2$(Nb, Ti, Ta)$_2$O$_7$**
Samarskite crystallizes in the orthorhombic system as prismatic crystals or compact masses. The colour is black to brown with a black or reddish-brown streak. The lustre is resinous. H 5–6; SG 5.2–5.7
*Occurrence.* Occurs in granite pegmatites associated with columbite.
*Localities.* From Brazil; Malagasy Republic; Riverside Co., California; North Carolina; and elsewhere.
*Treatment.* Do not try to remove coatings.
*Fashioning. Uses*: faceting or cabochons; *cleavage*: imperfect, brachypinacoidal; brittle; *cutting angles*: crown 30°–40°, pavilion 37°–40°; *heat sensitivity*: low.

## Phosphates

**Stercorite**
**Na(NH$_4$)H(PO$_4$).4H$_2$O**
Stercorite crystallizes in the triclinic system as masses and nodules, which are white, colourless, yellow or brown. They have a vitreous lustre. H 2; SG 1.5
*Localities.* Occurs in guano deposits off the coast of Peru and South-West Africa.

**Lithiophilite**
**Li(Mn$^{2+}$, Fe$^{2+}$)PO$_4$**
Lithiophilite crystallizes in the orthorhombic system as large crystals, but usually in cleavable masses, coloured reddish-brown. The streak is white or grey. There is a resinous lustre. H 4–5; SG 3.3
*Occurrence.* Occurs in granite pegmatites.
*Localities.* From Pala, San Diego Co., California; Namaqualand, South Africa; Argentina; etc.

**Triphylite Li(Fe$^{2+}$, Mn$^{2+}$)PO$_4$**
Triphylite crystallizes in the orthorhombic system as masses coloured greenish or bluish-grey with a colourless or grey streak. They have a resinous lustre. H 4–5; SG 3.4
*Occurrence.* Occurs in granite pegmatites.
*Localities.* From the Black Hills, South Dakota; Pala, California; France; Germany; Finland; etc.

**Sicklerite Li(Mn$^{2+}$, Fe$^{3+}$)PO$_4$**
Sicklerite crystallizes in the orthorhombic system as masses coloured yellow or brown, with a dull lustre. H about 4; SG 3.4
*Occurrence.* Occurs as a secondary mineral in granite pegmatites.
*Localities.* From Custer Co., South Dakota; Pala, San Diego Co., California; Sweden; Finland; etc.
*Treatment.* Clean with distilled water.

**Tavorite LiFe$^{3+}$PO$_4$OH**
Tavorite crystallizes in the triclinic system as prismatic crystals or granular masses. The colour is green or yellow, with a vitreous lustre. H not known; SG 3.3
*Localities.* Occurs in aggregates lining cavities in altered triphylite at the Tip-Top mine, Custer Co., South Dakota (some crystals are emerald-green); Malagasy Republic; Minas Gerais, Brazil; and elsewhere.
*Treatment.* Clean with distilled water.

**Pseudomalachite**
**Cu$_5$(PO$_4$)$_2$(OH)$_4$.H$_2$O**
Pseudomalachite crystallizes in the monoclinic system as prismatic crystals or as botryoidal masses; it has a perfect cleavage. The colour is dark green, with a vitreous lustre. H 4.5–5; SG 4.3
*Localities.* Occurs as a secondary mineral associated with quartz, malachite, etc, in the Rhineland, W. Germany; France; USSR; Canada; USA; and elsewhere.

**Cornetite Cu$_3$PO$_4$(OH)$_3$**
Cornetite crystallizes in the orthorhombic system as prismatic crystals or crusts. The colour is dark green or blue, and the lustre is vitreous. H 4.5; SG 4.1
*Localities.* Occurs with libethenite and malachite and other minerals at Yerington, Nevada; on an argillaceous sandstone at Bwana Mkubwa, Zambia; Etoile du Congo mine, Shaba, Zaire.
*Treatment.* Clean with distilled water.

**Libethenite Cu$_2$PO$_4$OH**
Libethenite crystallizes in the orthorhombic system as prismatic crystals or as crusts. The colour is light to dark green, with a vitreous lustre. H 4; SG 4.0
*Occurrence.* Occurs in the oxidation zone of copper-bearing ore deposits.
*Localities.* Found at Libethen, Romania; USSR; Zaire; San Benito Co., California; etc.

**Nissonite**
**Cu$_2$Mg$_2$(PO$_4$)$_2$(OH)$_2$.5H$_2$O**
Nissonite crystallizes in the monoclinic system as tabular and diamond-shaped crystals or as crusts. The colour is bluish-green. H 2.5; SG 2.7
*Localities.* Occurs with malachite, azurite and other minerals in metamorphic rocks in the Panoche Valley, California.
*Treatment.* Clean with distilled water.

**Turquoise**
**CuAl$_6$(PO$_4$)$_4$(OH)$_8$.4–5H$_2$O**
Turquoise crystallizes in the triclinic system as short prismatic crystals, rarely found; more commonly as masses, stalactites, veins or crusts. There is a perfect cleavage. The colour is bright blue to greenish-blue, green or grey. There is a waxy lustre. H 5–6; SG 2.6–2.8
*Occurrence.* Formed by the action of surface water on rocks containing aluminium.
*Localities.* Micro-crystals from Lynch Station, Campbell Co., Virginia; Arizona; Egypt; Iran, where the finest gem material comes from. Rashleighite, an iron-containing variety, from Cornwall.
*Treatment.* Clean with distilled water and a wetting agent.
*Fashioning. Uses*: cabochons, beads, carvings, tumbling, etc; *cleavage*: none in massive form; *heat sensitivity*: fairly high.

**Chalcosiderite**
**CuFe$_6$(PO$_4$)$_4$(OH)$_8$.4H$_2$O**
Chalcosiderite crystallizes in the triclinic system as prismatic crystals or crusts. There is a perfect cleavage. The colour is dark green, with a vitreous lustre. H 4.5; SG 3.2
*Occurrence.* Occurs as a secondary mineral in the oxidation zone of copper deposits.
*Localities.* From the Phoenix mine, Liskeard, Cornwall; and Seigen, Westphalia, W. Germany.
*Treatment.* Clean with distilled water.

*Left: Libethenite crystals from Rheinbreitbach, Germany*

**Andrewsite**
**$(Cu, Fe^{2+})Fe_3^{3+}(PO_4)_3(OH)_2$**
Andrewsite crystallizes in the orthorhombic system as botryoidal aggregates coloured blue or green, with a silky lustre. H 4; SG 3.5
*Localities.* Occurs with limonite and other minerals at the Phoenix mine, Liskeard, Cornwall.
*Treatment.* Clean with distilled water.

**Beryllonite $NaBePO_4$**
Beryllonite crystallizes in the monoclinic system as tabular prismatic crystals with polysynthetic twinning occurring. There is a perfect cleavage and a vitreous lustre. The colour is white, colourless or yellow. H 5.5–6; SG 2.8
*Occurrence.* Occurs in granite pegmatites.
*Localities.* From Newry and McKean Mountain, Maine.
*Treatment.* Clean with distilled water.
*Fashioning. Uses*: faceting or cabochons; *cleavage*: perfect // to basal pinacoid, distinct macropinacoidal; *cutting angles*: crown 40°–50°, pavilion 43°; *heat sensitivity*: fairly high.

**Moraesite $Be_2PO_4OH.4H_2O$**
Moraesite crystallizes in the monoclinic system as spherulitic masses. The colour and streak are white. H not known; SG 1.8
*Localities.* From vugs with beryl and with other phosphates at the Sapucaia pegmatite mine, Minas Gerais, Brazil.

**Faheyite**
**$(Mn, Mg, Na)Be_2Fe_2^{3+}(PO_4)_4.6H_2O$**
Faheyite crystallizes in the hexagonal system as tufts or botryoidal masses of fibres with a perfect cleavage. The colour is white to brown. H not known; SG 2.7
*Localities.* Occurs as a coating of quartz and other minerals at the Sapucaia pegmatite mine, Minas Gerais, Brazil.

**Hurlbutite $CaBe_2(PO_4)_2$**
Hurlbutite crystallizes in the orthorhombic system as prismatic crystals with striations, and a vitreous lustre. The colour is greenish white, yellow or colourless with a white streak. H 6; SG 2.9
*Localities.* Occurs with muscovite, smoky quartz and other minerals in pegmatite at the Smith mine, Newport, New Hampshire.
*Treatment.* Clean with distilled water.

**Roscherite**
**$(Ca, Mn, Fe)_3Be_3(PO_4)_3(OH)_3.2H_2O$**
Roscherite crystallizes in the monoclinic system as tabular crystals or platy aggregates. The colour is dark green or brown. H 4.5; SG 2.9
*Occurrence.* Occurs in pegmatites.
*Localities.* From Newry, Maine; Sapucaia, Minas Gerais, Brazil; Greifenstein, E. Germany.
*Treatment.* Clean with distilled water.

**Newberyite $MgHPO_4.3H_2O$**
Newberyite crystallizes in the orthorhombic system as prismatic crystals coloured grey, brown or colourless. They have a vitreous lustre. There is a perfect cleavage. H 3–3.5; SG 2.1
*Occurrence.* Occurs with hannayite in bat guano at the Skipton Caves, Ballarat, Victoria, Australia.
*Treatment.* Clean with distilled water.

**Monetite $CaHPO_4$**
Monetite crystallizes in the triclinic system as massive aggregates coloured white, yellow or colourless with a vitreous lustre. H 3.5; SG 2.9
*Localities.* Occurs with apatite on Ascension Island and elsewhere.
*Treatment.* Clean with distilled water.

**Whitlockite $(Ca, Mg)_3(PO_4)_2$**
Whitlockite crystallizes in the hexagonal system as rhombohedral crystals. The

*Left: A large specimen of turquoise in matrix from Mongolia, together with some polished samples*

*Right: Hopeite crystals from Broken Hill, Zambia*

*Far right: Variscite showing characteristic distribution of colour*

colour is pink, white, yellow or grey, and the lustre is vitreous. H 5; SG 3.1
*Occurrence.* In granite pegmatites.
*Localities.* From Oran, Algeria; Custer Co., South Dakota; etc.
*Treatment.* Clean with distilled water.

**Hydroxyapatite $Ca_5(PO_4)_3OH$**
Hydroxyapatite crystallizes in the hexagonal system as prismatic crystals or granular masses; they have a vitreous lustre. The colour is white, grey, yellow, green, violet, purple, red or brown. The streak is white. H 5; SG 3.0
*Localities.* Occurs in talc-schist, Cherokee Co., Georgia; in diallage-serpentine rock, Rossa, Ossola, Italy.
*Treatment.* Clean with distilled water.

**Goyazite $SrAl_3(PO_4)_2(OH)_5 \cdot H_2O$**
Goyazite crystallizes in the hexagonal system as rhombohedral or pseudocubic crystals with a perfect cleavage. May also occur as pebbles. The colour is yellow, pink or colourless. The lustre is resinous or pearly. H 4.5–5; SG 3.3
*Localities.* Occurs near Diamantina, Minas Gerais, Brazil; Simplon Tunnel, Switzerland; pegmatites in Maine; the tungsten area of Boulder Co., Colorado.
*Treatment.* Clean with distilled water.

**Palermoite**
**$(Li, Na)_2(Sr, Ca)Al_4(PO_4)_4(OH)_4$**
Palermoite crystallizes in the orthorhombic system as vertically striated prisms with a perfect cleavage coloured white or colourless. The streak is white and the mineral exhibits a white fluorescence under x-rays. There is a vitreous lustre. H 5.5; SG 3.2
*Localities.* Occurs with siderite and other minerals at the Palermo pegmatite, North Gordon, New Hampshire.
*Treatment.* Clean with distilled water.

**Gorceixite $BaAl_3(PO_4)_2(OH)_5 \cdot H_2O$**
Gorceixite crystallizes in the hexagonal system as botryoidal aggregates; also occurs as grains and pebbles. The colour is white or brown. H 6; SG 3.3
*Localities.* In novaculite at Hot Springs, Arkansas; in the diamond-bearing sands of Brazil, Guyana and Africa.

**Hopeite $Zn_3(PO_4)_2 \cdot 4H_2O$**
Hopeite crystallizes in the orthorhombic system as prismatic crystals or compact masses; it has a perfect cleavage. Parahopeite is dimorphous with hopeite, but crystallizes in the triclinic system. Hopeite is yellow, white, colourless or grey, with a white streak. There is a vitreous lustre. H 3.5; SG 3.0
*Occurrence.* Occurs in zinc ore deposits.
*Localities.* From Kabwe, Zambia; Hudson Bay mine, Salmo, British Columbia; Altenberg, W. Germany. Parahopeite from the same localities.

**Tarbuttite $Zn_2PO_4OH$**
Tarbuttite crystallizes in the triclinic system as prismatic crystals, often with deep striations or as crusts. There is a perfect cleavage, and a vitreous lustre. The colour is white, colourless, yellow, red, green or brown with a white streak. H 3.5; SG 4.1
*Localities.* Occurs with limonite and other minerals in the oxidation zone of the zinc ores, Shaba, Zambia.
*Treatment.* Clean with distilled water.

**Spencerite $Zn_4(PO_4)_2(OH)_2 \cdot 3H_2O$**
Spencerite crystallizes in the monoclinic system as tabular crystals or stalactitic masses. There is a perfect cleavage. The colour is white, and the lustre is vitreous. H 3; SG 3.1
*Localities.* In oxidized zinc ores at the Hudson Bay mine, British Columbia.

**Scholzite $CaZn_2(PO_4)_2 \cdot 2H_2O$**
Scholzite crystallizes in the orthorhombic system as prismatic or platy crystals. The colour is white or colourless. There is a vitreous lustre. H 3–3.5; SG 3.1
*Localities.* Occurs with quartz and other minerals in pegmatite at Hagendorf, Bavaria, W. Germany.

**Faustite**
**$(Zn, Cu)Al_6(PO_4)_4(OH)_8 \cdot 5H_2O$**
Faustite crystallizes in the triclinic system as compact apple-green masses with a waxy lustre. The streak is white or pale yellow. H 5.5; SG 2.9
*Localities.* Occurs at the Copper King mine, Eureka Co., Nevada.

**Phosphophyllite**
**$Zn_2(Fe, Mn)(PO_4)_2 \cdot 4H_2O$**
Phosphophyllite crystallizes in the monoclinic system as prismatic crystals with a vitreous lustre; they are often twinned and have a perfect cleavage. The colour is bright blue-green to colourless. H 3–3.5; SG 3.1
*Localities.* Occurs in vugs in massive sulphides at San Luis Potosi, Bolivia; in granite pegmatites at Hagendorf, Bavaria, W. Germany.
*Fashioning. Uses*: faceting or cabochons; *cleavage*: perfect orthopinacoidal, distinct clinopinacoidal; *cutting angles*: crown 40°, pavilion 40°; *heat sensitivity*: fairly high.

**Berlinite $AlPO_4$**
Berlinite crystallizes in the hexagonal system as granular masses. The colour is grey or pale pink. H 6.5; SG 2.6
*Localities.* Occurs with other phosphates at the Westanå iron mine, Näsum, Sweden.
*Treatment.* Clean with distilled water.

**Variscite $AlPO_4 \cdot 2H_2O$**
Variscite crystallizes in the orthorhombic system as octahedra but more commonly as masses, veins or nodules. The colour is pale to emerald-green and the lustre is waxy. The variety metavariscite crystallizes in the monoclinic system. H 3.5–4.5; SG 2.6
*Occurrence.* Occurs in aluminous rocks that have been altered by phosphatic waters.
*Localities.* From Fairfield, Utah; California, Nevada, Arizona; Germany; Austria; Spain; Brazil and elsewhere.
*Treatment.* Clean with distilled water only.
*Fashioning. Uses*: cabochons, carvings, beads, tumbling, etc; *cleavage*: none, material generally aggregated or massive; *heat sensitivity*: fairly high.

**Augelite $Al_2PO_4(OH)_3$**
Augelite crystallizes in the monoclinic system as tabular crystals or as triangular plates or as masses. There is a perfect cleavage. It is white, colourless, yellow, blue or pink with a white streak. There

is a vitreous lustre. H 4.5–5; SG 2.7
*Localities.* Occurs with andalusite at White Mountain, Mono Co., California; South Dakota; the Palermo mine, New Hampshire; Bolivia; and some other localities.
*Treatment.* Clean with distilled water.

**Bolivarite**
**$Al_2(PO_4)(OH)_3.4–5H_2O$**
Bolivarite is amorphous to 1,050°C and occurs as crusts and botryoidal masses, with a vitreous lustre. The colour is bright yellowish-green and there is a bright green fluorescence under ultra-violet light. H 2.5–3.5; SG 2.0
*Localities.* Occurs in granite near Pontevedra, Spain; from the pegmatite at Kobokobo, Kivu, Zaire.

**Wavellite $Al_3(OH)_3(PO_4)_2.5H_2O$**
Wavellite crystallizes in the orthorhombic system as radiating aggregates of acicular crystals, or as crusts. There is a perfect cleavage. The colour is green or white, yellow, brown, blue or colourless, with a vitreous lustre. H 3–4; SG 2.4
*Occurrence.* Occurs in hydrothermal veins or in phosphate rocks.
*Localities.* Fine specimens from Hot Spring Co., Arkansas; El Dorado Co., California; Barnstaple, Devon; and elsewhere.
*Treatment.* Wavellite should be cleaned ultrasonically.

**Evansite $Al_3PO_4(OH)_6.6H_2O$**
The formula quoted is not certain, and the crystal system is not known. Evansite occurs in massive stalactitic or botryoidal forms with a yellow green or blue colour; it may also be colourless. There is a vitreous lustre. The streak is white. H 3–4; SG 1.8–2.2
*Occurrence.* Occurs with allophane and limonite.
*Localities.* From the Coosa coal field, Alabama; Custer Co., South Dakota; Malagasy Republic.
*Treatment.* Clean with distilled water.

*Left: Radiating acicular wavellite crystals*

*Below: Brazilianite, discovered in this century. It is sometimes cut as a gemstone. This specimen is from Brazil*

*Left: A fine crystal of brazilianite with an unusually long prismatic form*

**Brazilianite $NaAl_3(PO_4)_2(OH)_4$**
Brazilianite crystallizes in the monoclinic system as short prismatic crystals with striations or as globules. The colour is pale yellow to yellowish-green or colourless with a colourless streak. There is a vitreous lustre. H 5.5; SG 3.0; RI 1.60–1.62
*Occurrence.* Occurs in pegmatites.
*Localities.* From Conselheira Pena, Minas Gerais, Brazil; Smith mine, Newport, New Hampshire.
*Treatment.* Clean with dilute oxalic acid.
*Fashioning. Uses*: faceting or cabochons; *cleavage*: perfect pinacoidal; *cutting angles*: crown 40°, pavilion 40°; *heat sensitivity*: low.

**Gordonite**
**$MgAl_2(PO_4)_2(OH)_2.8H_2O$**
Gordonite crystallizes in the triclinic system as sheaf-like aggregates: it has a perfect cleavage. The colour is white, pink, green or colourless with a white streak. H 3.5; SG 2.2
*Occurrence.* Occurs with crandallite at Fairfield, Utah.

**Overite $CaMg(H_2O)_4Al(OH)(PO_4)_2$**
Overite crystallizes in the orthorhombic system as plates or platy aggregates;

*Right: Tabular crystals of torbernite from Bois Noir, France.*

it has a perfect cleavage. The colour is light green to colourless with a vitreous lustre. H 3.5–4; SG 2.5
*Localities.* Occurs with crandallite at Fairfield, Utah.

**Montgomeryite $Ca_2Al_2(PO_4)_3(OH).7H_2O$**
Montgomeryite crystallizes in the monoclinic system as aggregates of plates coloured deep to pale green and with a perfect cleavage. There is a vitreous lustre. H 4; SG 2.5
*Localities.* Occurs with crandallite at Fairfield, Utah.

**Crandallite $CaAl_3(PO_4)_2(OH)_5.H_2O$**
Crandallite crystallizes in the triclinic system; it forms nodular masses and has a perfect cleavage. The colour is yellow or white. The lustre may be vitreous or dull. H 5; SG 2.8–2.9
*Localities.* Occurs with other phosphate minerals at Fairfield, Utah; Brazil; Senegal; Guatemala; etc.

**Wardite $NaAl_3(PO_4)_2(OH)_4.2H_2O$**
Wardite crystallizes in the tetragonal system as pyramidal crystals or fibrous aggregates. There is a perfect cleavage. The colour is pale green, bluish, white or colourless with a vitreous lustre. H 5; SG 2.8
*Localities.* Occurs with crandallite at Fairfield, Utah; with amblygonite at Pala, San Diego Co., California; and elsewhere.
*Treatment.* Clean with distilled water.

**Englishite $K_2Ca_4Al_8(PO_4)_8(OH)_{10}.9H_2O$**
Englishite is thought to crystallize in the monoclinic system; it forms layers and aggregates of curved plates with a perfect cleavage. It is colourless, with a vitreous lustre. H about 3; SG about 2.6
*Localities.* Occurs with crandallite at Fairfield, Utah.

*Below: Monazite, which crystallizes in the monoclinic system*

**Xenotime $YPO_4$**
Xenotime crystallizes in the tetragonal system as prismatic crystals or as rosettes. There is a perfect cleavage. The colour is yellow to reddish-brown, greenish or grey, and the lustre is vitreous. H 4–5; SG 4.4–5.1
*Occurrence.* Occurs in alkaline and igneous rocks and pegmatites.
*Localities.* From California; Colorado; Brazil; Malagasy Republic; etc.
*Treatment.* Clean with distilled water.

**Monazite (La, Ce, Y, Th)$PO_4$**
Monazite crystallizes in the monoclinic system as tabular crystals or granular masses with a resinous lustre. The colour is reddish-brown, brown, pink, yellow, green, white with a white or grey streak. H 5–5.5; SG 4.6–5.4
*Localities.* Occurs in placer deposits around the world. Fine crystals from Encampment, Wyoming, where they are found in association with euxenite; Norway; Finland; Switzerland; etc.

**Rhabdophane (Ce, Y, La, Di)$(PO_4).H_2O$**
Rhabdophane crystallizes in the hexagonal system as stalactitic encrustations with a greasy lustre. The colour is white, yellow or pink. H 3.5; SG 3.9–4.0
*Localities.* Occurs in a limonite deposit at Salisbury, Connecticut; Cornwall.

**Churchite (Y, Er)$PO_4.2H_2O$**
Churchite, sometimes known as weinschenkite, crystallizes in the monoclinic system as crusts or rosettes. There is a perfect cleavage. The colour is white, grey or colourless. H 3; SG 3.3
*Localities.* Occurs in a manganese-rich limonite deposit at Rockbridge Co., Virginia; with copper in Cornwall.

**Florencite $CeAl_3(PO_4)_2(OH)_6$**
Florencite crystallizes in the hexagonal system as rhombohedral pink or pale yellow crystals with a resinous lustre. H 5–6; SG 3.5–3.7
*Localities.* Occurs in mica schists at Ouro Preto, Minas Gerais, Brazil; in pegmatite at Klein Spitzkopje, South-West Africa; Malawi; etc.
*Treatment.* Clean with distilled water.

**Plumbogummite $PbAl_3(PO_4)_2(OH)_5.H_2O$**
Plumbogummite crystallizes in the hexagonal system as compact masses or stalactitic crusts. The colour is white, grey, yellow or greenish-blue, reddish-brown with a white or colourless streak. There is a resinous or dull lustre. H 4.5–5; SG 4.0
*Occurrence.* Occurs in the oxidation zone of lead ores.
*Localities.* From Inyo Co., California; Cumbria; Minas Gerais, Brazil; etc.

**Sincosite Ca $(VO)_2(PO_4)_2.5H_2O$**
Sincosite crystallizes in the tetragonal system as tabular crystals or compact masses. There is a perfect cleavage. The colour is green or yellow with a green streak. There is a vitreous lustre. H not known; SG about 2.8
*Localities.* Occurs in siliceous gold ore at Lead, Lawrence Co., South Dakota; Junin, Peru.
*Treatment.* Clean with distilled water.

**Meta-ankoleite $K_2(UO_2)_2(PO_4)_2.6H_2O$**
Meta-ankoleite crystallizes in the tetragonal system as plates; it has a perfect cleavage and is coloured yellow. It has a vitreous lustre. There is a yellow-green fluorescence in ultra-violet light. H not known; SG 3.5
*Localities.* Occurs with muscovite and quartz in the Mungenyi pegmatite, Uganda; Sebungive, Rhodesia.

**Uramphite $NH_4UO_2PO_4 . 3H_2O$**
Uramphite's crystal system is not known. It forms rosettes and plates coloured dark or pale green with a yellow-green fluorescence under ultra-violet light. They have a vitreous lustre. H not known; SG 3.7
*Localities.* From a uranium-coal deposit, USSR.

**Torbernite**
**$Cu(UO_2)_2(PO_4)_2 . 8–12H_2O$**
Tobernite crystallizes in the tetragonal system as tabular crystals or lamellar aggregates. There is a perfect cleavage. The colour is emerald-green and lighter shades with a pale green streak. There is a vitreous lustre. H 2–2.5; SG 3.2
*Localities.* Occurs in pegmatites at Spruce Pine, North Carolina; Cornwall; Puy-de-Dôme, France; E. Germany; and elsewhere.
*Treatment.* Remove iron stains with weak solution of sodium dithionate; otherwise use distilled water.

**Metatorbernite**
**$Cu(UO_2)_2(PO_4)_2 . 8H_2O$**
Metatorbernite crystallizes in the tetragonal system as thin tablets or lamellar aggregates. There is a perfect cleavage. The colour is pale to dark green, with a vitreous lustre. H 2.5; SG 3.7–3.8
*Occurrence.* Occurs in the oxidized zone of veins with uraninite and copper.
*Localities.* From Redruth, Cornwall; Lake Athabasca, Saskatchewan, Canada; Puy-de-dôme, France; Erzgebirge, E. Germany; etc.
*Treatment.* Clean with distilled water.

**Saléeite $Mg(UO_2)_2(PO_4)_2 . 8–10H_2O$**
Saléeite crystallizes in the tetragonal system as rectangular plates or platy aggregates. There is a perfect cleavage. The colour is yellow to yellowish-green, with a vitreous or dull lustre. There is a bright yellow-green fluorescence in ultra-violet light. H 2.5; SG 3.3
*Localities.* In a sandstone at Gull mine, Fall River Co., South Dakota; Schneeberg, E. Germany; Shinkolobwe, Shaba, Zaire; Rum Jungle, Northern Territory, Australia; etc.

**Autunite**
**$Ca(UO_2)_2(PO_4)_2 . 10–12H_2O$**
Autunite crystallizes in the tetragonal system as tabular crystals or crusts and aggregates. There is a perfect cleavage. The colour is bright yellow, pale or dark green, with a vitreous or dull lustre. There is a bright yellow-green fluorescence under ultra-violet light. Meta-autunite is a dehydration product. H 2–2.5; SG 3.0–3.2
*Occurrence.* Formed by the alteration of uraninite in pegmatites or granites.
*Localities.* From Rum Jungle, Northern Territory, Australia; E. Germany; St. Austell and Redruth, Cornwall, England; and other localities.

**Phosphuranylite**
**$Ca (UO_2)_4(PO_4)_2(OH)_4 . 7H_2O$**
Phosphuranylite crystallizes in the orthorhombic system as scales or plates, aggregates and crusts. There is a perfect cleavage. The colour is light golden

*Left: Autunite. Bright yellows are characteristic of radioactive minerals*

*Left: Autunite plates from Peveragno, Piedmont, Italy*

yellow to deep yellow. H about 2.5; SG 4.1
*Occurrence.* Occurs in the weathered zone of uraninite-bearing pegmatites.
*Localities.* From Rio Grande do Norte, Brazil; Margnac, Haute-Vienne, France; Palermo mine, New Hampshire; Mitchell Co., North Carolina; etc.

**Uranocircite**
**$Ba(UO_2)_2(PO_4)_2 \cdot 10\text{–}12H_2O$**
The crystal system is probably tetragonal and the mineral is found as tabular crystals or as aggregates. There is a perfect cleavage. The colour is yellow, with a green fluorescence under ultra-violet light. There is a pearly lustre. H 2–2.5; SG 3.5
*Localities.* Occurs at Farnwitte, Black Forest, W. Germany.

**Meta-uranocircite**
**$Ba(UO_2)_2(PO_4)_2 \cdot 6\text{–}8H_2O$**
Meta-uranocircite crystallizes in the tetragonal system as thin plates and aggregates with a perfect cleavage. They have a pearly lustre. The colour is yellow-green with a green fluorescence under ultra-violet light. H 2–2.5; SG 3.9
*Localities.* Occurs at Menzenschwand, W. Germany; the Banat, Romania; Harding Co., South Dakota; in an alluvial deposit near Antsirabe, Malagasy Republic; etc.

**Sabugalite**
**$HAl(UO_2)_2(PO_4)_4 \cdot 16H_2O$**
Sabugalite crystallizes in the tetragonal system as thin plates and crusts; it has a perfect cleavage. The colour is bright yellow with a similarly-coloured fluorescence under ultra-violet light. There is a vitreous lustre. H 2.5; SG 3.2
*Occurrence.* Occurs in sandstone-type uranium deposits and in uraninite veins.
*Localities.* From Mina da Quarta Feira, Beira Alta, Portugal; Margnac, Haute-Vienne, France; Arizona; Wyoming; etc.

**Parsonsite $Pb_2UO_2(PO_4)_2 \cdot 2H_2O$**
Parsonsite crystallizes in the triclinic system as prismatic crystals or tufts and fibrous masses. The colour is pale yellow to brown or pink, with an adamantine or greasy lustre. H 2.5–3; SG 5.7
*Localities.* Occurs with autunite at the Ruggles mine, Grafton Center, New Hampshire; with torbernite at Lachaux, Puy-de-Dôme, France; with metatorbernite at Shinkolobwe, Shaba, Zaire; etc.

**Renardite**
**$Pb(UO_2)_4(PO_4)_2(OH)_4 \cdot 7H_2O$**
Renardite crystallizes in the orthorhombic system as rectangular plates and lamellar masses with a perfect cleavage. The colour is light yellow to brown, with a vitreous lustre. H 3.5; SG 4.3
*Localities.* Occurs with torbernite at Shinkolobwe, Shaba, Zaire; Lignol, Morbihan, and Lachaux, Puy-de-Dôme, France; etc.

**Dumontite**
**$Pb_2(UO_2)_3(PO_4)_2(OH)_4 \cdot 3H_2O$**
Dumontite crystallizes in the monoclinic system as minute elongated crystals coloured pale to golden yellow. There is a weak green fluorescence under ultra-violet light. H not known; SG 5.6
*Localities.* Occurs with autunite at Nogales, Arizona; with parsonsite at Shinkolobwe, Shaba, Zaire.
*Treatment.* Clean with distilled water.

**Hureaulite**
**$H_2(Mn,Fe)_5(PO_4)_4 \cdot 4H_2O$**
Hureaulite crystallizes in the monoclinic system as prismatic crystals or fibrous masses. The colour is rose, red, yellow, orange, brown or colourless with a white streak. There is a vitreous lustre. H 3.5; SG 3.1
*Occurrence.* Occurs in granite pegmatites with other phosphate minerals.
*Localities.* From the Black Hills, South Dakota; the Palermo Mine, New Hampshire; Hagendorf, W. Germany.

**Stewartite**
**$MnFe_2(OH)_2(PO_4)_2 \cdot 8H_2O$**
Stewartite crystallizes in the triclinic system as tufts coloured yellow or brown. H not known; SG 2.9
*Occurrence.* Occurs in granite pegmatites with other phosphate minerals.
*Localities.* From the Stewart mine, Pala, San Diego Co., California; Alto Boqueiro, Rio Grande do Norte, Brazil; etc.

**Natrophilite $NaMnPO_4$**
Natrophilite crystallizes in the orthorhombic system as prismatic crystals and more commonly as granular masses. The colour is deep yellow, with a resinous lustre. H 4.5–5; SG 3.4
*Localities.* Occurs in a granite pegmatite at Branchville, Connecticut.

**Griphite**
**$(Na,Al,Ca,Fe)_3Mn_2(PO_4)_{2.5}(OH)_2$**
Griphite crystallizes in the cubic system as compact masses coloured brown to black, with a resinous lustre. H 5.5; SG 3.4
*Occurrence.* Occurs in granite pegmatites.
*Localities.* From Mt. Ida, Northern Territory, Australia; Pennington Co., South Dakota; etc.

**Reddingite $(Mn,Fe)_3(PO_4)_2 \cdot 3H_2O$**
Reddingite crystallizes in the orthorhombic system as octahedra or fibrous masses. The colour is pink, yellow, reddish-brown or white, and the lustre is vitreous. H 3–3.5; SG 3.2
*Occurrence.* Occurs as an alteration of lithiophilite in granite pegmatites.
*Localities.* From Fairfield Co., Connecticut; Buckfield, Maine.
*Treatment.* Clean with distilled water.

**Switzerite $(Mn,Fe)_3(PO_4)_2 \cdot 4H_2O$**
Switzerite crystallizes in the monoclinic system as flakes or bladed crystals with a perfect cleavage. The colour is pink or golden brown, with a pearly lustre. H about 2.5; SG 2.9
*Localities.* Occurs in a pegmatite at the spodumene mine, Kings Mountain, North Carolina.

**Beusite $(Mn, Fe, Ca, Mg)_3(PO_4)_2$**
Beusite crystallizes in the monoclinic system as prismatic crystals intermingled with lithiophilite. The colour is reddish-brown. H 5; SG 3.7
*Occurrence.* Occurs in granite pegmatites.
*Localities.* From Los Aleros, San Luis Province, Argentina.

**Triploidite $(Mn^{2+}, Fe^{2+})_2PO_4OH$**
Triploidite crystallizes in the monoclinic system as prismatic crystals with vertical striations or as fibrous aggregates. The colour is pink, yellow or brown to green. There is a vitreous lustre. The streak is white. H 4.5–5; SG 3.7
*Localities.* Occurs in granite pegmatites at the Ross mine, Custer Co., South Dakota; Branchville, Fairfield Co., Connecticut; etc.

**Salmonsite**
**$Mn_9^{2+}, Fe_2^{3+}(PO_4)_8 \cdot 14H_2O$**
Salmonsite probably crystallizes in the orthorhombic system as fibrous masses coloured light brown. H 4; SG 2.8
*Localities.* Occurs in granite pegmatite at the Stewart mine, Pala, California.

*Right: Uranocircite blades from Bergen, East Germany*

**Laueite $MnFe_2(PO_4)_2(OH)_2.8H_2O$**
Laueite crystallizes in the triclinic system as wedge-shaped crystals with a perfect cleavage. The colour is yellow, orange or brown, with a vitreous lustre. H 3; SG 2.4–2.5
*Localities.* Occurs in a pegmatite in eastern Bavaria, W. Germany; Palermo quarry, New Hampshire; Black Hills, South Dakota.
*Treatment.* Clean with distilled water.

**Strunzite**
**$MnFe_2(PO_4)_2(OH)_2.8H_2O$**
Strunzite crystallizes in the monoclinic system as tufts and coatings coloured yellow to brown. H not known; SG 2.5–2.6
*Localities.* Occurs in pegmatites containing triphylite at Hagendorf, Bavaria, W. Germany; Palermo, New Hampshire; Custer Co., South Dakota; and some other localities.

**Landesite**
**$Mn_{10}Fe_3^{3+}(PO_4)_8(OH)_5.11H_2O$**
Landesite crystallizes in the orthorhombic system as octahedra pseudomorphous after reddingite. The colour is brown. H 3–3.5; SG 3.0
*Occurrence.* In granite pegmatites.
*Localities.* From Poland, Maine.
*Treatment.* Clean with distilled water.

**Frondelite**
**$(Mn^{2+}, Fe^{2+}(Fe_4^{3+}(PO_4)_3(OH)_5$**
Frondelite crystallizes in the orthorhombic system as crusts and fibrous masses. There is a perfect cleavage. The colour is olive green to black. H 4.5; SG 3.5
*Occurrence.* Occurs in granite pegmatites as an alteration product of the mineral triphylite.
*Localities.* From the Black Hills, South Dakota; Minas Gerais, Brazil.

**Rockbridgeite**
**$(Fe^{2+}, Mn)Fe_4^{3+}(PO_4)_3(OH)_5$**
Rockbridgeite crystallizes in the orthorhombic system as prismatic crystals, more commonly as botryoidal crusts. There is a perfect cleavage. The colour is light to dark green becoming brown on oxidation. H 4.5; SG 3.3–3.5
*Occurrence.* Found in limonite, and in granite pegmatites with iron-manganese phosphate minerals.
*Localities.* From the Black Hills, South Dakota; Brazil; Germany; and from some other localities.

**Wolfeite $(Fe^{2+}, Mn^{2+})_2PO_4OH$**
Wolfeite crystallizes in the monoclinic system as prismatic crystals with vertical striations; also found as fibrous aggregates. There is a vitreous lustre. The colour is reddish or dark brown and the streak is white. H 4.5–5; SG 3.8
*Occurrence.* Occurs in granite pegmatites.
*Localities.* From Custer Co., South Dakota; Hagendorf, Bavaria, W. Germany; etc.

**Heterosite $(Fe^{3+}, Mn^{3+})PO_4$**
Heterosite crystallizes in the orthorhombic system in masses coloured red to purple with a similarly-coloured streak. Dull lustre. H 4–4.5; SG 3.4
*Occurrence.* Occurs as an alteration of triphylite in granite pegmatites.
*Localities.* From Custer Co., South Dakota; Germany; Australia; Erongo, South-West Africa; etc.
*Treatment.* Remove dark alteration coating with dilute hydrochloric acid.

**Purpurite $(Mn^{3+}, Fe^{3+})PO_4$**
Purpurite crystallizes in the orthorhombic system as masses coloured dark red to purple with a similarly-coloured streak. There is a dull lustre. H 4–4.5; SG 3.7
*Occurrence.* Occurs in granite pegmatites as an alteration of lithiophilite.
*Localities.* From Custer Co., South Dakota; Chanteloube, France; Wodgina, Western Australia; etc.
*Treatment.* Remove dark alteration coating with dilute hydrochloric acid.

**Dickinsonite $H_2Na_6(Mn, Fe, Ca, Mg)_{14}(PO_4)_{12}.H_2O$**
Dickinsonite crystallizes in the monoclinic system as tabular crystals or

foliated masses with a perfect cleavage. The colour is yellow to dark green with a white streak. There is a vitreous lustre. H 3.5–4; SG 3.4
*Occurrence.* Occurs in granite pegmatities in association with other phosphate minerals.
*Localities.* From Branchville, Connecticut; Poland, Maine.

**Fillowite**
**$H_2Na_6(Mn, Fe, Ca)_{14}(PO_4)_{12}.H_2O$**
Fillowite crystallizes in the hexagonal system as pseudorhombohedral crystals or granular masses; it has a perfect cleavage. The colour is yellow to brown with a white streak. There is a greasy lustre. H 4.5; SG 3.4
*Localities.* Occurs in granite pegmatites with reddingite, etc., at Branchville, Connecticut.

**Bermanite**
**$Mn^{2+}, Mn_2^{3+}(PO_4)_2(OH)_2.4H_2O$**
Bermanite crystallizes in the monoclinic system as tabular crystals, frequently twinned, or as lamellar masses; it has a perfect cleavage. The colour is pale red to brown, with a vitreous lustre. H 3.5; SG 2.8
*Occurrence.* Occurs in pegmatites with hureaulite and other phosphates.
*Localities.* From Custer Co., South

*Left: Eosphorite. The vitreous lustre is clearly visible in this fragment*

*Below left: Graftonite in a pegmatitic matrix*

Dakota; Sapucaia, Minas Gerais, Brazil; Malagasy Republic.
*Treatment.* Clean with distilled water.

**Graftonite**
**$(Fe^{2+}, Mn^{2+}, Ca)_3(PO_4)_2$**
Graftonite crystallizes in the monoclinic system as masses with a pink to brown colour and a vitreous lustre. H 5; SG 3.7–3.8
*Occurrence.* Occurs in granite pegmatites.
*Localities.* From Custer Co., South Dakota; Brissago, Switzerland; Olgiasca, Lake Como, Italy; etc.
*Treatment.* Clean with distilled water.

**Fairfieldite**
**$Ca_2(Mn^{2+}, Fe^{2+})(PO_4)_2.2H_2O$**
Fairfieldite crystallizes in the triclinic system as prismatic crystals or lamellar masses; it has a perfect cleavage. The colour is white or yellow to green with a white streak. There is a vitreous lustre. H 3.5; SG 3.1
*Occurrence.* In granite pegmatites.
*Localities.* From Branchville, Fairfield Co., Connecticut; Hühnerkobel, Bavaria, W. Germany.
*Treatment.* Clean with distilled water.

**Arrojadite**
**$(Na, Ca)_2(Fe^{2+}, Mn^{2+})_5(PO_4)_4$**
Arrojadite crystallizes in the monoclinic system as dark green masses with a vitreous lustre. H 5; SG 3.5
*Occurrence.* Occurs in granite pegmatites.
*Localities.* From Pennington Co., South Dakota; Serra Blanca, Picuhy, Brazil.

**Hagendorfite**
**$(Na, Ca)(Fe^{2+}, Mn^{2+})_2(PO_4)_2$**
Hagendorfite crystallizes in the monoclinic system as greenish-black masses. H 3.5; SG 3.7
*Localities.* Occurs in pegmatite at Hagendorf, Bavaria, W. Germany; and at Norro, Sweden.

**Eosphorite**
**$(Mn, Fe)AlPO_4(OH)_2.H_2O$**
Eosphorite crystallizes in the monoclinic system as prismatic crystals or radial

*Right: Translucent vivianite from Uncía in Bolivia. Vivianite is pleochroic*

aggregates. The colour is pink, yellow or colourless, red, brown or black; there is a vitreous lustre. H 5; SG 3.0
*Occurrence.* Occurs in granite pegmatites with other manganese phosphates.
*Localities.* From Minas Gerais, Brazil; Hagendorf, Bavaria, W. Germany; Branchville, Connecticut; Mt. Mica, Maine; Palermo mine, New Hampshire.
*Treatment.* Clean with distilled water.

**Childrenite**
**$(Fe, Mn)AlPO_4(OH)_2 . H_2O$**
Childrenite crystallizes in the orthorhombic system as tabular crystals or as plates. The colour is brown or yellow, with a vitreous lustre. H 5; SG 3.2
*Occurrence.* Found in hydrothermal vein deposits and in granite pegmatites.
*Localities.* From Cornwall, England; Custer Co., South Dakota; Minas Gerais, Brazil.
*Treatment.* Clean with distilled water.

**Vivianite $Fe_3(PO_4)_2 . 8H_2O$**
Vivianite crystallizes in the monoclinic system as flexible laminae; they have a perfect cleavage and are sectile. The mineral also occurs as crusts and earthy coatings. The colour is colourless, darkening on exposure to green or blue, purple or black. There is a pearly lustre. The streak is colourless altering to brown or dark blue. H 1.5–2; SG 2.7
*Occurrence.* In metallic ore veins and as an alteration product of phosphate minerals in pegmatites; also in sedimentary deposits.
*Localities.* From Lemhi Co., Idaho; Black Hills, South Dakota; Poopó, Bolivia; Cameroons; St. Agnes, Cornwall; USSR; Australia; and elsewhere.
*Treatment.* Clean with distilled water.

**Ludlamite $Fe_3(PO_4)_2 . 4H_2O$**
Ludlamite crystallizes in the monoclinic system as tabular crystals or granular masses. There is a perfect cleavage. The colour is bright to apple green, or colourless, with a vitreous lustre. H 3.5; SG 3.2
*Occurrence.* Occurs in the oxidation zone of ore deposits and as an alteration product of iron bearing phosphate minerals in granite pegmatites.
*Localities.* From Lemhi Co., Idaho; Custer Co., South Dakota; Wheal Jane mine, Truro, Cornwall; Hagendorf, Bavaria, W. Germany.
*Treatment.* Clean with distilled water.

**Lipscombite**
**$(Fe^{2+}, Mn^{2+})Fe_2^{3+}(PO_4)_2(OH)_2$**
Lipscombite crystallizes in the tetragonal system as aggregates of tiny crystals coloured dark green to black. H not known; SG 3.7
*Localities.* Occurs with metastrengite in frondelite at the Sapucaia pegmatite, Minas Gerais, Brazil, etc.

**Laubmannite**
**$Fe_3^{2+}Fe_6^{3+}(PO_4)_4(OH)_{12}$**
Laubmannite crystallizes in the orthorhombic system as botryoidal aggregates coloured bright yellow to green, with a vitreous lustre. H 3.5–4; SG 3.3
*Localities.* Occurs in novaculite on Buckeye Mountain, Polk Co., Arkansas; Amberg-Auerbach, Bavaria, W. Germany; Leveäniemi, Sweden.

**Barbosalite $Fe^{2+}Fe_2^{3+}(PO_4)_2(OH)_2$**
Barbosalite crystallizes in the monoclinic system as prismatic crystals or masses, or as crusts. The colour is greenish-blue to black, with a dull or vitreous lustre. H 5.5–6; SG 3.6
*Localities* Occurs in pegmatites with pyrite, Custer Co., South Dakota; and elsewhere.

**Phosphosiderite $FePO_4 . 2H_2O$**
Phosphosiderite crystallizes in the monoclinic system as tabular crystals or botryoidal crusts; interpenetration twins are common. The colour is red to violet or yellow; the lustre is vitreous. H 3.5–4; SG 2.8
*Localities.* Occurs with strengite in the Bull Moose mine, Custer Co., South Dakota; Pala, San Diego Co., California; Chanteloube, France; Hagendorf, W. Germany; etc.

**Strengite $FePO_4 . 2H_2O$**
Strengite crystallizes in the orthorhombic system as octahedra or spherical aggregates and crusts. The colour is pale to deep violet-red with a white streak. There is a vitreous lustre. H 3.5–4.5; SG 2.9
*Occurrence.* Formed by the alteration of phosphate minerals rich in iron.
*Localities.* From Custer Co., South Dakota; Pala, San Diego Co., California; Hagendorf, Bavaria, W. Germany; Mangualde, Portugal; etc.
*Treatment.* Clean with distilled water.

**Beraunite**
**$Fe^{2+}Fe_5^{3+}(OH)_5(H_2O)_4(PO_4)_4 . 2H_2O$**
Beraunite crystallizes in the monoclinic system as tabular crystals with vertical striations; more commonly as fibrous aggregates or crusts. The colour is red or brown with a yellow-brown streak. There is a vitreous lustre. H 3.5–4; SG 3.0
*Occurrence.* In iron ore deposits and in granite pegmatites.
*Localities.* From Pennington Co., South Dakota; Palermo mine, New Hampshire; Ireland, Germany; etc.

**Dufrenite**
**$Fe^{2+}Fe_4^{3+}(PO_4)_3(OH)_5 . 2H_2O$**
Dufrenite crystallizes in the monoclinic system as botryoidal masses or crusts; it has a perfect cleavage and is coloured dark green to black. H 3.5–4.5; SG 3.1–3.3
*Localities.* Occurs as a secondary mineral at Wheal Phoenix, Cornwall, England; Thüringer Wald, E. Germany; Cherokee Co., Alabama.

**Cacoxenite**
**$Fe_4^{3+}(PO_4)_3(OH)_3 . 12H_2O$**
Cacoxenite crystallizes in the hexagonal system as radial or tufted aggregates coloured golden yellow to brown. H 3–4; SG 2.3
*Occurrence.* Occurs as a secondary mineral associated with other phosphate minerals and with limonite.

*Localities*. From France; Germany; Sweden; Polk Co., Arkansas; Antwerp, New York, on hematite.

**Cyrilovite**
**$NaFe_3^{3+}(PO_4)_2(OH)_4.2H_2O$**
Cyrilovite crystallizes in the tetragonal system as very small squat crystals coloured orange to brown. H not known; SG 3.1
*Localities*. Occurs with metastrengite and leucophosphite at the Sapucaia pegmatite, Minas Gerais, Brazil; also from Cyrilov, Czechoslovakia; etc.

**Anapaite $Ca_2Fe^{2+}(PO_4)_2.2H_2O$**
Anapaite crystallizes in the triclinic system as tabular crystals or aggregates coloured green or white, with a vitreous lustre. H 3.5; SG 2.8
*Localities*. Occurs in phosphatic geodes at Bellaver de Cerdena, Spain; in a bituminous clay at Messel, W. Germany; from the Lewis Well, Kings Co., California.
*Treatment*. Clean with distilled water.

**Mitridatite**
**$Ca_3Fe_4^{3+}(OH)_6(H_2O_3)(PO_4)_4$**
Mitridatite crystallizes in the monoclinic system as tabular crystals or as crusts and veinlets. The colour is deep red with an olive-green streak, and the lustre is dull. H 3.5; SG 3.2
*Localities*. Occurs with jahnsite and collinsite in an altered triphylite in pegmatite, Custer Co., South Dakota; from Central Africa; etc.
*Treatment*. Clean with distilled water.

**Jahnsite $CaMn^{2+}Mg_2(H_2O)_8Fe_2^{3+}(OH)_2(PO_4)_4$**
Jahnsite crystallizes in the monoclinic system as well-developed crystals and as parallel aggregates, often twinned. The colour is brown, purple, yellow, orange or green. There is a vitreous lustre. H 4; SG 2.7
*Occurrence*. Occurs in granite pegmatites with other phosphate minerals.
*Localities*. From Custer Co., South Dakota; Palermo, New Hampshire.
*Treatment*. Clean with distilled water.

**Messelite**
**$Ca_2(Fe^{2+}, Mn^{2+})(PO_4)_2.2H_2O$**
Messelite crystallizes in the triclinic system as prismatic crystals or lamellar masses; it has a perfect cleavage. The colour is white, colourless, green or grey with a white streak. There is a vitreous lustre. H 3.5; SG 3.1
*Occurrence*. Occurs as a late hydrothermal mineral in granite pegmatites.
*Localities*. From Custer Co., South Dakota; Palermo, New Hampshire; King's Mountain, North Carolina.
*Treatment*. Clean with distilled water.

**Collinsite**
**$Ca_2(Mg, Fe)(PO_4)_2.2H_2O$**
Collinsite crystallizes in the triclinic system as prismatic crystals or as bundles; more commonly as crusts. There is a perfect cleavage. The colour is white, brown or colourless, with a vitreous lustre. H 3.5; SG 3.0
*Localities*. Occurs in altered phosphate nodules in a granite pegmatite at the Tip Top mine, Custer Co., South Dakota; and elsewhere.

**Phosphoferrite**
**$(Fe, Mn)_3(PO_4)_2.3H_2O$**
Phosphoferrite crystallizes in the orthorhombic system as octahedra or as granular masses. It is green or colourless, with a vitreous lustre. H 3–3.5; SG 3.3
*Occurrence*. Occurs in granite pegmatites as an alteration product of the mineral triphylite.
*Localities*. From Custer Co., South Dakota; Hagendorf, Bavaria, W Germany.
*Treatment*. Clean with distilled water.

**Metavauxite**
**$Fe^{2+}Al_2(PO_4)_2(OH)_2.8H_2O$**
Metavauxite crystallizes in the monoclinic system as prismatic crystals or as radial aggregates. The colour is white, green or colourless, and the lustre is vitreous. H 3; SG 2.3
*Localities*. Occurs with paravauxite and wavellite with quartz in the tin mines of Llallagua, Bolivia.
*Treatment*. Clean with distilled water.

Above: *Pyramidal crystals of lazulite, from Lincoln County, Georgia*

**Paravauxite**
**$Fe^{2+}Al(PO_4)_2(OH)_2.10H_2O$**
Paravauxite crystallizes in the triclinic system as prismatic crystals or radial aggregates. There is a perfect cleavage. The colour is greenish-white or colourless with a white streak, and there is a vitreous lustre. H 3; SG 2.4
*Localities*. Occurs in tin deposits at Llallagua, Bolivia.
*Treatment*. Clean with distilled water.

**Vauxite $Fe^{2+}Al_2(PO_4)_2(OH)_2.6H_2O$**
Vauxite crystallizes in the triclinic system as tabular crystals and as radial aggregates coloured pale to dark blue. The streak is white. There is a vitreous lustre. H 3.5; SG 2.4
*Localities*. Occurs with paravauxite and quartz in the tin deposits at Llallagua, Bolivia.
*Treatment*. Clean with distilled water.

**Leucophosphite**
**$KFe_2^{3+}(OH)(H_2O)(PO_4)_2.H_2O$**
Leucophosphite crystallizes in the monoclinic system as prismatic crystals or as lamellar masses. The colour is brown in pegmatite and greenish in sedimentary occurrences; there is a vitreous lustre. H 3.5; SG 2.9
*Localities*. Occurs in pegmatites at the Sapucaia mine, Minas Gerais, Brazil; in sedimentary deposits, Bomi Hill, Liberia; and elsewhere.

**Lazulite $(Mg,Fe^{2+})Al_2(PO_4)_2(OH)_2$**
Lazulite crystallizes in the monoclinic system as pyramidal crystals or as granular masses with twinning commonly found. The colour is deep or light blue, with a vitreous lustre. H 5.5–6; SG 3.1
*Occurrence*. Occurs in granite pegmatites, quartz veins and quartzites associated with garnet, andalusite and other minerals.
*Localities*. From Bolivia; Brazil; Malagasy Republic; Lincoln Co., Georgia; Mono Co., California; Hörrsjoberg, Sweden; etc.
*Treatment*. Clean with dilute hydrochloric acid only.

Left: *Strengite in matrix from Bavaria*

*Right: Tiny green crystals of euchroite from Lubietová, Czechoslovakia. The name means 'beautifully coloured'*

*Below right: Clinoclase from Gwennap, Cornwall*

*Fashioning. Uses*: usually cabochons or beads; *cleavage*: indistinct prismatic; *pleochroism*: strong; *heat sensitivity*: fairly high.

**Cassidyite**
**$Ca_2(Ni, Mg)(PO_4)_2 . 2H_2O$**
Cassidyite crystallizes in the triclinic system as crusts and spherules which are coloured bright green. H not known; SG 3.1
*Localities.* Occurs in weathered meteorites from Wolf Creek Crater, Western Australia

## Arsenates

**Olivenite $Cu_2AsO_4OH$**
Olivenite crystallizes in the orthorhombic system as prismatic crystals and as globular masses. The colour is olive green to yellow and brown. The lustre is vitreous or silky. H3; SG 4.4
*Occurrence.* Occurs in the oxidized zone of ore deposits with azurite and malachite.
*Localities.* From Tsumeb, South-West Africa; Majuba Hill, Nevada; and elsewhere.
*Treatment.* Olivenite should be cleaned with distilled water.

**Euchroite $Cu_2AsO_4OH . 3H_2O$**
Euchroite crystallizes in the orthorhombic system as prismatic crystals coloured bright emerald green. They have a vitreous lustre. H 3.5–4; SG 3.4
*Localities.* Occurs with olivenite in a sericite schist at Libethen, Hungary; from the Zapachitsa copper deposit, Bulgaria.

*Below Another Cornish mineral, olivenite*

**Cornwallite $Cu_5(AsO_4)_2(OH)_4 . H_2O$**
Cornwallite crystallizes in the monoclinic system as botryoidal crusts coloured light to dark green, with a dull lustre. H 4.5; SG 4.5
*Localities.* Occurs in Cornwall; Utah; Majuba Hill, Nevada; Germany; and other localities.

**Cornubite $Cu_5(AsO_4)_2(OH)_4$**
Cornubite crystallizes in the triclinic system as fibrous masses coloured light apple green. H not known; SG 4.6
*Localities.* Occurs in Cornwall, Devon and Cumbria, with malachite and olivenite.

**Clinoclase $Cu_3AsO_4(OH)_3$**
Clinoclase crystallizes in the monoclinic system as tabular crystals or rosettes; there is a perfect cleavage and the colour is dark green, blue or black. The streak is bluish-green. There is a vitreous lustre. H 2.5–3; SG 4.3
*Localities.* Occurs with olivenite in Cornwall; Tavistock, Devon; Majuba Hill, Nevada; Utah; etc.
*Treatment.* Clean with distilled water.

**Chlorotile $Cu_3(AsO_4)_2 . 6H_2O$**
Chlorotile crystallizes in the hexagonal system as prismatic crystals, more commonly as fibrous masses. The colour is pale to emerald green, with a dull lustre. H soft; SG 3.7
*Occurrence.* Occurs in the oxidation zone of ore deposits.
*Localities.* From Schneeberg, E. Germany; Dome Rock copper mine, South Australia; etc.

**Conichalcite $CuCaAsO_4OH$**
Conichalcite crystallizes in the orthorhombic system as prismatic crystals or as reniform masses and crusts. The colour is emerald-green or yellow. H 4.5; SG 4.3
*Occurrence.* Occurs in the oxidized zone of copper deposits with limonite and other copper minerals.
*Localities.* From South-West Africa; Mexico; Poland; Germany; Spain; Chile; South Dakota; Arizona; etc.

**Liroconite**
**$Cu_2Al(As, P)O_4(OH)_4 . 4H_2O$**
Liroconite crystallizes in the monoclinic system as wedge-shaped crystals or granular masses. The colour is blue to green, and the crystals have a

vitreous lustre. H 2–2.5; SG 2.9–3.0
*Occurrence.* Occurs in the oxidized zone of copper deposits with azurite and malachite.
*Localities.* From Cornwall and Devon; Germany; Inyo Co., California; and some other localities.

**Ceruléite**
**$CuAl_4(AsO_4)_2(OH)_8 . 4H_2O$**
Ceruléite's crystal system is not known. It is found as compact masses, blue in colour, resembling turquoise. SG 2.8
*Localities.* From Wheal Gorland, Cornwall; and from Chile.

**Chenevixite**
**$Cu_2Fe_2(AsO_4)_2(OH)_4 . H_2O$**
Chenevixite crystallizes in the orthorhombic system as compact masses with a greasy or dull lustre. They are coloured dark green with a greenish-yellow streak. H 3.5–4.5; SG 3.9
*Localities.* Occurs with azurite and chrysocolla at Klein Spitzkopje, South-West Africa; Tamanrasset, Algeria; Broken Hill, New South Wales; and some other localities.
*Treatment.* Clean with distilled water.

**Arthurite** **$Cu_2Fe_4(AsO_4, PO_4, SO_4)_4(O, OH)_4 . 8H_2O$**
Arthurite crystallizes in the monoclinic system as prismatic crystals or globular aggregates. The colour is apple green or emerald green, with a vitreous lustre. H not known; SG 3.0
*Occurrence.* Occurs as thin crusts with pharmacosiderite.
*Localities.* From Calstock, Cornwall; Majuba Hill, Nevada; Atacama Province, Chile.

**Rösslerite $MgH(AsO_4) . 7H_2O$**
Rösslerite crystallizes in the monoclinic system as fibrous crusts coloured white. H 2–3; SG 1.9
*Occurrence.* Occurs in arsenic-bearing ore deposits.
*Localities.* From Bieber, Hanau, W. Germany; Jachymov, Czechoslovakia; etc.

**Pharmacolite $CaHAsO_4 . 2H_2O$**
Pharmacolite crystallizes in the monoclinic system as botryoidal clusters or acicular crystals. There is a perfect cleavage. They are white or colourless. They have a vitreous or silky lustre. H 2–2.5; SG 2.7
*Localities.* Occurs with erythrite at San Gabriel Canyon, Los Angeles Co., California; Wittichen, Black Forest, W. Germany; Jachymov, Czechoslovakia; etc.
*Treatment.* Pharmacolite should be cleaned with distilled water.

**Sainfeldite $H_2Ca_5(AsO_4)_4 . 4H_2O$**
Sainfeldite crystallizes in the monoclinic system as rosettes coloured light pink or colourless. H not known; SG 3.0
*Localities.* Occurs in the Gabe Gottes vein, Ste. Marie-aux-Mines, Alsace, France; etc.

**Picropharmacolite**
**$H_2Ca_4Mg(AsO_4)_4 . 12H_2O$**
Picropharmacolite crystallizes in the monoclinic system as needles and encrustations. There is a perfect cleavage

*Left: Adamite crystals from the Ojuela mine, Mapimi, Mexico*

*Far left: Liroconite from Cornwall*

*Below left: Pharmacolite from Ste. Marie-aux-Mines, Alsace, France*

and the mineral is white or colourless. H not known; SG 2.6
*Localities.* Occurs on dolomite at Joplin, Missouri; also from Ste. Marie-aux-Mines, Alsace, France; etc.

**Köttigite $Zn_3(AsO_4)_2 . 8H_2O$**
Köttigite crystallizes in the monoclinic system as prismatic crystals or as crusts. There is a perfect cleavage. The colour is dark red to brown with a reddish-white streak. H 2.5–3; SG 3.3
*Localities.* Occurs at the Daniel mine, Schneeberg, E. Germany; Mapimi, Durango, Mexico.
*Treatment.* Clean with distilled water.

**Legrandite $Zn_2(OH)AsO_4 . H_2O$**
Legrandite crystallizes in the monoclinic system as prismatic crystals or as aggregates, coloured yellow to colourless. They have a vitreous lustre. H 4.5; SG 4.0
*Localities.* Occurs in a limonite matrix with adamite at Mapimi, Durango, Mexico.
*Treatment.* Clean with distilled water.

**Adamite $Zn_2AsO_4OH$**
Adamite crystallizes in the orthorhombic system as tabular crystals or as druses of interlocked crystals. The colour is bright yellowish-green, blue, violet or light red. There may be a fluorescence under ultra-violet light. The lustre is vitreous. H 3.5; SG 4.3–4.5
*Occurrence.* Occurs in the oxidation zone of ore deposits with limonite, calcite and other minerals.
*Localities.* From San Bernardino Co., California; Mapimi, Durango, Mexico; Laurion, Greece; and some other localities.
*Treatment.* Clean with distilled water.

**Paradamite $Zn_2AsO_4OH$**
Paradamite crystallizes in the triclinic system as aggregates or as rounded crystals. There is a perfect cleavage and the colour is pale yellow. There is a vitreous lustre. H 3.5; SG 4.5
*Localities.* Occurs with mimetite and adamite on limonite at Mapimi, Durango, Mexico.
*Treatment.* Clean with distilled water.

**Veszelyite**
**$(Cu, Zn)_3(PO_4)(OH)_3 2H_2O$**
Veszelyite crystallizes in the monoclinic system as prismatic crystals or granular aggregates. The colour is green to blue, the lustre vitreous. H 3.5–4; SG 3.4

*Right: Bayldonite from Tsumeb, South-West Africa*

*Localities.* Kabwe, Zambia; Kipushi, Shaba, Zaire; Banat, Romania; and other localities.
*Treatment.* Clean with distilled water.

**Austinite $CaZnAsO_4OH$**
Austinite crystallizes in the orthorhombic system as prismatic crystals or drusy crusts coloured white, pale yellow or bright green. They have an adamantine or silky lustre. H 4–4.5; SG 4.1
*Localities.* Occurs with adamite on limonite at Tooele Co., Utah; Mapimi, Durango, Mexico; Tsumeb, South-West Africa; etc.

**Chudobaite $(Na, K, Ca)(Mg, Zn, Mn)_2H(AsO_4)_2 \cdot 4H_2O$**
Chudobaite crystallizes in the triclinic system as small crystals coloured pink. H 2.5–3; SG 2.9
*Localities.* Occurs with conichalcite at Tsumeb, South-West Africa.

**Holdenite $(Mn, Zn)_6(AsO_4)(OH)_5O_2$**
Holdenite crystallizes in the orthorhombic system as tabular crystals coloured pink or yellowish-red to deep red. They have a vitreous lustre. H 4; SG 4.1
*Localities.* Occurs at Franklin, New Jersey. The only known specimen is found in a vein in franklinite.

**Chlorophoenicite $(Mn, Zn)_5AsO_4(OH)_7$**
Chlorophoenicite crystallizes in the monoclinic system as needles and fibres coloured light green in daylight and purple in artificial light. H 3.5; SG 3.5
*Localities.* Occurs with pyrochroite and other minerals in zinc-manganese-iron oxides in marbles at Franklin, New Jersey.
*Treatment.* Clean with distilled water.

**Retzian $Mn_2Y(AsO_4)(OH)_4$**
Retzian crystallizes in the orthorhombic system as prismatic crystals coloured dark brown with a light brown streak. They have a vitreous lustre. H 4; SG 4.1
*Localities.* Occurs in dolomite at Nordmark, Sweden.
*Treatment.* Clean with distilled water.

**Agardite $(Y, Ca)_2Cu_{12}(AsO_4)_6(OH)_{12} \cdot 6H_2O$**
Agardite crystallizes in the hexagonal system as acicular crystals, coloured blue to green. H 3–4; SG 3.7
*Localities.* From the oxidation zone of the copper deposit at Bou-Skour, Morocco; also from Utah; etc.
*Treatment.* Clean with distilled water.

**Cafarsite $Ca_3(Fe, Ti)_3Mn(AsO_4)_6 \cdot 2H_2O$**
Cafarsite crystallizes in the cubic system as well-formed crystals coloured dark or yellowish-brown. The streak is yellowish-brown. H 5.5–6; SG 3.9
*Localities.* Occurs on gneisses in Valais, Switzerland; Italy.

**Schultenite $PbHAsO_4$**
Schultenite crystallizes in the monoclinic system as rhombohedra, often with striated faces. They are colourless, with a vitreous lustre. H 2.5; SG 5.9
*Localities.* Occurs in association with anglesite and bayldonite in the Tsumeb area of South-West Africa.

**Bayldonite $(Pb, Cu)_3(AsO_4)_2(OH)_2$**
Bayldonite crystallizes in the monoclinic system as granular masses or as crusts. The colour is yellow to green; the lustre is resinous. H 4.5; SG 5.5
*Occurrence.* Occurs in the oxidation zone of copper ore deposits with azurite and other minerals.
*Localities.* From St. Day, Cornwall; Tsumeb, South-West Africa; etc.
*Treatment.* Clean with distilled water.
*Fashioning. Uses*: usually cabochons; *cleavage*: not significant; *heat sensitivity*: low.

**Duftite $CuPbAsO_4OH$**
Duftite crystallizes in the orthorhombic system as tiny crystals or as crusts coloured apple to dark green. H 3; SG 6.4
*Localities.* Occurs with wulfenite and malachite at Tsumeb, South-West Africa.

**Caryinite $(Ca, Na, Pb, Mn)_3(Mn, Mg)_2(AsO_4)_3(OH)$**
Caryinite crystallizes in the monoclinic system as granular masses with a yellow to brown colour. H 4; SG 4.3
*Localities.* Occurs in skarn at Långban, Sweden.

**Carminite $PbFe_2(AsO_4)_2(OH)_2$**
Carminite crystallizes in the orthorhombic system as minute crystals or as tufted aggregates. The colour is red to brown. H 3.5; SG 5.2
*Localities.* Occurs with anglesite and other minerals at Mapimi, Durango, Mexico; Calstock, Cornwall; Horhausen, W. Germany; Utah; Colorado; etc.

**Ludlockite $(Fe, Pb)As_2O_6$**
Ludlockite crystallizes in the triclinic system its crystals sometimes show lamellar twinning. The mineral is sectile and flexible. The colour is red with a light brown streak, and the lustre is adamantine. H 1.5–2; SG 4.4
*Localities.* Occurs with zinc in siderite at Tsumeb, South-West Africa.

**Atelestite $Bi_8(AsO_4)_3O_5(OH)_5$**
Atelestite crystallizes in the monoclinic system as tabular crystals or spherical crystalline aggregates. The colour is bright yellow to green with an adamantine lustre. H 4.5–5; SG 6.8
*Localities.* Occurs with bismutite at Schneeberg, E. Germany.
*Treatment.* Clean with distilled water.

**Mixite $Cu_{12}Bi_2(AsO_4)_6(OH)_{12} \cdot 6H_2O$**
Mixite crystallizes in the hexagonal system as needle-like crystals or as tufted aggregates coloured emerald green to white. The streak is lighter than the colour. H 3–4; SG 3.8
*Localities.* Occurs in Germany; Inyo Co., California; El Carmen mine, Durango, Mexico; etc.

**Walpurgite $(BiO)_4UO_2(AsO_4)_2 \cdot 3H_2O$**
Walpurgite crystallizes in the triclinic system as thin crystals, commonly twinned, or as aggregates. There is a perfect cleavage. The colour is yellow, and the lustre is adamantine. H 3.5; SG 5.9
*Localities.* Occurs with torbernite and other minerals in the oxidized zone of a uraninite vein, in the Walpurgis vein at the Weisser Hirsch mine, Schneeberg, E. Germany; etc.

**Trögerite $H_2(UO_2)_2(AsO_4)_2 \cdot 8H_2O$**
Trögerite crystallizes in the tetragonal system as tabular crystals or as aggregates. There is a perfect cleavage. The colour is lemon yellow and there is a similarly-coloured fluorescence under ultra-violet light. The lustre is vitreous. H 2–3; SG 3.5
*Localities.* Occurs with walpurgite in the Walpurgis vein, Weisser Hirsch mine, Schneeberg, E. Germany.
*Treatment.* Clean with distilled water.

**Abernathyite $KUO_2AsO_4 \cdot 3H_2O$**
Abernathyite crystallizes in the tetragonal system as tabular crystals or as coatings. There is a perfect cleavage; the colour is yellow and the streak pale yellow. There is a yellow-green fluorescence under ultra-violet light. The lustre is vitreous. H 2.5; SG 3.3
*Localities.* Occurs with scorodite in

sandstone at Temple Mountain, Utah; Harding Co., South Dakota.

**Heinrichite**
**$Ba(UO_2)_2(AsO_4)_2 . 10–12H_2O$**
Heinrichite crystallizes in the tetragonal system as tabular crystals coloured yellow-green and with a perfect cleavage. They have a vitreous lustre. There is a bright green fluorescence under ultra-violet light. H 2.5; SG 3.6
*Localities.* Occurs in an altered rhyolite tuff in Lake Co., Oregon; as an alteration of pitchblende at Wittichen in the Black Forest, W. Germany.

**Uranospinite**
**$Ca(UO_2)_2(AsO_4)_4 . 10H_2O$**
Uranospinite crystallizes in the tetragonal system as rectangular plates with a perfect cleavage. The colour is yellow to green with a pearly lustre. There is a bright yellow fluorescence under ultra-violet light. H 2–3; SG 3.4
*Occurrence.* Formed by the alteration of uraninite.
*Localities.* From the Weisser Hirsch mine, Schneeberg, E. Germany; Kane Co., Utah; etc.

**Zeunerite $Cu(UO_2)_2(AsO_4)_2 . 12H_2O$**
Zeunerite crystallizes in the tetragonal system as tabular crystals with a perfect cleavage. The colour is yellow to emerald-green, with a vitreous lustre. H 2.5; SG 3.4
*Occurrence.* Occurs in the oxidized zone of uraninite and arsenic-bearing deposits.
*Localities.* From the Weisser Hirsch mine, Schneeberg, E. Germany; etc.
*Treatment.* Clean with distilled water.

**Uranospathite**
**$Cu(UO_2)_2[(As, P)O_4]_2 . 12H_2O$**
It is not certain that uranospathite is a separate species. It probably crystallizes in the tetragonal system as groups of rectangular plates with a perfect cleavage. The colour is yellow to green or bluish-green. H not known; SG 2.5
*Localities.* Occurs with bassetite at Redruth, Cornwall.

**Sarkinite $Mn_2AsO_4OH$**
Sarkinite crystallizes in the monoclinic system as tabular crystals or as spherical granular masses. The colour is dark red or yellow with a red or yellow streak. There is a greasy lustre. H 4–5; SG 4.1–4.2
*Localities.* Occurs with hausmannite in Sweden at Långban and with jacobsite and other minerals at Pajsberg, Sweden.
*Treatment.* Clean with distilled water.

**Eveite $Mn_2(OH)(AsO_4)$**
Eveite crystallizes in the orthorhombic system as tabular crystals coloured apple-green with a white streak. H 4; SG 3.8
*Localities.* Occurs in fractures in hausmannite from Långban, Sweden.

**Brandtite $Ca_2Mn(AsO_4)_2 . 2H_2O$**
Brandtite crystallizes in the monoclinic system as prismatic crystals or as reniform masses and radial groups. There is a perfect cleavage and the colour is white or colourless. There is a vitreous lustre. H 3.5; SG 3.7
*Localities.* Occurs with rhodochrosite at Sterling Hill, New Jersey; etc.
*Treatment.* Clean with distilled water.

**Berzeliite**
**$(Ca, Na)_3(Mg, Mn)_2(AsO_4)_3$**
Berzeliite crystallizes in the cubic system as trapezohedra; more commonly as grains or in masses. The colour is orange-yellow. H 4.5–5; SG 4.1
*Localities.* Occurs in limestone with rhodonite and other minerals at Långban, Sweden.

**Hematolite**
**$Mn_4Al(OH)_2(AsO_4)(AsO_3)_2$**
Hematolite crystallizes in the hexagonal system as tabular or rhombohedral crystals with horizontal striations on the rhombohedral faces. There is a perfect cleavage. The colour is brownish-red to black, and the lustre is vitreous. H 3.5; SG 3.5
*Localities.* Occurs in crystalline limestone with jacobsite and other minerals at Nordmark, Sweden.
*Treatment.* Clean with distilled water.

**Symplesite $Fe_3(AsO_4)_2 . 8H_2O$**
Symplesite crystallizes in the triclinic system as small crystals or as spherical aggregates; it has a perfect cleavage. The colour is light blue or green to deep blue, with a vitreous lustre. H 2.5; SG 3.0
*Localities.* Occurs as a powder filling cavities in löllingite in a pegmatite at Custer Mountain Lode, Custer Co., South Dakota; from Lobenstein, E. Germany; Italy; Tasmania; etc.

**Scorodite $FeAsO_4 . 2H_2O$**
Scorodite crystallizes in the orthorhombic system as pyramidal crystals or as crusts or masses. The colour is pale green, yellow to brown or violet. The lustre is vitreous. H 3.5–4; SG 3.3
*Occurrence.* Formed by the oxidation of arsenic-bearing minerals.
*Localities.* From Ouro Preto, Minas Gerais, Brazil; Ontario; California; Mexico; and elsewhere.
*Treatment.* Clean ultrasonically.

**Pharmacosiderite**
**$Fe_3(AsO_4)_2(OH)_3 . 5H_2O$**
Pharmacosiderite crystallizes in the cubic system as cubes with diagonal striations or tetrahedra. The mineral is sectile and is coloured olive to emerald-green or reddish-brown. It has an adamantine or a greasy lustre. H 2.5; SG 2.8
*Occurrence.* As an oxidation product of arsenic minerals.
*Localities.* From Cornwall; Utah; South Dakota; Germany; and elsewhere.
*Treatment.* Clean with distilled water.

**Arseniosiderite**
**$Ca_3Fe^{3+}_4(OH)_6(H_2O)_3(AsO_4)_4$**
Arseniosiderite crystallizes in the monoclinic system as masses or fibrous aggregates with a yellow or brown colour. The streak is yellow. H 4.4; SG 3.6
*Localities.* Occurs at Mapimi, Durango, Mexico; Tooele Co., Utah; France; Germany; etc.
*Treatment.* Clean with distilled water.

*Left: Bladed crystals of erythrite from Bou Azzer, Morocco*

**Liskeardite**
**$(Al, Fe)_3AsO_4(OH)_6 . 5H_2O$**
Liskeardite crystallizes in the monoclinic or orthorhombic systems as aggregates and crusts. The colour is white or greenish to black. H not known; SG 3.0
*Localities.* Occurs coating quartz at Liskeard, Cornwall; and other places.

**Erythrite $Co_3(AsO_4)_2 . 8H_2O$**
Erythrite crystallizes in the monoclinic system as prismatic crystals or as bladed aggregates; there is a perfect cleavage and the mineral is sectile. The colour is deep purple to pale pink. The streak is lighter than this. The lustre is adamantine or dull. H 1.5–2.5; SG 3.2
*Occurrence.* Occurs in the oxidation zone of cobalt ore deposits.
*Localities.* From Schneeberg, E. Germany; England; Sweden; Bou Azzer, Morocco; Cobalt, Ontario; California; Nevada; New Mexico; etc.
*Treatment.* Clean with distilled water.

*Left: Cubic crystals of pharmocosiderite from Cornwall*

*Right: Lavendulan from Meskani, Iran*

**Lavendulan**
**$(Ca, Na)_2Cu_5(AsO_4)_4Cl.4–5H_2O$**
Lavendulan crystallizes in the orthorhombic system as flaky aggregates coloured lavender-blue, with a vitreous lustre. H 2.5; SG 3.5
*Localities.* Occurs with olivenite at Tooele Co., Utah; with erythrite at Jachymov, Czechoslovakia; etc.

**Roselite $Ca_2(Co, Mg)(AsO_4)_2.2H_2O$**
Roselite crystallizes in the monoclinic system as prismatic crystals or as spherical aggregates. There is a perfect cleavage. The colour is dark red to pink, with a vitreous lustre. H 3.5; SG 3.5–3.7
*Localities.* Occurs with erythrite at Bou Azzer, Morocco; Schneeberg, E. Germany; Shapbach, W. Germany.
*Treatment.* Clean with distilled water.

**Annabergite $Ni_3(AsO_4)_2.8H_2O$**
Annabergite crystallizes in the monoclinic system as prismatic crystals or as crusts or powders. There is a perfect cleavage. The colour is white to intense yellow-green with the streak a lighter shade than the colour. There is an adamantine lustre. H 1.5–2.5; SG 3.1
*Occurrence.* Occurs in the oxidation zone of nickeliferous ore deposits.
*Localities.* From Schneeberg, E. Germany; Cobalt, Ontario; Sierra Cabrera, Spain; Laurion, Greece; Humboldt Co., Nevada; Inyo Co., California; etc.
*Treatment.* Clean with distilled water.

## Vanadates

**Volborthite $Cu_3(VO_4)_2.3H_2O$**
Volborthite crystallizes in the monoclinic system as compact masses; it has a perfect cleavage and frequently displays lamellar twinning. The colour is dark green. yellow or brown, with a vitreous lustre. H 3.5; SG 3.5–3.8
*Localities.* Occurs in sandstone at Richardson, Utah; in a sedimentary rock at Menzies Bay, Vancouver Island, Canada; Syssersk, Urals, USSR.
*Treatment.* Clean with distilled water.

**Pascoite $Ca_2V_6O_{17}.11H_2O$**
Pascoite crystallizes in the monoclinic system as granular crusts coloured orange-yellow with a yellow streak and soluble in water. H 2.5; SG 1.9
*Localities.* Occurs in the vanadium deposit at Minas Ragra, Peru; Mesa Co., Colorado; etc.

**Hewettite $CaV_6O_{16}.9H_2O$**
Hewettite probably crystallizes in the orthorhombic system as aggregates and coatings coloured deep red. H not known; SG 2.5
*Localities.* Occurs in the oxidized zone of the vanadium deposit at Minas Ragra, Peru; etc.

**Hummerite $KMgV_5O_{14}.8H_2O$**
Hummerite crystallizes in the triclinic system as tabular crystals or as crusts with a bright orange colour. H not known; SG 2.5
*Localities.* Occurs in grey clay at the Hummer mine, Montrose Co., Colorado; also from South Dakota.

**Sherwoodite**
**$Ca_3(V^{4+}O)_2V^{5+}_6O_{20}.15H_2O$**
Sherwoodite crystallizes in the tetragonal system as polycrystalline aggregates coloured dark blue to black, altering to yellow-green. H about 2; SG 2.8
*Localities.* Vanadium mines in Colorado.
*Treatment.* Clean with distilled water.

**Hendersonite**
**$Ca_2V^{4+}_{1+x}V^{5+}_{8-x}(O, OH)_{24}.8H_2O$**
Hendersonite crystallizes in the orthorhombic system as platy crystals or as fibrous aggregates coloured dark green to black with a brownish-green streak. H 2.5; SG 2.8
*Localities.* Occurs in oxidized ore with sherwoodite at vanadium mines in Colorado and in New Mexico.
*Treatment.* Clean with distilled water.

**Steigerite $AlVO_4.3H_2O$**
Steigerite's system is not known. It forms plates of a yellow colour, with a waxy lustre. H and SG not known.
*Localities.* Occurs with gypsum in fractures in corvusite, San Miguel Co., Colorado.
*Treatment.* Clean with distilled water.

**Vanalite $NaAl_8V_{10}O_{38}.30H_2O$**
Vanalite's crystal system is not known; it forms bright yellow to orange crystals with a waxy or dull lustre. SG 2.3–2.4
*Localities.* Occurs as encrustations with clay minerals at Kara-Tau, Kazakhstan, USSR.
*Treatment.* Clean with distilled water.

**Wakefieldite $YVO_4$**
Wakefieldite crystallizes in the tetragonal system as yellow masses. H 5; SG 4.2
*Localities.* Occurs with quartz and other minerals at Wakefield, Quebec.
*Treatment.* Clean with distilled water.

**Chervetite $Pb_2V_2O_7$**
Chervetite crystallizes in the monoclinic system as twinned crystals or as pseudomorphs after francevilleite. The colour is grey to brown or colourless with a white streak. There is an adamantine

lustre. H about 2.5; SG 6.3–6.5
*Occurrence.* Occurs with francevillite in the oxidation zone of uranium deposits.
*Localities.* From Mounana, Gabon.
*Treatment.* Clean with distilled water.

**Mottramite $Pb(Cu, Zn)VO_4OH$**
Mottramite crystallizes in the orthorhombic system as prismatic crystals or as aggregates or crusts. The colour is light to dark green to black; the lustre is vitreous. H 3.0–3.5; SG 5.9
*Occurrence.* Occurs in the oxidation zone of ore deposits.
*Localities.* From Mottram St. Andrew, Cheshire; Crestmore, Riverside Co., California; Sardinia; Bolivia; Chile; and elsewhere.
*Treatment.* Clean with distilled water.

**Descloizite $Pb(Zn, Cu) VO_4OH$**
Descloizite crystallizes in the orthorhombic system as prismatic crystals or as aggregates or crusts. The colour is orange-red to brown or green, with a vitreous lustre. H 3.5; SG 6.2
*Occurrence.* Occurs in the oxidation zone of ore deposits with pyromorphite, calcite and other minerals.
*Localities.* From Tsumeb and Otavi, South-West Africa; Rhodesia; Mexico; Galena, South Dakota; and some other localities.
*Treatment.* Descloizite should be cleaned with distilled water.

*Left: A fragment of amblygonite*

*Below left: A group of descloizite crystals from Tsumeb, South-West Africa*

**Pucherite $BiVO_4$**
Pucherite crystallizes in the orthorhombic system as small crystals with curved faces, or as masses. There is a perfect cleavage. The colour is yellow to brown with a yellow streak. There is a vitreous lustre. H 4; SG 6.2
*Localities.* Occurs in the oxidized portion of a bismuth-bearing vein in the Pucher shaft of the Wolfgang mine, Schneeberg, E. Germany; Brejauba, Minas Gerais, Brazil; etc.
*Treatment.* Clean with distilled water.

**Carnotite**
**$K_2(UO_2)_2(VO_4)_2 . 1\text{–}3H_2O$**
Carnotite crystallizes in the monoclinic system as tiny crystals or as compact masses or aggregates. There is a perfect cleavage. The colour is bright golden yellow, with a pearly or dull lustre. H not known; SG 4.7
*Occurrence.* In sedimentary rocks.
*Localities.* From Kambove, Shaba, Zaire; El Borouj, Morocco; Radium Hill, South Australia; Wyoming; and some other localities.

**Sengierite $Cu(UO_2)_2(VO_4)_2 . 6H_2O$**
Sengierite crystallizes in the monoclinic system as thin plates with a perfect cleavage coloured green, with a vitreous lustre. H 2.5; SG 4.0
*Localities.* Occurs with malachite and oxides of copper and other minerals at Shaba, Zaire; Bisbee, Arizona.

**Tyuyamunite**
**$Ca(UO_2)_2(VO_4)_2 . 5\text{–}8H_2O$**
Tyuyamunite crystallizes in the orthorhombic system as scales or compact masses with a perfect cleavage. They have an adamantine or dull lustre. The colour is green or yellow, sometimes with a weak fluorescence of a similar colour under ultra-violet light. H 2; SG 3.3–3.6
*Occurrence.* Occurs as a secondary mineral with other uranium and vanadium minerals.
*Localities.* From Ferghana, USSR; Wyoming; Texas; Colorado; Nevada.

**Vanuralite**
**$Al(UO_2)_2(VO_4)_2(OH) . 11H_2O$**
Vanuralite crystallizes in the monoclinic system as plates with a perfect cleavage and coloured yellow. H 2; SG 3.6.
*Localities.* Occurs with francevillite at Mounana, Gabon.

**Curienite $Pb(UO_2)_2(VO_4)_2 . 5H_2O$**
Curienite crystallizes in the orthorhombic system as powders coloured yellow. SG 4.9
*Localities.* Occurs in sandstones at Mounana, Gabon.

**Schubnelite $Fe_2(VO_4)_2 . 2H_2O$**
Schubnelite crystallizes in the triclinic system as tiny crystals coloured black; yellow in thin fragments. H not known; SG 3.3
*Localities.* From Mounana, Gabon.

## Phosphates, Arsenates and Vanadates with other anions

**Amblygonite $(Li, Na)AlPO_4(F, OH)$**
Amblygonite crystallizes in the triclinic system as prismatic crystals or as masses; it has a perfect cleavage. The colour is white to yellow or pink, with a vitreous lustre. H 5.5–6; SG 3.1; RI 1.61, 1.64
*Occurrence.* In granite pegmatites.
*Localities.* From Newry, Oxford Co., Maine; Brazil; France; Sakangyi, Burma; etc.
*Treatment.* Clean with distilled water.
*Fashioning. Uses*: faceting or cabochons; *cleavage*: perfect // to basal pinacoid, distinct macropinacoidal; *cutting angles*: crown 40°, pavilion 40°; *heat sensitivity*: fairly high.

**Herderite $CaBePO_4(F, OH)$**
Herderite crystallizes in the monoclinic system as prismatic or tabular crystals or as fibrous aggregates. The colour is pale yellow or green with a vitreous lustre. H 5–5.5; SG 3.0
*Occurrence.* In granite pegmatites.
*Localities.* From Newry and other places in Oxford Co., Maine; Minas Gerais, Brazil; Bavaria, W. Germany and Saxony, E. Germany; Mursinsk, USSR.
*Treatment.* Remove iron stains with dilute oxalic acid.

**Wagnerite $(Mg, Fe, Mn, Ca)_2PO_4F$**
Wagnerite crystallizes in the monoclinic system as prismatic crystals or

masses. The colour is yellow, grey to brown, with a vitreous lustre. H5–5.5; SG 3.1
*Localities*. Occurs in quartz veins with magnesite near Salzburg, Austria; in pegmatite at Mangualde, Portugal; Mt. Vesuvius, Italy; etc.
*Treatment*. Clean with distilled water.

**Apatite $Ca_5(PO_4)_3F$**
Apatite crystallizes in the hexagonal system as prismatic crystals or as compact masses. The colour is white, colourless, green, yellow, dark blue, purple, brown or reddish-brown. The streak is white. There is a vitreous lustre. H 5; SG 3.1; RI 1.63–1.64
*Occurrence*. Occurs in igneous rocks and pegmatites; also in hydrothermal veins and as detrital deposits.
*Localities*. From Durango, Mexico; South Dakota; Ontario; Quebec; Panasqueira, Portugal; Spain; Germany; Norway; Malagasy Republic; Burma, etc.
*Treatment*. Clean with distilled water.
*Fashioning*. *Uses*: faceting or cabochons; *cleavage*: imperfect basal; very brittle; *cutting angles*: crown 40°, pavilion 40°; *dichroism*: strong in Burmese stones; weak in other stones, except in deeper colours; *heat sensitivity*: high, use low-temperature dop wax.

*Right: Violet apatite crystals showing tabular form. From Ehrenfriedersdorf, East Germany*

*Right: A hexagonal prism of apatite from Mexico*

**Triplite $(Mn^{2+}, Fe^{2+}, Mg, Ca)_2(PO_4)(F, OH)$**
Triplite crystallizes in the monoclinic system as masses coloured reddish-brown. The streak is white or brown. There is a vitreous lustre. H 5–5.5; SG 3.5–3.9
*Occurrence*. Occurs in granite pegmatites and in high-temperature vein deposits.
*Localities*. From Rhodesia; Germany; France; South-West Africa; Arizona; Colorado; and elsewhere.
*Treatment*. Clean with distilled water.

**Svabite $Ca_5(AsO_4)_3(F, Cl, OH)$**
Svabite crystallizes in the hexagonal system as prismatic crystals or as masses. It is yellow or colourless, with a vitreous lustre. H 4–5; SG 3.5–3.8
*Localities*. Occurs in zinc ores at Franklin, New Jersey; Långban, Sweden.
*Treatment*. Clean with distilled water.

**Durangite $NaAlAsO_4F$**
Durangite crystallizes in the monoclinic system as pyramidal crystals coloured light orange to red. There is a vitreous lustre. The streak is yellow. H 5; SG 3.9–4.1
*Localities*. Occurs in tin mines with cassiterite and topaz, etc, at Durango, Mexico.
*Treatment*. Clean with distilled water.

**Pyromorphite $Pb_5(PO_4)_3Cl$**
Pyromorphite crystallizes in the hexagonal system as hexagonal prisms or more commonly as reniform or globular masses. The colour is green, yellow, brown and the streak is white. Its lustre is adamantine. H 3.5–4; SG 7.0
*Occurrence*. Occurs in the oxidation zone of lead ores.
*Localities*. From England; Scotland; France; Broken Hill, New South Wales;

Bad Ems, W. Germany; Burma; Zaire; and elsewhere.
*Treatment.* Clean with distilled water.

**Mimetite $Pb_5(AsO_4)_3Cl$**
Mimetite crystallizes in the monoclinic system as acicular crystals or as granular masses with a vitreous lustre. The colour is bright yellow, orange or colourless. H 3.5–4; SG 7.3
*Occurrence.* Occurs in the oxidation zone of lead ore deposits.
*Localities.* From Tsumeb, South-West Africa; Mapimi, Durango, Mexico; Leadhills, Scotland; California; Utah; Nevada; Arizona; Germany; and elsewhere.
*Treatment.* Clean with distilled water.
*Fashioning. Uses*: usually cabochons; *cleavage*: imperfect pyramidal; brittle; *heat sensitivity*: high, dop with care or use low-temperature wax.

**Vanadinite $Pb_5(VO_4)_3Cl$**
Vanadinite crystallizes in the hexagonal system as prismatic crystals or as globular masses. The colour is bright red or orange to yellow with a white or yellow streak. The lustre is resinous. H 3; SG 6.9
*Occurrence.* Occurs in the oxidation zone of lead ore deposits.
*Localities.* From Scotland; Sardinia; Miblacen, Morocco; Arizona; New Mexico; Colorado; etc.
*Treatment.* Clean with distilled water.

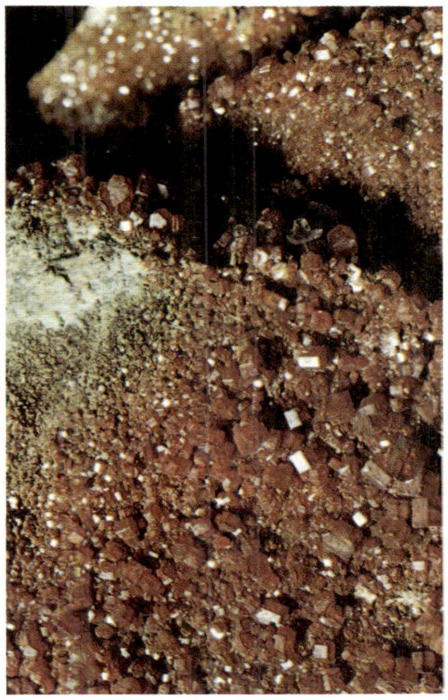

Left: Vanadinite crystals from the Old Yuma mine, Arizona

Far left: Mimetite from Johanngeorgenstadt, East Germany

**Chalcophyllite $Cu_{18}Al_2(AsO_4)_3(SO_4)_3(OH)_{27}.36H_2O$**
Chalcophyllite crystallizes in the hexagonal system as tabular crystals or foliated masses and rosettes with a perfect cleavage. The colour is emerald green to bluish-green. The streak is lighter than the colour. There is a vitreous lustre. H 2; SG 2.7
*Occurrence.* Chalcophyllite is found in

Far left: Hexagonal prism of pyromorphite from Czechoslovakia

Below: Fine hexagonal tabular crystals of chalcophyllite from Cornwall

*Right: Fornacite with dioptase from Renéville, Zaire*

the oxidation zone of copper ore deposits.
*Localities.* From Cornwall; France; Germany; Bisbee, Arizona; Utah; Nevada; etc.
*Treatment.* Clean with distilled water.

**Woodhouseite $CaAl_3PO_4SO_4(OH)_6$**
Woodhouseite crystallizes in the hexagonal system as pseudocubic crystals with curved or striated faces. There is a perfect cleavage and the colour is white to pink, with a vitreous lustre. H 4.5; SG 3.0
*Localities.* Occurs in veins with quartz and topaz in an andalusite deposit near Bishop, California.
*Treatment.* Clean with distilled water.

**Hinsdalite $(Pb, Sr)Al_3PO_4SO_4(OH)_6$**
Hinsdalite crystallizes in the hexagonal system as pseudocubic crystals or as granular masses. There is a perfect cleavage. The colour is yellow, green or colourless; the lustre is vitreous. H 4.5; SG 3.6
*Localities.* Occurs on covelline at Butte, Montana; Hinsdale Co., Colorado.
*Treatment.* Clean with distilled water.

**Hidalgoite $PbAl_3(AsO_4)(SO_4)(OH)_6$**
Hidalgoite crystallizes in the hexagonal system as masses coloured white, grey, or light green, with a dull lustre. H 4.5; SG 4.0
*Localities.* Occurs with iron oxides in ores at Tooele Co., Utah; Cap Garonne, France; etc.

**Beudantite $PbFe_3AsO_4SO_4(OH)_6$**
Beudantite crystallizes in the hexagonal system as rhombohedral crystals coloured dark green to black with a green streak; there is a vitreous lustre. Pseudocubic forms are also found. H 3.5–4.5; SG 4–4.3
*Occurrence.* Occurs in the oxidation zone of ore deposits.
*Localities.* From Tiger, Arizona; Laurion, Greece; Western Australia; etc.
*Treatment.* Clean with distilled water.

**Destinezite $Fe_2PO_4(SO_4)(OH).5H_2O$**
Destinezite crystallizes in the triclinic system as crusts or masses, sometimes stalactitic. The colour is deep yellow to brown. H 3–4; SG 2.0–2.4
*Localities.* Occurs in mine workings in San Benito Co., California; Black Hills, South Dakota; and elsewhere.

**Pitticite** near **$Fe_2^{3+}AsO_4SO_4OH.nH_2O$**
Pitticite's crystal system is not yet established; it occurs as crusts or as stalactitic masses light or dark brown in colour. They have a vitreous lustre. The streak is yellow to white. H 2–3; SG about 2.3
*Localities.* Occurs as a deposit from springs; found as an alteration product of arsenopyrite at Devil's Gulch, California; Nevada; England; Romania; Germany; etc.

**Tsumebite $Pb_2Cu(PO_4)(SO_4)(OH)$**
Tsumebite crystallizes in the monoclinic system as tabular crystals or crusts. The crystals are twinned as trillings or as more complex groups. The colour is emerald green, with a vitreous lustre. H 3.5; SG 6.1
*Localities.* Occurs with smithsonite and other minerals at Tsumeb, South-West Africa; and other places.
*Treatment.* Clean with distilled water.

*Below: Tyrolite. The foliated structure of the mineral can be clearly seen in these crystals from Penamellera, Spain*

**Tyrolite $Ca_2Cu_9(AsO_4)_4(OH)_{10}.10H_2O$**
Tyrolite crystallizes in the orthorhombic system as scales or as reniform masses with a foliated structure. There is a perfect cleavage. Pseudohexagonal aggregates are found. The colour is pale green to blue, with a vitreous lustre. H 2; SG 3.2
*Occurrence.* In the oxidation zone of copper deposits.
*Localities.* Found with chalcophyllite at Majuba Hill, Nevada; England; France; Italy; Austria and elsewhere.

**Vauquelinite $Pb_2Cu(CrO_4)(PO_4)(OH)$**
Vauquelinite crystallizes in the monoclinic system as wedge-shaped crystals and as fibrous aggregates. The colour is brown to black, and the lustre adamantine. H 2.5–3; SG 6.0–6.1
*Localities.* Occurs with mimetite at Beresov, USSR, and other places.
*Treatment.* Clean with distilled water.

**Embreyite $Pb_5(CrO_4)_2(PO_4)_2.H_2O$**
Embreyite crystallizes in the monoclinic system as crystalline crusts made up of tabular crystals showing multiple twinning. The colour is orange with a yellow streak. H 3.5; SG 6.4
*Localities.* Occurs with crocoite and vauquelinite at Beresov, USSR.

**Fornacite $(Pb, Cu)_3[(Cr, As)O_4]_2(OH)$**
Fornacite crystallizes in the monoclinic system as prismatic crystals coloured dark green with a yellow streak. H not known; SG 6.3
*Localities.* Occurs with dioptase at Renéville, Congo and other places.

## Arsenites

**Trippkeite $CuAs_2O_4$**
Trippkeïte crystallizes in the tetragonal system as prismatic crystals coloured brilliant greenish-blue. There is a perfect cleavage. H not known; SG 4.8
*Localities.* Occurs in copper deposits at Copiapó, Chile.
*Treatment.* Clean with distilled water.

**Heliophyllite $Pb_3AsO_{4-n}Cl_{2n+1}$**
Heliophyllite crystallizes in the orthorhombic system as pyramidal crystals with horizontal striations; more commonly found as granular masses. The colour is yellow to green. The lustre is vitreous. H about 2; SG 6.9
*Localities.* Occurs with ekdemite at Jacobsberg, Sweden.
*Treatment.* Clean with distilled water.

**Trigonite $Pb_3Mn[AsO_3]_2[AsO_2(OH)]$**
Trigonite crystallizes in the monoclinic system as tabular crystals with a perfect cleavage and a vitreous lustre. The colour ranges from yellow to brown or black. H 3; SG 6.1–7.1
*Localities.* Occurs with native lead in a

dolomite-haussmannite ore found at Långban, Sweden.
*Treatment.* Clean with distilled water.

**Magnussonite $(Mn, Mg, Cu)_5(AsO_3)_3(OH, Cl)$**
Magnussonite crystallizes in the cubic system as encrustations coloured emerald or grass-green with a white streak. H 3.5–4; SG 4.3
*Localities.* Occurs in fine-grained hematite at Långban, Sweden.

**Reinerite $Zn_3(AsO_3)_2$**
Reinerite crystallizes in the orthorhombic system as blue to yellow-green crystals with a vitreous lustre. H 5–5.5; SG 4.3
*Localities.* Found with chalcocite and bornite at Tsumeb, South-West Africa.

## Antimonates and Antimonites

**Stetefeldtite $Ag_{2-y}Sb_{2-x}(O, OH, H_2O)_{6-7}$**
Stetefeldtite crystallizes in the cubic system as brown masses with a shining streak. H 3.5–4.5; SG 4.6
*Localities.* Found with chalcocite and pyrite at Belmont, Nevada, etc.

**Roméite $(Ca, Fe, Na)_2(Sb, Ti)_2(O, OH)_7$**
Roméite crystallizes in the cubic system as octahedra or as masses. The colour is yellow to brown with a pale yellow streak; there is a vitreous lustre. Lewisite is a titanium-rich variety. H 5.5–6.5; SG 4.7–5.4
*Occurrence.* Found in manganese ores and with cinnabar.
*Localities.* From Minas Gerais, Brazil; Långban, Sweden; etc.
*Treatment.* Clean with distilled water.

**Nadorite $PbSbO_2Cl$**
Nadorite crystallizes in the orthorhombic system as tabular crystals or divergent groups with a perfect cleavage. The colour is brown to yellow, and the lustre is resinous. H 3.5–4; SG 7
*Localities.* Occurs with smithsonite and bindheimite at Djebel Nador, Constantine, Algeria; Långban, Sweden; as an alteration of jamesonite at the Bodannon mine, St. Endellion, Cornwall.
*Treatment.* Clean with distilled water.

**Bindheimite $Pb_2Sb_2O_6(O, OH)$**
Bindheimite crystallizes in the cubic system as cryptocrystalline masses or as crusts or pseudomorphs. The colour is yellow to reddish-brown or may be greenish to white. H 4.5; SG 4.6–7.3
*Occurrence.* Occurs in the oxidation zone of lead-antimony deposits.
*Localities.* From San Bernardino Co., California; Black Hills, South Dakota; England; Bolivia; USSR; Australia; and elsewhere.

## Sulphates

**Thenardite $Na_2SO_4$**
Thenardite crystallizes in the orthorhombic system as tabular dipyramidal crystals with a perfect cleavage. Also found as crusts. The colour is white, brown or reddish. There is a vitreous lustre and a salty taste. H 2.5–3; SG 2.7
*Occurrence.* Occurs in salt lake deposits and around fumaroles.
*Localities.* From Searles Lake, San Bernardino Co., California; Nevada; Spain; USSR; Sicily; etc.

**Mirabilite $Na_2SO_4 . 10H_2O$**
Mirabilite crystallizes in the monoclinic system as prismatic or acicular crystals or as fibrous masses or crusts. There is a perfect cleavage. It is colourless or white, has a bitter taste with a vitreous lustre. H 1.5–2; SG 1.4
*Occurrence.* Occurs as a saline lake deposit or as a deposit from hot springs.
*Localities.* From the Great Salt Lake, Utah; Albany Co., Wyoming; Spain; Sicily; USSR; etc.
*Treatment.* Store in a sealed container.

**Aphthitalite $K_3Na(SO_4)_2$**
Aphthitalite crystallizes in the hexagonal system as tabular crystals or as pseudohexagonal twins or as masses or crusts. The colour is colourless or white with a vitreous lustre. There is a bitter taste. H 3; SG 2.7
*Localities.* Occurs with borax at Searles Lake, San Bernardino Co., California; Carlsbad, New Mexico; Stassfurt, E. Germany; in fumaroles at Mt. Vesuvius and Mt. Etna, Sicily; etc.

**Chalcanthite $CuSO_4 . 5H_2O$**
Chalcanthite crystallizes in the triclinic system as prismatic crystals or as stalactites or veins, also as granular masses. The colour is pale to dark blue and the lustre is vitreous. There is a colourless streak. The taste is metallic. H 2.5; SG 2.3
*Occurrence.* Occurs in the oxidation zone of copper ore deposits.
*Localities.* From England; Ireland; Germany; Chile; California; New Mexico; Arizona; and elsewhere.
*Treatment.* Store in a sealed container.

**Boothite $CuSO_4 . 7H_2O$**
Boothite crystallizes in the monoclinic system as masses coloured light blue, with a vitreous or silky lustre. Metallic taste. H 2–2.5; SG about 2.1
*Localities.* Occurs with copper sulphates at Alameda Co., California; Sain-Bel, Rhône, France.

*Above: Brochantite from Chuquicamata, Chile*

**Antlerite $Cu_3SO_4(OH)_4$**
Antlerite crystallizes in the orthorhombic system as tabular crystals or as fibrous aggregates. There is a perfect cleavage. The colour is emerald green to dark green with a pale green streak and a vitreous lustre. H 3.5; SG 3.9
*Occurrence.* Occurs in the oxidation zone of copper deposits especially in hot dry regions.
*Localities.* From Chuquicamata, Chile; Coahuila, Mexico; Bisbee, and the Antler mine, Mohave Co., Arizona; etc.

**Brochantite $Cu_4SO_4(OH)_6$**
Brochantite crystallizes in the monoclinic system as prismatic or acicular crystals or as crystalline aggregates, commonly with twinning. There is a perfect cleavage. The colour is emerald green to black with a vitreous lustre. There is a pale green streak. H 3.5–4; SG 4.0
*Occurrence.* Occurs in the oxidation zone of copper deposits.
*Localities.* From Bisbee, Arizona; Chile; Mexico; England; Zaire; USSR; and elsewhere.
*Treatment.* Clean with distilled water.

*Left: Thenardite from Borax Lake, California*

*Above: Epsomite from Hérault, France*

*Above right: Anhydrite from Aussee, Styria*

**Langite $Cu_4SO_4(OH)_6 . 2H_2O$**
Langite crystallizes in the orthorhombic system as small twinned crystals or as crusts. There is a perfect cleavage. The colour is blue to green, with a vitreous or silky lustre. H 2.5–3; SG 3.3
*Localities.* Occurs with gypsum and copper sulphate at St. Just and St. Blazey, Cornwall; with chalcopyrite at Mollau, Haut Rhin, France; etc.
*Treatment.* Clean with distilled water.

**Devilline $CaCu_4(SO_4)_2(OH)_6 . 3H_2O$**
Devilline crystallizes in the monoclinic system as six-sided plates or as crusts. There is a perfect cleavage. The colour is emerald-green with a pale green streak. H 2.5; SG 3.1
*Occurrence.* Occurs with copper ores.
*Localities.* From Cornwall; Montgomery Co., Pennsylvania; Czechoslovakia; USSR.
*Treatment.* Clean with distilled water.

**Cyanotrichite $Cu_4Al_2SO_4(OH)_{12} . 2H_2O$**
Cyanotrichite crystallizes in the orthorhombic system as coatings or aggregates with a pale to dark blue colour. The streak is pale blue. H not known; SG 2.7–2.9
*Occurrence.* Occurs in the oxidation zone of copper ore deposits.
*Localities.* From Coconino Co., Arizona; Nevada; Utah; Greece; Scotland; USSR; South Africa; etc.

**Woodwardite $Cu_4Al_2SO_4(OH)_{12} . 4–6H_2O$**
Woodwardite's crystal system is not determined. It is found as rounded concretions coloured blue to green. H not known; SG 2.4
*Localities.* Woodwardite occurs in Cornwall; Nantlle, Caernarvonshire, Wales; Trentino, Italy.

**Kieserite $MgSO_4 . H_2O$**
Kieserite crystallizes in the monoclinic system as granular masses with a perfect cleavage. The colour ranges from white to grey, yellow or colourless. H 3.5; SG 2.6
*Occurrence.* Occurs in sedimentary deposits in association with halite.
*Localities.* From Carlsbad, New Mexico; Texas; USSR; Sicily; Poland; Germany; Austria; etc.
*Treatment.* Store in a sealed container.

**Hexahydrite $MgSO_4 . 6H_2O$**
Hexahydrite crystallizes in the monoclinic system as tabular crystals, more commonly as fibrous or columnar masses; it has a perfect cleavage. The colour is white to pale green with a vitreous lustre. There is a salty taste. H not known; SG 1.8
*Localities.* Occurs as a dehydration product of epsomite from Saki salt lakes, Crimea, USSR; Bonaparte River, British Columbia; Oroville, Washington.

**Epsomite $MgSO_4 . 7H_2O$**
Epsomite crystallizes in the orthorhombic system as fibrous crusts; it has a perfect cleavage and a vitreous lustre. It is colourless, white, greenish to pinkish with a salty taste. H 2–2.5; SG 1.7
*Occurrence.* Occurs as an efflorescence in mine workings and in salt lakes.
*Localities.* From Epsom, Surrey; Oroville, Washington; Mt. Vesuvius, Italy; and elsewhere.
*Treatment.* Clean with alcohol and store in a sealed container.

**Vanthoffite $Na_6Mg(SO_4)_4$**
Vanthoffite crystallizes in the monoclinic system as aggregates or grains. The mineral is colourless. H 3.5; SG 2.7
*Localities.* Occurs in potash deposits at Stassfurt, E. Germany; Carlsbad, New Mexico.

**Blödite $Na_2Mg(SO_4)_2 . 4H_2O$**
Blödite crystallizes in the monoclinic system as prismatic crystals or as compact masses, blue-green, colourless or grey. There is a salty taste. H 2.5–3; SG 2.2
*Occurrence.* Occurs in salt deposits and in the Chilean nitrate deposits.
*Localities.* From Atacama, Chile; Soda Lake, California; Germany; USSR; Austria; Poland; India.
*Treatment.* Clean with alcohol. Store in sealed container.

**Pickeringite $MgAl_2(SO_4)_4 . 22H_2O$**
Pickeringite crystallizes in the monoclinic system as acicular crystals or fibrous masses or as encrustations. It is colourless, white or yellowish to reddish. H 1.5; SG 1.8
*Occurrence.* Occurs as a product of the weathering of pyrite rocks; from coal veins.
*Localities.* From Inyo Co., California; Colorado; New Mexico; Germany; Austria; and elsewhere.
*Treatment.* Store in sealed container.

**Anhydrite $CaSO_4$**
Anhydrite crystallizes in the orthorhombic system as tabular crystals or granular masses; it has a perfect cleavage. It is white, grey, bluish, or colourless. There is a vitreous lustre. The streak is white. H 3.5; SG 3.0
*Occurrence.* Occurs as a rock-forming mineral in salt beds, in limestone or dolomite or in hydrothermal vein deposits.
*Localities.* From Carlsbad, New Mexico; Bancroft, Ontario; Germany; France; India; England; etc.
*Fashioning. Uses*: faceting or cabochons; *cleavage*: distinct to perfect // to the macro-, brachy- and basal pinacoids; very brittle; *cutting angles*: crown 40°–50°, pavilion 43°; *pleochroism*: weak; *heat sensitivity*: high; *mechanical sensitivity*: diamond saws and normal grinding techniques should not be used.

*Right: A section of gypsum*

**Gypsum $CaSO_4 . 2H_2O$**
Gypsum crystallizes in the monoclinic system as tabular crystals or granular masses with twinning common and a perfect cleavage. There is a vitreous lustre. The colour is white, colourless, greenish or yellowish to brownish. There may be a greenish fluorescence and phosphorescence under ultra-violet light. H 2; SG 2.3
*Occurrence.* Occurs in sedimentary deposits, in saline lakes and in volcanic deposits.
*Localities.* From the London area, Sussex and Kent; California; Colorado; New Mexico; Chihuahua, Mexico; Chile; France; USSR; and elsewhere.
*Treatment.* Remove iron stains with dilute oxalic acid.
*Fashioning. Uses*: cabochons, carvings, bowls, etc; *cleavage*: perfect, clinopinacoidal; *heat sensitivity*: low, but avoid overheating during dopping, etc.

*Above: Tabular gypsum crystal from Wiesloch, West Germany*

*Above left: Twinned gypsum crystals that have taken sand into their structure during growth*

*Left: Acicular gypsum crystals from Sicily*

*Right: Celestine with sulphur (bright yellow) from Sicily*

**Glauberite $Na_2Ca(SO_4)_2$**
Glauberite crystallizes in the monoclinic system as tabular crystals or groups. There is a perfect cleavage. The colour is yellow, grey or colourless with a white streak and a salty taste. There is a vitreous lustre. H 2.5–3; SG 2.8
*Occurrence.* Occurs in salt deposits.
*Localities.* From Spain; France; Chile; Canada; Searles Lake, San Bernardino Co., California; and elsewhere.

**Polyhalite $K_2MgCa_2(SO_4)_4 . 2H_2O$**
Polyhalite crystallizes in the triclinic system as fibrous or foliated masses; it has a perfect cleavage. It is white or grey and may be coloured pink or red from inclusions of iron oxide. Its lustre is vitreous. H 3.5; SG 2.8
*Occurrence.* Occurs in sedimentary deposits with anhydrite, halite and other salts.
*Localities.* From Carlsbad, New Mexico; England; France; USSR; Germany; and elsewhere.

**Ettringite $Ca_6Al_2(SO_4)_3(OH)_{12} . 24H_2O$**
Ettringite crystallizes in the hexagonal system as hexagonal bipyramids or as fibres. There is a perfect cleavage and a vitreous lustre. It is colourless. H 2–2.5; SG 1.8
*Localities.* Occurs in metamorphosed limestones near Ettringen, Germany; Franklin, New Jersey; Arizona; Scawt Hill, Moyle, Ireland.

**Celestine $SrSO_4$**
Celestine crystallizes in the orthorhombic system as tabular crystals or as nodules or granular masses. There is a perfect cleavage. The colour is white, light blue, yellow, orange, red to brown. There is a vitreous lustre. Some specimens may fluoresce under ultra-violet light. H 3–3.5; SG 4.0
*Occurrence.* Occurs in limestones, and in hydrothermal vein deposits.
*Localities.* From Matehuala, San Luis Potosi, Mexico; in geodes, Malagasy Republic; Yate, Gloucestershire; Germany; Switzerland; Italy; USSR; Egypt; and elsewhere.
*Treatment.* Clean with dilute acid.
*Fashioning. Uses*: faceting or cabochons; *cleavage*: perfect prismatic and // to basal pinacoid; very brittle; *cutting angles*: crown 40°, pavilion 40°; *pleochroism*: weak; *heat sensitivity*: very high; *mechanical sensitivity*: very fragile.

**Baryte $BaSO_4$**
Baryte crystallizes in the orthorhombic system as tabular crystals or as aggregates; lamellar or fibrous masses, sometimes stalactitic. There is a perfect cleavage. It is white, grey, colourless, yellow, bluish, brown, with a vitreous lustre. It may fluoresce and phosphoresce under ultra-violet light. H 3–3.5; SG 4.5
*Occurrence.* Occurs in hydrothermal vein deposits; in sedimentary rocks, cavities in igneous rocks and as a deposit from hot springs.
*Localities.* From Meade and Pennington Counties, South Dakota; Cumbria and Derbyshire; Germany; France; Romania; and elsewhere.
*Treatment.* Remove iron stains with dilute oxalic acid.
*Fashioning. Uses*: faceting or cabochons; *cleavage*: perfect, prismatic and // to basal pinacoid; very brittle; *cutting angles*: crown 40°, pavilion 40°; *pleochroism*: weak; *heat sensitivity*: very high; *mechanical sensitivity*: very fragile.

**Goslarite $ZnSO_4 . 7H_2O$**
Goslarite crystallizes in the orthorhombic system as granular masses; it has a perfect cleavage. It is white, colourless, greenish to brown, with a vitreous lustre. Metallic taste. H 2–2.5; SG 2.0
*Occurrence.* Occurs as an efflorescence in mines containing zinc minerals.
*Localities.* From Mexico; Argentina; Peru; New Mexico; California; Sweden; Germany; France; etc.
*Treatment.* Store in sealed container.

**Ktenasite $(Cu, Zn)_3(SO_4)(OH)_4 . 2H_2O$**
Ktenasite crystallizes in the monoclinic system as tabular groups coloured blue to green, with a vitreous lustre. H 2–2.5; SG 3.0
*Localities.* Occurs with serpierite and smithsonite at Laurion, Greece.
*Treatment.* Clean with distilled water.

*Right: Orthorhombic baryte crystal from Piacenza, Italy*

**Serpierite**
**$Ca(Cu, Zn)_4(SO_4)_2(OH)_6 . 3H_2O$**
Serpierite crystallizes in the monoclinic system as crusts and rounded masses. There is a perfect cleavage. The colour is blue. H not known; SG 3.1
*Localities.* Occurs with smithsonite at Ross Island, Killarney, Ireland; Laurion, Greece; etc.
*Treatment.* Clean with distilled water.

**Alunogen $Al_2(SO_4)_3 . 16H_2O$**
Alunogen crystallizes in the triclinic system as prismatic crystals, more commonly as crusts, efflorescences or masses. There is a perfect cleavage. The colour is white, yellow or colourless, with a vitreous lustre. There is an acid taste. H 1.5–2; SG 1.8
*Occurrence.* Occurs as an efflorescence in formations with iron sulphides, and in the oxidation zone of iron ore deposits.
*Localities.* From North Carolina; Utah; Colorado; New Mexico; Canada; Chile; Peru; France and elsewhere.
*Treatment.* Clean with alcohol.

**Aluminite $Al_2SO_4(OH)_4 . 7H_2O$**
Aluminite crystallizes in the monoclinic or orthorhombic systems as nodular masses coloured white to grey, with a dull lustre. H 1–2; SG 1.7–1.8
*Localities.* From Newhaven, Sussex; Green River, Utah; Halle, E. Germany; Salt Range, Punjab, India; etc.
*Treatment.* Clean with distilled water.

**Felsöbanyite $Al_4SO_4(OH)_{10} . 5H_2O$**
Felsöbanyite probably crystallizes in the orthorhombic system, with a perfect cleavage. It forms spherulitic aggregates with a yellow colour and a vitreous lustre. H 1.5; SG 2.3
*Localities.* Occurs with marcasite and quartz at Felsöbanya, Romania.
*Treatment.* Clean with distilled water.

**Basaluminite $Al_4SO_4(OH)_{10} . 5H_2O$**
Basaluminite probably crystallizes in the hexagonal system as microcrystalline masses coloured white with yellow or orange staining. H not known; SG 2.1
*Localities.* Occurs at the Lodge Pit siderite deposit, Irchester, Northamptonshire; Clifton Hill, Brighton, Sussex; Epernay, France; Utah; Kansas; etc.

**Ammonia alum**
**$NH_4Al(SO_4)_2 . 12H_2O$**
Ammonia alum crystallizes in the cubic system as octahedra or as fibrous masses. The colour is white or colourless and there is a sweetish taste. It has a vitreous lustre. H 1.5; SG 1.6
*Localities.* From brown coal at Tschermig, Czechoslovakia; Lake Co., California; Italy; Zaire; etc.
*Treatment.* Clean with alcohol.

**Potash alum $KAl(SO_4)_2 . 12H_2O$**
Potash alum crystallizes in the cubic system as masses of cubic or octahedral crystals. There is a vitreous lustre. It is white or colourless. Taste sweet. H 2–2.5; SG 1.7
*Occurrence.* Occurs in argillaceous rocks or in brown coals.
*Localities.* From England; Scotland; France; Germany; South Dakota; etc.
*Treatment.* Clean with alcohol.

*Left: An aggregate of alunogen from Czechoslovakia*

**Soda alum $NaAl(SO_4)_2 . 12H_2O$**
Soda alum crystallizes in the cubic system as octahedra. They are colourless. Vitreous lustre. H about 3; SG 1.7
*Localities.* From California; Colorado; Argentina.
*Treatment.* Clean with alcohol.

**Anglesite $PbSO_4$**
Anglesite crystallizes in the orthorhombic system as tabular crystals or as masses. The colour is white, colourless, yellowish, pale green or blue with a colourless streak. There is a vitreous lustre. May fluoresce yellow under UV light. H 2.5–3; SG 6.4– RI 1.87, 1.89
*Occurrence.* Occurs as a secondary mineral in lead deposits, and formed by the oxidation of galena.
*Localities.* Matlock, Derbyshire; Leadhills, Lanarkshire, Scotland; Anglesey, Wales; Chihuahua, Mexico; Tsumeb, South-West Africa; Australia; Wheatley Mine, Chester Co., Pennsylvania; Idaho; New Mexico; and elsewhere.
*Treatment.* Clean with distilled water.
*Fashioning. Uses*: faceting or cabochons; *cleavage*: distinct, prismatic and // to basal pinacoid; *cutting angles*: crown 40°, pavilion 40°; *heat sensitivity*: very high, with a cold setting cement; *mechanical sensitivity*: very fragile.

*Left: Anglesite crystals from Sardinia showing a large number of cleavage planes*

*Right: Linarite crystals from Leadhills, Scotland*

**Lanarkite $Pb_2SO_5$**
Lanarkite crystallizes in the monoclinic system as prismatic crystals or as masses. There is a perfect cleavage. The colour is grey to yellow with an adamantine lustre. There is a white streak. May fluoresce yellow under ultra-violet light. H 2–2.5; SG 6.9
*Occurrence.* In the oxidation zone of lead ore deposits.
*Localities.* From Leadhills, Lanarkshire, Scotland; Harz Mountains and the Black Forest, Germany; France; Chile; etc.
*Treatment.* Clean with distilled water.

**Linarite $PbCuSO_4(OH)_2$**
Linarite crystallizes in the monoclinic system as tabular crystals or as aggregates, frequently showing twinning. There is a perfect cleavage. The colour is dark blue, with a vitreous lustre. H 2.5; SG 5.3
*Occurrence.* In the oxidation zone of lead and copper deposits.
*Localities.* From Leadhills, Lanarkshire, Scotland; Mammoth mine, Tiger, Arizona; Spain; USSR; Canada; Argentina; and elsewhere.
*Treatment.* Clean with distilled water.

**Beaverite $Pb(Cu, Fe, Al)_3(SO_4)_2(OH)_6$**
Beaverite crystallizes in the hexagonal system as friable masses of hexagonal plates coloured yellow. H not known; SG 4.4
*Occurrence.* Occurs in the oxidation zone of lead-copper deposits.
*Localities.* From Beaver Co. and Salt Lake Co., Utah; also from Nevada.

**Plumbojarosite $PbFe_6(SO_4)_4(OH)_6$**
Plumbojarosite crystallizes in the hexagonal system as compact masses coloured yellow to brown, with a dull lustre. H not known, but soft; SG 3.6
*Occurrence.* Occurs in the oxidation zone of lead ore deposits.
*Localities.* From western USA; Laurion, Greece; Bolivia; Anatolia, Turkey; and other localities.

**Zippeite $(UO_2)_2(SO_4)(OH)_2 . 4H_2O$**
Zippeite crystallizes in the orthorhombic system as compact masses, often with twinning. The colour is orange-yellow to brown, with a dull lustre. There is a variable fluorescence in ultraviolet light. H not known; SG 3.7
*Occurrence.* As an efflorescence in mines.
*Localities.* From Cornwall; Colorado; Utah; Příbram, Czechoslovakia; etc.
*Treatment.* Clean with distilled water.

**Meta-uranopilite $(UO_2)_6SO_4(OH)_{10} . 5H_2O$**
Meta-uranopilite crystallizes in the orthorhombic system as needles coloured green or yellow. There is a yellow-green fluorescence under ultra-violet light. H and SG not known.
*Localities.* Occurs at Jachymov, Czechoslovakia; Cornwall.

**Uranopilite $(UO_2)_6SO_4(OH)_{10} . 12H_2O$**
Uranopilite probably crystallizes in the monoclinic system as crusts coloured bright yellow, fluorescing a strong green under ultra-violet light. They have a silky lustre. H not known; SG 4.0
*Localities.* Occurs with johannite and zippeite, San Juan Co., Utah; Wheal Owles, Cornwall; Příbram, Czechoslovakia; Grury, France; Northwest Territory, Canada; etc.

**Johannite $Cu(UO_2)_2(SO_4)_2(OH)_2 . 6H_2O$**
Johannite crystallizes in the triclinic system as tabular crystals or as aggregates. The colour is emerald green to yellow with a pale green streak. There is a vitreous lustre. H 2–2.5; SG 3.3
*Occurrence.* Occurs in the oxidized zone of uranium-bearing veins.
*Localities.* From Great Bear Lake, Canada; Jachymov, Czechoslovakia; Colorado; USSR; etc.

**Mooreite $(Mg, Zn, Mn)_8SO_4(OH)_{14} . 3\text{–}4H_2O$**
Mooreite crystallizes in the monoclinic system as tabular or platy crystals with a perfect cleavage. It is colourless, with a vitreous lustre. H 3; SG 2.5
*Localities.* Occurs with calcite at Franklin, New Jersey.
*Treatment.* Clean with distilled water.

**Torreyite $(Mg, Zn, Mn)_7SO_4(OH)_{12} . 4H_2O$**
Torreyite crystallizes in the monoclinic system as granular masses coloured blue. H 3; SG 2.7
*Localities.* Occurs with calcite at Franklin, New Jersey.
*Treatment.* Clean with distilled water.

**Melanterite $FeSO_4 . 7H_2O$**
Melanterite crystallizes in the monoclinic system as prismatic crystals or stalactitic crusts. The colour is green or blue with a colourless streak. There is a vitreous or silky lustre. H2; SG 1.9
*Occurrence.* Occurs as a weathering product of pyrite.
*Localities.* From Rio Tinto, Spain; South Dakota; Colorado; etc.
*Treatment.* Store in sealed container.

**Butlerite $Fe^{3+}SO_4OH . 2H_2O$**
Butlerite crystallizes in the monoclinic system as tabular crystals or as octahedra. There is a perfect cleavage. The colour is orange, the lustre vitreous. The streak is pale yellow. H 2.5; SG 2.5
*Localities.* Occurs with copiapite at Calf Mesa, Utah; Jerome, Arizona; La Alcaparrosa, Argentina; and elsewhere.

*Below right: An encrustation of zippeite, a typically brightly coloured uranium mineral*

*Below: A coating of johannite crystals*

**Amarantite $Fe^{3+}SO_4OH.3H_2O$**
Amarantite crystallizes in the triclinic system as prismatic crystals or as aggregates of needle-like crystals. There is a perfect cleavage. The colour is red or orange-yellow with a vitreous lustre. There is a yellow streak. H 2.5; SG 2.2
*Localities.* Occurs with copiapite at Blythe, California; South Dakota; Chuquicamata, Chile.

**Copiapite**
**$(Fe, Mg)Fe_4^{3+}(SO_4)_6(OH)_2.20H_2O$**
Copiapite crystallizes in the triclinic system as tabular crystals or as aggregates. There is a perfect cleavage; the colour is golden yellow or orange to green with a pearly lustre. H 2.5–3; SG 2.1–2.2
*Occurrence.* Formed by the oxidation of pyrite or other sulphides.
*Localities.* From Chuquicamata, Chile; Utah; California; Nevada; France; Spain; Germany; etc.
*Treatment.* Store in a sealed container.

**Natrojarosite $NaFe_3^{3+}(SO_4)_2(OH)_6$**
Natrojarosite crystallizes in the hexagonal system as minute tabular crystals or as crusts. There is a perfect cleavage. The colour is yellow or brown with a pale yellow streak. H 3; SG 3.2
*Occurrence.* Occurs as a secondary mineral in iron-bearing rocks, particularly ore deposits.
*Localities.* From the Black Hills, South Dakota; Nevada; Chile; Mexico; USSR; and elsewhere.
*Treatment.* Clean with distilled water.

**Voltaite $K_2Fe_5^{2+}Fe_4^{3+}(SO_4)_{12}.18H_2O$**
Voltaite crystallizes in the cubic system as octahedra or dodecahedra and as granular masses. The colour is dark green to black with a resinous lustre. There is a grey-green streak. H 3; SG 2.7
*Localities.* Occurs with sulphates at Bisbee, Arizona; Mt. Vesuvius, Italy; Bolivia; Chile; Japan; etc.

**Botryogen $MgFe^{3+}(SO_4)_2OH.7H_2O$**
Botryogen crystallizes in the monoclinic system as prismatic crystals or as botryoidal masses. There is a perfect cleavage. The colour is orange, the lustre vitreous. H 2.5; SG 2.1
*Localities.* Occurs with copiapite at the Redington mine, Napa Co., California; Chuquicamata, Chile; Santa Elena mine, San Juan, Argentina; France; Germany; Sweden; etc.
*Treatment.* Clean with distilled water.

**Halotrichite $Fe^{2+}Al_2(SO_4)_4.22H_2O$**
Halotrichite crystallizes in the monoclinic system as acicular crystals or as aggregates. They are white, colourless, yellow to greenish; the lustre is vitreous. There is a sharp taste. H 1.5; SG 1.9
*Occurrence.* Occurs as a weathering product of pyrite and in coal veins.
*Localities.* From Chile; France; Germany; Utah; and elsewhere.
*Treatment.* Store in sealed container.

**Bieberite $CoSO_4.7H_2O$**
Bieberite crystallizes in the monoclinic system as stalactites and crusts; it has a perfect cleavage. The colour is red; becomes opaque on dehydration. There is a vitreous lustre. H 2; SG 1.9
*Localities.* Occurs on pyrrhotine, Trinity Co., California; Siegen, Germany; Chalanches, France; etc.

**Morenosite $NiSO_4.7H_2O$**
Morenosite crystallizes in the orthorhombic system as stalactitic crusts. The colour is white or green with a greenish-white streak; there is a vitreous lustre. H 2.5; SG 2.0
*Occurrence.* Occurs as an alteration product of nickel-bearing sulphides.
*Localities.* From the Copper King mine, Boulder Co., Colorado; with erythrite at Julian, San Diego Co., California; Peru; France; Italy; Ontario, Canada, etc.
*Treatment.* Store in a sealed container.

**Retgersite $NiSO_4.6H_2O$**
Retgersite crystallizes in the tetragonal system as tabular crystals or as crusts. There is a perfect cleavage; the colour is emerald-green and the streak greenish-white. There is a vitreous lustre. The taste is bitter. H 2.5; SG 2.1
*Occurrence.* Formed as a secondary mineral from other nickel-bearing minerals.
*Localities.* From Lancaster Co., Pennsylvania; Minas Ragra, Peru; Lobenstein, Thuringia, Germany.
*Treatment.* Store in a sealed container.

**Connellite**
**$Cu_{19}Cl_4SO_4(OH)_{32}.3H_2O$**
Connellite crystallizes in the hexagonal system as groups of blue or blue-green acicular crystals with a vitreous lustre. The streak is pale blue. H 3; SG 3.4
*Occurrence.* Occurs in the oxidation zone of copper ore deposits.
*Localities.* From Cornwall; Bisbee, Arizona; South Africa; etc.
*Treatment.* Clean with distilled water.

**Spangolite**
**$Cu_6AlSO_4(OH)_{12}Cl.3H_2O$**
Spangolite crystallizes in the hexagonal system as prismatic or tabular crystals

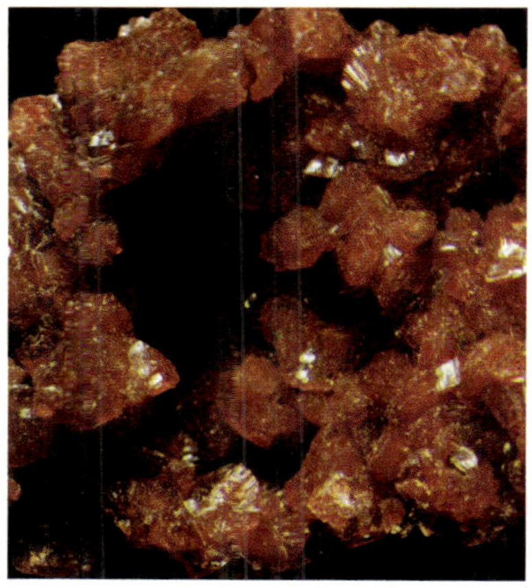

with a perfect cleavage. The colour is dark or emerald-green with a pale green streak. There is a vitreous lustre H 3; SG 3.1
*Occurrence.* Occurs in the oxidized zone of copper ore deposits.
*Localities.* From the Blanchard mine, Socorro Co., New Mexico; St. Day, Cornwall; Arenas, Sardinia.
*Treatment.* Spangolite should be cleaned with distilled water.

**Creedite**
**$Ca_3Al_2SO_4(F, OH)_{10}.2H_2O$**
Creedite crystallizes in the monoclinic system as prismatic or acicular crystals with a perfect cleavage. It is white or colourless and has a vitreous lustre. H 4; SG 2.7
*Localities.* From the tin veins of Colquiri, Bolivia; Colorado; Chihuahua, Mexico.
*Treatment.* Clean with distilled water.

## Chromates and Molybdates

**Tarapacaite $K_2CrO_4$**
Tarapacaite crystallizes in the orthorhombic system as tabular pseudohexagonal crystals coloured bright yellow. H not known; SG 2.7
*Localities.* Occurs with lopezite in nitrate deposits at Antofagasta Province, Chile.

**Lopezite $K_2Cr_2O_7$**
Lopezite crystallizes in the triclinic system as spherical aggregates; it has a perfect cleavage, and is orange-red in colour and has a vitreous lustre. H 2.5; SG 2.7
*Localities.* In a nitrate rock at the Maria Elena mine Antofagasta, Chile.

*Left: Amarantite crystals from Sierra Gorda, Chile*

*Below left: An aggregate of botryogen crystals from Knoxville, California*

*Far left: Copiapite from Copiapó, Chile*

*Right: The characteristic colour of crocoite. This specimen comes from its classic locality of Dundas, Tasmania*

*Below left: Wulfenite showing tabular form*

*Below right: Stolzite from Broken Hill, Australia*

**Crocoite $PbCrO_4$**
Crocoite crystallizes in the monoclinic system as prismatic crystals or as masses or aggregates. The colour is bright red or orange with an orange-yellow streak. Adamantine lustre. H 2.5–3; SG 6.0
*Occurrence.* Occurs in the oxidation zone of lead and chromium ores.
*Localities.* From Inyo Co., California; Mammoth mine, Tiger County, Arizona; Dundas, Tasmania; Beresov, USSR; Minas Gerais, Brazil; etc.
*Treatment.* Clean ultrasonically.
*Fashioning. Uses*: faceting or cabochons; *cleavage*: distinct, prismatic; sectile; *cutting angles*: crown 30°–40°, pavilion 37°–40°, *heat sensitivity*: very high, stones should be dopped with a cold-setting cement; *mechanical sensitivity*: very fragile.

**Powellite $Ca(Mo, W)O_4$**
Powellite crystallizes in the tetragonal system as pyramidal crystals or as crusts or masses. The colour is yellow, brown, grey, blue or black, the lustre is adamantine or greasy. There is a golden yellow fluorescence. H 3.5–4; SG 4.2
*Occurrence.* Occurs in the oxidation zone of ore deposits.
*Localities.* From Isle Royale, Michigan; Utah; Arizona; Turkey; USSR; Morocco.
*Treatment.* Clean with distilled water.

**Wulfenite $PbMoO_4$**
Wulfenite crystallizes in the tetragonal system as tabular crystals or granular masses. The colour is yellow or orange to brown with a white streak. There is a resinous lustre. H 2–3; SG 6–7
*Occurrence.* Occurs in the oxidation zone of ore deposits.
*Localities.* From Morocco; Tsumeb, South-West Africa; South Dakota; Utah; Austria; Mexico; and elsewhere.
*Treatment.* Clean ultrasonically.
*Fashioning. Uses*: faceting or cabochons; *cleavage*: distinct, pyramidal; brittle; *cutting angles*: crown 30°–40°, pavilion 37°–40°; *heat sensitivity*: high.

## Tungstates

**Cuprotungstite $Cu_2WO_4(OH)_2$**
Cuprotungstite's crystal system is not known; it forms masses and crusts coloured emerald-green or brown, with a vitreous lustre. H not known; SG 5.4
*Localities.* Occurs in a copper deposit at South Peacock mine, Adams Co., Idaho; Chile; Transvaal, South Africa; etc.
*Treatment.* Clean with distilled water.

**Scheelite $CaWO_4$**
Scheelite crystallizes in the tetragonal system as octahedral or tabular crystals or as granular masses. They are white, colourless, orange-yellow, green or purple. The lustre is adamantine or vitreous. There is a bright bluish-white fluorescence under short-wave ultraviolet light. The streak is white. H 4.5–5; SG 6.1; RI 1.92, 1.93
*Occurrence.* Occurs in contact metamorphic deposits and in hydrothermal veins and pegmatites.
*Localities.* From Cochise Co., Arizona; Inyo Co., California; Peru; England; Japan; Korea; and elsewhere.
*Treatment.* Clean with dilute acid.
*Fashioning. Uses*: faceting or cabochons; *cleavage*: distinct, pyramidal; brittle; *cutting angles*: crown 40°, pavilion 40°; *heat sensitivity*: low.

**Stolzite $PbWO_4$**
Stolzite crystallizes in the tetragonal system as tabular or dipyramidal crystals coloured yellow, red, brown or green with a colourless streak. There is a resinous lustre. H 2.5–3; SG 7.9–8.3
*Occurrence.* Occurs in the oxidation zone of tungsten ore deposits.
*Localities.* From England; Brazil; Broken Hill, New South Wales; Utah; Arizona; Massachusetts; etc.
*Treatment.* Clean with distilled water.

**Raspite $PbWO_4$**
Raspite crystallizes in the monoclinic system as tabular crystals coloured light yellow or brown with a perfect cleavage. They have an adamantine lustre. H 2.5–3; SG 8.5
*Localities.* Occurs with stolzite at Broken Hill, New South Wales; Minas Gerais, Brazil; in tin veins at Cerro Estano, Guanajuato, Mexico.
*Treatment.* Clean with distilled water.

**Russellite $Bi_2WO_6$**
Russellite crystallizes in the tetragonal system as compact masses coloured yellow-green. H 3.5; SG 7.3
*Localities.* Occurs with native bismuth at Castle-an-Dinas, St. Columb Major, Cornwall.
*Treatment.* Clean with distilled water.

**Hübnerite $MnWO_4$**
Hübnerite crystallizes in the monoclinic system as prismatic crystals and as groups of parallel crystals. There is a

Left: An aggregate of wolframite crystals, each prismatic but tending towards a tabular habit

perfect cleavage. The colour is yellow or reddish-brown with a reddish-brown or greenish-grey streak. The lustre is resinous. H 4–4.5; SG 7.2
*Occurrence.* In hydrothermal ore veins.
*Localities.* From Silverton, San Juan Co., Colorado; Idaho; Nevada; New Mexico; France; Peru; etc.
*Treatment.* Clean with distilled water.

**Wolframite (Fe, Mn)$WO_4$**
Wolframite crystallizes in the monoclinic system as prismatic crystals or as groups of crystals or lamellar masses. There is a perfect cleavage. The colour is grey or black with a reddish-brown streak. The lustre is metallic. H 4–4.5; SG 7.4
*Occurrence.* Occurs in high-temperature ore veins and quartz veins in granite.
*Localities.* From Panesqueira, Portugal; South Dakota; New Mexico; Arizona; England; France; and elsewhere.
*Treatment.* Clean with dilute acid.

**Chalcomenite $CuSeO_3 . 2H_2O$**
Chalcomenite crystallizes in the orthorhombic system as prismatic or acicular crystals of minute size. The colour is bright blue, with a vitreous lustre. H 2–2.5; SG 3.3
*Localities.* Formed by the oxidation of copper and lead selenides at Sierra Famatina, Argentina; also from Bolivia.
*Treatment.* Clean with distilled water.

## Tellurites, Iodates and Oxalates

**Cliffordite $UTe_3O_8$**
Cliffordite crystallizes in the cubic system as octahedra coloured bright yellow with an adamantine lustre. H 4; SG 6.6

Left: Pyramidal scheelite crystal from the Traversella mine, near Ivres, Italy

*Above: A large specimen of amber from the Baltic coast*

*Localities.* Occurs with tellurium at Moctezuma, Sonora, Mexico.
*Treatment.* Clean with dilute acid.

**Emmonsite $Fe_2(TeO_3)_3 . 2H_2O$**
Emmonsite crystallizes in the monoclinic system as compact masses; it has a perfect cleavage. The colour is yellowish-green, the lustre is vitreous or dull. H 5; SG 4.5
*Occurrence.* Occurs in the oxidation zone of deposits with native tellurium.
*Localities.* From Cripple Creek, Colorado; Nevada; New Mexico; Honduras.
*Treatment.* Clean with distilled water.

**Salesite $CuIO_3OH$**
Salesite crystallizes in the orthorhombic system as prismatic crystals with a perfect cleavage and bluish-green in colour. They have a vitreous lustre. H 3; SG 4.8
*Localities.* Occurs in oxidized ore at Chuquicamata, Chile.
*Treatment.* Clean with distilled water.

**Whewellite $CaC_2O_4 . H_2O$**
Whewellite crystallizes in the monoclinic system as crystalline masses coloured white, colourless, yellow or brown. There is a vitreous lustre. H 2.5–3; SG 2.2
*Occurrence.* Occurs in coal seams and also in sedimentary nodules and concretions.
*Localities.* From Zwickau and Burgk, E. Germany; San Juan Co., Utah; Alsace, France; USSR.
*Treatment.* Clean with distilled water.

## Appendix: some organic materials

**Amber**
A fossil resin with a chemical composition close to $C_{10}H_{16}O$ and containing some $H_2S$. It is most commonly brown or yellow but may also be green, reddish or close to white. It commonly displays a bluish-white fluorescence under long-wave ultraviolet light; under short-wave radiations the fluorescent colour inclines to green. H about 2; SG about 1.08; RI 1.54
*Occurrence.* From pine trees of the Oligocene period, notably *Pinus succinifera*.
*Localities.* The major locality is the Kaliningrad area of the USSR; also from the Baltic coast; the east coast of England; Burma; Sicily; Romania; etc.
*Treatment.* Clean with soap and water.
*Fashioning. Uses*: faceting, cabochons, carvings, beads, etc; *cleavage*: none; splintery; *cutting angles*: crown 40°–50°, pavilion 43°; *heat sensitivity*: very high, softens at about 150°C.

**Jet**
A fossil wood close in composition to brown coal. It is black and has a shining conchoidal fracture. It burns with a smell of coal. H about 2.5; SG about 1.33; RI about 1.66
*Localities.* From the Upper Lias of east Yorkshire, particularly from the Whitby area; Asturias, Spain; Aude, France; Utah.
*Treatment.* Clean with soap and water.
*Fashioning. Uses*: cabochons, carvings, beads, tumbling, etc; *cleavage*: none; *heat sensitivity*: low, but avoid overheating during dopping.

**Ivory**
Ivory is mainly a phosphate of calcium and includes both organic and mineral matter. Most of the worked ivory seen comes from the elephant; in transverse section it shows curved lines, the lines of Retzius, resembling the arcs formed by engine-turning. Other ivories come from the walrus, hippopotamus and whale. Ivory fluoresces under ultraviolet light with a bluish-white fluorescence. H just above 2; SG 1.7–1.9; RI 1.54

*Right: A branch of red coral, Corallium rubrum*

*Localities.* The best elephant ivory comes from Africa, particularly from the Cameroons.
*Treatment.* Clean gently with methylated spirits.

**Vegetable ivory**
From the nut of the Ivory Palm (*Phytelephas macrocarpa*). The composition is close to $C_6H_{10}O_5$. It fluoresces bluish-white under ultraviolet light, but much more faintly than elephant ivory. It shows no lines of Retzius. H about 2.5; SG 1.42; RI 1.54
*Localities.* Ivory Palm is found in Peru and Colombia.

**Bone**
The commonest simulant of ivory. Like ivory, it fluoresces bluish-white under ultraviolet light. In transverse section it displays cavities, surrounded by dark dots, called the Haversian systems and quite different from ivory's lines of Retzius. H about 2.5; SG about 2; RI about 1.54
*Treatment.* Clean gently with methylated spirits.

**Tortoise-shell**
The composition of tortoise-shell is close to the protein keratin, containing oxygen, carbon, nitrogen, sulphur and hydrogen. The brown mottling seen on the shell is shown by the microscope to consist of dots of colour. It is sectile. H about 2.5; SG 1.29; RI 1.55
*Localities.* From the shell of the hawk's-bill turtle, *Chelone imbricata*, an inhabitant of the Malay archipelago, the West Indies and other tropical centres.
*Treatment.* Clean in tepid water.

**Coral**
Coral is made up of the skeletons of coral polyps, which belong to the class Anthozoa. Chemically, coral is almost completely calcium carbonate with some magnesium carbonate, and also contains some iron oxide and organic matter. The colour may be a fine red, pink or white, but there are also black and blue varieties. H about 3.5; SG 2.6–2.7; RI about 1.5
*Localities.* Red varieties from the Mediterranean; black from the Indian Ocean and off Hawaii; blue from the Cameroons.

**Pearl**
Pearls are a product of pearl oysters, bivalve molluscs that are not true oysters. They are found in both sea water and fresh water. The chemical composition of pearl is largely calcium carbonate in the form of aragonite, with some conchiolin ($C_{32}H_{48}N_2O_{11}$) and water. Natural and artificial pearls are distinguished with x-rays. SG 2.6–2.7
*Localities.* Pearls are found in the Persian Gulf, the Gulf of Manaar between Ceylon and India, the Red Sea, the Gulfs of Mexico and Panama, and the waters off Australia and Venezuela. Fresh-water pearls are found in many rivers, including those of Scotland and North America – in particular the Mississippi river.
*Treatment.* Pearls should not be stored in too dry an atmosphere.

*Living coral.
When dried this species
is one of those suitable
for carving*

# Identification Tables

Mineral specimens are often difficult to identify because their crystal system is not immediately apparent, their colour is unusual because of surface coatings, and so forth. The customary form of mineral identification table, in which one property such as hardness is taken as a standard and the others related to it, has therefore not been adopted in this book. Instead, each major property has been allocated a separate table. This method has the advantage of making available alternative paths to identification. For example, a specimen whose hardness is not easily determined may be referred to the table of colour; a specimen whose crystal form is distorted beyond immediate recognition may be referred to the table of specific gravities; and so on.

Not all minerals included in the Mineral Kingdom section are included in these identification tables. This is partly to keep the size of the tables within reasonable bounds and partly because many of the minerals described in The Mineral Kingdom are rare or too difficult to identify without more sophisticated methods of testing being employed. The minerals listed in the tables therefore comprise only a part of the whole, but do include the commoner materials that are most likely to be encountered by the collector in the field.

Sometimes a mineral shows more than one set of characteristics, and then appears in several parts of a given table; for example, blende occurs in a variety of colours. Where numerical constants are given they represent general figures; values of some properties can vary widely within a particular mineral species.

Table 1
**Form and habit**
A form is a basic shape that a crystal can take, which has all the symmetries of the crystal's system. Several forms may be combined in a crystal. The overall shape of a crystal or group of crystals is largely due to the relative development of the forms present and is called the crystal's habit

| System | Form | Minerals |
|---|---|---|
| Cubic system | cubes | acanthite boracite diamond pyrite galena cuprite fluorite uraninite halite cerargyrite pharmacosiderite |
| | dodecahedra | diamond garnet magnetite copper amalgam cuprite sodalite |
| | icositetrahedra | garnet leucite |
| | interpenetrant twins | fluorite |
| | masses or wires | gold silver copper platinum bornite acanthite smaltite skutterudite sodalite lazurite uraninite chloanthite |
| | octahedra | ~~diamond gold~~ magnetite cuprite spinel franklinite fluorite chromite periclase pyrochlore uraninite |
| | pyritohedra | pyrite cobaltite gersdorffite hauerite |
| | tetrahedra | tetrahedrite blende boracite diamond (rarely) |
| Tetragonal system | dipyramids | cassiterite scheelite wulfenite zircon apophyllite |
| | masses | cassiterite pyrolusite |
| | prismatic | zircon idocrase scapolite apophyllite phosgenite |
| | tabular | torbernite autunite wulfenite |
| Orthorhombic system | bladed | diaspore strontianite goethite |
| | masses | iolite variscite prehnite olivine |
| | prismatic | arsenopyrite goethite chrysoberyl aragonite stibnite löllingite bournonite cerussite baryte anglesite danburite natrolite enargite celestine adamite olivenite wavellite |
| | prismatic dipyramidal | topaz andalusite staurolite olivine |
| | pseudohexagonal twins | chrysoberyl chalcocite cerussite aragonite |
| | wedge-shaped | azurite gypsum orpiment wolframite sphene monazite |

**Form and habit**
continued

| System | Habit | Minerals |
|---|---|---|
| | tabular | sulphur chalcocite marcasite hemimorphite columbite tantalite |
| Monoclinic system | bladed | erythrite vivianite sphene tremolite |
| | masses | jadeite nephrite actinolite malachite serpentine |
| | prismatic | gypsum actinolite tremolite azurite realgar manganite spodumene epidote clinozoisite pyroxenes amphiboles orthoclase |
| | pseudohexagonal tabular | muscovite lepidolite phlogopite biotite |
| Triclinic system | bladed | kyanite albite |
| | masses | ulexite turquoise rhodonite microcline |
| | wedge-shaped | axinite |
| Hexagonal system | hexagonal and trigonal prismatic | corundum tourmaline willemite dioptase apatite mimetite quartz beryl vanadinite calcite pyrargyrite millerite proustite pyromorphite |
| | rhombohedra | hematite cinnabar siderite calcite chabazite dolomite |
| | scalenohedra | calcite rhodochrosite smithsonite |
| | tabular | phenakite benitoite graphite molybdenite pyrrhotine covelline corundum—variety ruby ilmenite beryl apatite |

Table 2
**Lustre and colour**
The colour of a mineral specimen is the easiest property to observe. Unfortunately, a mineral's colour is often highly variable from specimen to specimen. It is a more valuable guide to identity when taken in conjunction with lustre, the quality of the reflected light

| Lustre | Colour | Minerals |
|---|---|---|
| adamantine | white and colourless | diamond zircon cassiterite scheelite cerussite anglesite |
| | brown | pyromorphite zircon blende sphene diamond cerussite wulfenite monazite scheelite |
| | black | diamond rutile zircon cassiterite cerussite blende |
| | red | cinnabar realgar proustite rutile cuprite vanadinite |
| | reddish-brown | rutile monazite blende cuprite zircon descloizite |
| | orange | zircon crocoite wulfenite scheelite mimetite |
| | yellow | sphene wulfenite blende rutile orpiment mimetite |
| | green | sphene vanadinite blende andradite zircon |
| metallic | white (silver- or tin-white) | silver arsenic antimony mercury arsenopyrite bismuth cobaltite skutterudite chloanthite smaltite |
| | greyish-white | galena stibnite |
| | steel-grey | platinum arsenopyrite |
| | blue-grey | galena stibnite tetrahedrite molybdenite |
| | purplish-grey | covelline bornite |
| | dark-grey | chalcocite platinum graphite acanthite galena enargite tennantite |
| | golden-yellow | gold chalcopyrite pyrite |
| | reddish-brown to black | goethite rutile tantalite |

| Lustre | Colour | Minerals |
|---|---|---|
| | black | rutile hematite ilmenite uraninite pyrolusite manganite wolframite goethite columbite tantalite acanthite enargite graphite magnetite chalcocite |
| | red | copper niccolite |
| | brownish-red | bornite |
| | yellow | pyrrhotine millerite pyrite marcasite |
| pearly (usually seen on cleavage surfaces) | white or colourless | gypsum stiibite muscovite albite apophyllite |
| | brown or reddish-brown | stilbite muscovite phlogopite biotite erythrite |
| | yellow, yellow-green or green | torbernite autunite kyanite chlorite microcline vivianite |
| | blue or purple | kyanite vivianite |
| resinous | white or colourless | nepheline halite gypsum apatite |
| | brown to black | axinite willemite wurtzite pyromorphite serpentine |
| | orange-yellow | orpiment sulphur willemite serpentine blende |
| | green | serpentine apatite mottramite |
| | blue | sodalite |
| vitreous | white or colourless | fluorite corundum grossular calcite baryte quartz orthoclase danburite topaz spodumene stilbite beryl idocrase leucite celestine gypsum apophyllite natrolite scapolite dolomite hemimorphite phenakite datolite petalite |
| | brown | corundum tourmaline calcite chrysoberyl baryte quartz topaz staurolite andalusite stilbite epidote clinozoisite idocrase |
| | black | quartz hornblende olivine spinel andradite |
| | red and pink | corundum spinel fluorite tourmaline rhodochrosite rhodonite almandine pyrope spodumene erythrite strengite topaz |
| | orange | spessartine topaz corundum calcite grossular |
| | yellow | corundum topaz chrysoberyl calcite fluorite orthoclase smithsonite beryl andradite quartz spodumene apatite aragonite colemanite brazilianite amblygcnite |
| | green | corundum tourmaline chrysoberyl fluorite beryl olivine spodumene jadeite orthoclase apatite epidote idocrase diopside dioptase andalusite andradite quartz tremolite actinolite adamite |
| | blue | corundum spinel fluorite smithsonite topaz baryte celestine benitoite sodalite beryl lazulite apatite tourmaline kyanite vivianite cordierite phosphophyllite |
| | purple | corundum fluorite cordierite spodumene spinel almandine kyanite |
| waxy | blue or blue-green | turquoise variscite |

Table 3
**Cleavage and parting**
Cleavage is the tendency shown by many minerals to split readily in directions parallel to possible or actual crystal faces. The cleavage is described in terms of the form defined by the cleavage faces. Only minerals with a perfect cleavage are listed here. Where twinning is present, even if not apparent, specimens may also part readily in certain preferred directions

| | | |
|---|---|---|
| cubic system | cubic | galena halite cobaltite periclase sylvine |
| | dodecahedral | blende sodalite |
| | octahedral | diamond fluorite |
| tetragonal system | basal | anatase apophyllite boléite |
| orthorhombic system | basal | topaz celestine baryte |
| | prismatic | anthophyllite enargite erythrosiderite hemimorphite natrolite wavellite |
| monoclinic system | basal | muscovite phlogopite biotite chlorite lepidolite epidote clinozoisite |
| | prismatic | amphibole spodumene glaucophane |
| triclinic system | pinacoidal | kyanite rhodonite ulexite amblygonite |
| hexagonal system | rhombohedral | calcite dolomite rhodochrosite |

Table 4
**Fluorescence in ultraviolet light**
Some minerals emit visible light when they are illuminated with radiation of shorter wavelength, such as ultraviolet light. Different colours may be emitted according to the wavelength band of the ultraviolet light

| | | |
|---|---|---|
| whitish | long-wave | amblygonite colemanite quartz (some chalcedonies) aragonite ulexite |
| | short-wave | anglesite scheelite |
| red | long-wave | beryl (a few chrome rich emeralds) corundum (variety ruby) spinel (red variety) |
| | short-wave | calcite spinel (red variety) |
| orange | long-wave | corundum (yellow varieties from Ceylon) diamond lapis-lazuli (in patches) sodalite (in patches) spodumene (variety kunzite) zircon |
| | short-wave | corundum (colourless varieties) diamond |
| yellow | long-wave | anglesite diamond apatite phosgenite scapolite zircon |
| | short-wave | opal powellite zircon |
| greenish-yellow | long-wave | autunite uranocircite adamite |
| | short-wave | autunite uranocircite adamite |
| green | long-wave | adamite willemite autunite |
| | short-wave | opal willemite chalcedony (some) |
| blue | long-wave | diamond fluorite danburite witherite |
| | short-wave | benitoite fluorite scheelite diamond |
| violet | long-wave | fluorite scapolite |
| | short-wave | fluorite |

Table 5
**Phosphorescence following illumination with ultraviolet light**
The emission of light under the stimulation of shorter-wave radiation is called phosphorescence when it persists after the stimulus has ceased

| | |
|---|---|
| white | gypsum opal ulexite |
| brown | albite—after short-wave irradiation (rare) |
| pink | calcite diopside |
| red | wollastonite |
| orange | blende spodumene (variety kunzite) |
| orange-yellow | scapolite |
| green | adamite willemite |
| bluish-white | celestine zircon |
| pale blue | amblygonite cerussite diamond |
| blue or violet | fluorite |

Table 6
**Thermoluminescence**
These minerals may emit visible light when heated to a temperature below red heat

| | |
|---|---|
| white | calcite oligoclase |
| greenish-white | willemite |
| pink | corundum (variety ruby) |
| red | smithsonite |
| orange | calcite topaz tourmaline (some red varieties) |
| yellow | calcite |

Table 7
**Hardness according to Mohs' scale**
Mohs' original scale was defined by ten selected minerals. Intermediate values are now employed. Each mineral will scratch those below it on the scale

| Hardness | Minerals |
|---|---|
| 1 | talc |
| 1–2 | graphite covelline realgar orpiment vivianite |
| 1.5–2.5 | sulphur erythrite stibnite gypsum |
| 2–2.5 | cinnabar proustite argentite bismuth autunite torbernite chlorite galena pyrargyrite halite ulexite |
| 2.5–3 | copper gold silver chalcocite anglesite crocoite vanadinite bournonite phlogopite biotite lepidolite muscovite serpentine wolfenite |
| 3 | enargite bornite cerussite olivenite |
| 3–3.5 | calcite antimony millerite celestine descloizite mottramite |
| 3–4 | tetrahedrite arsenic strontianite adamite chalcopyrite blende siderite rhodochrosite dolomite malachite wurtzite cuprite mimetite wavellite pyromorphite strengite variscite pyrrhotine |
| 4 | aragonite fluorite stilbite chabazite manganite |
| 4–4.5 | platinum smithsonite wolframite |
| 4.5–5 | pectolite turquoise colemanite hemimorphite scheelite apophyllite kyanite |
| 5 | apatite dioptase analcime |
| 5–5.5 | goethite lazurite niccolite monazite |
| 5.5–6 | ilmenite uraninite actinolite tremolite cobaltite löllingite datolite willemite arsenopyrite lazulite skutterudite natrolite opal leucite |
| 6 | orthoclase sodalite scapolite magnetite hornblende diopside rhodonite olivine sphene |
| 6–6.5 | columbite tantalite pyrite marcasite rutile benitoite pyrolusite |
| 6.5–7 | cassiterite zircon hematite jadeite nephrite idocrase andradite prehnite diaspore spodumene axinite |
| 7 | quartz danburite epidote clinozoisite grossular staurolite |
| 7–7.5 | pyrope spessartine tourmaline almandine |
| 7.5–8 | phenakite beryl |
| 8–8.5 | spinel topaz chrysoberyl |
| 9 | corundum |
| 10 | diamond |

Table 8
**Streak**
The colour of a mineral in its powdered form is called its streak. It can be observed by drawing a specimen across a piece of unglazed porcelain to leave a trace

| Specimen | Streak | Minerals |
|---|---|---|
| Specimen with metallic lustre | silver | arsenic bismuth silver |
| | grey | platinum |
| | golden-yellow | gold |
| | red | copper |
| Specimen with non-metallic lustre | grey | bornite chalcocite galena covelline stibnite pyrrhotine cobaltite löllingite marcasite arsenopyrite enargite bournonite graphite antimony molybdenite |
| | brown | blende wurtzite tetrahedrite rutile |
| | black | pyrolusite tetrahedrite magnetite columbite |
| | red to reddish-brown | cinnabar cuprite hematite manganite pyrargyrite proustite tennantite tantalite |
| | orange | realgar descloizite |
| | orange-yellow | crocoite |
| | yellow | orpiment vanadinite autunite torbernite |
| | green | malachite vivianite mottramite torbernite |
| | blue | azurite lazurite |
| | purple | vivianite |

Table 9
**Refractive index and birefringence**
In most cases the upper and lower limits of a range are quoted. Where significant, the birefringence (the difference between the two indices in a doubly refractive material) is given in brackets

| Mineral | Refractive index |
|---|---|
| fluorite | 1.43 |
| opal | 1.45 |
| borax | 1.46 |
| sodalite | 1.48 |
| chabazite | 1.48 |
| natrolite | 1.49 |
| stilbite | 1.49–1.50 |
| calcite | 1.49–1.66 (0.172) |
| lazurite | 1.50 |
| dolomite | 1.50–1.76 (0.179) |
| leucite | 1.51 |
| orthoclase | 1.52–1.53 (0.006) |
| strontianite | 1.52–1.66 |
| gypsum | 1.53 |
| plagioclase feldspars | 1.53–1.59 (0.051) |
| quartz (chalcedony) | 1.53–1.54 |
| cordierite | 1.53–1.55 |
| lepidolite | 1.55 |
| aragonite | 1.53–1.69 (0.155) |
| nepheline | 1.53–1.55 |
| apophyllite | 1.54 |
| scapolite | 1.54–1.58 |
| phlogopite | 1.54–1.58 |
| biotite | 1.54–1.58 |
| halite | 1.54 |
| muscovite | 1.56 |
| quartz | 1.54–1.55 (0.009) |
| serpentine | 1.56–1.60 |
| beryl | 1.56–1.59 (0.004–0.007) |
| chlorite | 1.57–1.59 |
| vivianite | 1.58–1.65 |
| variscite | 1.58 |
| colemanite | 1.59–1.61 |
| rhodochrosite | 1.60–1.82 (0.219) |
| tremolite | 1.60–1.68 |
| actinolite | 1.60–1.68 |
| nephrite | 1.62 |
| lazulite | 1.60–1.64 |
| topaz | 1.62–1.64 |

**Refractive index and birefringence**
continued

| Mineral | Refractive index (birefringence) |
|---|---|
| hemimorphite | 1.62–1.64 |
| tourmaline | 1.62–1.65 (0.014–0.020) |
| smithsonite | 1.63–1.84 (0.228) |
| turquoise | 1.62–1.63 |
| celestine | 1.62–1.63 |
| hornblende | 1.63–1.65 |
| erythrite | 1.63–1.70 |
| datolite | 1.64–1.67 |
| prehnite | 1.63 |
| danburite | 1.63–1.64 |
| apatite | 1.63–1.64 |
| siderite | 1.63–1.87 (0.240) |
| andalusite | 1.63–1.65 |
| baryte | 1.64–1.65 |
| phenakite | 1.65–1.67 |
| jadeite | 1.66 |
| spodumene | 1.65–1.67 |
| peridot | 1.65–1.69 (0.036) |
| dioptase | 1.65–1.71 |
| axinite | 1.68–1.69 |
| willemite | 1.69–1.73 |
| idocrase | 1.70–1.73 |
| clinozoisite | 1.71–1.72 |
| spinel | 1.71–1.80 |
| augite | 1.71–1.75 |
| kyanite | 1.72–1.74 |
| adamite | 1.73–1.75 |
| rhoconite | 1.73–1.75 |
| pyrope | 1.74 |
| azurite | 1.73–1.84 (0.107) |
| grossular | 1.74–1.75 |
| epidote | 1.74–1.77 |
| staurolite | 1.74–1.76 |
| chrysoberyl | 1.75–1.76 |
| corundum | 1.76–1.78 (0.008) |
| malachite | 1.77 |
| almandine | 1.77–1.83 |
| monazite | 1.79–1.85 |
| spessartine | 1.79–1.81 |
| cerussite | 1.80–2.08 (0.275) |
| zircon | 1.84–1.99 (0.059) |
| sphene | 1.84–2.09 (0.142) |
| anglesite | 1.88–1.89 |
| andradite | 1.89 |
| scheelite | 1.92–1.94 |
| sulphur | 1.96–2.25 (0.29) |
| cassiterite | 2.0–2.1 |
| pyromorphite | 2.05–2.06 |
| mimetite | 2.13–2.14 |
| descloizite | 2.19–2.35 |
| mottramite | 2.21–2.33 |
| wulfenite | 2.28–2.40 |
| crocoite | 2.29–2.66 |
| blende | 2.37 |
| orpiment | 2.40–3.02 (0.62) |
| vanadinite | 2.35–2.42 |
| diamond | 2.42 |
| realgar | 2.54–2.70 |
| rutile | 2.61–2.69 (0.287) |
| proustite | 2.79–3.09 (0.295) |
| cuprite | 2.85 |
| pyrargyrite | 2.88–3.08 |

Table 10
**Specific gravity**
A material's specific gravity is the ratio of its density (weight per unit volume) to the density of water. It is numerically equal to the material's density in grams per cubic centimetre. Only the specific gravities of the commoner minerals are given here, and mean values only are quoted

| Mineral | Specific gravity |
|---|---|
| borax | 1.7 |
| ulexite | 1.9 |
| opal | 2.1 |
| chabazite | 2.0–2.1 |
| sulphur | 2.0 |
| stilbite | 2.1 |
| graphite | 2.1 |
| halite | 2.1 |
| natrolite | 2.2 |
| sodalite | 2.2–2.3 |
| gypsum | 2.3 |
| apophyllite | 2.3 |
| wavellite | 2.4 |
| lazurite | 2.4–2.5 |
| leucite | 2.4–2.5 |
| colemanite | 2.4 |
| serpentine | 2.5–2.6 |
| variscite | 2.5 |
| nepheline | 2.5–2.6 |
| cordierite | 2.5–2.7 |
| microcline | 2.5–2.6 |
| orthoclase | 2.5–2.6 |
| scapolite | 2.7 |
| turquoise | 2.6–2.9 |
| albite | 2.6 |
| plagioclase feldspars | 2.6–2.7 |
| quartz | 2.6 |
| oligoclase | 2.6 |
| beryl | 2.6–2.9 |
| vivianite | 2.6–2.7 |
| chlorite | 2.7–2.9 |
| calcite | 2.7 |
| labradorite | 2.7 |
| muscovite | 2.8–2.9 |
| lepidolite | 2.8–2.9 |
| prehnite | 2.8–2.9 |
| datolite | 2.8–3.0 |
| dolomite | 2.8–3.0 |
| biotite | 2.8–3.4 |
| phlogopite | 2.8–3.4 |
| aragonite | 2.9–3.0 |
| phenakite | 2.9–3.0 |
| tremolite | 2.9–3.1 |
| danburite | 3.0 |
| erythrite | 3.0 |
| nephrite | 3.0 |
| tourmaline | 3.0–3.3 |
| hornblende | 3.0–3.4 |
| lazulite | 3.1–3.2 |
| apatite | 3.1–3.2 |
| autunite | 3.1–3.2 |
| andalusite | 3.1–3.2 |
| actinolite | 3.1–3.3 |
| spodumene | 3.1–3.2 |
| fluorite | 3.1 |
| axinite | 3.2–3.3 |

| Mineral | Specific gravity |
|---|---|
| olivine | 3.2–4.3 |
| torbernite | 3.2 |
| jadeite | 3.3 |
| diopside | 3.2–3.3 |
| dioptase | 3.2–3.3 |
| diaspore | 3.3–3.5 |
| clinozoisite | 3.3–3.4 |
| idocrase | 3.3–3.6 |
| goethite | 3.3–4.3 |
| hemimorphite | 3.4–3.5 |
| rhodochrosite | 3.4–3.6 |
| epidote | 3.4–3.6 |
| sphene | 3.4–3.5 |
| augite | 3.4–3.5 |
| orpiment | 3.4 |
| diamond | 3.5 |
| topaz | 3.5 |
| rhodonite | 3.5–3.7 |
| realgar | 3.5 |
| spinel | 3.5–3.9 |
| grossular | 3.6 |
| malachite | 3.6–4.0 |
| benitoite | 3.6 |
| kyanite | 3.6–3.7 |
| pyrope | 3.6–3.8 |
| staurolite | 3.7–3.8 |
| chrysoberyl | 3.7 |
| strontianite | 3.7 |
| azurite | 3.7 |
| siderite | 3.8–3.9 |
| andradite | 3.8–3.9 |
| willemite | 3.8–4.1 |
| blende | 3.9–4.1 |
| zircon | 3.9–4.7 |
| almandine | 3.9–4.3 |
| celestine | 3.9 |
| corundum | 3.9–4.0 |
| smithsonite | 4.0–4.5 |
| chalcopyrite | 4.1–4.3 |
| spessartine | 4.1–4.2 |
| rutile | 4.2 |
| manganite | 4.3 |
| adamite | 4.3–4.5 |
| baryte | 4.5 |
| enargite | 4.4–4.5 |
| pyrolusite | 4.4–5.0 |
| pyrrhotine | 4.6 |
| molybdenite | 4.6–4.7 |
| covelline | 4.6–4.7 |
| tennantite | 4.6–4.9 |
| monazite | 4.6–5.4 |
| stibnite | 4.6 |
| ilmenite | 4.7 |
| marcasite | 4.8 |
| tetrahedrite | 4.9–5.1 |
| pyrite | 5.0 |
| bornite | 5.0 |

| Mineral | Specific gravity |
|---|---|
| columbite | 5.1–6.5 |
| magnetite | 5.1 |
| hematite | 5.3 |
| millerite | 5.5 |
| chalcocite | 5.5–5.8 |
| proustite | 5.5 |
| arsenic | 5.7 |
| bournonite | 5.8 |
| pyrargyrite | 5.8 |
| mottramite | 5.9 |
| scheelite | 5.9–6.1 |
| crocoite | 6.0 |
| arsenopyrite | 6.0 |
| skutterudite | 6.1–6.9 |
| cuprite | 6.1 |
| descloizite | 6.2 |
| cobaltite | 6.3 |
| anglesite | 6.3 |
| wulfenite | 6.5–7.0 |
| vanadinite | 6.5–7.1 |
| uraninite | 6.5–9.7 |
| cerussite | 6.5 |
| tantalite | 6.5–8.0 |
| antimony | 6.7 |
| cassiterite | 6.8–7.1 |
| pyromorphite | 7.0 |
| argentite | 7.2–7.4 |
| mimetite | 7.2 |
| wolframite | 7.3 |
| löllingite | 7.4 |
| galena | 7.5 |
| niccolite | 7.7 |
| cinnabar | 8.1 |
| bismuth | 9.7 |
| silver | 10–11 |
| platinum | 14–19 |
| gold | 15–19 |

# Conversion Tables

**Linear measure**

| | | |
|---|---|---|
| 0.001 inch | = 0.0254 | millimetre |
| 1 inch | = 2.54 | centimetres |
| 12 inches = 1 foot | = 0.3048 | metre |
| 3 feet = 1 yard | = 0.9144 | metre |
| 5,280 feet = 1 (statute) mile | = 1.6093 | kilometres |

| | | | |
|---|---|---|---|
| | 1 millimetre | = 0.03937 | inch |
| 10 millimetres | = 1 centimetre | = 0.3937 | inch |
| 10 centimetres | = 1 decimetre | = 3.937 | inches |
| 10 decimetres | = 1 metre | = 39.37 | inches or 3.2808 feet |
| 10 metres | = 1 decametre | = 393.7 | inches |
| 10 decametres | = 1 hectometre | = 328.08 | feet |
| 10 hectometres | = 1 kilometre | = 0.621 | mile or 3,280.8 feet |
| 10 kilometres | = 1 myriametre | = 6.21 | miles |

**Square measure**

| | | | |
|---|---|---|---|
| | 1 square inch | = 6.452 | square centimetres |
| 144 square inches | = 1 square foot | = 929.03 | square centimetres |
| 9 square feet | = 1 square yard | = 0.8361 | square metre |
| | 1 square mile | = 259.00 | hectares or 2.590 square kilometres |

| | | | |
|---|---|---|---|
| | 1 square millimetre | = 0.00155 | square inch |
| 100 square millimetres | = 1 square centimetre | = 0.15499 | square inch |
| 100 square centimetres | = 1 square decimetre | = 15.499 | square inches |
| 100 square decimetres | = 1 square metre | = 1,549.9 | square inches or 1.196 square yards |
| 100 square metres | = 1 square decametre | = 119.6 | square yards |
| 100 square decametres | = 1 square hectometre | = 2.471 | acres |
| 100 square hectometres | = 1 square kilometre | = 0.386 | square mile or 247.1 acres |

**Volume measure**

| | | | |
|---|---|---|---|
| | 1 cubic inch | = 16.387 | cubic centimetres |
| 1,728 cubic inches | = 1 cubic foot | = 0.0283 | cubic metre |
| 27 cubic feet | = 1 cubic yard | = 0.7646 | cubic metre |

| | | | |
|---|---|---|---|
| 1,000 cubic millimetres | = 1 cubic centimetre | = 0.06102 | cubic inch |
| 1,000 cubic centimetres | = 1 cubic decimetre | = 61.023 | cubic inches or 0.0353 cubic foot |
| 1,000 cubic decimetres | = 1 cubic metre | = 35.314 | cubic feet or 1.308 cubic yards |

**Weight**

| | | | |
|---|---|---|---|
| 437.5 grains | = 1 ounce | = 28.3495 | grams |
| 16 ounces or 7,000 grains | = 1 pound | = 453.59 | grams |
| 100 pounds | = 1 US hundredweight | = 45.36 | kilograms |
| 112 pounds | = 1 Imp. hundredweight | = 50.80 | kilograms |
| 2,000 pounds | = 1 US ton | = 907.18 | kilograms |
| 2,240 pounds | = 1 Imp. ton | = 1,016 | kilograms |

| | | | |
|---|---|---|---|
| 10 milligrams | = 1 centigram | | |
| 10 centigrams | = 1 decigram | | |
| 10 decigrams | = 1 gram | = 0.035274 | ounce |
| 10 grams | = 1 decagram | = 0.3527 | ounce |
| 10 decagrams | = 1 hectogram | = 3.5274 | ounces |
| 10 hectograms | = 1 kilogram | = 2.2046 | pounds |
| 10 kilograms | | = 22.046 | pounds |
| 1,000 kilograms | = 1 metric ton | = 2,204.6 | pounds |
| | | = 1.1023 | US tons |
| | | = 0.9842 | Imp. ton |

# Important Addresses

**Australia**

*Gemmological Association of Australia*, GPO Box 149, Sydney, New South Wales 2001
*Geological and Mining Museum*, 36 George Street North, Sydney, New South Wales 2000

**Canada**

*Royal Ontario Museum*, 100 Queen's Park, Toronto, Ontario
*Geological Survey of Canada*, 601 Booth Street, Ottawa, Ontario

**Czechoslovakia**

*Lapidarium Historické Múzeum*, Park Kultury a oddechu Julia Fučika, Praha

**France**

*Musée de l'Ecole Supérieure des Mines*, 60 Boulevard Saint-Michel, Paris 75006

**Iran**

*Bank Melli*, Tehran (in the custody of the Bank Markazi, Supervisory Board for the Crown Jewels Collection)

**Switzerland**

*Geologische und Mineralogisch-Petrographische Sammlung der Technischen Hochschule*, 8000 Zürich

**UK**

*Institute of Geological Sciences and Geological Museum*, Exhibition Road, London SW7 2DE
*British Museum (Natural History)*, Cromwell Road, London SW7 5BD
*Mineralogical Society of Great Britain and Ireland*, 41 Queen's Gate, London SW7 5HR
*Gemmological Association of Great Britain*, St. Dunstan's House, Carey Lane, London EC2V 8AB
*Geological Society of London*, Burlington House, Piccadilly, London W1V 0JU
*Geologists' Association*, 278 Fir Tree Road, Epsom, Surrey

**USA**

*Smithsonian Institution*, 1000 Jefferson Drive, Washington, DC 20560
*American Museum of Natural History*, Central Park West, New York, NY 10024
*Geological Survey of the United States*, 12201 Sunrise Valley Drive, Reston, Virginia 22092
*Gemological Institute of America*, 11940 San Vincente Boulevard, Los Angeles, California 90049
*Mineralogical Society of America*, 1707 L Street, NW, Washington, DC 20036
*American Federation of Mineralogical Societies*, 704 SW 31st Street, Pendleton, Oregon 97801
*International Mineralogical Association*, 2018 Luzerne Avenue, Silver Spring, Maryland 20910

**USSR**

*Mining Museum of the G V Plekhanov Mining Institute*, Vasilievsky ostrov, Leningrad V 26

**West Germany**

*Bayrisches Geologisches Landesamt*, Prinzregentenstrasse 28,8 München 22
*Geologisches Landesamt in Baden Württemberg*, Albertstrasse 5,Freiburg Ei.Br.
*Geologisches Landesamt Nordrhein-Westfalen*, Postschliessfach 1080, 415 Krefeld
*Geologisches Landesamt Schleswig-Holstein*, Mecklenburgerstrasse 22/24, 23 Kiel-Wik
*Geologisches Landesamt Rheinland-Pfalz*, Flachsmarktstrasse 9, 65 Mainz
*Hessisches Landesamt für Bodenforschung*, Leberberg 9, 62 Wiesbaden
*Deutsches Edelsteinmuseum*, D658 Idar-Oberstein
*Deutsche Gemmologische Gesellschaft*, Gewerbehalle, Postfach 2260, D658 Idar-Oberstein

# Bibliography


**Chemistry, Crystallography, Geochemistry, Physics**

Bishop, A C, *An Outline of Crystal Morphology* Hutchinson, London, 1967.
Intended for students of geology.

Burns, R G, *Mineralogical Applications of Crystal Field Theory*, University Press, Cambridge, 1970.
A lucid book on the nature of chemical bonding applied to mineralogy and geochemistry.

Cotton, F A and Wilkinson, G, *Advanced Inorganic Chemistry*, 3rd edition, Interscience Publishers, New York and London, 1972.
The standard text.

Ditchburn, R W, *Light*, 3rd edition, Blackie, London, 1963.
First-year undergraduate-level textbook.

Donnay, J D H, *Crystal Data: Determinative Tables*, 3rd edition; vol 2, *Inorganic Compounds*, National Bureau of Standards, Washington, 1973.

Evans, R C, *An Introduction to Crystal Chemistry*, 2nd edition, Cambridge University Press, 1964.

Gleason, S, *Ultraviolet Guide to Minerals*, Ultra-Violet Products, San Gabriel, California, 1972.
A useful guide with coloured illustrations.

Goldschmidt, V M, *Geochemistry* (edited by Alex Muir), Clarendon Press, Oxford, 1958.
The standard work on geochemistry; supplements, closely linked to this original work, are also published.

Hartshorne, N H and Stuart, A, *Crystals and the Polarizing Microscope*, 4th edition, Edward Arnold, London, 1970.
The standard work in the field.

Lonsdale K, *Crystals and X-Rays*, G Bell & Sons, London, 1948.
A most lucid account of X-ray diffraction by crystals. Out of print but worth a search.

Sidgwick N V, *The Chemical Elements and their Compounds*, Clarendon Press, Oxford, 1950. Two volumes.

**Geology and Mineralogy—general**

Blyth, F G H, *Geology for Engineers*, 6th edition, Edward Arnold, London, 1975.
An excellent applied geology.

Chalmers, R O, *Australian Rocks, Minerals and Gemstones*, Angus and Robertson, Sydney, 1967.
The best guide to Australian gems and minerals.

Dana, E S, *A Textbook of Mineralogy*, 4th edition, revised by W E Ford, John Wiley, New York and London, 1932.
The instructional part of the great Dana series of mineralogical texts. Somewhat overtaken by new minerals, occurrences and research but still useful.

Dana, J D and E S, *The System of Mineralogy*, 7th edition by Palache, Berman and Frondel, 1944–. John Wiley and Sons, New York.
Three volumes so far published. Most works on minerals are based on the classification adopted for this book on its original publication in 1837.

Dana, J D, *Manual of Mineralogy*, John Wiley & Sons, New York. Various editions.
A simplified guide based on the textbook by E S Dana and others.

Deer, W A, Howie, R A and Zussman, J, *Rock-forming Minerals*, Longman, London, 1962. Five volumes.
Full details are given of the common minerals of igneous, sedimentary and metamorphic rocks. *An Introduction to the Rock-forming Minerals* is a digest in one volume.

Desautels, P E, *The Mineral Kingdom*, Paul Hamlyn, London, 1969.
Based on the collections of the Smithsonian Institution this book is a lucid introduction to the beauty of the mineral world.

Hamilton, W R, Woolley, A R and Bishop, A C, *The Hamlyn Guide to Minerals, Rocks and Fossils*, Paul Hamlyn, London, 1974.
The best of the pocket-sized field guides to minerals.

Hey, M H and Embrey, P, *Index of Mineral Species arranged Chemically*, British Museum (Natural History), London, 1955–1974.
Includes two supplements. The spine reads *Chemical Index of Minerals*.

Hurlbut, C S, *Minerals and Man*, Thames and Hudson, London, 1969.
An account of the economic use of minerals.

Institute of Geological Sciences, *British Regional Geology*, London, 1935–.
Continuously revised.

Michele, V de, *The World of Minerals*, Orbis Publishing Ltd, London, 1976.
Introduction to minerals, illustrated with high-quality colour photographs.

Moorhouse, W W, *The Study of Rocks in Thin Section*, Harper and Row, New York, 1964.
An introductory text.

Nature Conservancy (Great Britain), *List of Protected Geological Sites*.

Orbis Publishing Ltd, *Crystals*, London, 1976.
High-quality colour photographs, with an introduction.

Roberts, W L, Rapp, G R and Weber, J, *Encyclopedia of Minerals*, Van Nostrand Reinhold Co., New York and London, 1974.
Very useful up-to-date references for each mineral.

Rodgers, Peter R, *Agate Collecting in Britain*, Batsford, London, 1975.

Sinkankas, J, *Gemstone and Mineral Data Book*, Winchester Press, New York, 1972.
Contains all possible data needed for the identification and preservation of gems and minerals.
—*Prospecting for Gemstones and Minerals*, Van Nostrand Reinhold, New York and London, 1970.
Contains information on the recognition of gem-bearing geological formations, handling specimens, etc.

Traill, R J, *A Catalogue of Canadian Minerals*, Geological Survey of Canada, 1970 (Paper 69–45).
Updates R A A Johnston's Memoir 74 of 1915.

Vlasov, K, *Mineralogy of Rare Elements*, (Vol. 2 of the series *Geochemistry and Mineralogy of Rare Elements and Genetic Types of their Deposits*, translated from the Russian), Israel Program for Scientific Translations, 1966.

Wells, A F, *Structural Inorganic Chemistry*, 3rd edition, Clarendon Press, Oxford, 1962.
A standard reference-work of great clarity.

Winchell, A N and Winchell, H, *Elements of Optical Mineralogy*, 4th edition, John Wiley, New York, 1951.
The best work in this field.

## Periodicals and Serials


*Acta Crystallographica*, Munksgaard, Copenhagen, for the International Union of Crystallography, 1948–.
In 2 sections: A—theoretical; B—structural.

*American Mineralogist*, Journal of the Mineralogical Society of America.
The official American mineralogical journal.

*Australian Gemmologist*, Gemmological Association of Australia, Sydney.
Reports from university and government research bodies on Australian gem materials, particularly on opal.

*Bulletin Association Française de Gemmologie*, Paris.
The official French gemmological journal. Contains reports of new occurrences of gem materials, especially from the Malagasy Republic and Brazil.

*Bulletin of the Geological Survey of Great Britain*, HMSO, London.
Irregular.

*Canadian Mineralogist*, Mineralogical Association of Canada, 555 Booth St., Ottawa. Semi-annual.

*Gemmological Newsletter*, 7, Hillingdon Avenue, Sevenoaks, Kent.
A weekly bulletin of new gem finds, new testing methods, book reviews and other material.

*Gems and Gemology*. Gemological Institute of America, Los Angeles.
Especially noteworthy for reports of unusual gems tested at the GIA laboratories in Los Angeles and New York.

*Geochimica et Cosmochimica Acta*. Pergamon, New York, 1950–.

*Geological Magazine*, Cambridge University Press, six times a year.

*Geologists' Association Guides*, Benham & Co., Colchester, Essex, 1958–.

*Geoserials*, Geosystems, London, 1969–.
A world list of current geoscience serial publications. Supplements published in Geoscience Documentation.

*Geoscience Documentation*, Geosystems, London, 1969–.
Articles, news and bibliographies.

*Journal of Gemmology*, Gemmological Association of Great Britain.
The official British gemmological journal with material of a good standard.

*Journal of the Geological Society of London*, Geological Society of London, Burlington House, Piccadilly, London W1V 0JV. Six issues a year.

*Journal of Petrology*, Clarendon Press, Oxford, 1960–.

*Lapidary Journal*, PO Box 80937, San Diego, California 92138.
The best journal devoted to fashioning and also containing up-to-date reports on the occurrence of new gem materials.

*Memoirs*, Geological Society of Great Britain, London, 1958–.

*Memoirs*, Geological Survey of Great Britain, London, 1864–. In sheets.

*Mineral Digest*, Mineral Digest Ltd, PO Box 341, Murray Hill Station, New York, NY 10016.
A serial issued irregularly though with periodical-type numeration. Contains magnificent coloured illustrations. Seven issues extant at the time of writing.

*Mineralogical Abstracts*, Mineralogical Society of Great Britain, London SW7, and the Mineralogical Society of America.
Reviews all relevant literature in the fields of descriptive mineralogy, gemmology, crystallography, etc.

*Mineralogical Magazine*, Mineralogical Society of Great Britain, London, SW7.
Essential for the serious student of mineralogy.

*Mineralogical Record*, John S White, Jr, PO Box 783, Bowie, Maryland 20715. Six issues a year.

*Monthly List of New Publications* [of the US Geological Survey], US Dept. of the Interior, Geological Survey, National Center, Stp 329, Reston, Virginia 22092.

*Synthetic Crystals Newsletter*, 7, Hillingdon Avenue, Sevenoaks, Kent.
An occasional bulletin of information on new synthetic materials, particularly those of gemmological interest.


## Gemmology


Anderson, B W, *Gem Testing*, 8th edition, Butterworths, London, 1971.
The classic manual on the scientific identification of gemstones. Admirably lucid.

Gübelin, E, *Internal World of Gemstones*, ABC Edition, Zürich, 1974.
The best book extant on the inclusions found in gemstones; fine-quality coloured illustrations and a good bibliography.

Kalokerinos, A, *Australian Precious Opal*, Nelson, Melbourne, 1971.
Illustrated with fine-quality coloured plates. The author's nomenclature is sometimes non standard.

Liddicoat, R T, *Handbook of Gem Identification*, 10th edition, Gemological Institute of America, Los Angeles, 1975.
An excellent American textbook.

Rutland, E H, *An Introduction to the World's Gemstones*, Country Life, London, 1974.
The best simple introduction available in English.

Sinkankas, J, *Gemstones of North America*, D Van Nostrand Co., Princeton and London, 1959.
The best guide to the gem materials that occur in North America.
—*Van Nostrand's Standard Catalog of Gems*, D Van Nostrand Co., Princeton and London, 1968.
Gives tables of values, now dated, of rough and cut gem material; still very useful for the criteria upon which the values are based.

Smith, G F Herbert, *Gemstones*, 14th edition, revised by F Coles Phillips, Chapman and Hall, London, 1972.
One of the first and best scientific studies of the gem.

Webster, R, *Gems*, Newnes-Butterworths, London, 1975.
A comprehensive survey of the gem materials.
—*Practical Gemmology*, NAG Press, London. Various editions.
Based on the examination syllabus of the Gemmological Association of Great Britain and including questions.
—*The Gemmologists' Compendium*, NAG Press, London. Various editions.
For use as an adjunct to the laboratory examination of gemstones. Contains useful tables.


## Gem-cutting


Sinkankas, J, *Gem Cutting*, 2nd edition, Van Nostrand Reinhold Co., New York and London, 1962.
An excellent work on the fashioning of gemstones.

Vargas, G and M, *Faceting for Amateurs*, published by the authors, Thermal, California, 1969.
Another well written guide to gem fashioning.

# INDEX

*Numbers in italics refer to illustrations*

9.10.82